ENDURING EMPIRE

ARTICULATIONS STUDIES IN RACE, IMMIGRATION, AND CAPITALISM

EDITORS
Cedric de Leon
Pawan Dhingra

ENDURING EMPIRE

U.S. Statecraft and
Race-Making in the Philippines

katrina quisumbing king

STANFORD UNIVERSITY PRESS
Stanford, California

Stanford University Press
Stanford, California

Library of Congress Cataloging-in-Publication Data

Names: Quisumbing King, Katrina, 1985– author
Title: Enduring empire : U.S. statecraft and race-making in the Philippines
 / Katrina Quisumbing King.
Other titles: Articulations (Stanford, Calif.)
Description: Stanford, California : Stanford University Press, [2025] |
 Series: Articulations | Includes bibliographical references and index.
Identifiers: LCCN 2025002044 (print) | LCCN 2025002045 (ebook) | ISBN
 9781503642676 cloth | ISBN 9781503643253 paperback | ISBN 9781503643260
 ebook
Subjects: LCSH: Racism—United States—History—20th century |
 Philippines—History—1898–1946 | Philippines—Colonial influence |
 Philippines—Foreign relations—United States | United States—Foreign
 relations—Philippines
Classification: LCC DS685 .Q53 2025 (print) | LCC DS685 (ebook) | DDC
 305.800973/0904—dc23/eng/20250313
LC record available at https://lccn.loc.gov/2025002044
LC ebook record available at https://lccn.loc.gov/2025002045

Cover design: Susan Zucker
Cover art: Frances Segismundo
Typeset by Newgen in 10/14.75 Minion Pro

The authorized representative in the EU for product safety and compliance is:
Mare Nostrum Group B.V. | Mauritskade 21D | 1091 GC Amsterdam | The
Netherlands | Email address: gpsr@mare-nostrum.co.uk | KVK chamber of
commerce number: 96249943

CONTENTS

For my parents and grandparents.

ACKNOWLEDGMENTS

This book is but a stop on a long and winding journey. When I started graduate school, I did not plan to do historical research or to write about U.S. empire or the Philippines. While this project seemed to take me off the path I traveled, it also brought me home. As the child of immigrants, I grew up with the ambiguous sense of national belonging that many Asian Americans feel. My father's family, driven by my grandfather's nationalist sympathies, left China in the wake of World War II and after the rise of the People's Republic of China. Like many refugees, they experienced immeasurable loss and spoke little of their past. Their grief left my father with little knowledge to pass on to me.

Whereas my connection to China was tenuous at best, my mother—a self-declared nationalist who organized for democracy in the Philippines— explicitly taught me I was Filipina. (Here, I know she, ever concerned about accurate family histories, will also say that she taught me I was Filipina-Chinese, but Filipina first because she is the one who taught me.) I was fortunate to visit the Philippines regularly from a young age, and I grew up thinking of the Philippines as another home. While fitting in there was no less complicated than finding my place in my country of birth, experiences in both the United States and the Philippines gave me the opportunity to think about history and belonging from a young age. My *lola*'s stories also taught me about Spanish, American, and Japanese rule and my family's history in World War II.

Learning from my mother and her family, I tried to recover my Chinese family's history. Fifty years after my grandparents, toddler aunt, and infant father fled China, my grandfather shared their story. I learned from my mother and father's families that both what we share and what we omit shapes who we can become. In our reconstructed memories, through war, across oceans, and over generations, we bridge countries. We bind the past and present. These insights—although told differently—are also reflected in this book. I found visual representation of these intuitions in Frances Segismundo's stunning and evocative work. I thank Frances for her openness to my interpretation of her art and for allowing me to use it on this book's cover.

Along the way, I have benefited from and enjoyed the support from a great number of people. This book began at the University of Wisconsin–Madison. Mara Loveman taught me to read generously and widely, and she gave me the freedom to develop my ideas and my authorial voice. Pamela Oliver challenged me to think about how my work speaks more broadly across the discipline and how people outside my subfields might receive it. Myra Marx Ferree helped me realize my priorities and develop as an independent scholar. Jenna Nobles encouraged my early critical engagement with the sociology of migration. I am also grateful to Franco Scarano and Mike Cullinane for their guidance on historical research and U.S. colonial history early in this project. Cindy I-Fen Cheng graciously joined my committee at the last hour and shared her insights on immigration and citizenship with great enthusiasm.

Although they did not serve on my committee, Rick Baldoz, Julian Go, Paul Kramer, and Lanny Thompsons's work shaped this project from its early days. Once I decided to pursue a project about U.S. empire and the classification and racialized exclusion of Filipinos, I turned to their books. Rick, Julian, and Paul generously responded to an email from an unknown graduate student. They each met with me at conferences when I was early in this project. I was fortunate to meet Lanny Thompson as I was in the final stages of writing the book. I still return to their work, now layered with notes, underlining, and tabs from over a decade of rereading.

Beyond UW–Madison, grants and fellowships provided invaluable time and support. Research for this book was supported by the National Science Foundation under Grant No. 1519125, an MIT School of Humanities, Arts, and Social Sciences Diversity Predoctoral Fellowship, a Foreign Language and Area Studies Fellowship in Tagalog, University of Wisconsin Graduate School

Research Travel Grants, the Harry S. Truman Library Institute, the Franklin D. Roosevelt Institute, and the Association of Centers for the Study of Congress. During a postdoctoral fellowship at USC, Janet Hoskins at the Center for Transpacific Studies at USC supported an early book workshop. Rhacel Parreñas offered thoughtful professional advice, which guided me as I transitioned from graduate student to postdoc to assistant professor. I was also lucky to have encouraging mentors wrapping up their own historical projects on U.S. empire. At MIT, Chris Capozzola was always excited to talk big conceptual, sociological ideas and get into the nitty-gritty of archival material on the U.S. military. At USC, Sam Erman welcomed me into an interdisciplinary legal history community at the Center for Law, History, and Culture. He helped me brainstorm directions for an early version of the book.

Archivists, librarians, and Filipino community members offered practical help for navigating the many collections and data sources I consulted. Thanks to Eric Vanslander, Charles Miller, William Greene, Randy Sowell, Edwin Alberto, Rowena Mahinay, Eimee Lagrama, John Cahoon, Simon DeLeon, James Zobel, William Creech, Robert Cruthirds, Robert Spindler, Patrick Fahy, Casie Azuma, William Baehr, and Anne Zald. I am especially grateful to Franco Arcebal, Arturo Garcia, Pepi Nieva, and Cecilia Gaerlan for sharing personal, family, and political history with me.

I finished this book at Northwestern University, where incredibly kind colleagues welcomed me. I am grateful to have landed in a department that supports my research and writing. Special thanks to Tony Chen, who helped me plan and facilitate a book manuscript workshop. He and Jim Mahoney provided thoughtful written comments on the entire manuscript. I also thank colleagues and students in the Comparative Historical Social Science workshop, including Ann Orloff, who read and discussed a chapter with me. Michael Rodríguez-Muñiz, Mary Patillo, Wendy Espeland, and Bruce Carruthers offered much-needed advice on workshops and publishing to this first-time book author. A year leave at the Alice Kaplan Institute for the Humanities allowed me to finish writing and revising.

I am extremely grateful for the excellent research assistance of Kalliope Kobotis and final proofreading by Henry Chen. Rose Ernst's constructive feedback on the book's framework provided a necessary sanity check in the last stage of revising. At Stanford University Press, I thank Marcela Cristina Maxfield, who believed in this project early on. She read two chapters and offered clarifying guidance for a first-time book author. Thanks also to Justine Sargent, Chris Peterson, Charlie Clark, Melissa Jauregui Chavez, Claire Maby, and the production and marketing teams at Stanford for their attention in preparing the manuscript for publication.

Feedback is a gift, and I am thankful for the support of so many colleagues. I thank Cecilia Menjívar, Cristina Mora, and Yến Lê Espiritu for reading an early version of this book and helping me realize it was about more than just ambiguous membership. I benefited from Rick Baldoz, Julian Go, Moon-Kie Jung, and Simeon Man's historical expertise as I wrestled with how to write transnational and historical sociology for different audiences. Their sub-ject-area expertise in U.S. empire, the Philippines, the Pacific, immigration, and race also helped me clarify the contribution of the book. Stephanie Mudge generously read the entire manuscript and provided detailed and invaluable feedback that guided this project to a close. I am also deeply indebted to the anonymous reviewers of this book. Their close engagement and incredible comments renewed my energy to finish.

Colleagues in sociology and other disciplines have provided encour-agement, offered professional advice, and become important interlocutors. Thanks to Johanna Quinn, Esther HsuBorger, Sasha White, Rici Hammer, Heidi Nicholls, Jordanna Matlon, Marcelo Bohrt, Jake Watson, Mark John Sanchez, Adrian De Leon, Cybelle Fox, Tom Guglielmo, Nitsan Chorev, Mi-chelle Huang, Daniel Immerwahr, Nitasha Sharma, Kalyan Nadiminti, Nikki Spigner, Sulafa Zidani, Hana Brown, Jenn Jones, Tara Gonsalves, Julia Beh-rman, Aliza Luft, Anna Skarpelis, Annabel Ipsen, and Heather O'Connell. Casey Stockstill and Daanika Gordon have been regular writing compan-ions since graduate school. Together, we learned to be graduate students, race scholars, writers, job applicants, and professors. They have helped me sort through many professional and intellectual questions, and together we have celebrated each other's accomplishments.

Amanda McMillan Lequieu has read nearly every word of this manu-script. She has accompanied me through all stages of this project. As I wrote my first memo, processing data from the Truman Library, she sat across from me. She drove with me from the Truman to the Lilly Library, listening to my early ideas about this project. For the last eight years, we have exchanged drafts every two weeks. I am lucky to have a friend with whom I can process my inchoate ideas and refine my developed ones. I cannot imagine my work without her attention to clear writing and telling a good story.

Finally, I thank all those who supported me on the long journey of this project: Sophia Hasenfus, Linda Marie Pheng, Tony Tran, Samson Awosan, Yejin Lee, Ben Fuller-Googins, Nick Fuller Googins, Lizzy Mulkey, Eric Ares, Yelena Zeltser, Ayman Alvi, Liz Bradley, Elizabeth Genovese, Amy Kunkel, Kat Gutierrez, Tao Xie, Allen King, Agnes Quisumbing, Jesus Noel (Joel) Villaseñor, Ma. Lourdes (Marilou) Quisumbing Baybay, Angelo (Gelo) Baybay, Ma. Visitacion (Vising) Quisumbing, Scott Yara, and Vonceil Chun-Yara. My parents, Ma. Socorro (Cora) Quisumbing-King and Walter King, were the first to teach me to be an independent thinker. They encouraged me to ask questions, instilled in me a strong sense of self, and stoked my commitment to social justice. I cannot repay all they have given. This book is dedicated to them and their parents, Lourdes Reynes Quisumbing, Carlos Emilio Corrales Quisumbing, Hsien-Tsu King, Mona Chow, and Eosin Chu.

September 2024

INTRODUCTION

MAKING WAR, MAKING RACE

On February 21, 1902, the United States House Committee on Insular Affairs met to hear testimony about their newly acquired colony, the Philippines.[1] In addition to discussing the need for a U.S.-run civil government in the war-ravaged territory, representatives also considered the citizenship of Filipinos. Just eight months prior, the U.S. Supreme Court decided that territories acquired from Spain, including Puerto Rico and the Philippines, were "foreign in a domestic sense," meaning that while they "belong to," they are "not part of the Union."[2] This definition puzzled lawmakers charged with managing the Philippines. If the territory was foreign in a domestic sense, how would the United States define the Filipino people? Given that the United States claimed sovereignty over the Philippines, were its people citizens?

When Chairman Henry A. Cooper (R-WI) asked U.S. Governor-General of the Philippines William H. Taft—who would become U.S. president in 1909—if the legislation for a civil government in the Philippines should have a bill of rights, Taft responded affirmatively. He added, "I think it might be very well to declare in the act, what is also the law, that residents of the Philippine Islands owing allegiance to the United States should enjoy all the rights of citizens of the United States with respect to foreign countries." This would also allow Filipinos who legally migrate to the United States "to be

1

entitled to naturalization as citizens of the United States." Asking for clarification, Cooper interjected: "Some such provision is necessary, is it not, unless we modify the law as it now exists to enable a Filipino to secure a passport, passports being limited to citizens of the United States?" How could Filipinos migrate to the United States if they were not yet citizens? In his response, Taft was unsure of current naturalization and citizenship provisions as they applied to the Philippines. Representative Robert R. Hitt (R-IL) responded that there was not yet a law declaring Filipinos as U.S. citizens who owed allegiance to the United States.[3] Despite U.S. sovereignty over the islands, citizenship remained an open question and one that confused politicians.

In a later session, on May 31, 1902, the Committee on Insular Affairs heard a statement from Felipe Buencamino, the former secretary of state in the short-lived First Philippine Republic of 1899 and a member of the Civil Service Board in the Philippines. When asked about the proposed civil government for the Philippines, Buencamino turned the Committee's attention to what he believed was the most important political question: "We would like to know what we are as citizens, because the question of nationality should supersede the political questions. Are we Americans, or are we Filipinos?"[4] The Committee did not directly answer him. While Buencamino worried about the status of Filipinos under their new imperial overlord, U.S. representatives evaded the question of Filipino membership. During the hearings, U.S. legislators neither had a grasp of naturalization law nor did they take a clear stance on the membership of Filipinos. In the end, however, the 1902 Organic Act, which created a civil government in the Philippines, stipulated "that all inhabitants of the Philippine Islands . . .shall be deemed and held to be citizens of the Philippine Islands, and as such entitled to the protection of the United States."[5] The U.S. Congress did not grant citizenship to Filipinos.

At the heart of this decision was the pervasive concern that incorporating new nonwhite people would degrade the nation. Bound by the Fourteenth Amendment, which promised equal citizenship to all those under the jurisdiction of the United States, Southern and West Coast legislators thought of Filipinos as similar to Black Americans. In the same year that the United States took the Philippines, Senator Furnifold McLendel Simmons (D-NC), a staunch Southern conservative and chairman of the Democratic Executive Committee of North Carolina, began an explicit campaign to restore white supremacy against what he saw as domination by freed Black people. In North Carolina, he proposed an amendment to disenfranchise Black voters.[6] In debates over the Philippines, Simmons applied a similar logic of racial exclusion. He called Filipinos "only half civilized" and argued that they lacked "any just comprehension of the principles of self-government." Admitting them to the United States was impossible without "degrading the citizenship of the nation and inviting countless dangers."[7] Because of Filipinos' supposed inherent inferiority, legislators restricted the rights of Filipinos in the metropole. Although the Organic Act made Filipinos citizens of the Philippines, the Philippines was not a sovereign country. Over the next four decades, U.S. federal state actors—presidents, legislators, bureaucrats, and court justices—grappled with questions of racial exclusion and what it meant for the Philippines to be both foreign and domestic and for its people to be citizens of a non-sovereign colony.[8]

The case of U.S. rule over the Philippines—lasting from 1898 to 1946—challenges conventional knowledge about race, state formation, and the United States. It both upsets the myth that the United States is a nation state and draws attention to the role of ambiguity in statecraft. As the United States went to war and claimed new territories abroad, its leaders faced questions about who belonged and what their rights would be. Rather than grant Filipinos equal citizenship, U.S. state actors saw them as racially inferior colonial subjects who should not have the same rights as U.S. citizens. At the same time, U.S. colonization of the Philippines is but one instance of U.S. racial-imperial rule. Since British colonization of North America, white settlers and politicians have debated questions of race and political membership. U.S. state actors abridged the sovereignty of Native nations and enslaved Black people. In the nineteenth century, through wars of expansion, federal state actors confronted if and how to incorporate new nonwhite people into the political boundaries of the country. They fought violent wars to suppress Indigenous people. White politicians and former slaveholders restricted the rights of Black people after the Civil War, and white legislators limited migration and naturalization for Asian migrants.

While U.S. rule over the Philippines is an episode in a longer racial-imperial history, it also powerfully illuminates the importance of ambiguity to state formation. Different groups—with different resources, interests, norms, and ideas of race and governance—struggle for control. Conflict and compromise over who and what constitutes the polity are at the heart of modern state formation.[9] Even as U.S. state actors agreed to exclude nonwhite people and define the country as white, they disagreed about the terms of rule and relied on a range of strategies. Among them were ambiguous definitions like "foreign in a domestic sense." Unclear and equivocal definitions allowed U.S. state actors to reach political compromises and expand their power. They could both claim sovereignty over more territory and deny rights to people it brought under U.S. control. The Philippines was a U.S. territory, but its people were not U.S. citizens. Ambiguous definitions of membership are not unique to the Philippines, however. For instance, in 1831, the U.S. Supreme Court defined American Indian nations as "domestic dependent nations,"[10] claiming that tribes were neither foreign governments nor were they separate from the Union. Just as ambiguity is not particular to rule over the Philippines, it is not unique to the United States. Scholars of empire have long emphasized that imperial regimes rely on ambiguity, hybridity, and flexibility.[11] Nevertheless, the centrality of ambiguity to U.S. state formation is understudied. Ambiguity allowed U.S. state actors to resolve the problem of claiming new territory and excluding unwanted nonwhite people.

Enduring Empire traces both the debates that gave rise to and the consequences that emerged from ambiguity in U.S. rule of the Philippines. In the early years of rule, federal state actors like Taft who sought imperial expansion disagreed with people like Simmons, whose concerns about Filipinos' racial fitness led them to oppose U.S. rule of the archipelago. Unable to resolve the tensions between expansion and racial exclusion, the U.S. Supreme Court institutionalized ambiguity. Ambiguity accommodated a range of policies toward the Philippines and Filipinos. The United States not only claimed sovereignty over the archipelago while excluding its people from U.S. citizenship; in the 1930s and 1940s legislators also simultaneously defined Filipinos as citizens, nationals, and aliens. Both state actors in favor of and opposed to overseas empire had latitude to act as they pleased toward the Philippines with little interference from the other side. Institutionalized ambiguity granted state actors flexibility as they debated the terms of rule, reclassified the territory and people of the Philippines, and cemented a system of racial difference into state structure. The terms of rule evolved, but the foundational structure of inequality endured.[12]

Institutionalized ambiguity created a durable and flexible system that could adapt to state actors' diverse and changing concerns. In this way, the legal and administrative structure of U.S. racial-imperial rule is like grammar.[13] The metaphor of grammar illustrates how deep organizing structures, principles, and rules—like those of law—endure and adapt. On the one hand, structure can evolve with debate and through use. On the other, the rules of grammar are capacious and can accommodate different terms and vocabularies. As a system of rules, grammar refers to prescriptive norms.[14] It tells us how to order words and how different parts of the system—like subjects and objects—relate. It provides the mechanics—as in the conventions and organization—of communication. Grammar shapes how we see, know, and communicate about the world, and in this way, it serves a normalizing function. Although grammar provides a set of shared rules, it is not static. The agreed-upon rules of grammar evolve. Making changes official, however, usually requires debate and rarely upsets the deep structure. In other words, while people may change the use of pronouns, ignore the placement of prepositions, or dispose of antiquated tenses,[15] the fundamental aspects of language remain in place to make it mutually intelligible to different speakers over decades of transformation. Grammar thus provides a framework, shared rules, and structure while also being flexible and adaptable.

The metaphor of grammar illustrates how structures—like that of U.S. racial-imperial rule—rely on ambiguity to endure. Rather than a weakness, ambiguity is a feature of structures like grammar, law, and administration. Within the parameters of a given structure, ambiguity enables experimentation, interpretation, and discretion. Thus, ambiguity helps systems change without becoming obsolete. In the case of U.S. rule of the Philippines, state actors relied on ambiguity as they built a system of laws and an administrative structure for managing the Philippines. Their system of racial-imperial rule proved to be both flexible and durable. State actors repeatedly reclassified the Philippines, its people, and their relationship to the United States, often in contradictory ways. The terms of rule were mercurial, but the underlying structure of inequality persisted.

To interrogate how U.S. racial-imperial rule endured, this book charts the conditions that gave rise to ambiguity and the transformations that emerged. Over forty-eight years—beginning with the Spanish–American War and ending with rehabilitation from World War II—federal state actors made war and debated the boundaries of U.S. sovereignty and citizenship. U.S. presidents, federal legislators, administrators, and justices rarely agreed about what kind of state the United States should be, the place of nonwhite people in the polity, or about the best way to maintain U.S. white hegemony. As they debated, they relied on ambiguity to define the United States' geographic and demographic boundaries and remake law and administrative structure. Although the United States recognized Philippine independence in 1946, the flexible racial-imperial grammar enabled U.S. state actors to renew their control over the archipelago. U.S.–Philippine relations remained hierarchical. Tracing the institutionalization of ambiguity and its consequences for state formation reveals how the United States ostensibly decolonized the Philippines while maintaining unequal and racially differentiated rule.

Like socio-legal history and historical sociological studies of race, migration, citizenship, and the state,[16] this book focuses on how ideas of human difference unfold over time and shape state structures. I trace U.S. racial and imperial formations—as in cultural and sociohistorical processes that make and unmake structures of race and economic and geopolitical influence—over time.[17] I analyze how federal state actors make war and expand the state's boundaries, the vocabularies they use to debate, how they resolve their conflicts, how they cement their ideas into state structure, and how these structures continue to shape future political action. Unable to resolve conflicts wrought through war, U.S. Supreme Court justices and administrators institutionalized ambiguity. Ambiguity allowed future administrators and legislators to bifurcate imperial rule and disguise imperial relations in non-explicitly hierarchical terms. Together, institutionalizing ambiguity, bifurcating rule, and disguising empire explain how the United States changed the terms of rule while maintaining the underlying structure of inequality after formal independence.

Of the many racial, political, economic, and strategic considerations that allowed the U.S. empire to endure, I focus on the debates and conflicts among U.S. federal state actors.[18] As scholars have documented, Filipino elites and politicians were also critical figures in making U.S. empire. Under the constraints of foreign sovereignty, Filipinos resisted, accommodated, and adapted the structures of U.S. rule.[19] As Leia Castañeda Anastacio and Julian Go show, Filipinos reinterpreted the meaning of tutelage, democracy, and U.S. constitutionalism, thus reshaping the U.S. colonial project in the Philippines in ways that their colonizers did not anticipate.[20] What remains less understood, however, is how conflict among metropolitan state actors over different racial ideologies shaped U.S. racial-imperial state formation. When considered alongside insights about Filipinos' role in shaping the colonial project, attention to U.S. state actors' diverse positions on white hegemony reveals that the

U.S. metropole did not simply impose rigid mandates on its colony. Ambiguity enabled U.S. state actors to configure power in myriad and durable ways.

Charting the conflicting and evolving metropolitan practices of racial-imperial rule necessitates consideration of a diverse cast of actors. Overseas rule implicated multiple state actors in different branches of government and agencies. U.S. federal state actors across the political spectrum debated U.S.-Philippine relations. During nearly fifty years of rule, new politicians entered the debate, and key U.S. actors also changed their position on the Philippines. To capture the conflictual and changing political landscape, this book relies on primary source material from nearly twenty libraries and archives in the United States and the Philippines as well as existing secondary sources. I not only analyze the files of the United States *de facto* colonial office—the Bureau of Insular Affairs—but also records from a variety of sources and on topics not always understood as the sites to study overseas empire. Sources include records of the Immigration and Naturalization Service, the U.S. military, the Joint Chiefs of Staff, the Departments of State and Interior, Veterans Affairs, the U.S. Congress, as well as papers of U.S. legislators, U.S. and Philippine presidents, and executive administrators. By drawing on a variety of sources that not only discuss questions of immigration and naturalization but also trade tariffs and military policy, this book attends to both the foreign and domestic sites of U.S. empire.[21] In short, *Enduring Empire* pays attention to the variation across agencies and branches of government as well as practices of empire abroad in the colony and at home in the metropole.

In what follows, I first outline how war-making shapes racial-imperial grammar. By raising concern over the best way to maintain white hegemonic rule, state actors translated ideas of difference into state structures. They relied on a range of strategies, including ambiguous law. This is clear in the War of 1898 and in World War II as well as in better-known historical moments of U.S. state formation.[22] Episodes of war-making prior to 1898 are important for understanding U.S. history, race, and empire in their own right. At the same time, war-making prior to 1898 lay foundations that set the terms for debates about the Philippines. After discussing how war-making raises questions about race and membership, which state actors then cement into state structure, I outline the ethnoracial terminology used in this book and my approach to the study of race. The introduction ends with an overview of the rest of the book.

WAR-MAKING AND THE GRAMMAR OF RULE

The story of U.S. empire in the Philippines is bookended by war and its af-
termath. In 1898, the United States went to war with Spain and acquired the
Philippines. In 1946, as the United States recovered from World War II, it both
recognized Philippine independence and renewed imperial influence over the
archipelago. Because war raises questions across multiple state institutions, it
is an especially active site of state formation. State actors debate intervention
or neutrality, consider allies and enemies, mobilize, rebuild, rehabilitate, and
cement their victories and influence after wars. They consider questions of
extraterritorial conquest, settlement, taxation, military activity, trade, and the
membership and rights of conquered people. Through resource extraction,
taxation, and building standing armies, for example, state actors build new
state institutions, laws, and capacities.[23] As a totalizing activity, war braids
together foreign and domestic concerns and translates them into state structures.[24] Implemented across branches of government and state institutions,
the consequences of war-making are far-reaching. From the 1944 G.I. Bill—
which rewarded veterans for their service in World War II and built the white
middle class—to the expansion of U.S. military bases worldwide, war reshapes
people's rights and the state's geopolitical position.[25]

War-making not only involves different state institutions, but it is also
all-encompassing because it precedes and follows war. W.E.B. Du Bois wrote
that "the cause of war is preparation for war."[26] Seeking markets, raw materials, and outlets for capital, European states have gone to war. As J. A. Hobson,
Vladimir Lenin, and George Padmore showed, imperial competition leads
to war.[27] Even when not formally at war, state actors lay foundations for war
through building state security and military capacity. Political activity informs and constitutes war, just as the former extends and emerges from the
latter.[28] Wartime is a prolonged event or "chronic conflict."[29] Wartime and
peacetime, thus, are not discrete events; the lines between them are blurry.[30]
War-making has consequences that shape life and state formation after war.[31]

Just as war pervades state activities before, during, and after combat, state
actors also engage in symbolic and classificatory struggles as they make war.[32]
They redefine the geographic and demographic boundaries of the polity. Perhaps most obviously, as a result of war treaties, the United States has gained
sovereignty over new territories, bringing the foreign into the domestic. At the

same time, state actors also debate who the enemy is and why "we" must defeat "them." As Nikhil Singh writes, "The prospect of state violence, even war, has never been far from either the figuration or the conceptualization of race as a form of social relation."[33] Through war-making, state actors debate and concretize ideas of human difference. Making war animates debates and feeds anxieties about racial threats.[34] Paul Kramer argues that the Philippine–American War, which followed the Spanish–American War, was the foundational moment of colonial race-making.[35] Even as U.S. imperial conquest of the Philippines defined racial formations, classifications of race and citizenship, and colonial state structures, by continuing to make war, U.S. state actors transformed the discourse and practices of U.S. racial-imperial rule. Generations of state actors addressed three fundamental questions about U.S. identity: What is the United States' orientation to global affairs? What is the relationship of the United States to the Philippines and its people? And what is the place of the Philippines and Filipinos in the United States' global strategy? As U.S. state actors considered the geographic and demographic boundaries of the U.S. polity, they built a new structure of overseas rule and adapted its terms.

Whether during the Indian Wars, the Mexican–American War, the Civil War, the Spanish–American War, the Philippine–American War, or World War II, the United States has encountered questions of who and what makes up the United States. As U.S. state actors made war, they expanded U.S. sovereignty across the continent and globe. The Civil War, Reconstruction, and its end demonstrate that white hegemony and racial exclusion are fundamental to the U.S. state. The case of the Civil War is not only a history about slavery and the status of Black people but also one of imperial war-making that drove the United States to a sectional conflict.[36] Throughout U.S. history, state actors have tied together questions of race and empire through war-making.

The history of war, race, empire, and state formation prior to the Spanish–American War is important to the story of U.S. imperial rule of the Philippines. Prior practices and legal constraints shaped debates over the exclusion or incorporation of the new colony. Politicians, settlers, and elites defined the United States as a country for white men. Prior to the Civil War, U.S. state actors shared an understanding of many aspects of the U.S. racial-imperial grammar. The 1789 Constitution excluded American Indians and made chattel slavery legal. The Naturalization Act of 1790 limited the right of naturalization to freeborn whites. The rule of hypodescent maintained a rigid color line by defining people who were even "one drop" Black to be Black. At the same time, conflicts over expansion and the institution of slavery reshaped the U.S. system of rule and introduced new constraints into the strategies of white racial rule. After the Civil War, state actors continued to abridge Native sovereignty, institutionalize ambiguous law, and make tenuous political compromises. To manage the constraints of the Fourteenth Amendment, they also enabled discretion, and reinterpreted law that guaranteed racial equality, stripping it of its substantive meaning. These practices, detailed below, lay the groundwork for political debates over the War of 1898 and U.S. overseas rule of the Philippines.

Abridging Native Sovereignty and Institutionalizing Ambiguous Law

From the time of the British colonies through the first century of U.S. state formation, war-making drove conquest, treaties, annexation, land purchases, and violent dispossession. These activities shaped the U.S. racial-imperial grammar in durable ways. As U.S. state actors brought new land and people under the sovereignty of the United States, they not only defined the United States as a white country but also built federal state capacity. Prior to the War of 1898, they engaged in practices of Indian removal, preemption (which allowed settlers to occupy public land and then to receive government relief), and white homesteading. As they would again in the Philippines, the U.S. Supreme Court used ambiguous legal decisions to define nonwhite people as subordinated outsiders. In the case of continental expansion and tribes, the Court also relied on the doctrine of discovery. Wars of expansion, denial of sovereignty, exclusion from citizenship, and growth of federal power were also features of U.S. rule of the Philippines.

Prior to the Civil War, the country favored violent expansion as a strategy for securing white hegemony. As Ned Blackhawk notes, "the history of Indian-white relations, particularly in the eighteenth and nineteenth centuries, reads like a series of constant wars."[37] In instances where they believed the western territories to be under threat of Native attacks, the federal government supported white settlement.[38] Judges favored federal policies for preemption as a strategy for whitening and civilizing Native lands. For example, in *Johnson v. M'Intosh* (1823), the Supreme Court ruled that the doctrine of discovery gave the United States sovereignty over Native lands, as tribes were mere occupants.[39] The Court thus facilitated white property ownership and settlement. In 1830, Congress passed the Indian Removal Act, which formalized the role of the federal government in forcibly removing American Indians from east of the Mississippi.[40] By going to war, the United States expanded geographically and defined itself through the dispossession and exclusion of Native people.

The doctrine of discovery and forcible removal were not the only strategies employed by the U.S. federal government in managing expansion and demographic questions. At times, the United States recognized the sovereignty of American Indian nations. Often, however, this recognition was used to exclude tribes from making claims on the U.S. state. In two U.S. Supreme Court cases, *Cherokee Nation v. Georgia* (1831) and *Worcester v. Georgia* (1832), the justices decided that American Indians were not a part of the United States. Instead, the Court defined them as "domestic dependent nations," which limited tribes' sovereign claims and placed them under a trust relationship with the federal government. The U.S. government, not American Indians, would determine what was in the best interest of the tribes. These strategies, while departing from the doctrine of discovery precedent in *Johnson v. M'Intosh*, expanded U.S. state power. Exclusion and denial of U.S. citizenship was ultimately less a recognition of tribal sovereignty and more a way to expand the power of the federal government above states and settlers and keep out unwanted nonwhite populations. By the 1830s, dispossession and exclusion were core to the U.S. racial-imperial grammar.

During successive conflicts—or what Brian DeLay calls the War of a Thousand Deserts—among the Comanche, Kiowa, Apache, Diné, Mexico, and the United States,[41] the U.S. federal government expanded its power to manage new territory, people, and eventually incorporate more territories, including Texas (1845), the Oregon Territory (1846), and those from the Mexican Cession (1848). Congress increased opportunities for white settlers to gain political privileges and economic opportunities.[42] During the Civil War, the Union continued to engage in wars against Native people. The federal government virtually abandoned treaties and land purchases and instead plunged into more violent wars against Native tribes, including the Diné, Cheyenne, and Arapaho. In 1863, Union forces killed over 250 Northern Shoshone. In 1864, Union volunteers massacred Cheyenne and Arapaho at Sand Creek.[43] Alongside violent campaigns, the federal government continued Indian removal and lowered the cost of homesteading for white settlers. Wars of westward expansion built a system that provided economic opportunities to white people while abridging tribal sovereignty and excluding nonwhite people.

Making Tenuous Legislative Compromises over Slavery

Through wars of westward expansion, state actors, elites, and settlers not only threatened Native sovereignty and institutionalized ambiguous legal decisions, they also confronted questions about the institution of slavery and the rights of Black people in new territories. These debates would also inform the U.S. racial-imperial grammar. Prior to the Civil War, as they would again in rule of the Philippines, U.S. state actors relied on compromise to manage conflicts and divergent interests formed through wars of expansion. In the case of the antebellum United States, legislators made tenuous agreements, and the U.S. Supreme Court disrupted these arrangements.

Due to growing sectional divides, U.S. state actors turned to compromise to deflect conflict. The Missouri Compromise of 1820, for example, attempted to manage the delicate balance between slave and free states in the United States. Any state admitted above the 36°30' parallel except for Missouri would prohibit slavery, while those below would permit it. While this compromise held for several years, new wars with Mexico reanimated debates over race and membership in the United States. After annexing Texas in 1845 and winning new territories from Mexico in the 1848 Treaty of Guadalupe Hidalgo, U.S. state actors again confronted the question: would new territories become free or slave states? For many Southern planters, westward expansion had been an opportunity to expand their power and privilege. While Northern business and political elite formerly saw westward expansion as an opportunity for capital accumulation, in considering the Treaty of Guadalupe Hidalgo, they worried that too much territory could increase the power of Southern states in Congress.[44] Nevertheless, Northerners and the growing number of Western politicians supported racial restrictions to western land policies. Westward settlement was for white men.

The Compromise of 1850 again attempted to resolve conflicts emerging from wars of westward expansion. California was admitted as a free state, but other parts of the area won from Mexico remained U.S. territories. Popular sovereignty would determine whether they would eventually join as free or slave states. The compromise, however, did not fully resolve the tensions. Southerners worried that homesteaders would outnumber slave owners in the new territories.[45] Because of Southern concerns about western settlement, the Kansas–Nebraska Act (1854) repealed the Missouri Compromise (1820) in the territories of Kansas and Nebraska. In the act, Congress agreed that, following on the Compromise of 1850, the western states would use popular sovereignty to determine if they would be free or slave states.

While the growth of the institution of slavery was up for debate, expansion remained a key aspect of the U.S. racial-imperial grammar. Throughout this period and after the Kansas–Nebraska Act, Southerners looked to secure their interests farther south into Mexico, the Caribbean, and other parts of Latin America. From the 1820s to 1850s, presidents Thomas Jefferson, James Monroe, John Quincy Adams, James Polk, Franklin Pierce, and James Buchanan believed that these southern territories—which they construed as more populated than western territories—could help bolster the U.S. economy. In the twenty years preceding the Civil War, proslavery politicians, administrators, and their allies controlled the executive branch. They, along with planters from the Mississippi Valley, hoped that southern expansion could strengthen their economy based on slavery.

Amid Southern concern about westward expansion, attempts at conquest and annexation accelerated in the 1850s. Filibusters and proslavery imperialists launched missions to Cuba in 1851 and Nicaragua in 1855. In 1854, President Pierce's administration drafted the Ostend Manifesto, which argued that if Spain would not part with Cuba, then the United States would rely on military intervention to "detach" Cuba from Spain.[46] Cuba, they argued, was a natural extension of the United States. Both it and Nicaragua could provide new lands and markets for expanding white ownership of both land and enslaved people. Perhaps slaveholders could even reopen the slave trade, they hoped.[47]

As Southerners and the U.S. executive branch looked for new sites of expansion and considered war, the growing conflicts over Southern power and the institution of slavery upset the U.S. racial-imperial grammar. In 1857, the U.S. Supreme Court justices broke the tenuous compromise of the Kansas–Nebraska Act. In *Dred Scott v. Sandford*, they struck down the Missouri Compromise as unconstitutional and held that the word "citizens" did not include emancipated slaves.[48] The Court decided Congress did not have the power to restrict the expansion of slavery to new territories (for it infringed on the rights of slaveholders). The decision from *Dred Scott* put the rights of Southern states and slaveholders over the rights of Black people born in the

United States. By taking a stance on the rights of white slaveholders, the Court catalyzed the Civil War.

Thus, through wars of western colonization, U.S. state actors not only confronted questions about the status of American Indians but also about the institution of slavery.[49] On the one hand, because they agreed about the relationship of the United States to tribes, making war enabled U.S. state actors to limit tribal sovereignty and institutionalize ambiguous law that subordinated and excluded Indigenous people. On the other, U.S. state actors could not agree about the institution of slavery. They thus turned to temporary and tenuous legislative compromise. These attempts to keep the peace did not resolve any fundamental conflicts over expansion and slavery. Nevertheless, prior to the Civil War, compromise, ambiguity, and limiting Indigenous sovereignty were key foundations of the U.S. racial-imperial grammar.

Creating New Rules, Enabling Discretion, and Reinterpreting Law
The effects of the Civil War and Reconstruction continued to shape how the United States managed race and empire. As state actors created and confronted new rules about what and who made up the country, they used compromise to manage unwanted nonwhite populations. Legislators also enabled regional, state, and local discretion. The Court reinterpreted law, erasing its substantive meaning. In this period of post-war rehabilitation, the United States both re-inscribed and revamped the structure of racial-imperial rule.

The greatest innovation to the U.S. racial-imperial grammar came at the end of the U.S. Civil War when the U.S. federal government passed new legislation and amended the U.S. Constitution. A predominantly Republican Congress ratified the so-called Civil War or Reconstruction Amendments in 1865 and 1866. The Thirteenth Amendment abolished slavery and expanded the power of the federal government.[50] The Fourteenth Amendment provided citizenship and equal protection of freedmen (and all born on U.S. soil), the effects of which continue to reverberate in conflicts of national boundaries and membership to this day. And the Fifteenth Amendment provided voting rights to Black men. Together with the amendments, the 1866 Civil Rights Act, which created new rights for formerly enslaved people, reflected a radical shift in political culture and practices that, at least on the surface, suggested greater demographic inclusivity.[51] Seemingly, U.S. racial-imperial rule became more inclusionary.

These amendments, however, erased neither earlier debates about the status of Black people nor earlier exclusionary practices. The formal rules changed, but many in the United States remained committed to white supremacy.[52] Conflicts between the Republican and Democratic parties shaped how the country interpreted and applied the new rules. In response to a dispute about the election of Republican Rutherford B. Hayes to the U.S. presidency, the Compromise of 1877 withdrew U.S. military rule from the South. Northern- and Republican-led Reconstruction ended. While secured on the books, Southern Democrats rolled back the rights of Black Americans as they restored their control.[53] The compromise between North and South had disastrous effects for Black people in the United States. Southern white backlash gave way to a system of segregation, anti-miscegenation laws, and disenfranchisement known as Jim Crow. Informal, local, and state-level discrimination and subordination—as seen in the Black Codes (which limited the rights of Black Americans to hold certain jobs or own property)—were commonplace.[54] U.S. state actors recommitted to white supremacy through compromise, discretion, and creating new rules.

At the federal level, state actors reinterpreted the Reconstruction Amendments, bringing them in line with the antebellum racial-imperial grammar. The Supreme Court repeatedly ruled in ways that interpreted the Fourteenth Amendment's Equal Protection Clause as *not* being a means to combat discrimination.[55] *De jure* citizenship did not translate into a full extension of *de facto* rights for nonwhite and non-Indigenous populations.[56] In *Plessy v. Ferguson* (1896), the Court held that laws segregating whites and people of African descent were legal—people could be "separate but equal." The reinterpretation of law undermined the brief possibility of racial equality. Equal citizenship was but a weak promise. These approaches would again prove useful in accommodating U.S. overseas empire.

Enduring Ambiguity and Violence

Whereas the Court reinterpreted new rules and removed the substantive meaning from the post-war Amendments, another aspect of the U.S. racial-imperial grammar remained remarkably durable. In the post-bellum period, through ambiguous classification and ongoing war, the United States continued to displace and subordinate American Indian nations through projects of white settler colonialism.[57] Court decisions and acts of Congress both diminished tribal sovereignty and defined the United States as white.[58] In accordance with the decisions in both *M'Intosh* and the Cherokee cases, in 1886, the Court decided in *United States v. Kagama* that the United States had title to the land and that tribes were "semi-independent" wards. Building on the Court's decision, in 1887, Congress passed the Dawes Act, which divided reservations and created more land for white settlers. The U.S. federal government classified American Indians as tribal and semi-independent nations to whom the Fourteenth Amendment did not apply.[59] Such an alternative classification that placed some people outside the scope of the Constitution was another strategy that the United States would adapt in the Philippines.

As the Court excluded and defined American Indians in ambiguous ways, the executive branch continued campaigns of violence. After dividing the Great Sioux Reservation in what would become South Dakota, President Benjamin Harrison's administration (1889–1893) promoted white settlement and development. Facing a dire situation, the Lakota turned to the Ghost Dance to call for the abundance and relationships with the natural world that existed prior to settlement. Federal agents and settlers grew fearful. Confronted with the potential loss of western settler support, President Harrison ordered the U.S. Army to move in and prevent a Lakota uprising. When one man refused to give up his gun on December 29, 1890, the army shot at him and his disarmed companions. After the rest of the population panicked and attempted to flee, U.S. soldiers tracked and slaughtered almost three hundred people. Those who survived were brought under the control of the federal government's agency, the Indian Office.[60] Using executive oversight to manage populations wracked by state violence, the federal government reaffirmed its commitment to white nationalism.

The history of imperial and sectional wars in the United States reveals how, in making war, state actors wrestle with the best ways to maintain white hegemony. By looking at the practices that arose from making war, we can better understand transformations in racial-imperial forms. Settler colonial expansion and the Civil War lay down an unabashedly white supremacist racial-imperial grammar. At the same time, however, the promise of equal citizenship fundamentally transformed the structure of racial-imperial rule. Reconstruction created new rules on the books, and yet the United States continued to rely on practices of abridging sovereignty, institutionalizing ambiguity and tenuous compromise. U.S. state actors also used discretion and reinterpreted law to exclude and subordinate nonwhite people.

Widely recognized as an important period of U.S. state- and race-making,[61] nineteenth-century wars also shaped debates over another episode of war-making in the Philippines. Precedents for managing expansion and the membership of nonwhite people were not easily translated to the question of ruling the Philippines in the post–Civil War era. When the United States went to war with Spain, U.S. state actors debated and sought new approaches to manage the contradictions between expanding the U.S. territory and limiting the rights of nonwhite people. They disagreed on the terms of rule, classified territory and people in new ways, and institutionalized new rules into U.S. racial-imperial grammar. In the next chapter, I synthesize the different positions on war, concerns about threats to white hegemony, and how, through these considerations, war-making again reshaped state structures.

ETHNORACIAL TERMINOLOGY AND THE STUDY OF RACE

This book is about how, in making war, one population conceived of and debated the racial status of another and cemented these ideas of race into state structure. When I speak of race, I am concerned with how people draw boundaries between their imagined community and another,[62] or how they conceive of "us" and "them."[63] The drawing of boundaries—a process that Max Weber referred to as closure—matters for the distribution of rights and resources.[64] In making war and classifying Filipinos, U.S. state actors not only constructed Filipino-ness but also whiteness. Over the half century of U.S. rule of the Philippines, U.S. state actors sought to maintain and expand white hegemony. In their vision of a racial state, they defined themselves as white and Anglo-Saxon and superior to Filipinos. Over time, they developed different vocabularies for speaking of themselves and Filipinos.

When writing about people of European descent, in this book, I use the terms white and Anglo-Saxon. I use these words not because they reflect real human groupings but because it is how most state actors referred to their ideal population and the constituencies for whom they spoke. The term Anglo-Saxon rose in popularity by the middle of the nineteenth century. Originally, it referred to people living within England; later, it came to mean people who spoke English. In the race science zeitgeist, European Americans in the United States conceived of themselves against Black, Native, Mexican,

and Asian people. In relation to these people whom they believed to be inferior, they defined themselves as Anglo-Saxon and part of a superior race of
people. Even if they were not originally English or English-speaking, Europeans in the United States were conceived of as white.[65] And they could become
Anglo-Saxon by explicitly linking claims of their superiority to U.S. expansion.[66] Thus, for this period, I treat white and Anglo-Saxon as synonyms.

In the current U.S. context, it may be surprising that I refer to Filipinos as
a race or discuss racism directed at them. Today, few people think of Filipinos
in these terms, instead thinking of them as an ethnic or national group that
belongs to the Asian race.[67] Nevertheless, when referring to Filipinos and the
ideas that U.S. politicians and elite had about them, I use the terms "race"
and "racism" to accurately reflect the language of difference and belonging of
the time. In the early twentieth century, social thinkers and state actors considered Filipinos to be a racial problem. Only some U.S. state actors thought
Filipinos belonged to an Oriental, Asiatic, or Mongolian race. Others claimed
they were Malay, and the U.S. Census designated Filipinos in their own category, which remains true to this day.[68] Use of the term "race" is polysemous,
and how Filipinos came to be seen as Asian is part of the story of this book.[69]

For these reasons, I do not sharply distinguish race from ethnicity, nor do
I wish to reify what I consider a problematic analytical distinction between
the two.[70] As many Latin Americanists have noted, the meaning of the terms
"race" and "ethnicity" varies across time and space and cannot be reduced to
U.S. bureaucratic categories.[71] In the early twentieth century, the term "race"
was often used to denote fundamental differences, whether conceived of in
biological or cultural terms. Ideas of cultural and biological difference coexist and are co-constituted.[72] This is especially clear in the language of early-
twentieth-century imperialists discussed in Part I. At the same time, ideas
of both race and ethnic difference are situated in power relations.[73] Therefore,
I think of both as terms that people use to mark difference that they see as
pertaining to culture, heritage, origin, phenotype, and biology. The meaning
of race and ethnicity and which categories are salient are empirical questions,
not analytical givens.

Because this book details how ideas of human difference mattered for systems of rule, law, politics, and intervention, I take seriously the words that
politicians used.[74] The production of racial and imperial knowledge is itself
a form of power.[75] The way politicians spoke of Filipinos reveals how they

thought Filipinos should be treated in law and practice. Depending on their ideas of race, state actors reshaped U.S. laws and institutions to serve both nativist-isolationist and imperialist aims. In this book, I refer to two types of racial ideologies: vulgar and polite.

On the one hand, anti-imperialists, isolationists, protectionists, and nativists espoused vulgar racist arguments, based not only in explicit claims of biological difference and inferiority but also characterized by racialized exclusion, a denial of the possibility of assimilation, and a rejection of nonwhite peoples' individual subjecthood.[76] For example, Senator Stephen R. Mallory II (D-FL), a former member of the Confederate Army and Navy, complained about "the indefinite number of islands 10,000 miles distant from the capital of this country, seven thousand and odd miles distant from the nearest coast of the United States." He argued they were "inhabited by a very large population of mixed and different races, different in language, different in customs, different in religion, and to a large extent not only uncivilized, but even barbarous and savage." He warned that if the United States took the Philippines, then "seven to ten million of savages, barbarians, semicivilized, civilized, and partially enlightened people who constitute the population of the Philippine Islands" could not "be confined to the Philippine Islands." In Mallory's assessment of the U.S. Constitution, "it is out of the power of this Congress to deprive one of them of his liberty to pass from the confines of the Philippines and to go anywhere else on God's footstool he may choose to go."[77] Because the rule of law would require the United States to grant rights and liberties to "savage" Filipinos, the United States should not keep the islands. Legislators like Mallory opposed incorporating Filipinos into the U.S. polity and worked to constrain U.S. imperial expansion.

On the other hand, although imperialists and interventionists in the executive branch agreed Filipinos were racially inferior, they relied on paternalistic ideas. Their "polite" racist vocabulary was based on ideas of cultural difference, inclusionary discourse, and historicist arguments about the possibility of civilization and assimilation.[78] An ardent defender and architect of U.S. empire in the Philippines, William H. Taft served as President of the Philippine Commission and Governor General of the Philippines before he was elected U.S. president in 1909. In 1902, Taft testified in Congress that although Filipinos were not yet capable of self-rule or deserving of the rights guaranteed under the U.S. Constitution, they could be trained "by a gradual course."[79] On this basis, he suggested that the United States maintain control over the islands and allow executive branch administrators to manage overseas rule without the oversight of the U.S. Congress. As they tried to convince their reticent colleagues that overseas empire was in U.S. interests and would not threaten white hegemony at home, imperialists relied on polite racist claims. Their ideas of race were reflected in legal reform and administrative restructuring in the metropole and economic development and militarization in the colony.

The empire built in 1898 was at once supported by explicitly racial arguments and the outcome of different racial ideologies, one vulgar and one polite. U.S. state actors like Mallory and Taft spoke in different terms. They disagreed about the nature of Filipinos' inferiority and the practices of racial-imperial rule. This book charts how racial ideologies and their attendant vulgar and polite vocabularies changed over time and how they informed the laws, policies, and state institutions of U.S. racial-imperial rule in the Philippines.

Enduring Empire also raises questions yet to be tapped by U.S. social science of race and ethnicity. In studying race in formation, this book looks to race outside of the presumed U.S. national borders, rejects the myth of the U.S. nation state, and recenters the fact of empire.[80] In much of the U.S. sociology on race, ethnicity, and immigration, questions of racialization, belonging, membership, and inclusion are conceived as problems that begin when migrants cross the border into the United States.[81] This book draws on the work of scholars who study migration as a site where the foreign and the domestic intersect.[82] Border patrol and enforcement, immigration, and naturalization laws, for example, are not simply matters of defense or national interest but ways of keeping the foreign out.[83] How states decide who to let in or keep out is not only a domestic decision but also a matter of managing foreign relations.[84] I extend attention to how migration imbricates the foreign and domestic by showing that, through imperial conquest and war-making, U.S. settlers and state actors create racial "problems" at home and abroad by moving borders over people.

U.S. imperial management of the Philippines presents an opportunity to study the construction of racial difference, its consequences, and transformations over a half century. Prior to the War of 1898, few Americans even knew what or where the Philippines was. Neither had the Philippines been a significant source of immigration to the United States. War and the conquest of the

Philippines presented a new racial problem for the United States, one that both existed outside of U.S. national borders and that also could not easily be understood using the existing continental framework. U.S. state actors thought of the Philippine territory and Filipinos as both foreign and domestic. They compared the colony and its people to metropolitan, colonial, and foreign populations. While the historical record provides ample evidence of white supremacy in U.S. history prior to 1898, this book does not start a priori with anti-Filipino racism already existing. Instead, it draws attention to the formation of Filipinos as a race in the eyes of U.S. federal state actors. It charts how, through war-making, the meaning and terms of racial difference changed and how this mattered for state structures and imperial transformation.

BOOK OVERVIEW

Chapter 1 follows this introduction and offers a conceptual framework for understanding how U.S. rule of the Philippines both endured and changed. To arrive at this framework, Chapter 1 considers how the existing scholarship on U.S. empire and foreign relations and the scholarship on race make sense of racial-imperial transformation. Finding both sets of literature wanting, I put them in conversation with studies of the co-constitution of race and empire and theories of institutional change. By focusing on how different state actors in different parts of the federal government debate war and white hegemony, I outline how conflict shaped the early years of U.S. rule of the Philippines, which, in turn, created the foundations for eventual consensus and the transition to the informal empire of 1946.

The remaining chapters of the book are organized into three parts, each with paired empirical chapters. Part I covers 1898 to 1916. The War of 1898 and the United States' transition to an overseas empire catalyzed debates over white hegemony, Filipinos, and U.S. state structures. Chapters 2 and 3 address the challenges that U.S. state actors encountered in the transition to overseas empire. Specifically, these chapters show how, faced with conflict, the U.S. Supreme Court and executive branch administrators institutionalized ambiguity and lay a durable and flexible foundation for overseas rule.

War, first against Spain in Cuba and then for eight more years against Filipinos, raised new questions for U.S. state actors and elites.[85] First, what would overseas imperial rule mean for U.S. rule of law? And second, how could the United States administer the new colonies? Chapter 2, focused on 1898 to 1904, addresses the first question. It shows how in the *Insular Cases*, U.S. Supreme Court justices used old tools of the U.S. racial-imperial grammar. They translated their racial concerns and conflicts into ambiguous law. They enabled discretion to avoid settling seemingly intractable conflicts. They also created ostensibly race-neutral categories to evade the promises of the Fourteenth Amendment. In short, the justices transformed the U.S. Constitution to accommodate overseas colonial rule. Chapter 3 overlaps temporally with the events of Chapter 2 and extends into 1916. In the early 1900s, a dedicated band of imperialists in the executive branch built administrative structures to accommodate an ambiguous and flexible form of overseas empire. The executive branch not only used unclear definitions to facilitate overseas empire like their judicial counterparts, but they also centralized executive control of the Philippines as their predecessors had done with American Indian tribes. Together, these chapters reveal that conflicts over the scope of U.S. imperial sovereignty and the maintenance of white hegemony led state actors to institutionalize ambiguity in ways that both reinscribed and expanded the tools of the U.S. racial-imperial grammar.

Whereas Part I begins with the U.S. entrance to overseas empire in the Spanish–American War, Part II begins with another series of catalyzing events: World War I and party changes in the legislative and executive branches. It ends with the entrance to World War II. And while Part I traced how U.S. state actors institutionalized ambiguity into the legal and administrative structure of the U.S. state, Part II explores the contradictory and divergent political ramifications that emerged from ambiguity. Specifically, it shows how, by hiding empire at home and hiding race abroad, legislators and executive branch administrators bifurcated the foreign and domestic aspects of imperial rule.

Through two world wars and an interwar period, U.S. state actors disagreed about the geographic and demographic boundaries of the United States. These years raised questions about how the United States would continue to do empire. First, what would be the place of colonial subjects in the U.S. metropole? And second, what role would the colonies play in U.S. global strategy? Chapter 4, focused on 1928 to 1940, addresses the first question, showing how and why nativist-isolationists sought to exclude Filipinos from migration, settlement, and naturalization in metropolitan United States. Hostile toward the presence of Filipinos in the United States, nativist-isolationists redefined Filipino colonial subjects as foreign "Asians," obscuring the fact of ongoing colonial relations in domestic politics. Chapter 5, focused on 1934 to 1941, demonstrates how, in response to Japanese attacks on Hawai'i and the Philippines, U.S. legislators shifted their understandings of Filipinos and the Philippines in the global arena. At this time, the United States began to redefine its empire. The Philippines became geostrategically important to the United States. In this light, U.S. state actors saw Filipinos who served in the U.S. military as "good" Asians and loyal service members, not racialized outsiders. Even formerly nativist-isolationist politicians decoupled the imperial project from racial claims. Ambiguous and flexible definitions of the relationship of the United States to the Philippines—key outcomes of the political conflict document in Part I—enabled both sides to get what they wanted. Securing racial exclusion at home and imperial influence abroad facilitated the transition from explicitly racial-imperial rule to polite, informal imperial rule in the Philippines.

Part III picks up where Part II left off with the close of World War II. It also considers another important event: forthcoming Philippine independence. While the book began with the Spanish–American War and U.S. state actors' debates over the terms of inclusion of a new overseas territory, the book ends with the conclusion of another war and transition to informal empire in the Philippines. As empire took on new meanings in the post–World War II era, U.S. state actors altered the terms of rule. Part III shows how—building on the racial-imperial grammar founded in Part I and proliferated in Part II— members of the U.S. executive and legislative branches reached compromises and disguised U.S.–Philippine relations in terms that evaded explicit reference to hierarchical rule.

In response to the end of the war and plans for Philippine independence, U.S. state actors reevaluated their positions on U.S. hegemony. They wrestled with two questions. First, what would be the relationship of the United States to their soon-to-be former colonial subjects? Second, what would be the relationship of the United States to the new Philippine state? To answer these questions, U.S. politicians had to consider their positions on imperial rule (or decolonization), political influence abroad, and racial equality at home. Chapter 6, by analyzing legislative debates over migration and naturalization between 1945 and 1946, addresses the first question. It shows how legislators and the administrator of Veterans Affairs denied rights and rescinded promises made to Filipinos during World War II. Chapter 7, by attending to debates over trade, aid, and military bases between 1945 and 1947, answers the second question. This chapter shows how formerly divided members of the legislative and executive branches united around the importance of U.S. global hegemony. Through economic and military arrangements that were built during decades of formal colonial rule, U.S. state actors abridged Philippine sovereignty. They reframed the civilizing mission of formal empire as a democratizing one and disguised U.S.–Philippine relations in two other ways. Racial divides between white and nonwhite people became political ones between democratic and communist countries.[86] And rights and colonial relations became aid.

The book concludes by considering how Philippine independence was not a new dawn for the United States or the Philippines. The racial-imperial grammar of the United States remains in place today. Ambiguous sovereign relations persist. After 1946, from the archipelago to the United States' mandate over Japan and its former colonies and U.S. interventions in Korea, Vietnam, Latin America, and Southwest Asia, the U.S. empire endures.

As a whole, this book addresses how U.S. state actors transformed the terms of ruling the Philippines while maintaining its deep structure. In charting this metamorphosis, it becomes clear that formal empire and informal empire are undergirded by logics of racial differences and the desire to maintain white hegemony. At the same time, in the case of the Philippines, informal empire was built on the scaffolding of formal empire. Through war-making, federal state actors encountered human difference and perceived threats to U.S. white hegemony. They debated their visions for how to best maintain white racial rule at home and abroad. Race and the management of colonial subjects were central to how the United States fashioned overseas rule. Ambiguity was the key foundation that enabled flexibility in racial-imperial rule. Renovations to law and administrative structures provided opportunities for legislators to exclude Filipinos from the metropolitan United States and for members of the executive branch to include the Philippine territory in geopolitical and military strategy. These foundations were durable, lasting through two world wars and shaping the postcolonial relations between the United States and the newly independent Philippine state.

ONE TRANSFORMATIONS IN RACIAL-IMPERIAL RULE

The United States formally ruled the Philippines for forty-eight years, and after Philippine independence, U.S.–Philippine relations remained racial and imperial. Nevertheless, some aspects of rule changed. Even Theodore Roosevelt, a former jingoist and unapologetic imperialist, came to question if the United States should keep the Philippines. Before he became U.S. president, Roosevelt pushed for military intervention in the Caribbean and Pacific. As assistant secretary of the navy under President William McKinley (1897–1898), he believed that through empire, the United States could strengthen its character and shape the trajectory of civilization.[1] Filipinos, Roosevelt argued, were "backward" and lesser men than Anglo-Saxons.[2] In 1899, he gave a speech to the Hamilton Club of Chicago and claimed that the Philippines—composed of "half-caste and native Christians, warlike Moslems, and wild pagans" who were "utterly unfit for self government"—needed the United States' "wise supervision."[3] Then in 1900, as he accepted the nomination for vice president at the Republican National Convention, Roosevelt praised U.S. control of the islands. He claimed that without the United States, the archipelago would fall into tyranny. "The minute we leave," he stated, "it ceases to be stable."[4] He continued, "The Philippines are now part of American Territory. To surrender them would be to surrender American territory." Roosevelt believed the

Philippines was an integral part of the United States, and he viewed empire and racial rule as the responsibility of Anglo-Saxons and the United States.

While his ideas of race and civilization made him an early enthusiastic supporter of U.S. empire in the Philippines, as Roosevelt considered the United States' geopolitical position and naval strategy in the Pacific, his position on the Philippines changed.[5] In 1907, Roosevelt wrote that the United States "shall have to be prepared for giving the islands independence of a more or less complete type much sooner than I think advisable if this country were prepared to look ahead fifty years and to build the navy and erect fortifications which in my judgement it should." Without a strong navy, he continued, "the Philippines form our heel of Achilles. They are all that make the present situation with Japan dangerous."[6] By 1915, as the U.S. Congress considered a path toward Philippine independence, Roosevelt admitted that the United States could not sustain its empire in the same terms. Lamenting the lack of U.S. defense support for the archipelago, he wrote: "it has been very bitter for me to have to grow to feel, as I have grown to feel, that the attitude of the American people was such as to make it unwise for us to retain [the Philippines]." Without a clear commitment to strong U.S. foreign intervention, Roosevelt bemoaned that it now became "imperative to abandon the Philippines, as part of a policy of abandoning all intervention of asserting our ability to do the work of a strong nation overseas." While attempting to balance militarization, U.S. foreign relations with Japan, and U.S. racial-imperial rule of the Philippines, Roosevelt doubted the feasibility of maintaining the latter. Although he was an influential figure, his waning support of empire did not mean the end of U.S. rule in the Philippines. The United States retained the islands for thirty-one more years.

Roosevelt's evolving stance on the Philippines did, however, foreshadow future transformations to U.S.–Philippine relations. In 1941, the threat of Japan proved real when the rising empire state attacked the Philippines and Hawaiʻi. As they prepared to go to war against Japan, U.S. state actors again grappled with how to best maintain white hegemony at home and abroad. Considering the new threat, they reached consensus about whether and on what terms to include the Filipino people and territory in definitions of the United States. The Philippines became geostrategically important and its people loyal allies in war. In 1946, when the United States recognized Philippine independence, it did not—as Roosevelt had reluctantly suggested—wholly abandon the islands. Instead, the imperial power maintained informal control.

Both the continuation of U.S. empire and Roosevelt's shifting position demonstrate how empires are not just political entities or types of states, but they are processes, or as Ann Laura Stoler and Carole McGranahan put it, "states of being, becoming, and deferral."[7] As they considered threats to U.S. white hegemony, it was not only Roosevelt who changed. Federal state actors—some nativist, isolationist, and protectionist and others expansionist, interventionist, and imperialist—evolved from 1898 to 1946. As they changed their positions on the best way to maintain U.S. hegemony, U.S. state actors maintained a durable system of racial-imperial rule.

To explain both the transformations to U.S.–Philippine relations that Roosevelt came to believe were necessary and how the U.S. empire endured, this book analyzes how state actors weighed geostrategy, debated the scope of white hegemony, and defined the relationship of the United States to both the Philippines and its people. Over nearly five decades, U.S. state actors transformed their concerns and disagreements into state structures that accommodated a range of positions, facilitated change, and allowed them to maintain U.S. empire in the Philippines.

In making sense of racial-imperial state formation, predominating studies of U.S. foreign relations and U.S. empire, on the one hand, and studies of race, on the other, take different approaches. The former analyzes the formal economic and geopolitical relations between polities. Asking how economic and geopolitical factors shape extraterritorial rule, they interrogate whether states are empires and discuss the differences between formal and informal rule. They do not, however, consider race, or they treat it as epiphenomenal. Sociological studies of race in the United States, meanwhile, even when analyzing changes in racial patterns or ideologies, tend to confine their analyses of state formation to presumed national boundaries, thus missing how empire and foreign affairs shape racial formation. On their own, these approaches have not sufficiently addressed transformations in racial-imperial rule. Each offers an incomplete picture of how the United States transitioned from the empire of 1898 to that of 1946.

In this chapter, I first briefly summarize key differences and similarities between the empire of 1898 and that of 1946. I then review historical and social scientific approaches to the study of imperial and racial transformation. I discuss how they offer insights to and limit our understanding of how racial-imperial states evolve. After drawing attention to the importance of tracking state actors' positions, I discuss the different sets of actors who shaped U.S. rule over the Philippines. I briefly sketch their conflicts, as their changing and divergent ideas about white hegemony and race propel the story forward in subsequent chapters. Building on the overview of how state actors took different positions on the Philippines and Filipinos, I offer a conceptual framework to explain how the terms of U.S. rule over the Philippines changed while leaving the racial-imperial grammar intact.

EMPIRE FROM 1898 TO 1946

In 1898, the United States became a formal overseas empire and claimed sovereignty over the Philippine Islands. It justified its rule over its new colony in explicitly racial terms. Less than fifty years later, in 1946, the United States recognized Philippine independence and, on its surface, eschewed vulgar racial arguments about the islands and Filipino people. Formal U.S. racial-imperial rule of the Philippines ended, and yet U.S. control over the archipelago remained racial and imperial. The United States continued to exercise power over subordinated people outside the original political boundaries of the state, but state actors changed the terms of rule. U.S. state actors could turn away from explicit racial-imperial rule because they embedded reference to racial difference and inferiority in state structures. Although they no longer spoke of Filipinos as savages by 1946, over decades of formal rule, state actors' debates about how to best maintain white hegemony shaped state formation.

When the United States claimed sovereignty over the Philippines, the central question facing U.S. federal state actors was how to incorporate a new faraway territory with its nonwhite inhabitants into the political boundaries of the United States. This wasn't just a question about the racial fitness of Filipinos; it was also a question about the best strategy and practices for white racial rule. Virtually all federal state actors shared a tacit understanding of the U.S. racial structure. They agreed with Roosevelt: Filipinos were racially inferior outsiders. Despite their shared reliance on explicit racial arguments, U.S. elites, politicians, and legal experts could not agree on how the United States should relate to the Philippines. Anti-imperialists, isolationists, protectionists, and nativists, primarily in the U.S. Congress, saw Filipinos in vulgar terms and opposed U.S. imperial expansion. Others—imperialists and interventionists in the executive branch—agreed that Filipinos were racially inferior, but they also tried to convince their reticent colleagues that overseas empire was in the United States's interest and would not threaten white hegemony at home. The United States could train and civilize Filipinos. The conflict seemed intractable.

Forty-eight years later, however, U.S. state actors reached consensus about whether and on what terms to include the Filipino people and territory in definitions of the United States. In 1946, the United States relinquished sovereignty over the Philippines, something that former anti-imperialists, nativists, and isolationists long hoped for. After decades of conflict, the Philippines gained its independence, and its people became citizens of their new republic, no longer colonial subjects of the United States. In discussions about Philippine independence, former nativists and isolationists exchanged explicitly vulgar and racially denigrating vocabulary about Filipinos for narratives of Filipinos' loyalty to the United States and capacity for self-rule. The racial lexicon narrowed. U.S. state actors redefined their project not as one of white racial rule, as they had in the late nineteenth and early twentieth centuries, but as a project of spreading democracy and maintaining allies against communism. And yet, the structure of racial difference founded in the early years of rule continued to undergird the United States' informal empire.

Philippine independence was a transition in name but not in power relations between the United States and its former colony. U.S. state actors secured military bases, favorable trade deals, and natural resource development and investment rights in the Philippines to maintain extraterritorial control. Although Filipinos had long struggled for their independence, when it arrived, it was less a break with the past than the term "decolonization" might suggest. The imperial and racial grammar set in the early twentieth century continued to organize U.S. domination of Filipinos.

BRINGING RACE TO STUDIES OF FOREIGN RELATIONS

The story of the U.S. empire in the Philippines is one that transits a formal empire in 1898 to an informal one in 1946. The prevailing scholarship on empire, foreign relations, diplomatic history, and the United States in the world has provided helpful conceptual distinctions of imperial forms. Nevertheless, it suffers from two problems that limit our ability to make sense of the United States' enduring empire. First, it mistakes the myth of the United

States as a nation with how the state works in practice. Thus, this body of work minimizes the fact of U.S. empire and denies episodes of formal rule or treats the United States as exceptional. Second, it overlooks the importance of race and racial ideas in imperial state formation.

The scholarship on empire highlights differences in the exercise of political and economic influence. Some scholars distinguish between formal and informal rule. In formal empire and direct rule, states claim political sovereignty. In informal or indirect, they do not. Another related distinction in the literature is colonial and neocolonial. Kwame Nkrumah argued that, under neocolonialism, states had nominal sovereignty but were still subject to political, economic, and military influence from outside. Often, these forms of control operated through promises of aid from a former colonial or neocolonial overlord.[8] For some scholars, informal, indirect empire or neocolonial rule—exercised through military force, proxies, aid, or structural adjustments—involves less coercion and power from the metropole. Michael Mann, for example, calls informal empire a "lighter" form of coercion.[9] Others underscore the continuities between imperial forms. Julian Go writes, "We must not be too stark in our distinctions. Formal and informal empire might be better thought of as two ends of a blurry continuum."[10] Although primarily attentive to economic, military, and political arrangements and distinctions, this body of work captures how forms of power are hierarchically organized.[11]

Scholarship on U.S. foreign relations also foregrounds attention to economic, military, and political influence. It has long approached the United States as an exceptional empire,[12] underplaying the existence and persistence of U.S. empire. The common story goes like this: the United States, if it was ever an empire, decolonized the Philippines. The Philippines gained its independence. Filipinos learned how to run their own democratic country. From the conquest of the Philippines to its independence, the United States was a leader in democratizing the world.[13] In the bluntest accounts, if the United States was ever an empire, it was one only briefly.[14] Post-1946, then, the relationship between the United States and the Philippines was not imperial but one of foreign affairs between two independent states. This approach treats the United States as a democratic nation state and overlooks how state actors pursue foreign relation goals through empire.

Alongside explanations that minimize the history of U.S. empire, others argue that the term "empire" has too much baggage and doesn't adequately describe the United States' foreign and extraterritorial activities.[15] Some emphasize the liberal or democratic features of U.S. empire,[16] while others claim that the United States isn't like the old world empires or that U.S. imperial domination has gotten "lighter" and "milder" with time.[17] Others still argue that the United States is not like European empires of old but practices "new imperialism" of free trade and militarism without formal colonial control. They cite practices like Secretary of State John Hay's Open Door Policy toward China; President William H. Taft's dollar diplomacy in the Caribbean, Latin America, and China; President Franklin D. Roosevelt's Good Neighbor policy; and President Harry S. Truman's Inter-American Alliance and Cold War policy as evidence of a milder form of imperialism.[18] By focusing on the differences between formal imperial rule and decolonization and by comparing the U.S. empire to old world empires, even these more critical perspectives also treat the U.S. empire as exceptional.[19] At best, these perspectives only consider the United States an informal empire. They also incorrectly periodize U.S. empire. As a settler colonial empire that then expanded into both formal overseas colonialism and informal imperialism abroad, the United States endures as an empire state.

Because these perspectives do not consider the United States to be an empire state like others, they cannot ask how the United States maintained its empire, how it transitioned from formal to informal, nor can they analyze the structures and relations of imperial rule that lay beneath the words of politicians. They miss the continuities between the United States' own formal and informal empires and overlook the structured persistence of unequal relations.[20] It is important not to confuse the myth of the United States as a nation with how the state has actually operated. In practice, state actors translated explicit hierarchical rule into the polite language of foreign relations. This recognition of how state actors disguise empire in other terms is consequential for the study of race, empire, and geopolitics.

Rather than take state actors' foreign policy aims at face-value and deny U.S. empire, I link a range of imperial activities from formal to informal to show how so-called international relations have their roots in racial-imperial systems. The story of empire starts with the European settlement of North America and continues to this day. The United States still holds formal colonies, including Puerto Rico, Guåhan, and American Sāmoa. Kānaka Maoli scholars have argued that the United States illegally occupies the Kingdom of Hawaiʻi.[21] Likewise, through executive control, economic arrangements (including free trade agreements and aid), political repression and influence, and militarization, the United States continues to exert its informal imperial influence around the world: from military bases and nuclear testing sites in the Pacific to the military interventions in Iraq and Afghanistan.[22] Rule over the Philippines is a case through which to consider how state actors translated explicit racial rule into a polite language of foreign or international affairs.

Despite the persistence of exceptionalist accounts of U.S. empire, scholars have shown how economic change, military strategy, geopolitical aims, and local participation shape the conditions under which empires expand or choose formal or informal modes of control. States are more likely to relinquish direct control when they can maintain economic advantages.[23] Anti-colonial collaboration or resistance has also determined forms of imperial control.[24] In the case of the United States, as it grew as an empire, it entered a world already colonized by existing empires. Thus, the United States could rely on formal imperial outposts and networks established by empires that came before. It did not need new colonies to achieve its goals of expanded trade and military control. When the United States grew as an informal empire after decolonizing the Philippines, anti-colonial mobilizations were strong and limited possibilities for geopolitical influence. To illustrate how the United States chose informal over formal methods of imperialism, Go offers the example of the Philippines in the 1950s. He highlights that the U.S. State Department decided not to "recolonize" the Philippines because it would push Philippine nationalists toward communism.[25] Studying anti-colonial national movements, the pursuit of markets, and preexisting imperial networks sheds light on when and why state actors choose to pursue different forms of empire.

Material and geopolitical factors do not operate independently of racial rule, however. And while there is work on U.S. empire that draws attention to questions of race, scholars tend to treat racial ideas as the outcome of imperial policy. They emphasize how the search for markets brings people under imperial influence, which then leads to demographic change, creates ideas of racial difference, and reshapes definitions of the U.S. nation and the national project.[26] In these accounts, it is market imperatives or the search for strategic sites—not ideas of racial hierarchy or white supremacy—that drive state transformation. Race, however, is not epiphenomenal. Ideas of race and civilization also shape foreign policy and international relations.[27]

Scholars of racial capitalism have long shown that ideas of human difference shape economic development.[28] Muriam Haleh Davis documents how civilizational distinctions—specifically between European and Muslim economic capacity—shaped the trajectory of development policy in French Algeria.[29] Focused on the colonial state and native policy, George Steinmetz shows that ideas of race represented in ethnographies and inter-elite conflict shaped colonial policy. In the case of German rule of Kiaochow, different elites, occupying different social and class positions, drew on different ethnographic representations as they translated economic and geopolitical considerations into policy.[30] Strategic and economic interests mattered, but they were not the only factors that explain imperial formation. In war, imperial rule, and the decolonization of the Philippines, U.S. state actors maintained a commitment to white racial rule. Their varying ideas for how to maintain their hegemony shaped imperial state formation. Their investment in ideas of race and racial difference mattered for state structures. Attention to the interaction between racial ideologies and the global field is important for understanding imperial transitions.

BRINGING THE GLOBAL TO STUDIES OF RACE

While long-standing approaches to the study of U.S. empire have attended to economic and geopolitical arrangements, they have not provided the tools to adequately address the *racial* transformations of racial-imperial forms. Perhaps the scholarship on race has something to say. After all, in the empire of 1946, U.S. federal state actors disguised U.S.–Philippine relations in terms that were not explicitly hierarchical. They turned away from vulgar racism and toward polite racism. As critical race scholars have noted, "racial patterns adapt in ways that maintain white dominance."[31] "Oppositional racial ideologies," contestation, and racial struggles can change the systems that link political rule to the racial classification of people.[32]

The social scientific literature identifies the Civil Rights Movement as a critical turning point in the U.S. racial order. According to Michael Omi and Howard Winant, prior to the Civil Rights Movement, the United States was a white supremacist racial dictatorship; afterward, it moved toward a racial democracy—egalitarian and democratic.[33] Since their landmark contribution, most social scientific scholarship has shown that after the Civil Rights

Movement, the United States disavowed explicit racism but articulated racism in coded or colorblind terms.[34] Other scholars have similarly argued that a new form of racism, based on cultural difference, emerged in the 1970s.[35] Claire Jean Kim, for example, shows that while the pre–Civil Rights era racialization occurred in explicit terms, it also created a blueprint for future coded articulations in cultural terms.[36]

While social scientific literature shows that there was a shift in racial forms, we have fewer empirical accounts of how change happens or even that it was possible before the 1960s.[37] Making sense of the changes to U.S. racial-imperial formation between 1898 and 1946, then, is difficult. We could see continuity: from 1898 to 1946, the United States was a racial dictatorship characterized, as Omi and Winant argue, by defining U.S. identity in terms of whiteness, organizing society to subjugate nonwhite people, and homogenizing the experiences of Black and Indigenous people.[38] While the United States has subjugated nonwhite people throughout its history, that the United States was racist in 1898 and was still racist in 1946 does not explain the transformations that transpired in these years.

At the same time, relying on the premise that the United States was one kind of racist before the 1960s oversimplifies racial motivations and how racism works. This is a different conceptual problem than that presented by the scholarship on empire and international relations. Whereas the aforementioned scholars who believe the United States decolonized cannot ask about how imperial forms persist, here, predominating sociological scholarship on race risks presuming that racism and racial logics were stable prior to the Civil Rights Movement. By not interrogating change over time, confining themselves to one type of explanation of change within the assumed U.S. boundaries, or temporally locating that change in the 1960s, scholars may unintentionally limit explanations of how racial formations change.

Against a binary formulation of U.S. racial orders, I disaggregate types of white supremacist aims. I am interested in the kind of knowledge U.S. state actors and elites produced about the Philippines and Filipinos, how they disagreed, and how they enacted their competing visions of white hegemony. This means accounting for varieties of racism and studying how different actors use and construct ethnoracial terms, ideas, and categories in practice. This approach reflects how white supremacist ideas and policy are not monolithic. Like Naomi Murakawa and other scholars of World War II and "postwar racial liberalism,"[39] I draw attention to how one racial ideology "came to over-shadow biological racism."[40] The case of U.S. rule of the Philippines demonstrates how race is constructed across a range of sites in multiple, competing, and coexisting registers, and how some racial ideologies win out over others. To understand the construction of race, how white supremacy operates, how it shapes laws, and how it affects people, we must study the various ways it works in practice. Doing so allows us to see how the United States constructed its white national identity in both vulgar and polite terms and built state power in relation to its colonial subjects.

In addition to temporally distinguishing the U.S. racial order between the pre– and post–Civil Rights era, predominating approaches to the study of the U.S. racial order remain confined to presumed U.S. national borders. Over one hundred years ago, W.E.B. Du Bois identified war and imperialism as structuring a global color line that divided white and nonwhite people.[41] Despite the important contributions of scholars like Du Bois, the assumption that U.S. borders correspond with the national borders of the U.S. "logo" map continues to prevail in the social scientific study of race in the United States.[42] This has two consequences. First, it narrows the range of places we analyze in our studies of race and racism. To be clear, what happens within the national territorial boundaries of the United States is important for understanding racism. Indeed, debates over the rights and racial character of Black Americans, American Indians, and Chinese in the United States informed some conversations about the Philippines.[43] A continental view, however, is partial. Second, as a consequence of taking national boundaries as a given, scholars risk overlooking the process by which the United States came to be the United States, both demographically and geographically. They miss the fact that empire, global wars, imperial expansion, and foreign affairs reshaped the U.S. racial order.

Although all social scientific work on race and racism need not analyze change over time or look beyond U.S. metropolitan borders, historical and comparative work reveals how forms of racism change and how racial logics transform law and state structure. Scholars who have studied transitions other than the Civil Rights Movement have drawn attention to "extra-racial sources of change,"[44] including war, labor movements, class interests, foreign policy, and global policy diffusion that reshape racial structures.[45] Takashi Fujitani charts how, prior to the 1960s, U.S. and Japanese World War II regimes changed their racial strategies, disavowing explicit, vulgar racism in favor of polite and inclusionary forms.[46] Scholars have also shown how, because foreign policy and immigration are closely linked, the former influences U.S. racial order and white hegemony.[47] Debates over immigration catalyzed transformations in how state actors and intellectuals conceived of race. As their ideas of racial difference changed, so too did the capacities of the federal government.[48]

Asian American studies, in particular, has provided fruitful insights into how racial orders change. Like comparative and historical sociologists, these scholars draw attention to how shifting geopolitical priorities and domestic labor struggles shaped discourses and policies about Asians and Asian Americans. For example, during the British Opium Wars in China (1839–1860) and Chinese labor migration in the mid- to late 1800s, white Americans targeted Chinese people with racist violence and exclusion policies. Seen as a "yellow peril," racially inferior and incapable of assimilation, the U.S. Congress passed the Chinese Exclusion Act of 1882. While war and labor migration brought Chinese workers to the United States and catalyzed white-led exclusion, another war and shifting geopolitical priorities changed how people in the United States thought about Chinese people. Against the enemy Japanese, the Chinese became important potential allies in Asia and in the United States. The U.S. Congress lifted Chinese exclusion in 1943. And in the post–World War II, Cold War period in the United States, white elites and politicians spoke of Asian Americans allied with the United States' anti-communist efforts as "good Asians," allies, or model minorities who were committed to achievement and the United States' goals of global democracy.[49] Just as foreign policy aims directed migration policy that would shape the demography of the United States, so too did foreign policy redefine the terms in which state actors spoke of outsiders.

Paying attention to how racial formations transform in response to global events, like war, helps reveal how the United States could change how it talked about its colonial subjects without disrupting the underlying grammar of rule. While empire in 1898 and 1946 both supported white hegemony, this is a much more complex story than simply the persistence of a U.S. racial dictatorship. Building on Fujitani and Frantz Fanon, I trace the roots of World War II–era polite racism to earlier logics of cultural difference, which imperialists instantiated in the early years of U.S. colonial rule in the Philippines.[50] Racial ideologies prior to the Civil Rights Movement were multiple and conflicting.

Over time and through war-making, U.S. state actors changed their attendant vocabularies in response to global politics. They accomplished racial transformation by embedding reference to racial difference and inferiority into durable and flexible state structures.

THE MUTUAL IMBRICATION OF RACE AND EMPIRE

While studies of foreign relations treat race as epiphenomenal to statecraft and studies of U.S. race-making confine analysis to the metropolitan boundaries of the "nation," scholars who study both race and empire have drawn attention to the mutual imbrication of racial and imperial formation. They draw attention to dynamics of colonial statecraft, the "imperial boomerang,"[51] the construction of imperial difference in domestic and intimate spaces, and imperial recursion. This interdisciplinary field demonstrates that anxieties about race are central to colonial rule and that empire has long-lasting durable effects not only in the colony but also in the metropole. At the same time, there is room to consider the mechanisms by which war and empire-making transform metropolitan state formation.

Attending to the multiplicity of factors shaping colonial statecraft, scholars have analyzed the formation of ideas of human difference in the colony among colonial elites, nationalist leaders, everyday people, and mixed-race individuals.[52] Ethnographic representations and ideas of human differences shaped "native" policy, colonial governance and law, and the formation of the colonial state.[53] Colonizers used racial classifications to erect and manage the colonial division of labor, wedding racism and capitalism.[54] In addition to classifying the local population as racial inferiors especially suited to manual labor, administrators relied on racial hierarchy to organize colonial bureaucracy.[55] Colonial administrators exercised discretion and thus wielded immense and arbitrary power to shape the lives of colonized people.[56] At the same time, colonized people participate, collaborate, cooperate, and resist colonizing projects.[57] National elites' sovereign claims about colonized peoples' capacity for self-governance also shaped colonial state formation.[58]

Scholars of race and empire have drawn attention to the exercise of colonial disciplinary power through moral reform and racialized notions of sexual decency. Practices pertaining to the intimate are not isolated to personal matters but also inform state policy and the exercise of power.[59] Colonial state actors poured administrative capacity into disciplining bodies, regulating the life process, and governing mixed unions and people.[60] Logics of intimacy and the affective underlie the colonial order. Race, of course, is made not only in the domestic, intimate realm, or "microsites of governance,"[61] but also in domestic law and institutions about matters that, on their surface, have nothing to do with race or bodies. Lisa Lowe applies the concept of intimacy as a heuristic to understand the linkages across the global political economy.[62] Ideas of race not only organize and justify accumulation, dispossession, and exploitation but also the financial systems (including those related to taxation, wages, debt, credit, monetary and banking systems, and currency reserve) that support colonial capitalism.[63] Ideas of race work through and construct institutions and law about the intimate and material.[64]

While the scholarship on the mutual imbrication of race and empire demonstrates how the politics of difference informs the regulation of life and exercise of power in the colony, other researchers have focused on the effect colonization has on the metropole.[65] Writing about World War I, Du Bois argued the brutalities of war in Europe were rooted in the violence enacted in Europe's colonization of the world.[66] Similarly, referring to how the atrocities like those of Hitler's Germany had already been committed against colonized people, both Aimé Césaire and Hannah Arendt drew attention to how colonial violence shapes metropolitan life. Michel Foucault referred to the return of colonial techniques, weapons, apparatuses, and institutions as a boomerang. Considering the U.S. overseas empire of 1898, scholars demonstrated how, through experimentation in the colonies, the United States forged new administrative capacity in policing, law, education, public health, environmental management, and the military.[67] Colonialism, in other words, shapes the politics, economics, and institutions of the metropole.

Colonialism not only impacts the metropole, its effects are long-lasting. Racial and imperial forms "reverberate" and "fold back on themselves."[68] Even after independence, colonialism continues to shape postcolonial society. Achille Mbembe, for example, argues that because the foundation of society is based in violence, once-colonized states reappropriate violent colonial forms of governance.[69] Categories of difference established in colonial rule continue to shape racial classification and categories after formal rule.[70] Discourses that distinguish the "West" from "the rest" endure. They are stubborn, sticky, and persistent. The organization of racial hierarchies and historical narratives are remarkably durable over long periods of transformation. They inform not only representations of human difference but also the laws and norms of new political and economic formations, including international and global governing bodies.[71] Scholars have referred to persistent underlying layers of social relations and systems of meaning as a palimpsest.[72]

Ideas of human difference forged through imperial encounters, through wars, in everyday life, and in intimate spaces shape colonial and postcolonial statecraft. As the following chapters will show, their durability is true in the colony abroad but also at home in the metropole. How do discourses and practices change even as an underlying structure remains in place? How do U.S. federal state actors, through their debates over ideas of race and white hegemonic rule, build a durable and flexible racial-imperial grammar? These questions anchor the next chapters.

CONFLICTS OVER WAR-MAKING, WHITE HEGEMONY, AND THE PHILIPPINES

Between 1898 and 1946, U.S. federal state actors addressed questions about the economic, geopolitical, and racial position of the United States in the world. In making war, the three branches of government, multiple agencies, and many state actors fashioned a new and durable form of racial-imperial rule. They considered laws and policies related to expansion, trade, natural resource development, military strategy, migration, and naturalization. In 1898, state actors instantiated a formal, explicitly racist empire, and in 1946, they disavowed both vulgar racism and formal sovereignty. In explaining this transformation, it could be tempting to conclude that U.S. state actors had unclear and shifting aims. After all, imperial rule is flexible, contradictory, hybrid, and ambiguous.[73] U.S. overseas empire in particular has relied on ambiguous and equivocal definitions of the relationship of the United States to conquered people and territory.[74] These accounts suggest that U.S. racial-imperial development looked the way it did because imperial rule is especially flexible and ambiguous. U.S. state actors could do as they pleased when it suited their interests: enact equivocal laws and act with discretion toward the territory and its people. In the early years of rule, they could disagree about the United States' relationship to the Philippines. At the end of formal rule, they could then give the Philippines its independence in name while also maintaining favorable trade, development, and military relations.

While this book builds on important insights about ambiguous and discretionary imperial rule to understand imperial state transformation, it also seeks to address how racial-imperial structures are not only flexible but durable. That rule is flexible and ambiguous does not mean it is arbitrary, opaque, or mystifying. I consider the different interests, logics, discourses, and commitments of U.S. federal state actors.[75] By asking for whom Filipinos and the Philippines were foreign or domestic and under what conditions, this book reveals patterns in how U.S. state actors relied on and translated ambiguity. In the case of U.S. rule over the Philippines, U.S. state actors in both the metropole and colony subscribed to conflicting ideas of racial difference. In this section, I provide an overview of U.S. state actors' positions on warmaking, white hegemony, and the Philippines. These different discourses and how they changed over time reshaped U.S. racial-imperial formation.

For three decades prior to 1898, the United States had halted annexation beyond the territory it already claimed. Although Republican President Ulysses S. Grant attempted to annex Santo Domingo in 1870 and white settlers in Hawai'i did the same again in 1893 and 1897, their attempts failed. U.S. state actors' approval of U.S. economic and military influence abroad—as evidenced in the Open Door Policy toward China—did not translate into support for direct colonial conquest. They favored protecting white hegemony at home. They argued against U.S. expansion in the Caribbean and Pacific after the Civil War. They pushed for the deportation of formerly enslaved Black Americans and passed Asian exclusion laws in the late 1800s and early 1900s.

Despite this period of continental isolation, after less than eight months of war with each other, the United States and Spain signed the Treaty of Paris in 1898. Spain relinquished sovereignty over Cuba, and the United States acquired new island territories of Guåhan, Puerto Rico, and the Philippines. The United States set down a new path of overseas imperial rule. The "Philippine Question," akin to the "Negro Question" of the time, raised concerns about expansion, race, and democracy. Whereas prior to the Civil War, U.S. state actors across the political spectrum favored expansion, at the onset of U.S. overseas empire in the Philippines, there were two camps: one opposed to direct, formal colonialism, and another in favor. This is the dividing line that

I focus on.[76] Neither camp was homogenous: not all Democrats were isolationists, nativists, or protectionists, nor were all Republicans imperialists, jingoists, or expansionists. The coalitions also shifted over time.[77] Nevertheless, over the course of U.S. imperial rule of the Philippines, divisions about the best ways to maintain U.S. white hegemony were primarily articulated in nativist-isolationist and imperialist terms.

Nativist-Isolationists
When the United States went to war with Spain, a heterogenous group of conservative and white supremacist Democrats, an older generation of liberal Republicans, and New England Mugwumps opposed overseas empire.[78] Among their ranks, they counted former abolitionists, populists, nativists, and isolationists, including Senators Benjamin Tillman (D-SC) and George Hoar (R-MA), Democratic presidential candidate William Jennings Bryan, and former Presidents Grover Cleveland (D) and Benjamin Harrison (R). They were united by the belief that the United States should not emulate European empires but maintain its republican values. Notably, while they did not think the United States should extend formal sovereignty beyond the U.S. continent, they did not have a problem with westward settler colonialism.[79]

Nativist-isolationists—who opposed colonial rule of the Philippines because it would incorporate nonwhite people into the "nation"—were the longest-lasting, strongest, and most vocal opposition to U.S. empire and rights for Filipinos. They were concerned with the rights of white farmers and laborers and the racial degradation of their ideal nation. Some, like Tillman—a fervent racist populist who served as governor of South Carolina from 1890 to 1894 and was a possible candidate for the Democratic presidential nomination in 1896—believed that incorporating new "backward" races would create a new "Negro problem" and add to the existing "white man's burden" in the South. After the Fourteenth Amendment ostensibly guaranteed citizenship to anyone born on U.S. soil, isolationists feared the browning of the nation and halted interventions that might result in territorial expansion.

Throughout the forty-eight years of U.S. imperial rule, nativist-isolationists were mostly Democrats, Southerners, or from the West Coast. They responded to the exclusionary calls of the media, influential labor leaders, bankers, and the California Joint Immigration Committee—a prominent nativist lobbying organization that emerged from the Asiatic Exclusion League and the Japanese Exclusion League.[80] West coast legislators, the most consistently nativist politicians, relied on vulgar racist claims and focused on domestic matters, including the demographic management of the "nation."

Sometimes I call nativist-isolationists simply nativists or isolationists. In referring to them as isolationists, I do not mean that they were unilaterally opposed to all U.S. foreign affairs or interventions. Rather, their commitment to a white nation and isolating the metropolitan United States from unwanted immigrants or colonial subjects defines their isolationist stance.[81] Isolationism, when it came to debates over U.S. expansion to the Philippines, was a racist-nativist stance. Ideas about racial difference and the inability of nonwhite people to assimilate shaped economic and geopolitical positions of these state actors.

Imperialists

The second camp—imperialists, expansionists, interventionists, and jingoists— claimed there were opportunities to spread white hegemony (masquerading as civilization and constitutional democracy) abroad. They favored expansion and intervention and did not see them as a threat to U.S. domestic interests. At the start of the Spanish–American War in 1898, Theodore Roosevelt formed a volunteer cavalry regiment, popularly known as the Rough Riders. He critiqued "government inefficiency" and "big business," terms that appealed to Democrats, populists, and nativists. Roosevelt represented a vision in which the United States could be for rugged individual white men who went to war for liberty and national interests.[82] After his return from Cuba, Roosevelt campaigned for McKinley and accepted the Republican party nomination for vice president in 1900. Roosevelt stepped in as president after McKinley was assassinated, and he continued to push for U.S. rule over the Philippines. Roosevelt was reelected in 1904.[83]

Although not all imperialists embodied the rugged jingoist individualism of Roosevelt, in the late 1800s and early 1900s, they tended to see both extraterritorial military deployments and formal colonial rule as extensions of U.S. continental expansion and as an opportunity for white Americans to claim more control over the globe. In the 1890s, the discourse of Christian humanitarianism emerged from the Union victory in the Civil War along with a belief that the federal government would play a key role in minimizing suffering and tyranny. As they justified U.S. foreign interventions and the spread of white hegemony, imperialists argued that the United States had a mission to civilize and uplift.[84] For example, speaking on Cuba, McKinley stated that the United States must go to war "in the interest of civilization, humanity, and liberty."[85] The most well-known articulation of the idea that white Americans could not only claim control over less civilized parts of the world but also help uplift them can be found in Rudyard Kipling's "The White Man's Burden," published in *McClure's* in February 1899. In this poem, Kipling called upon the United States to join the British empire in its civilizing mission.[86] Imperialists could thus claim that intervention served oppressed people and spread democracy.

Racial Vocabularies and State Structures

Both those committed to white hegemony at home and those interested in expanding it abroad relied on explicit racial arguments about Filipinos. Those who favored strict exclusion racialized nonwhite people in vulgar terms, invoking claims of inherent biological difference. Imperialists, meanwhile, drawing on the rhetoric of both rugged individualism and humanitarianism, argued that nonwhite others could be civilized and educated under white tutelage. Their vocabularies of cultural difference coexisted with the more exclusionary and vulgar racist claims.[87] As they conceived of Filipinos' inferiority in different registers, nativist-isolationists and imperialists built different structures and policies. The vulgar ideas of the former supported the complete exclusion of Filipinos from the polity and constrained imperial administration. The polite racist ideas of the latter supported the partial incorporation of Filipinos into the polity through training in U.S.-style government and administration.

While federal state actors initially spoke of Filipinos in different terms, after World War II and forty-eight years of U.S. rule, they limited their racial lexicon to speak in politely racist ways. By the 1940s, U.S. state actors across the political spectrum had disavowed racism in its explicit form.[88] They could abandon vulgar racism because, in state structures, they embedded reference to racial difference and inferiority. Thus, racism became "inevident" but "not absent," instead "operating beneath the surface of our language and institutions, structuring them."[89] Federal state actors not only avoided and obscured vulgar racism, but they also disavowed empire, at least in its formal terms. They recognized Philippine independence, arguing that Filipinos had proven themselves through martial sacrifice. Now, after forty-eight years of rule, the Philippines would enter the world stage as an allied nation state.

In some ways, it is perhaps not surprising that over the course of nearly fifty years, U.S. state actors changed how they did empire and how they thought of and treated the Philippines. After all, few of the justices, bureaucrats, and legislators from 1898 remained by 1946. And yet, as this book shows, the explicit racial arguments from 1898 persisted well into the first three decades of the twentieth century. Rather than a simple turnover of political actors, how U.S. state actors debated war-making and different visions of white hegemony and how they cemented their visions into state structure explains the differences between the empires of 1898 and 1946. Because earlier conflicts translated racial concerns into state structure, future state actors no longer needed to rely on explicit or vulgar racist logics of rule.

To summarize, when facing the Philippine Question, U.S. state actors consistently attempted to maintain white hegemony, but they did not do it in the same ways. State actors relied on different vocabularies and drew on vulgar, biological, and polite cultural claims about Filipinos' racial character to different ends. Thus, it is not enough to say that U.S. state actors were racist. Rather, it is crucial to understand in what terms they were racist, which visions of white hegemony they held, and when they agreed or disagreed with one another. Conflict enabled flexibility, which, in turn, helped the U.S. empire endure. Throughout the book, I track different visions of white hegemony and the different camps and state actors that supported these racial projects. Documenting the remarkable consistency in the internal composition of these camps and their eventual consensus reveals how U.S. state actors built a durable and flexible grammar of rule.

HOW RACIAL-IMPERIAL RULE ENDURES

Despite the persistence of U.S. empire, this is not a straightforward story in which imperialists got their way. Rather, in the early years of U.S. imperial rule over the Philippines, the conflict between those committed to white hegemony at home and those looking to expand abroad led to new state structures and imperial practices that outlasted the period of formal rule over the Philippines. Faced with conflict between vulgar and polite racial ideologies, state actors institutionalized ambiguity and decoupled domestic and foreign aspects of imperial rule. On the one hand, U.S. state actors concerned with demographic questions and racial exclusion at home could treat Filipinos as alien outsiders rather than colonial subjects. On the other, those concerned with extraterritorial expansion could strengthen U.S. influence without explicit reference to racial subordination. Enabled by ambiguity, state actors thus cast racial-imperial rule in the metropole as a matter of race relations and rule abroad as one of geopolitics. Charting how conflict leads to institutional transformations reveals that racial-imperial rule endures by distinguishing between colony and metropole, treating the former as foreign and the latter as a domestic nation.

To explain the endurance and transformations of U.S. imperial rule, I draw on the insights from studies of institutions. New institutionalism, for example, draws attention to how past experiences shape structures, practices, and "rules and organizing logics" in ways that endure. When explaining change, these approaches attribute rapid reconfigurations to external political influence, the entrance of new actors, conditions of uncertainty, or changing broader societal or economic norms.[90] In the case of U.S. rule over the Philippines, a new institutionalist account would point to war and changing sovereign claims as sources of change. This is certainly part of the story. Historical institutionalism and models of institutional change, meanwhile, look to endogenous sources of gradual institutional change, including how tensions and ambiguity create opportunities for structural reconfigurations. In these accounts, institutions, while durable, are also the outcome of compromise.[91] In the U.S. rule over the Philippines, endogenous sources of change are especially evident in the U.S. Supreme Court's management of the conflict between nativist-isolationists and imperialists. The early years of colonial rule also shaped future legal and political development of the Philippine state. U.S. colonial state-building provided a "disciplinary grid that structured and governed human thought and activity."[92] In a complementary fashion, I draw attention to how, as they confronted large-scale transformations wrought through making war, metropolitan state actors embraced ambiguity and redefined law and policy, laying the foundations for future state formation, but in flexible ways.

Through successive episodes of war-making, state actors confronted and created ideas about the enemy: who "we" are fighting and why "we" must defeat "them." As they debated the state's geographic and demographic boundaries to secure white hegemony, state actors institutionalized ambiguity, bifurcated rule, and disguised empire. Through these activities, illustrated in Figure 1.1,

1898

1941

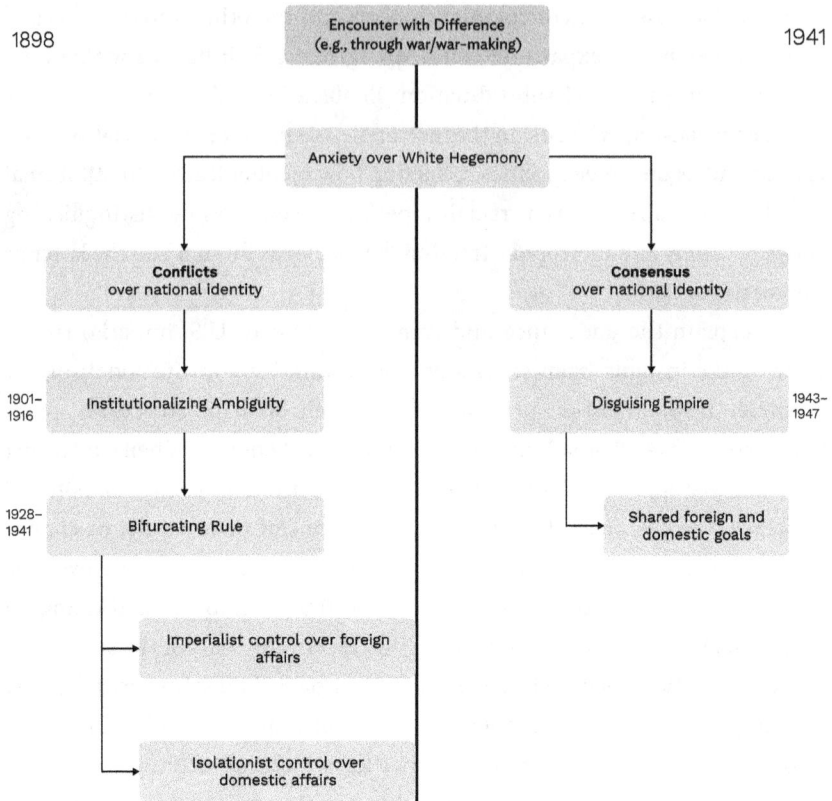

FIGURE 1.1.   Conflict, Consensus, and Racial-Imperial Transformation

they both sedimented racial concerns into laws and administrative structures and transformed the terms of rule, eventually reaching consensus. The years between 1898 and 1941 follow the left side of the figure and the years after 1941 follow the right side.

Encounters with human difference and anxieties over white hegemony are contingent events that shaped future institutional patterns. At the same time, ambiguity enabled not one path but many. In the case of the events that followed from the War of 1898, illustrated on the left side of the figure, state actors disagreed about going to war with Spain and the terms of territorial conquest. Earlier strategies for managing conflicts between expansion and incorporating nonwhite people did not facilely apply. The Fourteenth Amendment guaranteed citizenship to all those under the jurisdiction of the

United States. Citing ideas of racial difference in the early 1900s *Insular Cases*, however, the U.S. Supreme Court accommodated the competing interests of isolationists and imperialists and institutionalized ambiguity. Through ambiguous, unclear, or equivocal law and creating classifications that were not, on their surface, about race, U.S. Supreme Court justices sedimented racial concerns into the grammar of U.S. law and foreign affairs.

Conflicts over race and the scope of white racial rule provided a scaffolding for bifurcating imperial practices and treating the Philippines and Filipinos as both foreign and domestic. Because imperialists were in the executive branch, they vested the foreign aspects of imperial rule there. They worked to do so in isolation from their legislative counterparts. Meanwhile, nativist-isolationists in Congress gained control over imperial matters that concerned the domestic or metropolitan United States, such as regulating the demography of the ideal U.S. nation through immigration and naturalization law. Debates over what the imperial encounter meant for U.S. hegemony shaped both the United States' trajectory within a global political order and the structure of U.S. race relations. Due to the work of imperialists, the United States rose to the position of global hegemon. Their nativist-isolationist counterparts tightened restrictions for unwanted nonwhite populations.

The transition to the Philippine Commonwealth in 1934 is an important turning point from conflict to consensus that links the empires of 1898 and 1946. This moment, while emerging from initial conflict over how to treat the Philippine territory and people, built on the scaffolding of ambiguity and bifurcation. The 1934 Philippine Independence Act reclassified the Philippines as a U.S. Commonwealth, thus promising future independence and classifying Filipinos as aliens in the metropole. Although the Philippines remained a colony, the act equivocated in that the Filipino people were foreign while the territory remained domestic. After 1934, the United States could manage racial outsiders "at home" through restrictive migration as they had with Asian aliens before. The act created the conditions for future consensus over domestic and foreign goals.

By the time Japan attacked Hawai'i and the Philippines in 1941, nativist-isolationists successfully excluded Filipinos from demographic definitions of the United States. Imperialists, meanwhile, continued to manage the foreign aspects of imperial rule. While institutionalized ambiguity emerged from conflict over visions of white hegemony in the War of 1898, in 1941,

war-making and anxieties over white hegemony created an opportunity for
U.S. state actors to reevaluate their position on the Philippines, as illustrated
on the right side of Figure 1.1. While colonial officials had for decades warned
about the threat of Japan and argued for the importance of U.S. rule in the
Philippines as a defense, it was not until Japan's 1941 attack on Pearl Harbor
and Manila that legislators came to see the Philippines as a necessary part
of the United States. It no longer made sense to be an isolationist, even for
racist-nativist reasons. Now, building on the existing racial-imperial grammar that bifurcated foreign and domestic aspects of rule, formerly divided
state actors agreed about the greatest threat to U.S. white hegemony: the Japanese. With nativist-isolationists' successful exclusion of Filipinos from the
metropole, Filipinos in the Philippines now became important to defending
U.S. hegemony. Japanese imperialism and U.S. war-making against Japan
ushered in the transition to a new era of consensus and the empire of 1946.

Consensus about the Philippines, however, did not mean that U.S. state
actors suddenly became anti-racist or anti-imperial. Indeed, World War II
brought a new racial challenge to U.S. state actors. World War II was a war of
empires struggling to expand extraterritorial control. It was a war over moral
authority and about which country had the best vision for modern advancement. And finally, it was a race war.[93] The United States argued it was defending the world against German and Japanese tyranny and oppression. Together
with growing global pressure to decolonize, explicit racism and racial colonial rule threatened the United States' global position and reputation. U.S.
state actors now worked to reconcile their shared vision of white hegemony
with their global position in an era of decolonization. United around the new
shared threat of anti-colonial movements, the two formerly divided camps
converged on a new racial vocabulary rooted in the polite racist logics of the
imperialists.

U.S. state actors disguised U.S.–Philippine imperial relations. They disavowed explicit, vulgar racism. U.S. Congress created symbolic pathways to
inclusion through the 1946 Luce–Celler Act. By allowing one hundred Filipinos a year to migrate and naturalize in the United States, U.S. legislators
claimed they were lifting racial restrictions to citizenship. Imperialists, meanwhile, had spent nearly fifty years building economic and military imperialism in the Philippines, and the war had proven the benefit of extraterritorial
possessions. Committed to spreading white hegemony abroad, imperialists

TRANSFORMATIONS IN RACIAL-IMPERIAL RULE **49**

continued their project under the mantle of war and post-war rehabilitation. Through military bases and trade deals framed as aid, they extended
white hegemony. They transformed their racial vocabulary, leveraging polite
racism and a racial-civilizational mission into one of spreading race-neutral
democracy.

In sum, over the course of forty-eight years, U.S. racial-imperial rule over
the Philippines underwent large-scale transformations fashioned through
war. As they made and responded to the threats of war, U.S. federal state
actors also slowly reconfigured state institutions. The period of conflict immediately following 1898 created opportunities for nativist-isolationists to
control domestic aspects of imperial rule in the legislative branch and for imperialists to control foreign ones in the executive branch. Later, a period of
consensus during World War II built on the existing conditions of ambiguity
and institutional bifurcation between the legislative and executive branches.
Structures that emerged from the early years of U.S. overseas rule lasted far
beyond the years of initial conflict. Forty-eight years after conquest, U.S. state
actors refashioned aspects of U.S–Philippine relations while barely deviating
from their racial-imperial grammar. In response to conflicts over war and debates over hegemonic visions, the United States disguised formal economic,
geopolitical, and racial rule over the Philippines as an ostensibly race-neutral
relationship between two independent republics.

CONCLUSION

Through making war, institutionalizing ambiguity, bifurcating rule, and disguising empire, U.S. state actors built a system of rule that was both durable
and flexible. War-making is an activity through which state actors confront
geographic and demographic questions. They debate what and who belongs.
They redraw boundaries and the terms of inclusion. In their conflicts, state
actors draw on distinct racial ideologies, and when faced with intractable conflict, they institutionalize new rules that shape future political development.

The study of race and empires requires attention to the mutual constitution of economic, geopolitical, and racial interests. As a starting point, we
must take the fact of U.S. empire seriously. Scholarship on state formation
needs to consider how factors that exceed the national boundaries of the
United States—such as changes in the global field, anti-colonial resistance,

and foreign policy aims—influenced state actors as they considered the terms of racial-imperial rule. Racial ideas are not epiphenomenal to imperial transformations. Likewise, understanding the transformations in U.S. racial-imperial rule requires questioning the periodization of so-called "colorblind" or polite racism. As this book shows, in the late 1800s, U.S. state actors held polite ideas of racism, and during World War II, war-making shaped the overwhelming turn to "polite racism" both abroad and at home.

Understanding racial-imperial transformations also requires eschewing methodological nationalism, and not treating the U.S. borders as the container for political processes. Finally, an account of racial-imperial state formation requires attention to the multiple and conflicting interests of those who make imperial policy. Studying state actors' positions on war, race, and foreign affairs reveals who and what they considered foreign or domestic. By analyzing how they draw boundaries between "us" and "them," classify people, and cement their ideas into law and policy, we can reveal how state actors both maintain and transform racial-imperial state structures.

PART ONE

INSTITUTIONALIZING AMBIGUITY, 1898–1916

The story of U.S. imperial rule in the Philippines began when the United States intervened in Cuban revolutionaries' battle for independence from Spain. For over thirty years, nativist-isolationists' concerns kept the United States out of wars of expansion and intervention. Entering war with Spain, thus, marked the beginning of a new era for the United States—one in which a band of dedicated imperialists gained power. Although the United States claimed sovereignty over the Philippines, Puerto Rico, and Guåhan, to many observers, this seemed an unlikely outcome. Through conflict with nativists and isolationists, imperialists transformed the terms and structures of rule.

The following two chapters chart how U.S. federal state actors laid new foundations for the United States' racial-imperial grammar. In the early years of rule over the Philippines, state actors established a formal overseas empire in which they debated and set the terms of rule in explicit racist language. As the United States waged imperial wars in Cuba and the Philippines, administrators, legislators, and justices faced new questions.[1] First, what would U.S. overseas intervention and sovereignty over the Philippines mean for the U.S. rule of law? And second, how would the United States administer the Philippines? Chapter 2 addresses the first question, showing that U.S. Supreme Court justices made decisions that accommodated a durable and flexible form of overseas empire and translated vulgar racial ideas into ostensibly race-neutral administrative categories. Chapter 3 demonstrates how, against the opposition of legislators, members of the executive branch centralized control over colonial affairs. Together, these chapters reveal that conflicts over how to best achieve white hegemony led state actors to institutionalize ambiguity. Through ambiguous legal decisions, ostensibly race-neutral categories, discretion, and centralized executive oversight, U.S. justices and War Department administrators laid durable foundations for U.S. overseas intervention for the century to come.

U.S. state actors created and contested dynamic ideas of racial difference, and these ideas structured specific practices of imperial rule of the Philippines and other U.S. colonies.[2] In these chapters, I draw attention to disagreements among U.S. federal state actors about how to achieve white hegemony. Their different visions—vulgar and polite—about the racial supremacy of the United States reshaped state institutions in ways that would last beyond the years of formal rule. I not only focus on the racial discourses of imperial officials, but also of justices, legislators, and other administrators. Some state actors, mostly legislators who were Southern and West Coast Democrats, aimed to maintain white hegemony at home. Republicans in the executive branch, meanwhile, believed that U.S. white hegemony could have a global reach. The former's vulgar racism shaped their characterization of Filipinos as similar to nonwhite domestic populations who should be excluded from the U.S. polity. The latter spoke in the terms of polite racism and saw Filipinos as childlike subjects over whom the United States could rule.

The divide in positions about the Philippines and Filipinos continued through the 1930s, as Part II will show. In this part of the book, I show that different state actors disagreed about how to maintain or expand white hegemony and that they instantiated their ideas in different U.S. political institutions. It was not only U.S. state actors' racial discourses that were refracted through law and administration, but their conflicts over war and racial threat also shaped the way U.S. state institutions developed. Before turning to the chapters, I first review the history of managing threats to white hegemony and the entrance into the war with Spain, as these were key background events that shaped the debate over U.S. colonial rule of the Philippines.

NEW THREATS TO WHITE HEGEMONY

U.S. war-making with Spain and the Philippines was not the first time that U.S. elites encountered questions of expansion and racial rule. The experience of managing nonwhite populations in the metropolitan and continental United States shaped both the debates about the Philippines and the terms of rule, as Chapters 2 and 3 will show. In popular imagination, liberty, equality, rule of law, and individualism are key features of the fundamental American creed.[3] In the territory we now recognize as the United States, however, state actors wove together the pursuit of liberty, freedom, and democracy with conquest, subordination, and exclusion of nonwhite others.[4] White supremacy is a core U.S. ideal, and the commitment to white settler expansion shaped U.S. laws and institutions since its founding.[5] As they built the U.S. state, white settler politicians adhered to three ideological commitments that set the terms of national-imperial conflicts. First, the United States is a white nation. Second, great nations are homogenous. And third, territorial expansion benefits white people.[6] Over the course of U.S. history, politicians and elites wrestled with building a white nation through or despite imperial expansion and war. The fear and prospect of obtaining territory inhabited by people deemed to be nonwhite spurred great national conflict.

Not only was the enduring commitment to white nationalism clear in the United States' approach to the sovereignty and rights of American Indians and the place of Black people in the newly reformed Union, but it also extended to the exclusion of new nonwhite migrants. The first wave of Chinese migrants came to the United States as laborers during the 1848 Gold Rush, and after the Civil War, many in the U.S. government raised concerns about the applicability of the Fourteenth Amendment to descendants of Chinese migrants. In the late 1800s and early 1900s, one way Congress addressed anxieties about Asian membership in the "nation" was by excluding Chinese and then other Asian nationals from migration and naturalization.[7] In the Immigration Act of 1875, also known as the Page Act, the U.S. Congress barred the migration of Chinese women, and in 1882, Congress passed the Chinese Exclusion Act barring the migration of Chinese male laborers as well. Congress affirmed the restriction of Chinese and others from the Asian region when they created the "Asiatic Barred Zone" in 1917 and again in 1924 with the National Origins Act, which limited Asian migration and naturalization.[8] In the 1910s and 1920s, justices and Congress also defined Asian migrants as nonwhite and therefore ineligible for naturalization. The United

States Supreme Court affirmed this classification of Asians in *Ozawa* (1922) and *Thind* (1923).[9] As U.S. nationals, Filipinos could freely migrate, but they could not naturalize as U.S. citizens, except in the special case of veterans, which I discuss in Chapters 5 and 6. U.S. state actors hoped to stop the flow and settlement of Asian nationals and thus limit children of Asian descent from being born in the United States and gaining citizenship. During this time, the U.S. federal government also expanded border patrol and deportation efforts.[10] The primary goal of these programs was to exclude Mexicans and Mexican Americans. Because, after 1898, Filipinos were under U.S. sovereignty and most were in the Philippines, state actors could not easily apply these strategies of wholesale exclusion. Nevertheless, they attempted to deport Filipinos as they did Mexicans.

Approaches like wholesale exclusion from migration that U.S. state actors used to manage nonwhite populations on the U.S. continent were not immediately translatable to the project of overseas empire. U.S. state actors turned instead to reinterpreting law in racially exclusionary ways and creating unclear categories of membership. In claiming sovereignty and ruling over the Philippines and other overseas possessions, U.S. state actors had to answer new questions about expansion, colonial rule, and race. As the next two chapters show, they adapted and developed new ways for managing the contradictions between the demographic and geographic definitions of the United States.

FROM ISOLATION TO INTERVENTION IN THE WAR OF 1898

How and why the United States intervened in Cuba set the terms for future claims about rule in the Philippines. While many authors have argued that Republican President William McKinley was reluctant to involve the United States in Cuba's struggle for independence and that he initially supported a plan for Cubans to control their domestic relations and in which Spain would maintain sovereignty,[11] the United States' long-standing interest in Cuba suggests otherwise. At different points in U.S. history, former presidents, legislators, and Southern planters saw Cuba as a natural extension of the United States. McKinley and Grover Cleveland (D) before him opposed Cuban attempts to cultivate U.S. support for their revolution. McKinley considered buying the island from Spain, and Spain even considered the offer. While they failed to take the island from Spain, U.S. state actors agreed that if Spain were to relinquish sovereignty over the island, the United States would be its rightful owner.[12]

Long-standing expansionist or imperialist factions not only believed the United States should claim Cuba, these groups were also warmongers. Their jingoist arguments gained traction in the wake of the 1893 to 1897 depression. As a Cuban victory looked more likely, more U.S. state actors worried about what independence could mean for U.S. interests. On February 15, 1898, the explosion of the U.S. battleship *Maine* in the Havana Harbor gave the United States occasion to intervene, not for Cuban independence, but for an end to Spanish rule. Expansionists claimed they had an opportunity in Cuba: intervention could lead to expanded economic influence and new markets. Imperialists also claimed this was an opportunity for the United States to assert its power in the world.[13]

On April 11, 1898, President McKinley requested Congressional authority for U.S. intervention to end the "hostilities" between the Spanish government and the people of Cuba and "to secure in the island the establishment of a stable government, capable of maintaining order and observing its international obligations." In this request, McKinley argued that U.S. intervention was "in the cause of humanity and to put an end to the barbarities, bloodshed, starvation, and horrible miseries" endured by Cubans.[14] The State Department advised him that military intervention would likely guarantee U.S. control over the island. Meanwhile, in Congress, the objections of pro-independence and anti-interventionist legislators who cautioned against U.S. territorial conquest waned. Support for redeeming the reputation of the United States after the insult of the *Maine* grew. Pro-war legislators critiqued McKinley's support of war as too meagre. Thus, on April 13, 1898, the House voted 311 to 6 and the Senate 42 to 35 to go to war with Spain.

The resolution for war passed and did not raise nativist-isolationist alarm because it included an amendment that became known as the Teller Amendment. Introduced by Senator Henry M. Teller (Silver Republican–CO),[15] the amendment gave the United States the responsibility to protect Cuban sovereignty. The United States could go to war but would not assert sovereignty over the island. The war, jingoists claimed, would not benefit U.S. business interests, but democracy and humanity.[16] Because the United States would leave control to Cubans after the war, nativist-isolationists need not worry about incorporating Cubans. On April 25, Congress formally declared war.

Initially, the war seemed to be contained in the Caribbean. Since Spain had territories in the Pacific, however, vocal jingoist Assistant Secretary of the Navy Theodore Roosevelt ordered Commodore George Dewey to depart for Hong Kong and await further instruction. On May 1, the U.S. Navy defeated the Spanish at Manila Bay. President McKinley ordered more U.S. troops to the Philippines, and on May 25, the first expedition left. As of July that year, almost eleven thousand U.S. soldiers were in the Philippines,[17] and on August 13, the U.S. Navy captured Manila, the principal city in the largest northern Philippine Island of Luzon.

Whereas intervention in Cuba initially did not raise concern about imperialism, now with victories in the Philippines, nativist-isolationists grew concerned. There was no Teller Amendment for the Philippines. What would prevent the United States from incorporating the faraway territory? Imperialists, meanwhile, argued that there could be geostrategic and economic advantages to claiming sovereignty over the Philippine Islands. On July 6, 1898, the United States annexed Hawai'i, another Pacific archipelago. Imperialists claimed that taking both territories could strengthen U.S. strategic and economic power in the Pacific and Asia. Japan, Russia, and European powers were already interested in cornering the Chinese market. Though initially hesitant take the Philippines, Senator Henry Cabot Lodge (R-MA) "wanted the East Asian markets opened for the benefit of the nation, his party, and his Massachusetts constituents—industrialists, merchants, missionaries, and the state's working classes."[18] Trade was not the only material benefit, however. Expansionists believed that U.S. business could develop hemp and sugar crops in the Philippines to supply the United States.[19] Taking the islands could serve geopolitical interests. If the United States held colonies in the region, it could help secure the balance of power in the region. Both Britain and Japan asked the United States to keep the Philippines lest Germany or Russia strengthen their position and a war break out. Germany and France also were concerned about the potential scramble for Pacific territory.[20]

For the next five months, the United States military occupied Manila until formal negotiations with Spain ended. Spain surrendered and signed the Treaty of Paris, which was ratified by the U.S. Senate in January 1899. By this treaty, Spain relinquished sovereignty over Cuba, and the United States gained the former Spanish territories of Guåhan, Puerto Rico, and the Philippines, paying $20 million for the latter. The United States claimed sovereignty over the Philippines, and President McKinley supported the annexation of the islands.

Although the treaty brought an end to the war with Spain, the United States was now embroiled in a bloody war with Filipinos, who sought their independence from their new colonial ruler. The Filipino struggle shaped the

U.S. imperial project. Together with revolts in the rural provinces and conflicts between the Spanish state and Catholic Church, the Propaganda Movement—composed of Filipinos who had studied in Europe and called for political reforms under Spain—now culminated in social unrest and the formation of revolutionary efforts. In 1892, the secret society known as the *Kataas-taasang, Kagalang-galangang Katipunan ng mga Anak ng Bayan* (The Highest and Most Honorable Society of the Children of the Nation), or the Katipunan, formed in Manila. Under the leadership of Andrés Bonifacio, the organization sought to overthrow Spanish rule. Although Tagalog-speaking people led the organization, they declared their fight as one for all Filipino people. In a speech, General Emilio Aguinaldo called on "all the natives, all the Spanish mestizos, as well as the Chinese mestizos of the Philippines" to be united for Philippine independence.[21] When, in 1896, Spanish authorities in the islands discovered the revolutionary activities of Filipinos, the Philippine Revolution was born.[22]

After the Treaty of Paris, to stake their own sovereign claim over the Philippines, Filipino elites held elections and formed the first Filipino legislature under General Emilio Aguinaldo, the Philippine president. The new government, known as the Malolos Republic, ratified a constitution on January 23, 1899. A week later, a representative of the newly formed republic, Felipe Agoncillo, lobbied for Philippine independence in the U.S. Senate. U.S. leaders and military, however, refused to recognize the Philippine Revolution or Republic. On February 5, 1899, Emilio Aguinaldo declared war against the United States. Filipino elites saw their newly formed nation and the war they fought against the United States as "being waged in the spirit of the Declaration of Independence," and therefore akin to the U.S. revolution against the United Kingdom.

Despite the Philippine independence movement, in July 1902, U.S. Congress organized a civil territorial government for the Philippines and President Roosevelt declared the Philippine–American War (or, as it was known to many in the United States, the Philippine Insurrection) over. With this, the United States asserted its sovereign claim to the Philippine territory. Guerilla resistance continued until 1906, however. Over 4,000 U.S. soldiers lost their lives in the Philippine–American War. Estimates on Filipino casualties vary, but by conservative estimates, at least 50,000 died. The Philippine–American War Centennial Initiative estimates that 22,000 soldiers and at least 500,000 civilians perished between 1899 and 1902.[23] Filipinos lost their lives struggling for independence, and the Philippines received a new colonial master.

The years of war and casualties were worth it for imperialists, who continued to claim that in the Philippines, the United States had opportunities for
resource development and extraction, trade, and securing a military foothold in
Asia. Secretary of War Elihu Root, for example, asserted that the hardwood forests of the Philippines, including "immense quantities of cedar, of mahogany,
and several hundred varieties of woods the names of which are unknown here,"
as well as rubber and gutta-percha trees were yet underdeveloped. He noted that
although the trees were "tapped by natives," Filipinos only transported lumber
"by water buffalo or loads carried on men's backs."[24] According to Root, the
forests of the Philippines could provide "enormous" investment and revenue
opportunities for the United States. Several U.S. state actors cited the islands as
rich not only in timber but also in minerals and soil. Governor General of the
Philippines William Howard Taft emphasized the islands were full of American
prospectors looking to develop mining, railroads, and other industries.[25] Naval
Captain Alfred Thayer Mahan argued that to secure the United States' commercial influence, the country needed military influence in the Pacific.[26]

Overseas conquest and rule were not merely opportunities for economic
development, however. Imperialists also saw expansion as a racial project. In
their claims, they wed the two: imperial rule over Filipinos imposed a racial
hierarchy for the material benefit and geopolitical aims of white Americans.
Henry Gannet, the chief geographer of the United States Geological Survey
and assistant director to the Philippine Census, even argued that "the question of profit in any form should not enter" into considerations of ruling the
islands. Instead, he claimed that "when we took the islands from Spain we assumed a duty, that of reducing them to order and of maintaining them as good
neighbors to other peoples of the earth." Despite his interest in civilizing the
Philippines, he admitted that the islands "will pay us in more ways than one."
Besides citing that ruling the islands with "the best of the English methods"
paid in self-respect and national pride, Gannet said that "even in the matter
of dollars and cents it is probable that the islands will ultimately pay us. . . .
When we see our people rapidly obtaining control of the commerce of the
Pacific" and when U.S. currency is "received as readily as gold in the Far East,
in China, and in Japan, we can realize what our advent in the Philippines has
done already and what it is leading to." He concluded, "Because of our possession of the Philippines we shall become the dominant power of the Pacific,
both politically and commercially."[27] U.S. military officials also supported

expansion. As imperialists saw it, through political and economic gain, U.S. expansion and intervention would secure white hegemony.

Despite the growing influence of imperialists after the Spanish–American War, nativist-isolationists did not disappear. Nativist politicians could acknowledge the possibilities of capital investment and development. For example, Senator Furnifold McLendel Simmons (D-NC) spoke in Congress, saying that "everybody knows it, we want these islands for purposes of exploitation, for purposes of commercial advantage." Agriculture could likewise be developed in the islands, and the goods and trade developed in the Philippines could open "a gateway to the markets of the Orient."[28] Even those critical of imperialism could not deny the economic possibilities of overseas imperialism. Simmons, however, opposed U.S. imperial rule. He argued against the acquisition of the islands, claiming that it would introduce problems of managing inferior races. For nativist-isolationists, then, the commercial benefit to claiming the islands was not worth the risk to the U.S. polity. Whereas support for intervention in Cuba brought together politicians from both sides of the aisle in a struggle to defend white American manhood, claiming sovereignty over the Philippines was another question entirely. Concerns over race, then, motivated the extended debates over empire. And against these racial concerns, imperialists had to justify and build their imperial project.

In sum, in the late nineteenth and early twentieth centuries, imperialists and expansionists struggled against isolationists, nativists, and protectionists. And as the former pursued war with Spain and continued to fight in the Philippines, they set the United States down a new path of overseas intervention and imperial rule. They had to justify their actions, which departed from the thirty-year precedent of continental isolation and nonintervention. To do this, imperialists argued not only for intervention based on economic or geostrategic interests. After all, isolationists acknowledged these potential benefits. Imperialists also justified imperial rule in racial terms. As Chapters 2 and 3 will detail, they argued that Anglo-Saxon Americans were especially racially fit and equipped to rule over nonwhite people like Filipinos. Imperialists and expansionists expressed their ideas about racial difference through new law and policy. As they did so, they not only transformed the United States from a settler colonial power to an overseas administrative one,[29] but they also lay the foundations of a durable and flexible racial-imperial grammar for the century to come.

TABLE PI.1. Timeline of Key Events in Chapters 2 and 3

	DATE	EVENT
1897	March 4	McKinley sworn in as president
1898	February 15	U.S. Battleship *Maine* explodes in Havana harbor
	April 11	McKinley requests Congressional authority for U.S. intervention in Cuba
	April 25	U.S. Congress declares war on Spain
	May 1	U.S. Navy defeats Spanish at Manila Bay
	August 14	U.S. Navy captures Manila from Spanish
	December 10	Treaty of Paris signed by Spain and the United States
	December 13	Division of Customs and Insular Affairs created in the War Department
1899	February 2	First Philippine Republic declares war on the United States
	April 11	Treaty of Paris goes into effect
	August 1	Elihu Root becomes secretary of war
1900	January 20	McKinley establishes the Schurman Commission to the Philippines
	March 16	McKinley establishes the Taft Commission to the Philippines
	April 2	Puerto Rican Organic Act enacted
	December 10	Division of Customs and Insular Affairs name changed to Division of Insular Affairs
1901	March 2	Spooner Amendment to the Army Appropriations Bill passes
	March 4	McKinley sworn into his second term
	May 27	*De Lima v. Bidwell, Downes v. Bidwell* decided
	September 14	McKinley assassinated and Roosevelt becomes president
	December 2	*Fourteen Diamond Rings v. United States* decided
1902	July 1	Division of Insular Affairs becomes Bureau of Insular Affairs
	July 2	Philippine Organic Act enacted
	July 4	Roosevelt declares Philippine–American War over
1903	March 2	First U.S. Census of the Philippines
1904	January 4	*Gonzales v. Williams* decided
	May 31	*Dorr v. United States* decided
1905	March 4	Roosevelt sworn in as president for second time
1909	March 4	Taft sworn in as president
1913	March 4	Wilson sworn in as president
1916	August 29	Jones Act (Philippine Autonomy Act) enacted

TWO   A FLEXIBLE LEGAL ARCHITECTURE, 1898–1904

On December 10, 1898, Spain and the United States signed the Treaty of Paris, concluding the short-lived Spanish–American War. Spain relinquished its claim of sovereignty over Cuba, and the United States walked away with new island colonies of Guåhan, Puerto Rico, and the Philippines. While U.S. and Spanish diplomats negotiated, concerns about what the war—and specifically what the Philippines—meant for the United States reverberated beyond Paris. William Day, the former secretary of state and chair of the U.S. peace delegation, summarized these questions in a letter to President McKinley:

> The acquisition of this great archipelago with eight or nine millions of absolutely ignorant and many degraded people, with a capacity for supporting a population of fifty millions, seems like a very great undertaking for a country whose pride it is to rest its Government on the consent of the governed.[1]

Day argued Filipinos' ignorance prevented them from consenting to U.S. governance. He was not the only one to raise concern. Soon-to-be President Theodore Roosevelt also spoke of the racial inferiority of Filipinos, calling them "'savages,' 'barbarians,' 'a savage people,' 'a wild and ignorant people,'

'Apaches,' 'Sioux,' and 'Chinese boxers.'"[2] Without question, to the vast majority of U.S. elites, Roosevelt's racial language was uncontroversial. Filipinos were racially inferior and unsuitable to include in the U.S. "nation" state.

Nevertheless, not all federal state actors agreed on what Filipinos' racial inferiority meant for the United States. The acquisition of the Philippine Islands reopened nineteenth-century questions about U.S. expansion and equal rights. For thirty years, the United States contained the promise of the Fourteenth Amendment through white nationalist backlash and isolation. What, then, would it mean for the country to take new overseas territories inhabited by nonwhite people? Was it possible for the United States to be both an overseas empire and a democratic nation that guarantees equal citizenship under the Fourteenth Amendment? Legal scholars, jurists, and politicians of the time wrestled with what these new possessions meant for U.S. rule of law.

Although committed to a white nation, the United States lacked consensus on handling expansion and nonwhite integration. As they did thirty years prior, politicians, legal experts, and the media debated issues of democracy and racial rule. This time, their concerns coalesced into the so-called Philippine Question. Some opposed overseas rule and warned of demographic threats to the United States. Others believed that the United States could continue its program of expansion beyond the continental boundaries. Within the U.S. metropolitan state, multiple racial discourses coexisted.

In this chapter, I first show that federal state actors in different structural positions drew on distinct racial repertoires to construct Filipinos as a racial problem. After discussing scholarly legal opinions on the Philippine Question, which informed the U.S. Supreme Court's decisions, I then turn to the *Insular Cases.*[3] Faced with conflicts over the relationship of empire to constitutional democracy, U.S. Supreme Court justices chose a middle road that accommodated U.S. empire. In these cases, justices worked out the constitutional terms of U.S. overseas empire. Alongside this overview of key cases, I discuss related legislative debates about definitions of territory and people. I then turn attention to how the U.S. Supreme Court, while drawing on explicit ideas of racial difference, institutionalized three foundational components of U.S. overseas empire, each characterized by non-definition in that they were politically open as opposed to legally closed: ambiguous law and mandates, ostensibly race-neutral categories, and discretion. In each section, I demonstrate that jurists, in conversation with legislative debates, accommodated the conflicts about white hegemony by evacuating explicit mention of race from the practices and categories of rule. While ideas of racial difference and Filipinos' racial inferiority shaped the new racial-imperial structure, the terms of empire, such as "unincorporated territory" and "nonaliens," did not, on their surface, reference race. These early years of U.S. colonial rule—in which U.S. state actors translated a racial problem into legal practices—are crucial to understanding how the United States eventually transitioned from an explicitly racist empire to one in which race was inevident, but not absent. This foundation was not only politically open in that it equivocated between different visions of white hegemony and racial rule, but it also laid the groundwork for future political and bureaucratic discretion, which I document in subsequent chapters of the book.

CONSTRUCTING THE FILIPINO PROBLEM

U.S. politicians and elites saw Filipinos as a racial problem, but what kind of problem were they? Tracing how elites answered this question not only sheds light on the different racial-imperial projects—vulgar and polite—that U.S. state actors pursued toward Filipinos and the Philippines, but also sets the stage for understanding how the U.S. Supreme Court institutionalized a new legal architecture for dealing with the colonies. Existing literature shows that U.S. media, elites, and politicians relied on different racial schemas to make sense of newly colonized people across the many sites of U.S. empire, including Puerto Rico, Cuba, Guåhan, American Sāmoa, Hawaiʻi, and the Philippines.[4] On-the-ground cultural repertoires and debates shaped local attempts at governance in the colonies.[5] When it came to U.S. rule of the Philippines, different U.S. politicians in the metropole subscribed to different visions of white hegemony and, therefore, of Filipinos' racial character. They relied on analogies and compared Filipinos to different nonwhite populations.

As U.S. scholars, elites, and state actors debated the relationship of the United States to a new place and population, they were informed by their own interests and experiences and thought of Filipinos in different terms. Those who made sense of Filipinos in light of their own continental experiences with race spoke of Filipinos in vulgarly racist terms, referencing innate and biological inferiority. They cast challenges with Black and Chinese people as foreboding evidence of what the incorporation of Filipinos could mean for the "nation." Their aim was to keep Filipinos out. They favored the complete exclusion of Filipinos from the United States empire. While some drew on analogies to domestic racial problems to argue that the United States should not govern the Philippines, others created new ideas of race as they understood the Philippines. They spoke of Filipinos as culturally different and historically or evolutionarily delayed compared to Anglo-Saxon Americans. Although they compared Filipinos to American Indians—another population the U.S. government was working to conquer—imperialists also portrayed Filipinos in ways that differed from both continental populations and from those of other former Spanish colonial subjects. They viewed Filipinos as a controllable population. These politely racist ideas justified overseas rule. The racial status of Filipinos was not a given. Rather, it was debated and constructed, illustrating the indeterminacy of racial categories. As subsequent chapters will show, enabled by ambiguity and discretion, U.S. state actors would continue to draw on these two racialized understandings of Filipinos as they made policy about the domestic and foreign aspects of imperial rule for the next forty-eight years.

Analogies to Black and Chinese People
When the United States first faced the Philippine Question, the country also encountered other so-called racial problems. Nativist-isolationists tried to understand Filipinos through these existing frameworks. Were they similar to Black people, whom the United States had reluctantly made citizens? Would Filipinos face the same restrictions as the Chinese, who were barred from naturalizing and whose migration was limited?[6] While Southern politicians made analogies to Black people, West Coast legislators representing white labor interests compared Filipinos to Chinese people.

In Congress, Senator Furnifold McLendel Simmons (D-NC), citing the education of "an inferior race," by which he meant Black people in the United States, argued that by trying to educate lesser people like Blacks and Filipinos, the United States would acquire little and improvement in the population would be "slight." He referred to Filipinos as "only half civilized," most of them lacking "any just comprehension of the principles of self-government." He argued it would be impossible to admit them to the U.S. Republic without "degrading the citizenship of the nation and inviting countless dangers." The cost, Simmons argued, of keeping the Philippines was greater than giving them up. By keeping the Philippines, the United States would have to educate the uncivilized people, subdue warring people from various islands, maintain an army for "an indefinite period of time," and develop and industrialize labor. Simmons argued that whereas previous continental expansion (read: settler colonialism) under Democrats "brought safety, not danger," the current acquisition of the Philippines—with its racially unfit inhabitants—would threaten U.S. republican institutions.[7] Given the constitutional guarantee of equal rights after the Civil War, Southern politicians and elites argued against Philippine incorporation by constructing Filipinos as a new "Negro problem" that would need to be solved. Extending rights to Black people was an error that must not be repeated.

Others, especially on the West Coast, expressed concerns that annexation would bring unwanted migration into the continental United States. Filipinos would be another Asiatic mass of invaders, threatening white men's job prospects. The president of the American Federation of Labor, Samuel Gompers, for example, commenting on U.S. intervention in the Philippines, referred to the existing "hordes of Chinese and semi savage races" as a problem for U.S. labor interests. He was well-known for his anti-imperial stance and concern about introducing "semi-barbaric laborers" into the United States.[8] Senator Edward Carmack (D-TN) questioned if Filipinos were "naturally treacherous toward the United States," as "that is the characteristic of all the oriental races."[9] By comparing Filipinos to Chinese and other "oriental races," Gompers and Carmack suggested Filipinos were racially similar to other Asians. While the determination of Filipinos' "race" was still an open question, these actors suggested that the same logics of exclusion could apply to Filipinos.

Given that Congress sought to solve possible Chinese membership in the "nation" through exclusion from migration and naturalization of Chinese nationals, some nativists wondered if they could do the same for Filipinos. Making the Philippines a U.S. territory would grant citizenship to Filipino children born there. In fact, even this basis for limiting the possibility of U.S. Chinese citizens was about to end. In 1898, the same year the United States acquired the Philippines, the U.S. Supreme Court was scheduled to rule on whether birthright citizenship, guaranteed by the Fourteenth Amendment, applied to people of Chinese descent born in the United States (in *Wong Kim Ark*). Anticipating a ruling that supported birthright citizenship, nativist lawmakers argued that if the United States acquired the Philippines, the government should restrict migration and citizenship from the outset. Senator Carmack (D-TN), for example, expressed concern that "the people of the Philippine Islands—islands populated with eight or ten million Asiatics—should be admitted to the full rights of American citizenship."[10] In the context of the post–Civil War Constitution, the acquisition of the Philippines worried nativists as the Fourteenth Amendment created the possibility of citizenship for both Black and Chinese people. Arguing against imperial expansion, nativist-isolationists leveraged preexisting racial ideas. To alleviate isolationists' concerns about Black and Chinese people, imperialists had to present a new racial-imperial project, disassociating it from vulgar and domestic racial analogies.

Are Filipinos Like American Indians?
If they could not be controlled like Black or Chinese people, could Filipinos be treated similarly to American Indians? As nonwhite people whose territory the United States had conquered, American Indians were a recognizable and salient comparison. Both nativist-isolationists and imperialists analogized Filipinos to American Indians, conceiving them as wards and savages while also emphasizing differences from Native American populations.

Those who argued that the United States should not rule the archipelago stressed that Filipino and American Indian political statuses were distinct. Legal scholar Carman F. Randolph—who opposed annexation of the Philippines—noted that while some might assume that the United States could treat Filipinos as "'wards,' 'dependent nations,' or 'tribal Indians,'" these statuses derived from "the fact that he [the American Indian] owes allegiance to a political organization other than though inferior to the United States." Because, according to the Treaty of Paris, Filipinos did not owe allegiance to a political organization or have sovereignty like American Indians, they could not be ruled in the same fashion as the latter. As a result, those opposed to overseas imperial expansion cautioned, under the Fourteenth Amendment, Filipinos could claim citizenship in the United States, an obviously undesirable outcome.[11]

While Randolph eschewed a facile comparison of Filipinos to American Indians, U.S. soldiers wrote home with accounts of Filipinos' savagery. Just as they compared Filipinos to Black people, they also saw similarities to American Indians. In a report shared by Roosevelt with Elihu Root, then secretary of war, Captain John Parker called Filipinos a "half civilized foe, who fights largely without regard to the conventions of civilized warfare, with the same methods devised for civilized warfare against people of our own race, country, and blood." Filipinos were, he wrote, "amenable only to fear" and not reason. He continued to suggest that the war in the Philippines was a lost cause, writing "as in the case of Geronimo, the Apache, there is no reasonable prospect that they can ever be 'pacified.'"[12] Both nativists and U.S. soldiers compared Filipinos to American Indians to suggest that Filipinos could not be incorporated.

Meanwhile, imperialists argued that Filipinos, while neither white nor Black, were, at least in some ways, a racial group like American Indians that could be conquered. In a letter to Elihu Root, Theodore Roosevelt compared conditions of war in the Philippines to the U.S. wars against American Indians, noting that the United States "had been far more merciful to the Filipinos than [General Miles] and the troops associated with him in the old days had been toward the Indians of the plains" and with Sitting Bull.[13] By comparing Filipinos to savage Indians, imperialists argued that not only could the United States conquer the Philippines, but that it would be easier than the Indian wars.[14]

Even as they characterized Filipinos as savages who could be conquered like American Indians, U.S. military officials also recruited Filipinos to serve in the U.S. military, like Indian Scouts on the continent. These soldiers demonstrated to U.S. audiences that Filipinos could be conquered, civilized, and incorporated. In June 1899, Lieutenant Matthew Batson and his servant, Jacinto, hatched a plan for the army to recruit Filipinos. After receiving permission from the commanding general in the Philippines, Major General Elwell Otis, this group became known as the Philippine Scouts. These Filipinos would serve alongside the U.S. military as guides and in combat against the Philippine independence movement.[15] In 1902, the U.S. Congress formalized the relationship of the Scouts to the United States military, offering them rights and benefits for their service. Although they were incorporated into the U.S. military and held up as examples of imperialists' civilizing project, U.S. officers still applied racial logics, segregating them by "tribes," or ethno-linguistic groups.[16]

Filipinos as a New Racial Type

Imperialists not only suggested that the country could learn from wars with American Indians to improve overseas rule, but they also argued that the people of the Philippines were distinct from American Indians and other continental populations. Imperialist politicians and legal thinkers emphasized three key differences: political status, race, and climate.[17] The first defining feature of Filipinos was that they were tribal and heterogenous. In making this claim, U.S. imperialists, like their nativist counterparts, argued that whereas American Indians had sovereignty, Filipinos did not. The latter lacked political unity. The second defining feature of Filipinos was that, besides not being American Indian, they were neither Black nor Chinese. They were, instead, a new mixture of racial types yet unknown in the United States. The third feature of Filipinos was that they were tropical people, which, according to social evolutionary thinking of the time, meant they were a racial type in an early stage of development. They were capable of growth. Owing to the particular political status, races, and climatic origins of Filipinos, imperialists claimed that the United States was dealing with a new type of people who could be treated differently than continental nonwhite populations.

For imperialist state actors, Filipinos were just as racially different from other island people as they were from Black people, Chinese people, and American Indians. Popular media and politicians portrayed Puerto Rico, Cuba, and Hawai'i as refined, virtuous, and beautiful, and therefore comfortably under U.S. dominion. The popular narrative of Cuba was that it was controlled by an elite white population. For Puerto Rico, U.S. media and state actors took pity on what they saw as a white, Black, and, mixed working-class people and believed that Puerto Ricans could move toward whiteness. For Hawai'i, metropolitan actors' concerns about racial problems and the native population were assuaged by the history of white settlers and the overthrow of the Hawaiian monarchy. In the Philippines, Guåhan, and American Sāmoa, however, state actors did not easily make sense of the population in white and Black terms. They saw Guåhan and American Sāmoa as primitive and in need of protection. The Philippines, meanwhile, although tropical, were also seen as undesirable, hateful, and unruly.[18]

These were not merely ideas.[19] The United States institutionalized concepts of racial difference into systems of governance. In Cuba, U.S. state actors built an informal empire. In Hawai'i, they pursued white settlement and integration. In Guåhan and American Sāmoa, they both preserved systems of native rule and worked to minimize assimilation into all U.S. systems except the navy. In Puerto Rico, state actors worked toward cultural and economic assimilation. In the Philippines, questions of profound racial difference plagued rule. Imperialists, against the objections of their nativist-isolationist counterparts, worked to manage Filipinos under a project of tutelage, as Chapter 3 will show.

SCHOLARLY LEGAL OPINIONS ON U.S. EMPIRE

Competing ideas of race informed legal debates about what to do with the islands. In the months after the Treaty of Paris, four prominent legal scholars published their positions in the *Harvard Law Review*. Their opinions invoked the aforementioned ideas of race and accompanying legal doctrine for dealing with different nonwhite populations. One set of legal scholars and politicians argued that the United States could not take the territories, even for their potential benefits. Proponents of this first position, known as *ex proprio vigore* or "by its own force," argued that the rule of law, as defined by the U.S. Constitution, must follow the flag. If this were the case, territories must become states and their people be granted citizenship. It would be unconstitutional to not set the islands on a path toward statehood. According to these scholars, territory, membership, sovereignty, and citizenship must coincide. Invoking the Fourteenth and Fifteenth Amendments as warnings, these scholars cautioned that the people of the Philippines could have the same rights as "white men of civilized races" and that people "in the tropics" reproduce "more rapidly" than white men.[20] Lest the United States face an unmanageable racial problem in maintaining an "efficient government," the United States should not claim sovereignty over the Philippines.[21] This perspective, however, did not give the United States a justification for claiming the colonies that it already held.[22]

The second set of legal scholars and politicians, focusing on the potential benefits of claiming new overseas territory, argued for unabashed empire. Even as they did so, they did not eschew racial thinking. They claimed that the United States could take the territory as a subordinated colony and did not need to extend the rights of citizenship. They saw the Philippines' potential benefit as U.S. military outposts, a gateway to Asian markets, and extraction sites for natural resources. In their view, the Constitution did not apply to the colonies. Their position came to be known as the doctrine of extension. They argued that the state could rule the colonies through military or executive orders, as in the time of war. The Philippines could be treated as subordinate to other U.S. territories. According to these thinkers, because the Constitution did not apply to the colonies, the United States need not consider the membership, responsibilities, or rights of island inhabitants. The downside to this perspective was that it suggested Congress could arbitrarily bestow and take powers outside the terms of the Constitution, which would be undemocratic. Neither of these legal perspectives on the territories gave the United States judicial sanction to set some territories on a path to statehood as the United States had done with Texas, New Mexico, and California, for example, and to take others as subordinated territories.[23]

In the post–Civil War era, these two positions on the Philippines not only reflected preexisting divides over expansion and incorporating nonwhite people, but they also proved unable to reconcile the fact of overseas empire with white national aspirations. A year after the Treaty of Paris, a new third position emerged that attempted to both maintain the commitment to a white nation and resolve the foundational conflict over territorial expansion and the limitation of rights. This third view, which came to be known as the doctrine of incorporation, accommodated imperial tensions in a new and equivocal way. The author of this position, Abbott Lawrence Lowell, agreed that the Philippines was unsuitable as a state. At the same time, he challenged the assumptions in the preceding positions. By creating a new definition of U.S. territory, he decoupled birth on U.S. soil from the guarantee of equal rights. Creating a loophole to the Fourteenth Amendment, Lowell suggested some territories could be annexed to become part of the United States, while others could be acquired "as not to form part of the United States."[24]

Lowell proposed a legal definition of the United States as composed of two types of territories, those acquired prior to and after the writing of the Constitution. The territories organized before the Constitution followed it; those organized after followed treaties. It didn't matter if the Constitution followed the flag. The power to determine what happened to the territories rested, on the one hand, on Congress's power to make treaties, and on the other, on Congressional discretion in setting the terms of the treaties. For example, depending on the treaty in question, some territories (such as Florida and those once forming Mexico) would become states, while others—like the Philippines—could be managed as colonies.[25] Thus, Lowell created a legal argument for racially restricting citizenship while expanding sovereignty.[26] The academic debate in the *Harvard Law Review* both reflected and informed the positions of U.S. jurists and politicians. When these debates made their way to the United States Supreme Court and Congress, U.S. state actors equivocated on what U.S. overseas expansion meant for the United States as a "nation" and how the United States could do empire.

REDEFINING TERRITORY AND PEOPLE IN LAW

In a series of cases known as the *Insular Cases*, the U.S. Supreme Court justices decided about the constitutional relationship of the metropole to its insular (as in, island) possessions. These decisions were based in part on the definitions of territory and people debated and set in Congress. While both the Court and Congress attempted to define the status of colonial people and territory, the Court built the legal foundations for U.S. imperial sovereignty. While most of the *Insular Cases* centered on the status of Puerto Rico and the rights of Puerto Ricans vis-à-vis the United States, the decisions extended to other territories and were haunted by debates over the Philippines and Filipinos' racial status.[27] Justices invoked racial fears about Filipinos as they wrote their opinions. At the same time, the *Insular Cases* "did not suddenly inject racism into a hitherto nonracial practice of empire-state formation,"[28] but reflected the durable ideological and political commitment to white supremacy. When these cases went before the Supreme Court, they "aroused more political passion than any action by the Supreme Court since its decision in *Dred Scott v. Sandford* (1857)."[29] These cases "creat[ed] the constitutional underpinnings" of a new formation of U.S. empire.[30]

The *Insular Cases* address the constitutionality of U.S. policy in the new territories over three periods: during U.S. military occupation of the islands until the Treaty of Paris went into effect on April 11, 1899; the period between the Treaty of Paris and each territory's Organic Act; and after the Organic Acts. The Court faced several issues, including the collection of tariffs from territorial imports, which aspects of the Bill of Rights were guaranteed in the territories, and migration from the territories to the metropolitan United States. These cases addressed U.S. sovereignty over territories and people. The *Insular Cases*, as a corpus, marked a pivotal moment in U.S. empire. The U.S. Supreme Court established a new constitutional interpretation and a lasting foundation for rule. Like in the earlier scholarly debates, the justices were divided over the definition of the United States, the scope and applicability of the Constitution, the racial threat posed by nonwhite people, and these subjects' potential rights as members of the U.S. polity. Lurking in the background was the Philippine Question, or what it could mean for the United States to incorporate a large mass of distant, nonwhite people. Treating Puerto Rico like the United States for the purpose of tariffs would also apply to the Philippines. What would this mean for Filipinos? Would they also become part of the United States? Before discussing the legal foundations set in these cases, I provide background on five *Insular Cases* (*De Lima, Fourteen Diamond Rings, Downes, Dorr,* and *Gonzales*), the related debates in Congress, and the Philippine Organic Act.

Tariffs in De Lima, Fourteen Diamond Rings, *and* Downes

One of the first cases heard by the U.S. Supreme Court, *De Lima v. Bidwell* (1901), concerned sugar imports from Puerto Rico to the United States in the second period (after the Treaty of Paris and before the Puerto Rican Organic Act). The question the Court faced in *De Lima* was whether the import of sugar could be taxed under the Dingley Act. If Puerto Rico were a foreign country, the sugar could be taxed. If not, then the sugar could not be taxed. The question of sugar was important to U.S. state actors and businesses. Before acquiring Spanish territories, Republicans supported tariffs to promote domestic investment in new industries. Democrats viewed this as a burden for consumers seeking cheaper imports. According to them, tariffs favor industrialists but not consumers. They supported tariffs as long as they did not raise prices for consumers.

As the United States expanded westward and claimed new island territories, however, questions about race and including new people and territories reshaped the debate over the sugar tariff in new ways that did not neatly cohere to party lines. Thus, when the United States acquired the Philippines, politicians and jurists wrestled with the terms of including Filipinos in the U.S. territory for the purposes of migration and citizenship and of including the Philippine territory for the purposes of trade and taxation. Republicans mostly favored free trade of sugar, while Democrats wanted high sugar tariffs. Democrats worried that both foreign goods and laborers from abroad would degrade white America. They opposed preferential tariffs for the colonies.[31]

The confounding effects of U.S. imperial conquest also could be seen in debates among sugar producers and refiners. Initially, when the United States acquired new island territories in 1898, there were four sugar groups weighing in on tariffs. Two favored lower sugar tariffs: Cuba and U.S. sugar refiners.

Cuba wanted its goods to enter the United States. Low tariffs and duties could increase producers' profit margins. Sugar refiners wanted low prices and low tariffs for raw sugar. They also wanted high tariffs for the refined product, so it would not compete with their domestically produced refined sugar. Two others favored high sugar tariffs: metropolitan and colonial sugar producers. Beet and cane sugar producers in the continental United States wanted to keep foreign sugar out of the continental and metropolitan United States. Democrats tended to align with metropolitan producers, as they wanted to support domestic, metropolitan farmers. Perhaps surprisingly, cane sugar producers in the territories also wanted high tariffs. This is not because they wanted to keep sugar out of the metropolitan United States, but because they wanted a competitive advantage over sugar imports from non-U.S. territories.[32]

Metropolitan and colonial producers might have agreed on high tariffs on foreign sugar to benefit their industries, but they did not agree on what was foreign or what constituted the United States. Even as colonial sugar producers worked with the U.S. colonial office to advocate for high sugar tariffs, other imperialists and Republicans, including William Howard Taft, favored low raw sugar tariffs. Understanding this conundrum requires identifying how each of these groups defined the United States for the purposes of tax law. Article I, Section 8, Clause 1 of the U.S. Constitution states that "all duties, imposts and excises shall be uniform throughout the United States." But what was the United States? This is the question that the Court considered in *De Lima.*

In a 5–4 decision, the Court held that Puerto Rico, while occupied by the United States, was "treated as being domestic and not foreign territory." Therefore, taxes could not be collected. This is not the outcome that Democrats and domestic sugar producers hoped for. Justice Henry Billings Brown, citing previous cases of U.S. territorial acquisition, including Louisiana, Texas, California, and Alaska, argued that when the United States acquired a territory, it became domestic. Brown claimed that a territory could not "at the same time be both foreign and domestic."[33] In his dissent, Justice Joseph McKenna (Justices George Shiras, Jr., and Edward D. White concurring) argued, however, that the terms foreign and domestic have no absolute meaning but depend on the issue at hand.[34]

With *De Lima* alone, one might think that the former Spanish territories were clearly domestic. However, questions about the status of the territories, especially the Philippines, persisted. Opining on the outcome of the case,

Senators William Stewart (Silver Republican–NV), William Lindsay (D-KY), and Augustus Bacon (D-GA) claimed that the Philippines should be distinguished from Puerto Rico because the United States never meant to incorporate the Philippine territory or its people into U.S. citizenship.[35] If Congress had different intentions for the two territories, then did the ruling from *De Lima v. Bidwell* apply to the Philippines? This was the question before the court in *Fourteen Diamond Rings v. United States* (1901).[36]

In *Fourteen Diamond Rings*, the Court upheld the idea that the Constitution follows the flag. They addressed whether rings acquired by a U.S. soldier while in the Philippines and after the Treaty of Paris (but before the Philippine Organic Act of 1902) were considered imports from a foreign country and thus subject to payment of duties. The Court ruled 5–4 that *De Lima v. Bidwell* applied to the Philippines, just as it did to Puerto Rico. The same justices that dissented in *De Lima v. Bidwell* dissented again. According to Chief Justice Melville Fuller, delivering the opinion of the Court, the Philippines, by the language of the Treaty of Paris, was no longer Spanish and therefore no longer a foreign country. Rather, the islands were "under the complete and absolute sovereignty and dominion of the United States." Besides ruling that the Philippines was not foreign, this case determined that treaty meanings cannot be modified. Thus, even if nativist-isolationists in Congress continued to exclude the Philippines because of its "uncivilized tribes," the Court affirmed that the United States claimed sovereignty over the Philippines.[37] In *De Lima* and *Fourteen Diamond Rings*, the Court concluded that Puerto Rico and the Philippines were domestic, not foreign territories. This was, at least, prior to their Organic Acts.

The most famous *Insular Case*, *Downes v. Bidwell*, 1901, which concerns the third period, after the Puerto Rican Organic Act, however, institutionalized a new way of thinking about the former Spanish territories. Cases concerning this period set the terms for colonial rule. When read alongside *De Lima* and *Fourteen Diamond Rings*, *Downes* presents a confounding interpretation of territorial status. Again, the case concerned trade and tariffs. This time the question was whether the United States could collect taxes (per the terms of the Puerto Rican Organic Act)[38] on an import of oranges from Puerto Rico.[39] If Puerto Rico were annexed and considered domestic, then the Organic Act could not hold, meaning that imports would *not* be taxed. If it was foreign, imports would be taxed. Domestic producers favored defining the United

States in a way that excluded the territories, or considered them foreign to the United States. High tariffs, then, would apply not only to foreign countries but also to colonies. Territorial producers favored a broader interpretation of the United States in the uniformity clause. For them, the United States could include the colonies, and thus protect colonial products from foreign ones. Agricultural producers in the metropolitan and colonial United States were in a tenuous compromise over high tariffs, as they had different ideas of what should remain within the U.S. tariff wall.

Although the nine justices were hardly in agreement, the Court, in a 5–4 plurality decision,[40] decided that after the Organic Act, the former Spanish territories could be treated as foreign, and thus the import of oranges could be taxed. Justice Brown wrote the opinion for both *Downes* and *De Lima*. No other justice was in the majority/plurality decision for both cases. In *De Lima*, Brown's decision was that Puerto Rico was domestic, and in *Downes*, that it was foreign. Justice Brown elaborated, arguing that Puerto Rico (and by extension the other territories acquired from Spain) was "a territory appurtenant and belonging to the United States, but not a part of the United States."[41] In the language of Justice White, the territory was foreign, but "in a domestic sense." This status later became known as "unincorporated territories," and Brown's and White's arguments for ruling the colonies still hold to this day.

Everyone except Justice Brown switched sides: in *De Lima*, Fuller, John M. Harlan, Rufus W. Peckham, and David J. Brewer joined the majority (ruling that Puerto Rico was not foreign). In *Downes*, they dissented. The concurring opinions in *Downes* were written by White, joined by Shiras and McKenna (who joined each other in dissent in *De Lima*) and Horace Gray, who also dissented in *De Lima* (see Table 2.1). The difference in opinions between these two cases reflects the lack of consensus about how to treat the former Spanish territories before and after the Puerto Rican Organic Act. Brown's opinion, meanwhile, reflects a new way of approaching the tension between constitutional democracy and overseas empire.[42] Before the Organic Act, territories were not foreign, but domestic. After, they were foreign.

Rights for People in Dorr *and* Gonzales

Three years after *Downes*, the Court heard a case, *Dorr v. United States* (1904), concerning the applicability of the Bill of Rights to the territories in the second period—between the Treaty of Paris and the Philippine Organic Act. In a trial

TABLE 2.1. Justices' Opinions on Whether Puerto Rico and the Philippines Are Foreign, 1901

JUSTICE	*DE LIMA* AND *FOURTEEN DIAMOND RINGS* (PUERTO RICO AND THE PHILIPPINES ARE *NOT* FOREIGN)	*DOWNES* (PUERTO RICO IS FOREIGN)
Brown	Yes	Yes
Fuller	Yes	No
Harlan	Yes	No
Peckham	Yes	No
Brewer	Yes	No
White	No	Yes
Shiras	No	Yes
McKenna	No	Yes
Gray	No	Yes

in the Philippines, Fred Dorr, a U.S. citizen, was convicted of libel against the U.S. government and the insular government of the Philippines. Dorr appealed his case as he was denied a trial by jury, which he claimed was his constitutional right. Citing *De Lima* and *Downes*, the Supreme Court decided (8–1, with Harlan dissenting) that the constitutional right to trial by jury did not necessarily extend to the territories. Instead, the extension of rights was determined by Congress and through treaty-making.

Whereas the Court determined constitutional rights need not extend to the territories, in a subsequent *Insular Case* (*Gonzales v. Williams*, 1904),[43] the Court faced the question of citizenship for subjects of U.S. empire. U.S. state actors were still unclear on what rights colonial subjects had vis-à-vis the metropolitan state. In the 1900 Puerto Rican Organic Act and the 1902 Philippine Organic Act,[44] however, Congress defined Puerto Ricans and Filipinos as citizens of Puerto Rico and the Philippines respectively. The designation of Puerto Ricans and Filipinos as citizens of their own nations would seem to suggest that the territories had sovereignty over their people, but what did this mean, given that Puerto Rico and the Philippines were under the sovereignty of the United States? This was the question before the Court in *Gonzales v. Williams.*

In 1902, Isabel González left San Juan, Puerto Rico, for the United States. González expected to be admitted to the United States when she left Puerto Rico. When she arrived in New York, however, immigration officials barred her entry, claiming she was an undesirable alien. According to the Immigration and Naturalization Service, González, as a Puerto Rican, was "subject to the same examinations as are enforced against people from other countries over which the United States claims no right of sovereignty."[45] With the help of her uncle, Domingo Collazo (a New York journalist who previously sought to end Spanish rule of Puerto Rico),[46] she launched a suit against the Immigration and Naturalization Service. The Court unanimously decided that, in terms of U.S. citizenship law, colonial subjects were not aliens. While González could be admitted to the United States free from regulation by the Immigration and Naturalization Service, the Court did not affirmatively comment on the question of U.S. citizenship for inhabitants of U.S. territories acquired from Spain.

THREE RULES OF THE U.S. RACIAL-IMPERIAL GRAMMAR

Together, the decisions from *Gonzales* and the other *Insular Cases* established three important foundations for U.S. sovereignty over the new territories. First, *Downes* and *Gonzales* institutionalized ambiguous law. Second, *Downes* and *Gonzales* translated racial concerns into new race-neutral categories. And third, *Downes, Dorr,* and *Gonzales* also relied on broad definitions by enabling discretion for future legal and political decisions. Together, the Court imbued racial concerns into the legal architecture of the state and created a flexible and ambiguous structure of imperial rule that could accommodate the many and shifting interests of U.S. state actors for years to come. In what follows, I parse aspects of each case that created ambiguous law, ostensibly race-neutral categories, and discretion.

Ambiguous Law

In *Downes* and *Gonzales,* Justices created an ambiguous definition of the former Spanish colonies and their people. According to Justice Brown, Puerto Rico was "a territory appurtenant and belonging to the United States, but not

TABLE 2.2.   Three Cases and Three Rules of
the U.S. Racial-Imperial Grammar

| | AMBIGUOUS | OSTENSIBLY RACE-NEUTRAL | |
CASE	LAW	CATEGORIES	DISCRETION
Downes	X	X	X
Dorr			X
Gonzales	X	X	X

a part of the United States."[47] Justice White also argued for an ambiguous classification of the territories. He stated that territories fell into two categories: those that would become states and those that would not. The latter became known as unincorporated territories. White wrote that "in an international sense Puerto Rico was not a foreign country, since it was subject to the sovereignty of and was owned by the United States." Rather, he added, Puerto Rico "was foreign to the United States in a domestic sense, because the island had not been incorporated into the United States, but was merely appurtenant thereto as a possession."[48] The newly defined unincorporated territories were neither clearly foreign nor unequivocally domestic. Justices Brown, White, Shiras, and McKenna created an ambiguous definition of the Spanish territories that (1) belonged to but were not part of the United States and (2) were foreign in a domestic sense.

Not all justices agreed with this stance, however. Justice Harlan, famous for his dissenting opinions on the Court, drew attention to the lack of clarity in the Court's decision. He concluded his dissent by saying, "I am constrained to say that this idea of 'incorporation' has some occult meaning which my mind does not apprehend. It is enveloped in some mystery which I am unable to unravel."[49] Harlan argued that Brown, White, Shiras, and McKenna created an ambiguous definition of the Spanish territories. The new colonies were neither foreign nor domestic, but in an in-between state.

The Court's ruling changed the legal architecture of the United States. The United States could claim a territory as its own and provide for a civil government through an Organic Act but need never set it on a path to statehood. Once this happened, the territory was foreign in a domestic sense. According to this view, the Constitution guaranteed fewer rights in the colonies than in the metropole. Echoing the earlier opinion of Lowell, the Constitution would apply to the colonies, but only when dictated by treaty and federal statutes. The definition of the former Spanish territories as "unincorporated" and "foreign in a domestic sense" was capacious enough to allow the United States to both remain a constitutional democracy within the metropolitan borders and to engage in imperial activities. The decision in *Downes v. Bidwell* accommodated both imperial expansion and limiting rights.

Just as the Court evaded a clear definition of the colonial territory and its relationship to the metropolitan United States, the Court also did not settle confusion over the status of colonial people. Instead, they institutionalized another ambiguous classification. After the territories were deemed "foreign in a domestic sense," both the Court and Congress continued to wrestle with defining the people of the Philippines. Were they citizens or aliens? Nativist-isolationists objected to including Filipinos "in the body politic of the American Government," arguing they were "a race incapable of self-government."[50]

The Organic Act also stipulated, however, that as citizens of the Philippines islands, Filipinos were "entitled to the protection of the United States," unless they explicitly elected otherwise.[51] Even as Congress defined Filipinos as citizens of the Philippines, the substantive meaning of this citizenship was unclear. Senator Henry M. Teller (D-CO), for example, expressed his confusion by asking "What is the status of the people of the Philippines. I see that the bill provides that they are to be citizens of the Philippine Islands. I desire to know whether or not they are to be citizens of the United States or what is the theory of the pending bill in that regard?" When asked what were the rights of Filipinos and other colonial people in the United States if the Philippines was under U.S. sovereignty, Senator Henry Cabot Lodge (R-MA) replied inconclusively, stating that this phrasing "was adopted in the Porto Rican bill." Teller pressed, "It seems to me that we have reached a point where we should determine the status of these people." Lodge attempted to clarify, stating that "we determined that they were citizens of Porto Rico, entitled to the protection of the United States and owing allegiance to the United States." The Philippine Organic Act, he noted, followed that clause. Teller was not satisfied, arguing that this "is a new relation that these people bear to the Government of the United States," which Lodge denied. Teller continued, "It seems to me that it would be easy enough to determine whether it is policy to make them citizens or whether it is not policy to make them citizens. . . .To say that they are citizens of the Philippine Islands does not mean anything at all."[52] In a latter session, Senator Teller again raised the question of what Filipino citizenship meant, underscoring that because the Philippines had no sovereignty, "the Filipino must be left floating around uncertain whether he is a citizen of the United States or whether he is a man without a country."[53] Nevertheless, even with the ambiguity on the question of citizenship, the Philippine Organic Act passed, like the Puerto Rican one before it, and designated Filipinos as citizens of the Philippines but under U.S. sovereignty.

In *Gonzales v. Williams* (1904), the Court addressed but did not definitively settle colonial subjects' membership and rights in the metropole. González, the Court noted, was a citizen of Puerto Rico, and Congress had no intention "that the citizens of Porto Rico should be considered aliens, and the right of free access denied to them."[54] Colonial subjects, while citizens of their nation, were also not aliens of the United States. According to Chief Justice Fuller, writing for the opinion of the Court, after the Treaty of Paris, "their allegiance became due to the United States, which was in possession and had assumed the government, and they became entitled to its protection." Fuller continued, "The nationality of the island became American."[55] Refusing to make an affirmative decision on the terms of inclusion in the U.S. polity, Fuller emphasized that this case was about alienage, not citizenship. He wrote that "the general terms, 'alien,' 'citizen,' 'subject,' are not absolutely inclusive, or completely comprehensive." Nonalien status did not guarantee citizenship. Fuller argued that in ruling that González was not alien, the Court was not required to discuss whether she was a citizen. The Court created an ambiguous political subject who could not fully belong to the nation but was also not foreign.

In this period, the Court and Congress treated Filipinos as neither citizen nor alien but something in between. Justices and legislators drew legal boundaries to partially incorporate and partially exclude the former Spanish territories and their people. Their ambiguous status as neither aliens nor citizens meant that, despite the *de jure* exclusion of Chinese (and later others from the Asian region), Filipinos could freely migrate from 1898 until 1934 and held some rights given to U.S. citizens. The justices could have excluded Filipinos and former Spanish subjects or treated them as aliens ineligible for citizenship like Chinese migrants; instead, they accommodated both expansion and the limitation of rights by institutionalizing new ambiguous legal statuses.

Ostensibly Race-Neutral Categories

The ambiguous decisions of the *Insular Cases* like *Downes* and *Gonzales* also translated explicitly racial concerns and ideas into ostensibly race-neutral categories. While the category of unincorporated territory does not explicitly refer to race, the reasoning provided by the justices reveals that claims of race neutrality emerge from racial justifications. Constrained by the terms of the Fourteenth Amendment, the Court could not use race to exclude Filipinos from membership in the United States. By classifying Filipinos as citizens of another country (albeit one that did not have sovereignty) and as U.S. nationals, the Court enabled future state actors to call upon ideas of racial inferiority and superiority without directly wielding racial terms. Instead, throughout imperial rule, U.S. state actors could refer to Filipinos by their seemingly race-neutral bureaucratic classifications that were imbued with logics of racial difference and inferiority.

Although the determination of the Court in *Downes*—that oranges imported to the United States from Puerto Rico were subject to duties—seemingly had nothing to do with race, the Court in fact translated racial concerns into the race-neutral category of "unincorporated territories." The debates and the decision of the Court in *Downes* were informed by racial ideas of the Philippine Islands and its people. For example, Justice Brown, writing for the Court, argued that people from "outlying and distant possessions" were of "alien races," and raised questions of "race, habits, laws, and customs." These issues "may require action on the part of Congress," as rights under the U.S. Constitution may not have applied to people of a different race who were not accustomed to "Anglo-Saxon principles." He wrote that "the administration of government and justice, according to Anglo-Saxon principles, may for a time be impossible."[56]

In his statement for the Court, not only did Justice Brown racially differentiate colonial populations from the Anglo-Saxon United States, but he also reinterpreted the Thirteenth and Fourteenth Amendments. Justice Brown claimed it was the intent of the authors of both amendments to distinguish the United States from places within the jurisdiction of the United States "that are not part of the Union." In his interpretation, Puerto Rico and the other Spanish territories were under the jurisdiction of but not part of the United States. Brown argued that citizens were only born or naturalized within the United States. He leveraged text from the Thirteenth and Fourteenth Amendments to the Constitution—intended to guarantee equal rights to enslaved people emancipated at the end of the Civil War—to argue for a subordinated class of territory and people just over thirty years later. Brown's racial arguments supported his decision that the newly acquired territories were not "part of the United States," but unincorporated.

Concerns about racial suitability of Filipinos also informed the creation of new bureaucratic categories. When Congress passed the 1902 Philippine Organic Act, they concealed racial concerns about incorporating Filipinos in the category of Philippine citizen. After the Fourteenth Amendment, racial exclusions to citizenship for those born in the United States or under its jurisdiction were unconstitutional. Rather than explicitly exclude Filipinos from U.S. citizenship, however, Congress could exclude Filipinos by designating them as citizens of the Philippines. The fiction of Filipino citizenship—which implied that Filipinos were members of a sovereign nation—rested on a commitment to racial exclusion from U.S. citizenship by both isolationists and imperialists. In a Senate hearing before the Committee on the Philippines, Senator Carmack (D-TN) voiced his concern about giving citizenship to nonwhite people. He asked then Governor Taft about "the character of the people" of the Philippine Islands and whether they "shall be made an integral part of the United States" with "equal constitutional rights, and the full rights of citizenship." Taft responded that Filipinos should not be covered by all aspects of the U.S. Constitution as this would "very much interfere with the establishment of a stable and successful government . . .which ought to be established under American guidance." Taft, like his imperialist-leaning counterparts in the Court, evaded a clear response, saying that he would wait two or three generations before providing an answer to Carmack's question. Taft instead emphasized the need for "teaching them what individual liberty is and training them to a knowledge of self-government."[57] The designation of Filipinos as citizens of the Philippines both evaded a clear definition of Filipinos as citizens of the United States and obscured the racial motivations for such a designation.

Nevertheless, racial fears were the primary motivation for classifying Filipinos as citizens of their own country. Senator John T. Morgan (D-AL) summarized, "It is our reluctance to admit the Filipinos to citizenship that has caused them to believe that Congress regards them, either with pity or disdain, as an inferior people. And such is the fact." Morgan, a Southern Democrat and former slave owner who advocated for segregation under Jim Crow, was unlike many politicians of the day. He actually argued that Filipinos should be given citizenship. He noted that U.S. precedents—referring to the Fourteenth Amendment—"are all against the denial of citizenship on account of race or color." To deny Filipinos citizenship, Morgan asserted, was "the worst form imperialism."[58] Nevertheless, Congress translated racial concerns into the bureaucratic category of Philippine citizen and by extension denied Filipinos citizenship in the United States.

After the Court determined that Puerto Ricans and other inhabitants of unincorporated territories were nonaliens, Congress administratively defined Filipinos as U.S. *nationals*, who were not citizens but owed allegiance to the United States.[59] This term came from Frederic R. Coudert, Jr., the lawyer who argued for the plaintiff in *Downes* and the appellant in *Gonzales*. In the latter case, Coudert argued that because U.S. citizenship was already gradational and ambiguous, Puerto Ricans and island inhabitants could, in fact, be classified as citizens. Second-class citizenship was already a possibility in the United States, claimed Coudert. As Duffy Burnett notes, "In the ambiguity of the concept of citizenship, Coudert saw an opportunity. The lack of a clear definition, he argued, left room for 'various gradations or subdivisions of subjection.'"[60] In justifying a scale of membership, Coudert argued that U.S. law gave citizenship to people who had been or were subordinated, such as free Black people, American Indians, women, and children. In other words, "Coudert portrayed a U.S. citizenship which generally accompanied U.S. nationality and that, similar to nationality in other empires, was widespread and largely inconsequential."[61] Coudert distinguished between citizenship and full rights, highlighting the existing lack of clarity in definitions of citizenship in the United States. If the United States would not grant citizenship to Puerto Ricans, Coudert argued, then they could be designated as "nationals."[62] Akin to "subject," the term "national" created a status that was not alien but also not full citizenship. Congress adopted this. Thus, constrained by the Fourteenth Amendment, jurists and legislators created new administrative categories for territory and people that, while informed by the racial concerns about Filipinos, did not explicitly mention empire or define membership in terms of race.

Discretion

Not only did the Court create new legal categories that were both ostensibly race-neutral and ambiguous, but it also created a structural justification for discretionary decision-making in the political realm. The Court, rather than make a clear, unequivocal ruling on the place of Filipinos and the Philippines in the United States, decided that ambiguous law could be widely interpreted by legislators. In essence, they left the question of managing and incorporating new people and territory to legislators.

According to the opinion of the Court in *Downes*, U.S. Congress alone had the power to determine which parts of the Constitution would extend to the territories. Through Congress's plenary power[63]—or sole absolute power—to make treaties, legislators had the right to determine what became of the territories. Citing Justice John Marshall's opinion in *American Insurance Company v. Canter* (1828), White argued that the terms of treaties, which are themselves determined by Congress, define the relationship of rule between the United States and its territories, which were considered property of the United States.[64] Some members of Congress anticipated this outcome. Three months before the U.S. Supreme Court decided on *Downes*, Senator George Graham Vest (D-MO) referred to the question of whether the Constitution applies *ex proprio vigore* to the new territories. He stated, "It is rumored that the Supreme Court proposes not to decide that question at all." He continued, "The Court does not intend to decide at all whether the Constitution applies to the Philippine Islands, but will simply evade the question by saying it is a political question entirely, and within the jurisdiction of Congress."[65]

Justice Brown also supported the idea that Congress could decide the terms of U.S. imperial rule and argued that Congress's treaty-making power created special provisions regarding citizenship. In his opinion, Brown doubted whether "Congress would ever assent to the annexation of territory upon the condition that its inhabitants, however foreign they may be to our habitats, traditions, and modes of life shall become at once citizens of the United States."[66] To support his arguments for Congressional discretion, Brown argued that Congress did not intend to grant U.S. citizenship to former Spanish colonial subjects. He contrasted the 1898 Treaty of Paris with previous territorial acquisitions and treaties. With the Louisiana Purchase (1803) and Florida (1819), Brown noted, Congress stipulated that inhabitants of the territories would become citizens "as soon as possible." According to the Treaty of Guadalupe Hidalgo (1848), the inhabitants would be "admitted at the proper time to be judged of by the Congress of the United States." In the case of Alaska (1867), inhabitants would also be admitted, but "with the exception of uncivilized native tribes." Brown noted that in the case of the Philippines,

Puerto Rico, and Spain's other former colonies, however, Congress wrote "that the civil rights and political status of the native inhabitants . . .shall be determined by Congress." With earlier territorial acquisitions, Congress planned to admit inhabitants (except American Indians) to the United States; with the Spanish colonies, however, there were no plans for citizenship. Thus, according to Brown, such differences in treaties demonstrated Congress's plenary power. Brown affirmed that Congress not only had the right to determine if inhabitants of the territories became "immediately upon annexation, citizens of the United States," but also if "their children thereafter born, whether savages or civilized, are such entitled to all the rights, privileges and immunities of citizens."[67] Both Brown and White gave discretion to Congress and relied on racial logics of exclusion to do so. Through Congress's treaty making power, they also connected U.S. foreign relations and domestic race relations: treaties with foreign nations would determine the future civic status of newly conquered people.

Upholding Congressional power, however, was not a foregone conclusion. As previously mentioned, the opinion of the Court in *Downes* was written by one justice, reflecting the factional interests and interpretations about managing the U.S. empire. Chief Justice Fuller (joined by Brewer and Peckham) called White's opinion on Congressional discretion into question, stating "the contention seems to be that, if an organized and settled province of another sovereignty is acquired by the United States, Congress has the power to keep it, like a disembodied shade, in an intermediate state of ambiguous existence for an indefinite period." Fuller continued, writing "and more than that, that after it has been called from that limbo, commerce with it is absolutely subject to the will of Congress, irrespective of constitutional provisions"[68] In Fuller's opinion, the Court's decision to uphold Congressional discretion not only created ambiguity but also gave unconstitutional powers to Congress.

Justice Harlan also believed the Court's decision on Congressional power violated the Constitution. He argued racial concerns were not appropriate justifications for violating the Constitution. He wrote, "whether a particular race will or will not assimilate with our people, and whether they can or cannot with safety to our institutions be brought within the operation of the Constitution, is a matter to be thought of when it is proposed to acquire their territory by treaty." While Harlan thought Filipinos deserved equal rights, he argued that "a mistake in the acquisition of territory, although such acquisition seemed at the time to be necessary, cannot be made the ground for violating the Constitution or refusing to give full effect to its provisions."[69] He may not have approved of the initial acquisition of the Spanish territories, but Harlan saw no justification for breaking with the Constitution. He wrote that he "reject[s] altogether the theory that Congress, in its discretion, can exclude the Constitution from a domestic territory of the United States."[70] Although *Downes* affirmed Congressional discretion, not all justices endorsed Congress's plenary power as a justification for ruling the territories and for U.S. empire.

Harlan's opinion, however, was not widely shared. Members of the Court argued for discretion in determining not only the applicability of the Constitution to the new territories, but also the scope of citizenship. In his dissent in *De Lima v. Bidwell* (1901), Justice McKenna claimed it was not the duty of the Court to determine the "nationalization of uncivilized tribes." He wrote: "There may be no ready test of the civilized and uncivilized, between those who are capable of self-government and those who are not, available to the judiciary or could be applied or enforced by the judiciary." As he noted, the "whole matter is legislative, not judicial." McKenna also noted that the opinion written by White for *Downes*, which he joined, addressed these questions. In short, White, Shiras, and McKenna held that the applicability of the various provisions of the U.S. Constitution would be determined by Congress. Though McKenna was in the minority in *De Lima*, the Court institutionalized this argument in *Gonzales* when they refused to comment on González's citizenship, thus punting the question to Congress. Not only did the Court avoid deciding on the rights of colonial people, leaving this matter to Congress, but it also suggested that the geographic scope of constitutional rights was limited only to the metropole. In another case, *Dorr v. United States* (1904), the Court maintained its own judicial power to determine which aspects of the Bill of Rights applied in the unincorporated territories, but not the rights territorial subjects had in the metropole. The Court argued that the right of trial by jury does not extend to the territories unless explicitly written by Congress.[71] In their decisions in the *Insular Cases*, the Court translated racial concerns into the legal architecture of the state. This flexible system of rule evaded any clear decisions on how to treat colonial territory or people.

CONCLUSION

Faced with ruling new overseas territories and people, U.S. state actors and legal thinkers debated their visions of the U.S. "nation." Through this conflict, they institutionalized new terms of rule. Democrats, isolationists, nativists, and those opposed to U.S. expansion hoped to clarify the relationship of the United States to the Philippines and other former Spanish colonies so that the colonies, colonial exports, and colonial people would be excluded from the United States. Imperialists and their supporters, however, accommodated a flexible interpretation of the Constitution. They evaded clear, univocal definitions of the relationship between metropole and colony.

The decisions from the *Insular Cases* defied the post–Civil War Constitution and institutionalized ideas about Filipinos' racial inferiority into a flexible and durable grammar of racial-imperial rule. The Court established broad mandates and definitions through ambiguous law, ostensibly race-neutral categories, and discretion. In their ambiguous and equivocal decisions, the Court helped the United States manage the contradictions of claiming to be a constitutional democracy and having overseas territories. Rather than a clear ruling about the status of the colonies, the justices punted the authority to determine the relationship between the colonies and the metropolitan United States to Congress. Through the Court's decision to uphold Congressional plenary power over the territories, the justices decided that ruling the colonies was an open political question (rather than one that the Court would settle). Thus, by avoiding clear definitions, the Court enabled decades of debates and experimentation over how to treat the Philippines and Filipinos, as subsequent chapters will show. The United States Supreme Court created a new flexible strategy of non-definition for managing expansion and racial-imperial rule that would continue to shape U.S. imperial formation for decades to come.

THREE A DURABLE ADMINISTRATIVE STRUCTURE, 1898–1916

On December 21, 1898, President William McKinley issued a proclamation. In it, he asserted that the United States came to the Philippines "not as invaders or conquerors, but as friends, to protect the natives in their homes, in their employments, and in their personal and religious rights." In the Philippines, the U.S. military should show Filipinos that "the mission of the United States is one of benevolent assimilation."[1] Imperialists argued that the United States was a guardian or teacher that would educate and train Filipinos in the ways of the civilized world, including democratic governance. As Mark Elliot argues, this project of post-wartime rehabilitation "recalled Reconstruction, if in complex ways." McKinley's rhetoric "sounded eerily familiar to the rhetoric of sectional reconciliation" espoused by Union victors.[2] The United States claimed sovereignty over Philippine politics and society and tried to pacify a local population, claiming to build foundations of democracy and secure individual rights.

At the same time, McKinley's statement, which became known as the Benevolent Assimilation Proclamation, responded to and built on long-standing concerns about the racial incorporation of nonwhite people in the metropole.

As one legal thinker of the time argued, the United States Constitution "was made by a civilized and educated people" and could not apply to Filipinos. Referencing racial categories new to the United States, he argued that "to give the half-civilized Moros . . .or even the ordinary Filipino of Manila, the benefit of such immunities from the sharp and sudden justice or injustice which they have been hitherto accustomed to expect, would, of course, be a serious obstacle to the maintenance there of an efficient government."[3] In other words, the overseas administration of nonwhite people was a task that the United States should abandon. Nevertheless, as the last chapter showed, the United States had claimed the islands.

U.S. imperialists in the executive branch innovated and laid down new rules. Against nativist critics, they broke with past practices of foreign and colonial affairs. Led by newly appointed Secretary of War Elihu Root, they acted against a majority of legislators who wished to focus on domestic matters rather than overseas imperial projects. U.S. imperialists in the executive branch reshaped the administration of overseas affairs. Their commitment to expanding white racial rule transformed the metropolitan government. Colonial administrators produced new racial knowledge to fuel their project. Imperialists' ideas about race, in turn, shaped on-the-ground innovations in the colony. Each of these innovations to administrative structure, racial knowledge, and colonial administration defied the legal, administrative, and racial orders of the day.

My discussion of the administrative foundations of U.S. empire builds on Colin Moore's account of the U.S. colonial administration.[4] Moore shows that U.S. politicians and administrators built a system that laid the foundation for the "modern executive-dominated security state."[5] I join him in arguing that U.S. territorial expansion and empire set the terms for international intervention. Unlike Moore, in this and the previous chapter, I show that these are racial projects rooted in fears about and hostility toward including nonwhite others in the United States. I pay special attention to race. I emphasize that the conflict between vulgar racists concerned with white hegemony at home and polite racists invested in expanding white hegemony abroad not only shaped the legal compromises and ambiguities institutionalized by the U.S. Supreme Court, but also created opportunities to develop domestic and foreign affairs aspects of empire independently from each other. These conditions gave discretion to both Congress and the U.S. executive branch, and the latter took charge of building a durable administrative structure. The commitment to an overseas white hegemonic project created the conditions to amass new white supremacist racial knowledge, which shaped governance and development in the colony.

U.S. imperialists built a new administrative apparatus in the metropole that vested power in the executive branch and limited the control of the legislative branch. After demonstrating that imperial administrators solicited and constructed polite ideas about racial difference, rooted in the possibility of civilizing Filipinos, I show that, in the Philippines, they translated their racialized program of "benevolent assimilation" into policy. The restructured metropolitan and newly founded colonial administrative architecture persisted beyond the string of imperialist Republican presidents, which ended in 1913. I close this chapter by illustrating that these early years of imperialist and Republican-led rule were key foundations of a racial-imperial grammar that continued to shape U.S. state formation in the Philippines even after Republicans lost control of the executive and legislative branches.

BUILDING A NEW COLONIAL ADMINISTRATIVE STATE

As conflict between projects of domestic and global white hegemony shaped the U.S. Supreme Court's decisions in the *Insular Cases*, the U.S. executive branch pushed on with its aims for expanding U.S. influence abroad through imperial rule. At home in the metropole, U.S. imperialists created a new administrative system to manage overseas colonial affairs. Their innovations included centralizing colonial rule, relying on broad and ambiguous definitions, vesting power in the executive branch, and managing the information received by the legislative branch. As legislators noted, these practices broke with the past territorial administration. The grammar that U.S. imperialists built to accommodate their vision for overseas white hegemony would continue to structure U.S. colonial and foreign affairs decades after the Spanish–American War.

To manage the new project of overseas affairs, in 1899, President McKinley tapped Elihu Root, a private sector lawyer from New York, to serve as the new secretary of war. Root, in fact, authored McKinley's aforementioned Benevolent Assimilation Proclamation and is widely recognized as the architect of the United States' colonial administration, housed in the U.S. War Department. Serving in this capacity until 1904, Root reorganized imperial rule. Root instituted several new precedents that departed from prior U.S. imperial rule. First, he centralized territorial administration in a division of the War Department and endowed the division with broad powers. The Division of Insular Affairs, which later became the Bureau of Insular Affairs (BIA), oversaw the civil administration of the new Spanish territories.[6] Second, as Root centralized overseas rule in the BIA, he also redesigned the structure of reporting within the War Department so that the BIA reported directly to him.[7] In the newly formed BIA, the United States "tried to assume the role of colonizer simultaneously reconciling the same with American Republican and democratic traditions."[8] The BIA—though not in name—was the United States' colonial office. Third, Root vested power in the BIA by never clearly defining its role. Root gave the War Department and the BIA broad power to manage affairs ranging from diplomatic, financial, legal, agricultural, commercial, and others. For example, as they built the structures for U.S. overseas empire, the War Department liberalized law in the Philippines to encourage U.S. capital investment in infrastructure such as railroads and sugar mills, thus relying on public-private partnerships.[9] They tried to pass land laws for agricultural investment and development. To extract the maximum advantage for U.S. domestic industries, they also prioritized favorable free trade agreements for U.S. products in the Asian market.[10] The powers of the BIA were wide ranging and ill-defined. Root and the executive branch took advantage of ambiguous definitions to develop an autonomous external state that did not answer to legislators.[11]

As he built a new and powerful colonial administration, Root recruited more people for the imperialist project. Key among them was Charles Magoon, who served as the Law Officer of the Division of Insular Affairs (and then the Bureau) from 1899 to 1905. His service overlapped with years of the early *Insular Cases* discussed in Chapter 2, and his reports to Root and Congress on the legal status of the territories contributed to legal opinion of the time. As Law Officer, Magoon investigated legal matters related to military and civil affairs in the territories. He provided rationales for extending territorial boundaries and sovereign claims, the treatment of territorial inhabitants, and Congressional action in the territories. Like the U.S. Supreme Court's rulings in the *Insular Cases*, Magoon argued that although U.S. territorial boundaries extended to new possessions, including the Philippines, the U.S. Constitution did not extend to territorial inhabitants. He also claimed that Congress had the jurisdiction to legislate for the territories, and that legislation did not need to conform to the Constitution. As the United States transitioned from war to military government to civil government in the Philippines, Root and Magoon worked to maintain the broad powers of the executive. They did this by centralizing and justifying executive control and by influencing legislative action.

Expanding Executive Control

In shaping U.S. colonial administration, Root and Magoon used capacious definitions of wartime to manipulate the meaning of consent and constitutionalism.[12] They justified the executive branch's centralized and broad powers in three ways: by claiming that the Philippines was hostile territory, that they had effectively established the separation of powers (albeit all under the executive branch), and that the BIA was most equipped to rule because of its specialized knowledge. Defining the United States as still at war granted the executive branch more powers to manage the newly acquired territory. Magoon argued that the Philippines was a hostile territory and the United States a belligerent. Classifying the Philippines as a hostile territory relied on the idea that the Philippines was in an ongoing state of insurrection. This, Magoon argued, meant that to rule, the United States did not need the consent of Filipinos—who, as Chapter 2 showed, were racially inferior and could not understand civilized government.

In addition to deeming it a hostile territory, five months after *Downes*, in his October 30, 1901, report, Magoon emphasized that whether the Philippines was foreign was not the criteria to determine U.S. executive branch control. Instead, "the absence of Congressional action" allowed the executive to determine Philippine affairs. According to Magoon, the Philippine insurrection was "still potent" and "so long as this spirit shall prompt any considerable number of insurgents to continue the insurrection," then the United States could "rely upon the military branch . . .to maintain its authority in the Philippine islands."[13] Thus, the BIA drew on the idea that Filipinos could not consent to rule and on wartime categories to empower the U.S. executive branch.

Just as he classified the Philippines as a hostile territory, Magoon also cited the United States' status as a belligerent state as justification for military rule. He wrote that "so long as the United States is authorized to exercise the rights of a belligerent there are no limitations on such exercise excepting those imposed by the laws and usages of war."[14] As a belligerent state (at war with Spain), the United States gained rights to possess the former Spanish territories. Magoon added, "So long as the insurrection continues the President, as Commander in Chief of the military forces of the United States, will continue to have authority to regulate and control trade with the hostile territory by exercise of belligerent right."[15] That the United States was a belligerent state and the Philippines was a hostile territory meant that the U.S. executive could continue to control the archipelago.

The executive's claim to military authority over the Philippines also supported the judicial arguments discussed in Chapter 2 that the Constitution did not extend to the territories. Magoon reasoned that because the Philippines was under military control, and the military cannot incorporate territory, the Philippines could not become a state and the Constitution did not apply. There was "no question," he wrote, "that territory without the boundaries of the United States is not bound and privileged by our Constitution."[16] According to Magoon, "territory may be under the sovereignty and jurisdiction of the United States and yet not subject to the laws of the United States."[17] Because of wartime classifications and military rule, Magoon claimed the Philippines was not part of the United States.

In addition to relying on wartime classifications of a hostile territory and a belligerent state to rationalize the extension of U.S. executive power (but not the Constitution) abroad, the BIA claimed that executive-led rule over the Philippines was constitutional. As the United States prepared to transition from military to civil government, Elihu Root noted that the "chief objection to any unnecessary continuance of military government" was that executive, legislative, and judicial powers were all vested in the U.S. president. Despite acknowledging the importance of the separation of powers, Root argued the executive could maintain oversight in the Philippines because legislative, judicial, and executive powers would, in fact, be divided. The Philippine Commission (a group of educators, diplomats, and military officials appointed by President McKinley to survey the Philippines and make recommendations on governance and development) would act as the legislative branch. The BIA was establishing new courts, creating a judicial branch. Military leaders had executive authority. Each of these so-called branches of government, however, was under the control of the U.S. executive branch.[18] Thus, the executive branch separated sovereign rule from the people and bestowed vast powers upon itself.

As the BIA relied on wartime classifications and instituted a symbolic separation of powers, they also argued that they knew more about Filipinos than the U.S. Congress and were thus in a better position to manage overseas affairs. In fact, from the moment of U.S. conquest of the archipelago, the executive had created the conditions for monopolizing knowledge production. The U.S. president had appointed a commission to study Philippine affairs. Government commissions respond to and propose solutions to pressing and controversial social issues. As they collect information, they produce new social facts under the guise of impartiality.[19] In this case, because the president appointed the commission, they controlled information about the Philippines. Therefore, Root claimed, the executive branch should oversee rule. Root argued that to establish a government in the Philippines, the United States needed "full and accurate knowledge of the conditions and proceedings of all the governments in the islands," and that both the U.S. president and Congress must look to the War Department for this information. Only the War Department had received "every conceivable kind of information regarding the islands . . .in an uninterrupted stream."[20] The executive's monopoly of information about the colonies enhanced administrators' control over colonial affairs. Root and Magoon equipped the executive with more information to manage the Philippines.

Legislators, however, doubted the veracity of the accounts provided by the BIA. Senator Benjamin Tillman (D-SC) compared the executive's proclamations to "the dark days of reconstruction in South Carolina," his home state, "when carpetbaggers had full sway."[21] He stated Congress was "unable to determine just what the situation" in the Philippines "really is." Was the United States at war? According to Tillman, in the summer of 1900, the president proclaimed pacification, but then requested Congress to authorize a standing army to quash insurrection in the Philippines. "First we have peace, and then we have war, and now we have got peace again. . . .It appears that we have war or peace in the Philippines just as the political schemes of the Administration may require."[22] Tillman's remarks highlight how the BIA manipulated the definition of wartime and its accompanying classificatory schemes to enhance their own power. Tillman opposed federal power and what he saw as imposing Northern business interests on so-called common people. In comparing the Philippines to the end of white-ruled confederacy in the U.S. South, Tillman objected to Republican and executive-led intervention. For him, federal control abroad could spell the end of white segregationist policies in the South.[23] Tillman argued that the executive branch was manipulating information about conditions in the Philippines and that by evading the establishment of a territorial civil government, the executive branch co-opted the powers of Congress. The War Department and the president were imposing their will and control and seeking economic profits in places they ought not to—whether it be the recently defeated confederate South or the Philippines. Even as they made their arguments primarily in terms of opposition to the unconstitutional claims of the executive branch, the history of the Civil War and their commitment to excluding nonwhite people motivated Democratic senators' position on the Philippines.

Senate Democrats were not alone in questioning the veracity of information provided by the executive. The debates in a session of the House of Representatives demonstrate how legislators believed that political interests shaped the "facts" reported by the BIA. Representative John Dalzell (R-PA) submitted a report from a joint resolution to appoint a Congressional committee to visit Puerto Rico, the Philippines, and Cuba. Senator Leonidas Livingston (D-GA) asked the purpose of including the Philippines when the Taft Commission (appointed by the president) already existed and could travel not only to the Philippines but also to Puerto Rico and Cuba. Dalzell responded that the Congressional commission would "satisfy Congress as to the correctness or incorrectness of the report made by the Taft Commission." Representative James Daniel Richardson (D-TN) added that "it is absolutely essential in order for members to legislate intelligently with respect to our insular possessions to get it from partisan sources." He added that he did not favor information from nonpartisan sources and thought that partisan sources would "get all the truth." Richardson responded to other legislators who suggested that this was little more than Congressional junketing and that that there was no need for such a commission, saying he did not think "we have ever had the facts." In other words, Richardson implied that the Taft Commission and Bureau of Insular Affairs were selectively sharing information. Representative Oscar Underwood (D-AL) also joined in, arguing that his party could not give "full faith and credit to the report of any commission that has been appointed by the Executive to report the facts to us." He continued, commenting on the applicability of the decisions from the *Insular Cases* to Congressional law-making: "Regardless of what positions the Supreme Court may take on these important questions, whether they will hold the present law constitutional or unconstitutional, there is no man on the floor of this House who does not know next winter we will be called upon to legislate in some way with reference to those questions." Thus, Underwood argued, the House needed clear and trustworthy information about the U.S. colonies.[24] Nevertheless, BIA skeptics in Congress did not establish an alternative commission or source of information and were unsuccessful in wrestling control away from the executive.

Influencing the Legislative Branch

As they vested power to determine colonial relations in the executive branch, the Bureau of Insular Affairs also carefully managed their relationship with Congress. Root and the BIA sought both greater discretion from and influence over Congress in ways that broke with past territorial expansion. The BIA achieved this goal through drafting legislation about the colonies and seeking friendly sponsors.[25] Examining how Congress drafted and passed the Spooner Amendment to the Army Appropriations Bill of 1901—which gave the executive branch authority over military, civil, and judicial affairs in the Philippines—reveals the extent of BIA control, legislators' objections to it, and why it was so hard for Congress to manage territorial affairs.

The War Department, under Root, drafted the Spooner Amendment. While Senator John C. Spooner (R-WI) first tried to introduce the amendment as its own act, the Senate did not see it through.[26] Spooner then attached it to a large Army Appropriations bill, increasing the likelihood that the amendment would pass.[27] Senator John T. Morgan (D-AL) noted that "very suddenly, at the close of this session of Congress" Spooner attached the amendment "upon one of [the Senate's] own appropriation bills," which Congress needed to pass to keep the U.S. Army funded.[28] This hasty approach left Congress with little option but to pass bill with the amendment. The final version of the amendment in the Army Appropriations Act read that "until otherwise provided by Congress," "all military, civil, and judicial powers necessary to govern the Philippine Islands" would lie with people appointed by the president. The act continued that "until a permanent government shall have been established in said archipelago full reports shall be made to Congress" by said appointed people.[29] After the Spooner Amendment, then, Congress had little say in co-lonial affairs.

Democratic senators objected to the Spooner Amendment, as it broke with past territorial administration and gave too much power to the executive branch. Senators Tillman and Joseph L. Rawlins (D-UT) compared the acqui-sition and territorial rule of the Philippines to the 1803 Louisiana Purchase, the 1848 Treaty of Guadalupe Hidalgo, and the 1867 purchase of Alaska. They noted that with each of these territorial acquisitions, Congress had control over establishing a territorial government and over military, civil, and judicial powers in the new territory. Senator Donelson Caffery (D-LA) argued that this amendment was "a clear delegation of power to make laws granted by Congress to the President of the United States." Caffery cited that the Treaty of Paris was supposed to give Congress "unlimited jurisdiction and power under the Constitution to govern the Philippine Islands outside of the Constitution and beyond the Constitution, save only as to those personal rights which are guaranteed in the Bill of Rights." This amendment "goes a little further in the march of empire." Caffery continued, "It makes the President a virtual czar, unchecked, and uncontrolled by any supervisory power of Congress." Foreshadowing future U.S. foreign relations, Caffery warned, "I say we have not and no imperialist, however wild he was or however eager to grasp the territory of another people, ever made contention that the President of the United States could virtually be the lawmaking power either in these foreign territories or in any other place within the jurisdiction of the United States."[30] As Democratic senators argued, Republican-led imperial rule reshaped the structure of the U.S. federal government and laid down new executive-led practices for territorial and foreign governance.

To correct the unprecedented executive control endowed by the Spooner Amendment, Senator George Graham Vest (D-MO) proposed an amendment to Spooner's. It read: "no judgement, order, nor act by any of said officials so appointed shall conflict with the Constitution and laws of the United States."[31] While Spooner argued that such an addition was unnecessary, as the matter of the applicability of the U.S. Constitution would be determined by the U.S. Supreme Court, Senator Augustus O. Bacon (D-GA) raised concern that with-out Vest's addition, "there shall be committed into the hands of the President of the United States the unlimited power to organize, maintain, enforce, and administer a Government over 12,000,000 people, without any restraint or limitation whatsoever."[32] Thus, Bacon argued, Spooner's amendment without Vest's addition would be unconstitutional. Senator Tillman also argued that the Spooner Amendment was "a bald, naked investment of power in the President."[33] As imperialists attempted to assert more control over foreign affairs and concentrate this power in the executive, Democratic senators pushed back.

Despite legislators' protests, the BIA successfully passed the Spooner Amendment and continued to secure control over territorial affairs. In the 1902 Philippine Organic Act, Root designed the powers, structure, and relationships of the colonial government in the Philippines.[34] The Taft-led Philippine Commission submitted this proposal for civil government to the U.S. Congress, which Congress debated and eventually passed as the Organic Act (albeit with restrictions to economic development).[35] As Senators Tillman (D-SC) and Rawlins (D-UT) argued above, in prior territorial acquisitions, Congress had the power to establish a civil government, including oversight of military, judicial, and civil affairs in the new territory. It would not be so in the Philippines. Thus, in a break from past practices of territorial rule, the executive branch controlled not only the information Congress received about the Philippines but also the structure of government for the Philippine Islands. In sum, as U.S. imperialist bureaucrats built the structures of U.S. overseas rule, they encountered Congressional opposition to executive control. In response, they innovated. By managing the flow of information about the colonies and drafting legislation that vested power in the executive, the BIA built a strong external state like none seen before in the United States.

CONSTRUCTING RACIAL KNOWLEDGE FOR RULE

As the executive branch secured their hold on overseas affairs, they produced new racial knowledge not only to understand the unfamiliar territory and people but also to rationalize their rule. They both built on preexisting ideas of race rooted in experiences of U.S. settler expansion and constructed new ideas of race. In their capacity as members of commissions appointed by the U.S. president, U.S. politicians and academics collected data, took photographs, made maps, and reported on the status of the Philippines and Filipino people.[36] As part of the first Philippine Commission, known as the Schurman Commission, a zoologist from the University of Michigan, Dean Worcester, traveled the islands, documenting in photos and fieldnotes the bodies, clothing, housing, and customs of Filipino people. These legibility projects were attempts to make sense of what U.S. politicians and elites thought of as a foreign, savage, and hostile place. Collecting and systematizing information helped them make sense of and justify their project of rule.[37] For example, Worcester argued that Filipinos "collectively do not form a nation or a people." While we often think of legibility projects as clarifying, the claims that Filipinos were tribal, heterogenous, and tropical also helped justify ambiguous and polysemous rule.

The racial knowledge produced by executive branch commissions significantly departed from the preexisting continental racial knowledge discussed in Chapter 2. U.S. imperialists drew on popular "race science" of the time to argue that Filipinos were a different people. Worcester and the Schurman Commission reported that there were eighty-four tribes that were "wild" and lacked unity.[38] The eighty-four tribes could be divided into "three sharply distinct races—the Negrito race, the Indonesian race, and the Malayan race."[39] The latter were the majority and "more or less modified through intermarriage with Chinese, Indonesians, Negritos, Arabs, and, to a limited extent, Spaniards and other Europeans." These classifications drew on and extended Johann Friedrich Blumenbach's typologies. According to this system, Malay "were considered to be governed not so much by law as by opinion and caprice, who were thought to be racially incapable of the order necessary to live under the rule of the state."[40] Thus, Filipinos, as tribal and racially heterogenous people, should be ruled by the United States.

Besides tribal and racial divisions, the Schurman Commission distinguished "pagan" or animist hill tribes (the Aetas or Negrito) from "Mohammedan" Muslims and Christian Malays. The "pagan" hill tribes were seen as aboriginal, primitive, nearly extinct, and incapable of civilization. Muslims, as a fearsome type of Malay, meanwhile, were seen as cruel, warlike, and fanatical. The Schurman Commission argued that because Christian Filipinos descended from the intermixture of Malays and Catholic Spaniards and some Chinese, they were the most civilized. Those from Manila, who spoke Tagalog, were described as a "hybrid race." Filipino elite, for their part, registered their opinion that these numbers and systems of classification from the Schurman Commission were absurd. Sixto López, the former secretary of the Philippine mission to negotiate independence, said that the eighty-four tribes were a product of "imagination, bad spelling, translation, subdivision, and multiplication" from the Spanish records, which were already inaccurate.[41]

Nevertheless, the U.S. Census institutionalized ideas of heterogenous ethno-linguistic and ethno-religious tribes. In 1904, for example, Senator Henry Cabot Lodge (R-MA) presented a report to Congress entitled "The Philippine Islands and Their People," produced by Henry Gannet, the chief geographer of the United States Geological Survey and assistant director to the Philippine Census. Gannet wrote, "These brown people, both civilized and uncivilized, are separated into many tribes, and they are of all grades and degrees of civilization." He continued, "A classification of the natives by tribes is a rough index to the degree of civilization. The Tagalogs . . .are the most powerful and highly civilized."[42] According to the 1905 U.S. Census of the Philippines, there were twenty-five ethnolinguistic groups, which were the same as the tribes described by Gannet but notably differed from the number reported by the Schurman Commission.

As the Census institutionalized the language of tribes, they also departed from both existing continental descriptions of nonwhite people. The Census divided "civilized" (meaning Christian) and "wild" (pagan, animist, or Muslim) Filipinos.[43] Within this system of subdivision, the Census listed five skin color options, taking from the Spanish system: *blanco, amarillo, marrón, mestizo,* and *negro.*[44] Thus, the U.S. Census not only adopted ideas from the Schurman Commission but also relied on Spanish designations. Together, these distinct classification systems demonstrate that there was not a monolithic or dominant way of constructing Filipinos. Rather, U.S. administrators drew on preexisting and newly constructed ideas of race to justify their project of racial-imperial rule.

Imperialist politicians emphasized the ethnolinguistic diversity of the Philippine archipelago to call into question the capacity of a Philippine state to rule over racially unrelated tribes. Evidence from military rule supported these claims. Elihu Root, for example, referred to Tagalog rule of the island of Negros as "thoroughly disorganized." He continued, "All the turbulent and predatory elements of tribes ranging from barbarism to semi-civilization had been set free from the habit of obedience to law."[45] Tagalogs could not yet be trusted to rule over those in Negros. Later, he emphasized that "there is special need of means to make the people homogenous and capable of uniting in common self-government."[46] Referring to ethno-religious divisions, Theodore Roosevelt wrote:

The Philippines offer yet a graver problem [compared to Puerto Rico and Cuba]. Their population includes half-caste and native Christians, war-like Moslems, and wild pagans. Many of their people are utterly unfit for self-government and show no signs of becoming fit. Others may in time become fit but at the present can only take part in self-government under wise supervision.[47]

U.S. imperialists claimed Filipinos lacked unity to govern themselves due to their diverse tribes and ethnoreligious groups. As Worcester argued, Filipinos "collectively do not form a nation or a people."[48] Thus, despite Filipinos' decades-long struggle for independence, U.S. politicians cast Filipinos as lacking a national consciousness and the Philippines as an illegitimate state whose sovereignty could not be recognized. Imperialists argued that the ethno-linguistic and religious heterogeneity of the islands made the Philippines both unassimilable to the United States and incapable of being ruled by local leaders.

In addition to distinguishing Filipinos from known continental populations by emphasizing that they were a conglomeration of disparate tribes and new racial types, imperialists and their nativist-isolationist counterparts raised concerns about the tropical climate of the Philippines, but to different ends. For nativist-isolationists, the tropical archipelago was unsuitable to white settlement. One anti-expansionist legal scholar argued that "the character of its people" and the Philippines' "climatic conditions forbid the hope that Americans will migrate to it in sufficient numbers to elevate its social conditions and ultimately justify its admission as a state."[49] Another legal professional invoked the fiction that the territories of the continental United States were "vast, unpeopled areas"[50] and "virtually a wilderness"[51] to argue that the Philippines, as a densely populated tropical place, could not be incorporated.[52] Thus, isolationists argued that while Filipinos could not learn the ways of the United States, neither could white U.S. citizens settle in the Philippines. While the majority of inhabitants of both the Philippines and Hawai'i were nonwhite, nativists saw the Philippine climate as distinct from that of Hawai'i, which had already been settled. Given the fears about the Philippines' tropical climate, U.S. mass migration could not solve the problem of governance in the Philippines.

Imperialists meanwhile argued that the tropical climate was a sign of an early evolutionary stage and that Filipinos could improve. According to social evolutionary thinking of the time, race was, in part, conditioned by the climate. In contrast to the comparisons of Filipinos to Black Americans or portrayals of Filipinos as savage, imperialists thought of Filipinos' racial status as the product of environmental-historical factors. Thus, categorizing Filipinos as tropical was not only a climatic or geographic designation but also a racial one. Unlike Cubans and Puerto Ricans, U.S. state actors and the Census saw the Philippines as incomprehensible in Black-white terms. Their tropical status set them apart.[53] Imperialists likened people from more tropical climates to children. One U.S. official in the Philippines wrote that Filipinos "were locked in a 'feudal' or 'medieval' stage of development."[54] William Howard Taft, head of the Philippine Commission who would become the first governor of the Philippines and later the twenty-seventh U.S. president from 1904 to 1913, famously referred to Filipinos as "little brown brothers." Woodrow Wilson—a professor of Political Science at Princeton University who would later become the president of the university in 1902, governor of New Jersey in 1911, and the twenty-eighth president of the United States in 1913—wrote that Filipinos "are children and we are men in these deep matters of government and justice."[55] Because Filipinos were products of their history and environment, imperialists argued that Filipinos were also capable of growth. As Julian Go notes, this implied that "the colonized's inferiority was not in fact interminable." Imperialists relied on what Go calls a Lamarckian racial scheme, one in which "nurture trumped nature."[56] McKinley, for example, remarked that "Filipinos are a race quick to learn and profit from knowledge."[57] Imperialists claimed that in a few generations, Filipinos could improve and become capable of self-government.[58] This language of growth and self-improvement would again appear at the end of colonial rule, as seen in Chapter 7.

Characterizations of Filipinos as tropical and in an early stage of development supported justifications for the project of benevolent assimilation. If Filipinos were willing and pliable children, whites were disciplined fathers. In popular thinking of the time, Anglo-Saxons were the most fit to rule. They could supervise and educate children worldwide. Taft considered Anglo-Saxons to be "the most self-governing but also the most administrative of any race in history."[59] Rule over the colonies was an opportunity for the United

States—as Anglo-Saxon and as inheritors of the British empire—to civilize the rest of the world.[60] While Taft testified that Filipinos were not yet capable or deserving of the rights guaranteed under the U.S. Constitution, he also suggested that the United States could teach Filipinos to self-govern "by a gradual course."[61] Before gaining full rights, Taft argued, Filipinos must "learn a self-restraint that can only be learned after practice."[62] Civic officials argued that with the proper education and training by Anglo-Saxons, Filipinos eventually could evolve toward a (more) civilized state.

Not only could Filipinos improve under U.S. supervision, but imperialists also claimed that the Filipino masses, like children, were grateful and obedient subjects. In 1902, Luke Wright, then vice governor of the Philippines, wrote Colonel Clarence Edwards, the chief of the Division of Insular Affairs, with his assessments of Filipinos' receptivity to self-governance and the goals of U.S. rule over the islands: "The Filipinos, as you know, are not a warlike people; the great mass of them care but little under what form of government they live, and the educated and intelligent among them as a rule recognize their utter inability to maintain an independent government of their own and are ready to accept American sovereignty." He continued, assessing the ease with which the United States could rule the Philippines: "These people do not appear to me to be difficult to govern, and I believe they will readily accept a firm, kindly and fixed policy and will gradually become firmly attached to us."[63] Notably, Wright's accounts of Filipino passivity depart from the characterizations of Filipinos as hostile and barbaric people. When it came to justifying executive control, the BIA relied on wartime classifications, but when it came to justifying long-term rule, imperialists cast their project as a gradual and peaceful one.

To summarize, U.S. bureaucrats produced new racial knowledge and concretized Filipinos' tropical and primitive status into government categories. They mobilized ideas of tribal heterogeneity to justify that Filipinos did not have political sovereignty, at least at the present time. Heterogeneity also helped explain the varying interpretations of Filipinos—as both war- and childlike, as barbaric, but also teachable. Casting Filipinos as a new racial type was not only a response to nativist-isolationist concerns but also helped justify a new U.S. program of overseas tutelage. Filipinos' tribal and heterogenous nature meant they were unfit to rule themselves. Under the firm hand of the United States, they could benefit and grow to maturity.

THE U.S. PROGRAM OF IMPROVEMENT

Racial ideas not only justified overseas rule but also shaped the terms of on-the-ground colonial administration. After the Republican victory in the 1900 presidential election, the Taft Commission wrote that "conditions in these islands will grow steadily better." The report continued, "And however formidable the difficulties really are, the possibilities that present themselves of improving the condition of the people in education, wealth, comfort, and in the knowledge of how to govern themselves can not but awaken the deepest enthusiasm on the part of every friend of civilization familiar with the actual conditions."[64] In their reports, colonial administrators regularly wove together mentions of Filipinos' racial status, the United States' fitness to rule, and programs for colonial improvement.

By 1900, McKinley reported to Congress that business, agriculture, and the economy of the archipelago had improved. The Philippine Commission, McKinley wrote, was "encouraging the benefits of liberty and good government to the Filipinos, in the interest of humanity and with the aim of building up an enduring, self-supporting, and self-administering community in those far eastern seas."[65] The commission attempted to implement a program of Anglo-Saxon-led modernization and civilizational uplift, concentrating their efforts on colonial governance, militarization, public education programs, and economic development.

Although the U.S. Congress often stymied imperialists' goals, the polite racial logics and programmatic aims of U.S. imperialists and more specifically of the Philippine Commission shaped U.S. imperial structures. Following the Spanish–American War and through 1916, the second Philippine Commission under Taft oversaw Philippine affairs. Imperialists translated their polite racial ideologies into plans for the structures of governance, public education programs, the military, and economic development.[66] Logics of racial difference shaped each of these institutions, which also lasted beyond the early years of rule.

Government Administration

Drawing on ideas of the fundamental racial difference between Filipinos and U.S. Anglo-Saxons, imperialists cemented plans for gradual tutelage and development. According to the 1902 Philippine Organic Act, the Philippine judiciary, legislative, military, defense, trade, and natural resource matters were subject to oversight by members of the U.S. federal government.[67] As previously mentioned, all three branches of government were under the control of U.S. imperial administrators who were viewed themselves as "tutors in the art of self government."[68] The U.S. president would "continue to regulate and control commercial intercourse with and within said Islands [*sic*] by such general rules and regulations as he, in his discretion, may deem more conducive to the public interests and the general welfare."[69] As U.S. imperialists constructed Filipinos as racially inferior children in need of instruction, they limited Filipino sovereignty and self-determination.

Even as the United States trained some Filipinos in civilization and incorporated them into the colonial government, imperialists also cautioned that not all Filipinos could learn self-rule. Instead, imperialists determined that by gradual course, Filipinos could learn the art of governance. For example, from 1900 to 1907, the Taft Commission served as the legislative branch of the U.S. government in the Philippines, with Taft as the executive in the position of governor general. The Philippine Commission, while mostly composed of U.S. officials, included some Filipinos who had been part of the Revolutionary government. It was not until 1907—five years after the Organic Act established a civil government in the Philippines—that the Philippine Legislature added a lower house composed of elected Filipino officials. Officials appointed by the governor general of the Philippines continued to comprise the upper house. It was indeed a slow process by which U.S. colonial officials trained Filipinos and evaluated their fitness to take part in government.

At the same time, imperialists argued that some Filipinos were more equipped and capable of self-rule. U.S. colonial officials drew on the aforementioned tribalizing accounts and the Spanish system to divide the Christian Filipinos from the others, ruling with "dual mandates."[70] They argued that the more advanced Malay Filipinos should rule over other ethnolinguistic groups. Some imperialists believed that the heterogeneity of the Philippines meant an indefinite period of tutelage. The United States imperial government increasingly recognized Malay Catholic Filipinos to the exclusion of non-Christians, including Muslims and animists. For example, in a hearing before the House Committee on Insular Affairs, Chairman Henry Allen Cooper (R-WI), referring to the "Moros," asked Taft, "Then the Christian Filipinos are much the superior of the two, under present conditions at least?"

Taft responded, "Certainly they are for capacity for education and capacity for development of self-government."[71] Officials like Taft saw Christians as a step toward Anglo-Saxon civilization. The Christian Filipinos would be tutored in rule over the lesser "tribes." Bifurcated rule, while creating paths for recognizing and including some Filipinos, also taught Catholic Filipinos to rule over the non-Christian "tribes" in their own internal colonial project.[72] In other words, wielding ideas about Filipinos' early developmental stage and tribal heterogeneity, imperialists justified structures of colonial administration in the archipelago.

Education

U.S. imperialists also translated ideas of Anglo-Saxon superiority and Filipinos' gradual advancement into colonial practice through the institution of education. Elihu Root underscored the importance of colonial education. He believed that education "shall tend to fit the people for the duties of citizenship and for the ordinary activities of a civilized community."[73] As he asked to recruit more teachers and build more schools, Root claimed that "all the good influences of American civilization may enter through this door."[74] With this vision in mind, colonial administrators in the Philippines created a system of public education, recruited U.S. teachers to train Filipinos, and developed an exchange program for young Filipino men to benefit from U.S. university education.

On January 21, 1901, the Philippine Commission, acting as the legislative branch of the colonial Philippine government, passed Act 74 to establish a department of public instruction. Drafted by the newly appointed general superintendent of public instruction, Fred Atkinson, this Act provided for the training of U.S. teachers, the establishment of normal, trade, and agricultural schools, as well as schools for the instruction of English.[75] Atkinson appointed U.S. teachers, known as Thomasites, for the *Thomas* army transport ship on which many of them entered. They moved to the Philippines and trained young Filipinos in American education and norms.[76] The Second Philippine Commission wrote that "the desire for education by the Filipinos of all tribes is very strong and gives encouraging promise of the future mental development of a now uneducated and ignorant people."[77]

As head of the Commission, Taft believed that education was key to preparing people for the duties of citizenship. In 1900, he appointed David Barrows as the superintendent of schools in Manila. Barrows, who later served on the faculty and in the administration of the University of California–Berkeley, became the head of the education bureau in 1903 after Taft dismissed Atkinson. Barrows developed the U.S. program for education and social engineering in the Philippines. At the same time, Barrows believed that educating the masses would help combat the power of the Philippine aristocracy.[78] Instruction and literacy in English were key to Barrows's program. In a Senate Committee Hearing on the Philippines, he stated that "if the Filipino is to be enlightened at all, he has to have some medium of exchange from tribe to tribe and from himself with the white race, and it is an exceedingly fortunate thing I think that his ambition at the present time is to acquire English, and that he never acquired any deep attachment to the Spanish language."[79] English was the language of instruction, for, as Taft wrote, it was "the language of free institutions" and "business in the Orient."[80]

Drawing on Lamarckian ideas of race, in 1903, the Commission also gave scholarships to those deemed the most promising students. Known as *pensionados*, they were given the opportunity to pursue advanced degrees in the United States and to then return home to the Philippines and apply their newly acquired American education and skills in the colonial government.[81] The Act specified candidates must be "natives of the Philippine Islands, of good moral character." And when their education in the United States ended, the act specified they would return to take a civil service exam in the Philippines. As Sarah Steinbock-Pratt notes, this program "was intended to ensure the collaboration of Filipino elites with the colonial state, and the Americanization of the governing class."[82] The Philippine education system, then, was built on the idea that the United States could train Filipinos in the art of civilization.

Military

Ideas of racial difference not only shaped the terms and structures of colonial rule and the institution of education, but they also informed military recruitment and strategy. As U.S. military officials characterized Filipinos as savages who could be conquered like American Indians, they also recruited Filipinos to serve in the U.S. military. In June 1899, Lieutenant Matthew Batson and his servant, Jacinto, hatched a plan for the army to recruit Filipinos. After receiving permission from the commanding general in the Philippines, Major General Elwell Otis, this group became known as the Philippine Scouts. Like the Indian Scouts before them, these Filipinos would serve alongside the U.S. military as guides and in combat against the Philippine independence movement.[83] In 1901, U.S. Congress authorized the U.S. president to enlist up to twelve thousand Filipinos into the U.S. Army.[84] In 1902, the U.S. Congress formalized the relationship of the Scouts to the United States military, offering them rights and benefits for their service. Although Filipinos were incorporated into the U.S. military, U.S. officers still applied racial logics, segregating them by their respective "tribes," or ethno-linguistic groups.[85]

In forming the Scouts, the U.S. military and colonial officials drew on past continental practices with American Indians, putting these Filipinos on display as evidence of the United States' civilizing project. When deciding on what to include in the Philippine exposition at the 1904 St. Louis World's Fair, Taft suggested the Philippine Scouts. They would represent the civilizing benefits of U.S. imperial rule. The Scouts wore their U.S. uniforms. Their band played "The Star-Spangled Banner" and other patriotic U.S. songs. Together with the participation of *pensionados*, the display included the Scouts alongside "tribal" Filipino people. The juxtaposition suggested the uplifting effects of U.S. colonialism.[86] The recruitment of and reliance on colonial soldiers drew on racial logics of difference and institutionalized patterns imperial rule that would continue to shape U.S.–Philippine relations.

Economic Development

As U.S. imperialists translated their ideas of Anglo-Saxon superiority into the terms of colonial governance, the public education system, and the military, they also argued that the U.S. model of economic development would uplift Filipinos.[87] At the same time, their programs of uplift kept Filipinos subservient to the United States, reflecting the logics of racial colonial difference. As part of the aforementioned Act establishing a department of public instruction, the Philippine Commission also appropriated money for a trade school and an agricultural school.[88] Educational programs were not only for training in Western democracy and citizenship but also for industrial and economic development. The curriculum included morality lessons on thrift and land-ownership that supported U.S-led development.

Imperialists translated ideas of white superiority into strategies of rule. Superintendent Fred W. Atkinson designed industrial education in the model of Booker T. Washington's Tuskegee School, even visiting Tuskegee and the

Hampton Institute.[89] Washington believed Black Americans could improve through agricultural and industrial work. Atkinson wrote, "We must be aware of the possibility of overdoing the matter of higher education. . . .We should heed the lesson taught us in our reconstruction period when we started to educate the negro. The education of the masses here must be an agricultural and industrial one."[90] As Glenn May notes, "White Americans found industrial education for blacks appealing," as "it seemed to relegate blacks to an inferior position in society."[91] Luke Wright, acting governor of the Philippines in 1902, believed that the U.S. government, by educating and training Filipinos especially in manufacturing industries, was "fitting the native for the higher degrees and responsibilities of citizenship."[92] Unlike many U.S. colonial administrators, Wright was a former Confederate soldier and the only Democrat on the Philippine Commission. Thus, although U.S. colonial administrators claimed that colonial rule and education would civilize Filipinos, it would do so in a way that conformed with the aims of white hegemonic rule and corrected the perceived failures of Reconstruction. On this, Democrats and Republicans could agree.

At the same time, imperialists sought means to shape not only Filipinos' capacities in industry and agriculture, but also material benefits of Philippine economic development for Filipinos. They claimed that this could bring modern techniques to the islands and increase agricultural production. Taft argued that "nothing will civilize them so much as the introduction of American enterprise and capital here."[93] To facilitate modernization, the Commission recommended that U.S. capitalists acquire government-owned land. Alongside investing in agriculture, mining, and timber, Taft and his colleagues advocated for reduced tariffs so that goods from the colonial economy could enter the U.S. market at a lower price. Finally, the Taft Commission proposed the development of greater transportation infrastructure in the Philippines; rails, roads, and ports would facilitate economic extraction.[94]

Taft's perspectives on the sugar industry reveal how imperialists believed U.S. investment in the Philippines would benefit the United States. Sugar and agricultural tariffs were much debated and important issues in the late 1800s through the 1890s. Decisions about the sugar industry and tariff were crucial sites in which state actors arranged the pseudo-domestic relationship between the United States and the Philippines. According to Act No. 230 of the Philippine Commission, exports of sugar would be subject only to $0.05 duty on 100 kilos, much less than the $1.685 per hundredweight (or $3.317 per 100 kilos)

provided by the Dingley Tariff.[95] Taft hoped that the U.S. Congress would levy
favorable rates, such as a 50 or 75 percent reduction. Taft believed lowering
tariffs would help modernize both the United States and the Philippines while
also keeping the latter dependent on the former and providing investment opportunities for U.S. citizens. The Taft Commission suggested that by developing the sugar industry, the Philippines could eventually buy U.S. agricultural
tools and machinery. The Commission suggested Filipinos use steam plows
instead of water buffalos, as was the current practice and seen as "crude in the
extreme." The Commission was optimistic that they could develop the Philippine agricultural sector as a site to sell U.S. goods, as "the Filipinos are to a
considerable extent an imitative people."[96] In managing colonial economic development—including tariffs and the import of U.S. machinery—Taft and his
commission worked to treat the Philippines as domestic to the United States
and thus create an additional outlet for U.S. goods.

Nativist-isolationist sway in Congress constrained imperialists' aims to
modernize the Philippine sugar industry. As discussed in Chapter 2, Congress sought to protect domestic agricultural industries like sugar and tobacco
through tariffs. Democrats representing metropolitan sugar and other agricultural producers continued to oppose free trade and low tariffs for the Philippines, as they saw the colonies as outsiders. For example, Senator Murphy
L. Foster (D-LA) argued "by the importation of free sugar from our colonial
dependencies a conflict has been precipitated between the Anglo-Saxon of this
country on the one hand and the cooly labor of the Orient and the cheap labor
of the Tropics on the other."[97] Tariffs reflected exclusionary logics. The 1902
Philippine Revenue Act in the United States passed after both the Commission's Act No. 230 and the U.S. Supreme Court decision in *Downes* changed
the rate of duty of 75 percent foreign duties for Philippine goods, or only a 25
percent reduction.[98] In other words, while Taft and the Philippine Commission
hoped for the Philippines to be defined more in domestic terms, U.S. Congress
did not agree. Congress also forbade grants for small businesses, which limited
U.S. investment in the Philippines. As a result, imperialists struggled to implement their economic proposals for the so-called uplift of Filipinos.[99]

While Democrats, isolationists, and protectionists tried to keep the Philippines foreign to the United States, the view that the United States should
invest in and improve the islands outlasted the early years of conquest and war.
In 1910, W. Cameron Forbes, governor general of the Philippines, reflecting on

his work in the Philippines, wrote: "Fifty years from now these will be one of the most remarkable and progressive peoples in the world, with great wealth and beautiful surroundings, living better and thriving more than almost any peoples anywhere." Specifically referencing the U.S. approach to development, Forbes continued, "There will be thousands of miles of railroads, Manila a huge city and very beautiful, Baguio a small city and very beautiful; thirty-five millions [sic] of people, and a wealth, and production, imports and exports, nearly ten times as great per capita as today."[100] Beyond the initial years of U.S. conquest and rule, imperial state actors continued to speak of their project in the Philippines as one of benevolent assimilation. Through the structures of governance, formal education, the military, and programs for industrial and economic development, imperialists argued they would train Filipinos in self-rule while also cultivating dependence on the United States.

ENDURING IMPERIALIST CONTROL

Although benevolent assimilation was an imperialist project to justify the expansion of white racial rule, the practices of overseas affairs persisted beyond the initial years of Republican control. In 1912, Democrats gained control of the presidency and legislature. One might expect that the election of a Democrat to office could change the grammar of U.S. empire. After all, throughout this period, Democrats voiced their opposition to U.S. imperial rule over the Philippines and tried to exclude the people and territory of the Philippines. The 1904 Democratic Party Platform opposed the "indefinite, irresponsible, discretionary and vague absolutism and a policy of colonial exploitation, no matter where or by whom invoked or exercised." Regarding the Philippines, they aimed "to set the Filipino people upon their feet, free and independent, to work out their own destiny."[101] In 1908, the party platform called U.S. imperial rule in the Philippines a "blunder" that "laid our nation open to the charge of abandoning a fundamental doctrine of self government."[102] The 1912 platform reaffirmed the last two party platforms and condemned U.S. empire in the Philippines. It stated, "We favor an immediate declaration of the nation's purpose to recognize the independence of the Philippine Islands as soon as a stable government can be established."[103] In 1912, with successful election of Democrats to the presidency and both chambers of Congress, nativist-isolationists grew more hopeful that they could end U.S. imperial rule of the Philippines. Under Woodrow

Wilson's administration, aspects of colonial rule changed. Democrats were in charge and Filipinos gained more control over their domestic affairs.

The system of monopolistic control of imperial and overseas affairs by the U.S. executive branch continued, however. Wilson was not the anti-imperialist that some Democrats hoped for. Like the Republican presidents before him, Wilson too believed the United States should play a special role in the world and in U.S. (white) hegemony.[104] In the early years of U.S. empire, Wilson did not favor independence for the islands.[105] As mentioned in Chapter 2, he endorsed U.S. colonialism in the Philippines. When he accepted the Democratic nomination for president, however, he stated that he no longer wanted to hold on to the Philippines. He noted that the Philippines was "at present our frontier, but I hope we presently are to deprive ourselves of that frontier."[106] To avoid upsetting the more nativist-isolationist factions of his party, Wilson took a centrist position as he rose in political prominence. He neither gave in to the nativist-isolationists nor wholly favored permanent empire. As president, Wilson's public position on the Philippines was ambivalent, but he took advice from his cabinet and Henry J. Ford, a political science colleague from Wilson's time at Princeton. After his return from a mission to the Philippines, Ford, for example, recounted that the strong independence sentiments in the islands suggested that the Philippines become a republic.

Nevertheless, Ford's suggestions did not dramatically reshape the grammar of overseas rule laid down by Root and the BIA, foreshadowing that structures of colonial administration could last beyond even formal imperial rule. In what seemed to be a departure from the era of imperialist–Republican rule of the Philippines, Ford and Secretary of War Lindley Garrison (with the help of Felix Frankfurter, a law officer in the War Department) proposed a new policy of Filipinization. Officials appointed by the U.S. president would no longer comprise the upper house of the Philippine Legislature. Instead, Filipinos would be elected to the Senate of the Philippines. Filipinization would give Filipinos more control over their domestic politics. Notably, the War Department underscored, this change to the Philippine Legislature would not take any U.S. Congressional action. Because the legislative branch of the Philippine government was already under control of the U.S. executive, the president could make changes. The U.S. executive branch—whether explicitly endorsing imperialism or taking a more measured approach like Wilson—would maintain ultimate control, including veto power over the Philippine Legislature.

Despite the War Department's emphasis on continued executive control, it could have seemed to Democrats that an end to empire in the Philippines was near. In addition to framing Filipinization as an important step in moving the Philippines toward independence, Wilson appointed the first Democratic governor general of the Philippines—Francis Burton Harrison, a representative from New York—to facilitate the process of Filipinization. While known for his pro-Philippine independence position,[107] Harrison adopted the imperialists' language of benevolent assimilation to push for independence. The ideal of benevolent assimilation was flexible in that it could both justify U.S. rule and allow for the possibility of Filipino self-rule, albeit at an unspecified date. Upon arriving in Manila in 1913, Harrison declared that his administration believed in "the political capacity of these native citizens" of the Philippines, "who have already come forward to represent and lead their people in affairs."[108] According to Harrison, Filipinos had nearly reached capacity to run their own state. Activities in Congress also gave hope to nativist-isolationists. Around the same time in early 1914, Representative William A. Jones (D-VA), chairman of the House Insular Affairs Committee, worked on a bill promising independence to the Philippines. The measure gave more control over natural resource development, finance, and tariffs to Filipinos. It also proposed to take some power away from the U.S. executive branch by ensuring that Filipino people elected both the upper and lower houses of the Philippine Legislature and that the legislature had ultimate say over who would serve as the U.S. governor general in the Philippines.

Proposed changes to the authority of the U.S. executive branch over the Philippines became a point of conflict between U.S. Congress and the executive branch, however. The executive branch wanted to maintain its powers over foreign and colonial affairs. While one might expect Wilson's administration to support Jones's bill, as his administration too planned for greater Filipino control in the islands, the War Department and Wilson opposed legislative attempts to limit executive power. The conflict became about legislative and executive power, not Philippine independence alone. Thus, the Jones Bill did not advance in Congress.[109] The chief of the BIA, Frank McIntyre, intervened and edited the proposed bill. The War Department approved, and Wilson followed. In the revised bill, the U.S. president had veto authority over Philippine legislation. The executive branch would maintain control over imperial and foreign affairs. Although the bill still promised eventual independence, it did not specify a date. Its preamble, however, read: "It is, as it always has been, the purpose of the people of the United States to withdraw their sovereignty over the Philippine Islands and to recognize their independence as soon as a stable government can be established therein."[110] Wilson and the War Department hoped that including this statement would quell independence agitators both in the United States and in the Philippines.[111]

Although the Wilson administration attempted to walk a middle road, both imperialists and isolationists objected to the BIA-revised bill that Jones introduced in the House. Again, foreshadowing World War II and Philippine independence in the 1940s, imperialists warned of Japan's interest in the islands, arguing that independence for the Philippines would create problems for U.S. Pacific interests. Writing Roosevelt on his opposition to the Jones Bill, Forbes argued that pulling out of the Philippines would threaten security in the Pacific. He wrote that "the possession of the Philippines to us gave us an offensive value in dealing with Japan which to my mind is of supreme importance." Based on Japan's rising influence in Asia, Forbes foretold the events that would launch the United States into World War II. He argued that by retaining the Philippines, the United States "could put ourselves at reasonable expense in position to so threaten Japan that any attack overseas, even on our island possessions, such as Hawaiʻi and the naval stations between the Sandwich Islands and the Philippines, would be exceedingly hazardous." He continued, "The modern developments in naval warfare underseas seem to me to make the Philippine Islands a vantage ground from which we could go forth and practically annihilate Japan's commerce and it seems to me therefore strategically an element rather of strength than of weakness."[112] Yet Forbes's concern with Japan did not become the majority opinion of U.S. state actors until after the attack on Pearl Harbor twenty-five years later in 1941 (as discussed in Chapter 5). And in 1915, his commitment to overseas empire was not one that received much support.

Nativist-isolationists, meanwhile, criticized the Jones Bill for not bringing independence soon enough. Southern Democrats pushed for a specific date of independence. Senator James Clarke (D-AR), for example, proposed an amendment to withdraw from the Philippines in two years.[113] The War Department and the BIA strongly objected to this amendment, and even Wilson expressed that it was against his plans for the Philippines. After much debate, the bill finally passed in the Senate and promised eventual independence with no set date.[114] While he publicly spoke in favor of advancing the Philippines toward self-government, Wilson did not support a clear timeline for actual independence.

Overall, while not much shifted in terms of executive control of overseas affairs, the Jones Act did bring some important changes to the terms of imperial rule. These changes were those upon which the executive branch and imperialists and nativist-isolationists in Congress could agree. The Act reformed the Philippine Legislature to a body of elected Filipino people.[115] It also specified that "it is desirable to place in the hands of the people of the Philippines as large a control of their domestic affairs as can be given them without in the meantime impairing the exercise of the rights of sovereignty by the people of the United States, in order that by the use and exercise of popular franchise and governmental powers they may be the better prepared to fully assume the responsibilities and enjoy all of the privileges of complete independence."[116] This new form of colonial administration meant that Filipinos in the Philippines gained more control over domestic affairs. After all, this seemed like the logical extension of benevolent assimilation and tutelage. Filipinos had nearly come of age, or so the Democrats argued.

The disagreements among imperialists, most Democrats, and Wilson's administration laid the foundation for the future trajectory of U.S.–Philippine relations. Democrats' policy of Filipinization not only contributed to the growth of a Philippine political elite, who would increasingly call for Philippine independence, but also saw the investment of American business and privatization in the islands. Democrats, surprisingly like the imperial administrators before them, also advocated for economic development of the islands. Unlike imperialists, however, Democrats touted this as the path toward a viable independent Philippines. Thus, the possibility of seeing that the United States could benefit from economic development and resource extraction in the colony gained traction. This became clear during World War I, as demand increased for Philippine exports. Others in the government argued that the Philippines, while not a formal colony, could still be a strategic asset, and its population could be leveraged in times of war. For now, however, the Philippines remained a U.S. colony. Wilson, while he asked the United States "to keep our promise to the people of those Islands by granting independence which they so honorably covet,"[117] did not push for Philippine independence. It was not until the early 1930s that calls for independence accelerated.

CONCLUSION

Against the objections of nativist-isolationists, imperialists broke with the past and reshaped the structures of the federal government and overseas rule. Whereas the previous chapter documented how U.S. state actors and legal thinkers debated Filipinos' racial character and how their ideas of race shaped law, this chapter showed how the U.S. executive branch pursued and implemented a project of benevolent assimilation. Led by the Bureau of Insular Affairs, the executive branch centralized overseas colonial rule, gained broad powers, and managed legislative action. U.S. imperial actors not only reshaped the metropolitan systems for managing overseas affairs, but they also produced racial knowledge to justify their aims. They cemented these ideas into on-the-ground policies of governance, education, military, and economic development in the Philippines. Imperialists' visions of spreading white hegemonic rule abroad thus changed the structures and practices of U.S. governance both at home and abroad.

Conflicts over the scope of U.S. imperial sovereignty and achieving white hegemony were important for legal and administrative restructuring, as seen in these last two chapters. Although Republicans lost control in 1913 with the election of President Woodrow Wilson and a Congress controlled by Democrats, the foundations of the U.S. imperial state persisted beyond party change and shaped subsequent political development. Ideas of white superiority informed the making of ambiguous law, ostensibly race-neutral categories, discretion, and executive control over foreign affairs. From 1898 and through the next four decades, U.S. state actors treated the Philippines and Filipinos in ways distinct from how they treated states and incorporated territories, on the one hand, and citizens and aliens, on the other.

Imperialists and nativist-isolationists continued to disagree about the racial classification and treatment of colonial territory and its people. While U.S. imperialists focused on economic and military advantages of the territory, polite logics of the racial inferiority of Filipinos persisted in their arguments. Unsurprisingly, those concerned with white hegemony at home continued to cite vulgar ideas of racial difference to argue against empire and for the exclusion of colonial subjects. The legal and administrative structure of colonial rule was both durable and flexible. By institutionalizing ambiguity, justices enabled stepwise transformations in the terms of rule, accommodating both racial exclusion at home and the pursuit of interventionist aims abroad, as the next two chapters demonstrate.

PART TWO

BIFURCATING RULE, 1916–1941

Part I explored the U.S. entrance to overseas empire and how state actors institutionalized ambiguity as a foundation of racial-imperial rule. Chapter 2 discussed how U.S. Supreme Court justices translated racial concerns into ambiguous law, ostensibly race-neutral bureaucratic categories, and discretion. Chapter 3 focused on how War Department bureaucrats broke with the past and cemented a new administrative structure for U.S. colonial and foreign affairs. Part II reveals the divergent political ramifications of these early transformations and how U.S. federal state actors began to transform the terms of rule. In Chapters 4 and 5, I argue that building on the legal and administrative foundations of the early years of U.S. empire, U.S. legislators created two new definitions of Filipinos, one that applied at home and one that applied abroad. On the one hand, in the metropole, legislators racialized Filipinos as Asian aliens, thus hiding the imperial relationship of the United States to its subject people. Nevertheless, the United States maintained sovereignty over the Philippine territory. On the other, responding to the threat of Japanese imperial war-making, legislators treated Filipinos in the colony as loyal allies. Thus, as they hid empire at home, legislators also hid the explicit racial characterizations of Filipinos abroad.

The following two chapters tackle questions related to the domestic and foreign aspects of U.S. imperial rule over the Philippines. First, what would be the place of colonial subjects in the U.S. metropole? And second, what role would the colony play in U.S. global strategy abroad? Chapter 4 addresses the first question, showing how those concerned with protecting white hegemony at home continued to see Filipinos as a demographic problem. Legislators worked to exclude Filipinos from migration, settlement, and naturalization in the metropolitan United States. Invoking vulgar racist claims, they argued Filipinos would depend on the U.S. government, were a physical and moral contagion, and were racially ineligible for membership. When it came to their presence in the domestic sphere of the United States, U.S. state actors excluded the Filipino people by casting them as Asian foreigners.

Chapter 5 demonstrates how war-making changed the tide on U.S. nativism against Filipinos. In World War II, formerly nativist state actors joined their imperialist and interventionist counterparts, not only in the desire to go to war but also in recognizing the importance of the Philippines to U.S. global hegemony. When discussing the Philippine territory and Filipinos residing overseas, questions of economic interests, geopolitics, and military strategy rose to the fore. With exclusion secured at home and in making war, U.S. state actors depicted Filipinos who served in the U.S. military abroad in a redemptive light—as loyal service members, not racialized outsiders. This framing of Filipinos relied both on the imperialists' polite racist idea that Filipinos could be trained in the U.S. image and on the newfound consensus that the Japanese empire posed a greater threat to the United States than potentially migrating Filipinos. Through debates over the foreign or domestic status of the Philippines and Filipinos, U.S. state actors began to change the terms of U.S. imperial rule. No longer was it an explicitly hierarchical racial-imperial project, but U.S.–Philippine relations would become ostensibly race-neutral foreign affairs. The way U.S. legislators separated the foreign and domestic aspects of rule shaped the future of U.S. empire.

These two chapters draw attention to three key features of how U.S. state actors changed the terms of rule but maintained the foundational grammar. First, U.S. state actors bifurcated the domestic and foreign aspects of rule. Second, they racially recharacterized Filipinos. Third, they reached consensus about geostrategy. Together, these three shifts in policy toward the Philippines allowed U.S. state actors to hide empire at home and hide race abroad. Daniel

Immerwahr's *How to Hide an Empire* astutely shows that people in the United States have forgotten about their empire. Colonies are hidden or erased from maps and atlases. Libraries are organized in ways that obscure U.S. overseas intervention. The press dodged mentioning colonial actors and resistance, calling the U.S. empire by another name.[1] These practices are what Ann Laura Stoler calls "acts of obstruction."[2] As they conceal racial and imperial formations, state actors create opportunities to reform empire. Facilitated by the flexible decisions of the U.S. Supreme Court in the early 1900s—in which the territories were "foreign in a domestic sense" and the people were "noncitizens"—and Congressional and administrative discretion, U.S. federal state actors pursued their different visions of white hegemony. Colonial people became racialized outsiders. Colonial territory became geostrategically important and thus included.

Before turning to the chapters, I review key background events that occurred between the election of Woodrow Wilson in 1912 and the late 1920s and early 1930s debates over Filipino migration and Philippine independence. The 1912 elections did not radically transform executive control over imperial rule. Nevertheless, conflicts, war-making, and rehabilitation after World War I catalyzed new conversations about the place of the United States in the world and its relationship to the Philippines. Disagreements about intervention and internationalism shaped the polysemous classifications of Filipinos as citizens, nationals, and aliens, which will be explored in detail in Chapters 4 and 5.

WORLD WAR I AND CONFLICTS OVER U.S. INTERVENTION

World War I was a war of empires that revealed the fissures in the global imperial system and renewed debates about the place of the U.S. empire in the world.[3] While European powers and their colonies fought one another, the United States, for its part, remained neutral for the first two and a half years of the war. Still, the events of global war-making shaped U.S. racial-imperial rule of the Philippines. Foreign and domestic political developments wrought through war reshaped the United States' imperial ambitions and diminished U.S. commitment to formal empire in the Pacific.

World War I marked a shift in how U.S. state actors saw the place of U.S. empire in the world. During the war, U.S. colonial officials and Filipino elite saw an opportunity to demonstrate the importance of the Philippines to the

United States. Despite U.S. neutrality, in February 1917 Governor General of the Philippines Francis Burton Harrison seized twenty-three German ships.[4] In a demonstration of loyalty to the United States, on March 17, 1917, the Philippine Legislature passed the Militia Act, which created the Philippine National Guard and allowed the governor general to require military service in the Philippines.[5] Wilson's administration, however, paid little attention to Filipinos' and Harrison's interest in supporting the war.[6]

Afterward, U.S. state actors took different positions on how to rebuild in the wake of war. A global financial crisis and the fall of the Ottoman, Austro-Hungarian, German, and Russian empires demonstrated that empire might not be as resilient as once thought. Colonial workers, many of whom were promised rights and benefits in exchange for their wartime service found themselves without rights, which contributed to the rise of anti-colonial movements.[7] U.S. colonial officials, imperialists, and Filipino state actors also noted Japan's rising influence in the Pacific. Democrats and isolationists, meanwhile, worried about how post-war global cooperation might impact the United States' history of unilateralism. As U.S. agricultural exports fell and hurt U.S. farmers, Democrats and nativist-isolationists raised alarm. Republicans in Congress were forced to address rising concerns about competition with Philippine products, sugar and coconut oil. Alongside creating emergency tariff protections, members of Congress repeatedly introduced measures for Philippine independence. During the 67th Congress (1921–1923) alone, legislators submitted six measures, although none made it to the floor.[8]

In the wake of World War I, Wilson advocated for U.S. hegemony in polite terms. His plan for the League of Nations indicated his commitment to national self-determination, as he stated that "national aspiration must be respected."[9] Wilson also stated that he had no interest in remaining in the Philippines. "Self-determination" for Wilson, however, was not synonymous with national independence. This definition of self-determination did not become hegemonic until the 1960 UN General Assembly Declaration on the Granting of Independence to Colonial Countries and Peoples.[10] By contrast, in the 1910s and 1920s, the vision of self-determination that Wilson had could coexist alongside colonial tutelage. He did not believe all people were capable of self-rule, nor did he support anti-colonial political movements in Asia or Africa. Like imperialists before him, Wilson argued that self-government must be earned.

The U.S. Senate rejected Wilson's plan for the League of Nations, dealing a blow to interventionist and internationalist plans. Together with post-war devastation in the Atlantic world, U.S. intervention worldwide declined as did support for formal empire.[11] Although Republicans, once the party of imperialists, regained control of Congress in the 1918 election and the presidency in the 1920 election, empire did not look like it did twenty years earlier. Formerly vocal advocates for overseas rule, including Theodore Roosevelt, reluctantly admitted that the United States might not sustain its empire in the same terms.

While Congress rejected internationalist concerns, the executive branch's fears about foreign relations and the effects of global war-making reshaped debates about U.S. imperial rule. President Warren G. Harding, as well as Presidents Calvin Coolidge and Herbert Hoover after him, focused on recovering from the embarrassing failure of the League of Nations and global disarmament. In 1921 and 1922, the United States, Japan, France, Italy, and the United Kingdom, hoping to avoid another world war, agreed to limit expansion of naval bases and maintain a set ratio of warships (determined by tonnage).[12] It was not mere interstate agreements, however, that limited U.S. imperial ambitions in the Philippines. President Coolidge did not want to increase the resources of the navy in the Pacific. Likewise, President Hoover opposed increased military spending. He even decreased support for the navy in the Pacific.

Unlike Presidents Harding, Coolidge, and Hoover, colonial administrators W. Cameron Forbes and Leonard Wood maintained an explicitly imperialist vision for the world. Wood, who had lost the Republican presidential nomination to Harding, previously served as the military governor of the Moro Province in the Philippines from 1903 to 1906. Forbes served as governor general of the Philippines from 1909 to 1913. His term ended when Wilson became president. After Wilson's administration, President Harding sent both Forbes and Wood to the islands to report on conditions. The experienced colonial administrators underscored the frustrations of Filipinization and hoped to reinstall the Republican- and imperialist-led systems of rule in the islands. Harding appointed Wood governor general of the Philippines on October 15, 1921.[13]

While support for formal empire was waning in the metropole, the return to Republican colonial control of the islands brought with it virtually the same imperialist justifications and executive oversight as during the pre-Wilson years. Republicans continued to support formal empire in the colonies. Wood unabashedly worked to restore U.S. imperial control while in the archipelago. Wood advocated for U.S. control of the islands for access to Asian markets and spoke of moral obligations to civilize. He also advised against specific promises of independence. All Filipinos, Wood argued, did not want independence. Rather, he claimed that calls for independence only came from a few politicians in their attempts to gain political support.[14] Even those Filipinos who desired independence, Wood claimed, were not ready for it. In 1926, exercising his executive power in the islands, Wood rejected the Philippine Legislature's plebiscite for independence. So too did President Coolidge, vetoing the bill after the Legislature passed it. When Speaker of the Philippine House of Representatives Manuel Roxas told President Coolidge of the challenges Filipinos faced working with Wood, Coolidge supported Wood's power as governor general.[15] As Chapter 4 demonstrates, the U.S. executive's lack of support for Philippine independence continued through the mid-1930s. Even with changing priorities at home and around the world, administrative discretion and executive control supported the return to U.S. control over the islands.

THE POLYSEMOUS CLASSIFICATION OF FILIPINOS

The early decades of the twentieth century were an especially contentious period of U.S. imperial rule over the Philippines. This is apparent in the aforementioned debates among U.S. state actors about national priorities in the wake of World War I. The debates also reflected different camps' definitions of Filipinos and the Philippines. Because of the ambiguity discussed in Part I, U.S. state actors wrestled with the consequences of their own imperial activities abroad and how to manage rule over their subjects. For example, a memorandum by a State Department committee read, "Little assistance can be obtained from judicial decisions respecting the nationality status of the inhabitants of the possessions under discussion. Because of this lack of judicial guidance, the decisions of the administrative offices of the United States and of the Governments of the outlying possessions thereof have not always been consistent, and in many cases have been considered of doubtful legality."[16] In other words, what did it mean that Filipinos were U.S. nationals? Were Filipinos racial outsiders or loyal and deserving subjects? Was the Philippines a foreign nation or a colonial possession?

As a result of decades of changing administrations and conflicts over the relationship of the United States to the Philippines, legislators were understandably confused about the appropriate classification of the Philippine territory and people. In a 1932 Congressional Hearing, Senator Millard Tydings (D-MD) sought to confirm with Senator Royal Copeland (D-NY) whether Filipinos were, in fact, citizens of the United States. To this question, Copeland responded, "Not in the sense as are the citizens of Puerto Rico," and when asked to clarify which country they are citizens of, he asserted, "Of the Philippines." Tydings and Copeland agreed that the Philippines was part of the United States. "Then," Tydings pressed, "are not the Filipinos citizens of the United States?" To which Copeland responded, "They are technically." Tydings followed the inconclusive exchange by noting:

> What I can not [sic] understand is: If Filipinos have the right to come to this country and the immigration laws do not bar them from coming to this country, why they do not have more right in the voice of the Government if they are a part of the citizenship of the United States of America.[17]

If U.S. lawmakers were confused, the situation was not any clearer for Filipinos enduring U.S. empire. On April 8, 1930, Fred Feliciano wrote a letter to the editor of the *New York Times*, asking how Filipinos should answer question 24 of the U.S. Census, which asks "Are you naturalized or an alien?" Feliciano stated that "this appeared to me to be a perplexing question, as it is in reality to all Filipinos. . . .If we are not citizens, nor aliens, what are we and where do we stand?"[18]

With a government divided over the relationship of the United States to the Philippines, the U.S. Congress passed laws that conceived of and classified the Philippines and Filipinos in myriad ways. Legislators both barred Filipinos from the United States and included them in definitions of the territory. The Philippines and Filipinos were defined and treated as both foreign to and part of the U.S. empire. Classifying the Philippines as part of the United States meant that, technically, its people were like citizens who had both obligations and rights vis-à-vis the states. No classification of Filipinos overturned a previous one. Rather, various definitions of Filipinos and the Philippines coexisted (see Table PII.1).

Despite the apparent confusion and flexibility, this period is important for understanding the historical change in how the United States did empire. From the 1910s to 1940s, the United States participated in two global wars and continued to debate the relationship of the United States to the Philippines

TABLE PII.1.   Polysemous Classification of Filipinos, 1916–1942

ACT	ISSUE	TERRITORIAL CLASSIFICATION	CITIZENSHIP STATUS
1916 Jones Act	Philippine "autonomy"	Insular possession of the United States	Nationals
1934 Tydings–McDuffie Act	Ten-year trial period toward independence	Commonwealth	Aliens
1935 Repatriation Acts (and subsequent renewals through 1939)	Repatriation of Filipinos		Aliens
1939 Neutrality Act	Security and peace of the United States	United States includes the Philippines	Citizens
1940 Alien Registration Act	Documenting foreigners in the United States	United States includes the Philippines	Aliens
1940 Selective Service Act	Military draft	United States includes the Philippines	Omitted
1940 Nationality Act	Naturalization of aliens		Aliens
1942 Second War Powers Act	For the expedited naturalization of noncitizens		Noncitizens, eligible for naturalization through military service

and the broader world. In these different pieces of legislation, members of Congress considered much more than migration, wartime policy, and military service. Influenced by competing interests, Congress tried out different positions regarding the Philippines and ways of doing empire. The United States navigated their ideas of U.S. hegemony and foreign and domestic problems. And at the intersection of the foreign and domestic, the United States managed its relationship to its colony, the Philippines.

Parsing the confusing classifications of the Philippine territory and Filipino people is essential for understanding how the United States transformed
imperial rule. In making sense of this period, it is essential to track when and
how political actors leveraged explicit racial arguments and when they did
not. Nativist members of Congress discussed Filipinos' racial inferiority when
debating membership in the United States metropole. Race was still salient
in managing the ideal demographics of the United States. Filipinos were increasingly cast as foreigners rather than colonial subjects. Nativist legislators
endeavored to treat them like excluded Asians in the U.S. metropole, erasing
their forcible incorporation in the U.S. empire. While the race of Filipinos was
still seen as a barrier to their migration and settlement in the United States,
vulgar arguments about Filipinos' racial inferiority were absent from justifications for national security, military policy, and geostrategy. In other words,
when it came to international or foreign-facing aspects of empire, neither imperialist nor nativist members of Congress spoke about Filipinos' race.

In sum, this period of debates over U.S. intervention in war, visions for U.S.
internationalism, and systems of rule in the Philippines is crucial for understanding how the United States transitioned from explicitly racial-imperial
rule to an ostensibly decolonized world power. At the turn of the twentieth
century, as discussed in Part I, U.S. political and legal actors justified and debated empire using explicit racial arguments. By the 1910s, those in power had
already cemented the grammar of rule. Equivocal law and discretion set down
in the U.S. Supreme Court *Insular Cases* not only obscured the racial terms of
colonial rule but also gave state actors increasing autonomy over their distinct
concerns. They enacted unclear and inconsistent policies of imperial rule,
which informed the puzzling classifications of Filipino people. The events of
the 1910s to 1920s might suggest increasing incoherence of the U.S. empire.
The following two chapters will show, however, that through conflict, U.S.
state actors worked out a coherent and durable system of U.S. hegemony. They
hid empire at home and hid race abroad.

After World War I, more U.S. politicians from both sides worried about
the place of the United States in the world and favored abandoning formal
empire. Yet the United States did not desert its imperial ambitions or structures. In foreign affairs, U.S. state actors stopped making explicit arguments

TABLE PII.2.   Timeline of Key Events in Chapters 4 and 5

	DATE	EVENT
1928	May 19	Welch Bill (to exclude certain citizens of the Philippine Islands) introduced
1929	March 4	Hoover sworn in as president
1930	January 30	Second Welch Bill (to exclude certain citizens of the Philippine Islands) introduced
1933	January 17	Hare–Hawes–Cutting Bill for Philippine Independence enacted
1933	March 4	Franklin Delano Roosevelt sworn in as president
1934	May 1	Tydings–McDuffie Bill for Philippine Independence enacted
1935	July 10	First Filipino Repatriation Act enacted
1937	January 20	Roosevelt sworn in for his second term
1939	July 1	Powers of the BIA transferred to the Division of Territories and Island Possessions, Department of the Interior
	November 4	Neutrality Act enacted
1940	June 28	Alien Registration Act enacted
	September 16	Selective Service Act enacted
	October 14	Nationality Act enacted
1941	January 20	Roosevelt sworn in for this third term
	March 11	Lend-Lease Act enacted
	July 26	Roosevelt calls Philippine Commonwealth Army to under the U.S. Armed Forces in the Far East
	December 7	Japan attacks Hawai'i and the Philippines
	December 8	U.S. Congress declares war against Japan

about their project to civilize "little brown brothers." Now, they spoke of Filipinos in terms of loyalty and martial sacrifice. Filipinos were growing up. These transformations in the years leading up to and through World War II demonstrate how politicians from both camps tried on different strategies and relationships to empire, allowing them to make race and empire inevident in both domestic and international affairs.

FOUR HIDING EMPIRE AT HOME, 1928–1940

On May 17, 1934, Ambrocio Aclang, a twenty-one-year-old Filipino, went before a Board of Inquiry of the Immigration and Naturalization Service (INS) in San Francisco, California. The Board moved to deny Aclang's admission to the United States and deport him. During the hearing, the chairman of the Board argued Aclang was "likely to become a public charge, it being a well-known fact that many Filipinos now in the U.S. are unable to find employment, and are therefore on relief rolls."[1] The chairman also cited the recently passed Tydings–McDuffie Act, or Philippine Independence Act, according to which "citizens of the Philippine Islands, who are not citizens of the U.S., are considered as if they were aliens and are subject to the provisions of the Immigration Laws of the U.S."[2] This act was ratified on May 1, 1934, while Aclang was aboard the SS *President Hoover*. In other words, Aclang's eligibility for migration to and residency in the United States changed while he was aboard the ship.

The Board's decision could have been avoided. Less than one month before Aclang arrived, on April 24, 1934, the Bureau of Insular Affairs informed the Department of Labor (which oversaw the INS) of the Filipinos aboard the SS *President Hoover*. The Commissioner of Labor responded that "it would appear that the Act in question makes no provision for the possible permanent admission of Filipinos departing prior to the acceptance of the Act but not arriving until subsequent thereto." He continued, "However, if the group to which you refer should arrive," then "it is possible that some means may be found for their temporary admission if such admission is desired."[3] Nevertheless, neither Congress nor the Department of Labor created provisions for the admission of Filipinos already aboard the SS *President Hoover*. Like Isabel González, the Puerto Rican woman whose immigration case went before the U.S. Supreme Court, Aclang and other Filipinos on the SS *President Hoover* thought they could freely migrate to the United States. Indeed, this was the case until May 1, 1934.

The change in Aclang's status to an alien ineligible for admission demonstrates that, in the late 1920s through the 1930s, legal ambiguity enabled nativists to exclude Filipinos from the metropolitan boundaries of the nation.

FIGURE 4.1. No. 34028/14-8, Ambrocio B. Aclang. Photograph from the U.S. Department of Labor, Immigration and Naturalization Service. Source: In the Matter of Aclang, Ambrocio B., Filipino, At a Meeting of a Board of Special Inquiry, Hearing for Testimony, U.S. Department of Labor, Immigration Service, May 17, 1934, 3208 Aclang, Box 34028, SS *President Hoover*, RG 85, NARA–San Bruno, San Bruno, CA.

Together with the economic concerns stemming from the Great Depression, racialized fears about immigration and labor competition, and Filipinos' calls for independence, ambiguity created the conditions for reclassifying both the Philippines and its people. After World War I, more politicians viewed empire as a political liability. As the Great Depression arrived, U.S. state actors wed their economic concerns to nativist-isolationist aims.[4] The territory became a Commonwealth on its way to independence and the people were racialized as Asian outsiders. U.S. legislators who worried about unfettered migration invoked self-sufficiency as criteria for citizenship. They argued Filipinos like Aclang were likely to be dependents or wards of the state. Labor lobbyists and members of Congress also argued that Filipinos would both bring disease and threaten the white morals of the United States. Friends of U.S. labor, interested in protecting white jobs during the Depression, invoked the existing geographic and racial exclusions applied to Asians. Again, these attempts often failed because under U.S. law, as colonial subjects, Filipinos were not aliens but nationals, and according to prevailing "scientific" race knowledge of the time, Filipinos were not the same race as other Asians.

By the 1930s, however, nativists gained traction. A projected shift in geopolitical arrangements created the possibilities for long-awaited racial exclusion. A coalition of nativists, protectionists, friends of U.S. labor, and U.S. and Filipino politicians secured a pathway to Philippine independence. As the U.S. Congress reclassified the Philippines as a Commonwealth, they also barred U.S. residency, naturalization, and work opportunities for Filipinos in the United States. In other words, laws regarding territorial sovereign arrangements outside of U.S. national or metropolitan boundaries not only redefined Filipinos as non-colonial Asian outsiders but also shaped the domestic racial demographics of the United States. Nativists took advantage of changes in the imperial relationship to reshape their ideal nation. They braided vulgar notions of racial fitness together with arguments about political sovereignty.

Even though the Philippines remained a U.S. colony, in these debates over Filipinos' status in the metropole, explicit recognition of empire virtually disappeared. Hiding empire, or making it inevident in the metropole, relied on projections that the Philippines would soon be an independent nation. In anticipation of forthcoming independence, Filipinos could be treated as Asian aliens. These reclassifications of the Philippines and its people were possible because of the flexible racial-imperial grammar that jurists and bureaucrats laid down in the early 1900s. Now, in the 1920s and 1930s, nativist legislators leveraged racial concerns—which were still articulated in vulgarly racist terms—to create exclusionary definitions of citizenship. Domestic law limited the rights of overseas subjects who legislators saw as threatening white norms at home.

After discussing how nativists constructed Filipino migration as a social problem, I review legislators' attempts to solve this problem through exclusionary migration and naturalization laws. Opposition from colonial officials and Filipino elites was unsuccessful. I discuss how even as nativist legislators hid empire at home, ambiguity—a foundational component of the United States' racial-imperial grammar—endured. I then turn to detailing the four main rationales that nativists provided in arguing for Filipino exclusion: dependency, disease, immorality, and Asian ineligibility. Finally, I show how although nativists' opponents—those who defended Filipino migration and naturalization—spoke in more politely racist terms, their characterizations also elided Filipinos' colonial status.

THE FILIPINO MIGRATION PROBLEM

Global economic conditions contributed to making the Filipino migration problem, but so too was the "Filipino problem" a problem of racial capitalism. The competing interests of farm owners, white imperialists, agricultural companies, and anti-Asian nativists shaped the arrival of Filipinos to the U.S. metropole. In response, nativists raised alarm and attempted to restrict the migration and settlement of Filipinos in the United States.

Between 1920 and 1930, Filipinos' numbers in the continental United States rose from 5,603 to 56,000.[5] The tenfold increase in the Filipino population resulted, in part, from the collapse of the world's sugar supply during World War I. Philippine mills were not profitable and Filipino farmers sought stable work opportunities within the imperial ambit.[6] Labor recruitment first by the sugar industry in Hawai'i and then by California growers facilitated Filipino migration to Hawai'i, Alaska, and the metropolitan United States. Metropolitan agricultural recruitment of Filipinos rose even more dramatically after the United States limited the migration of others, notably the Japanese, in the 1924 Immigration Act.[7] Farm owners sought Filipinos as laborers, believing them specifically equipped to do farm labor.[8] As of 1930, nearly 60 percent of

Filipinos in the continental United States worked as farm laborers, typically in seasonal agriculture in California, Oregon, and Washington. Nine percent worked in Alaskan salmon canneries.[9]

Even as metropolitan actors created the conditions for nativists' alarm, the growing number of Filipinos in the United States and the faltering post–World War I economy drove nativists and West Coast labor to keep Filipinos out. The first documented case of racial violence against Filipinos in California happened in 1926. As Mae Ngai notes, "The perception of widespread job competition was, in fact, fueled by long-standing racial animus towards Asiatics," including Filipinos.[10] In 1927, a white mob rioted and attacked Filipinos, removing them from their homes in Yakima, Washington, and putting them on trains to another part of the state.[11] There were additional well-known riots in Exeter, California, in October 1929, and Watsonville, California, in January 1930.[12] In their attacks on Filipinos, nativists sought to protect their ideal white nation.

Nativists and West Coast labor not only pursued exclusion through local campaigns, boycotts, and extrajudicial violence, but also by referencing past experiences with Asian migrants. They argued that Filipinos were a social problem and a "third Asiatic invasion."[13] In 1929, E. G. Adams, a Democratic California state assemblyman, stated, "California because of its location on the western rim of this continent, always has had the duty, unpleasant perhaps, of leading the fight to stem the tides of the Orient....First it was the fight for Chinese exclusion, won in 1882; then, forty years later, it was the Japanese undertaking; and now beginning in 1929, it is the fight of this nation against Filipinos."[14] Laws limiting Asian migration, participation in the labor market, and settlement were already in place when Filipinos arrived. So too had West Coast governments enacted local and state anti-miscegenation laws and restrictions on property ownership for Chinese and Japanese migrants in the early 1900s.

Filipinos' colonial status and popular "race science" of the day, however, complicated nativists' attempts at exclusion. Although the U.S. Congress denied admission to migrants from Asia through the 1882 Chinese Exclusion Act, the 1917 "Asiatic Barred Zone," and the 1924 National Origins Act, these strategies of exclusion did not easily apply to Filipinos, who were not aliens but U.S. nationals. While this was an ambiguous category, it meant that Filipinos could freely migrate to the United States and were not subject to the rules or oversight of the Immigration and Naturalization Service. Similarly, most people thought Filipinos belonged to the "Malay" race and not the "Mongolian" one.[15] While the U.S. Supreme Court ruled that Japanese, as members of the latter race, were unassimilable aliens and ineligible for naturalization,[16] this classification did not facilely apply to Filipinos.

Nevertheless, nativist leaders endeavored to exclude to Filipinos at the state level. In the realm of intermarriage, California state actors struggled to reach a consensus about the racial classification of Filipinos and, therefore, how to limit their rights. While some lower California courts upheld that white and Filipino racial intermarriage should be illegal because Filipinos were Mongolian and perhaps mixed with Negrito blood, some counties continued to grant marriage licenses. Judges from the Los Angeles Superior Court could not agree on the racial classification of Filipinos. Some maintained that Filipinos were not Mongolian and therefore could intermarry, and others argued that they were obviously Mongolian and therefore could not marry white people.[17] On January 27, 1933, in the case *Roldan v. Los Angeles County and the State of California,* the California State Court of Appeals found that Filipinos were not Mongolians. Thus, California anti-miscegenation law did not apply to them. Referencing Johann Friedrich Blumenbach's racial typology, the court stated, "We find no dissent to the statement that the Filipino is included among the Malays." Although the state court acknowledged ongoing debates among ethnologists about the "subdivisions of the races of mankind," they noted that "the common use of the word 'Mongolian' in California" did not include Filipinos and thus supported their decision.[18] In response to the state court's decision, California legislators introduced bills to bar marriage between whites and Malay people. These resolutions passed in April 1933.[19]

While nativists saw Filipino migration and settlement in the United States as a social problem, the ambiguity of Filipinos' status in the metropole presented challenges not only for nativists' plans for exclusion but also for employers and Filipinos themselves. Filipinos, white civilians, and employers remained confused about Filipinos' status in the United States. They regularly wrote letters to the Bureau of Insular Affairs (BIA) inquiring whether Filipinos were aliens. As the BIA noted, Filipinos were not aliens, but as *Gonzales* decided, neither were they U.S. citizens. They were citizens of the Philippines who owed allegiance to the United States. Whether Filipinos could naturalize for citizenship was also unclear. In 1922 Assistant to the Chief of the Bureau of Insular Affairs Chas Walcutt wrote that "conflicting opinions as to the eligibility of Filipinos for naturalization laws have been handed down by the courts, and until the question is passed upon by the United States Supreme Court, it will, of course, remain in doubt and be a subject for varying decisions." He continued, "Filipinos have, however, upon application become United States citizens," and Walcutt advised that "one who desires such citizenship should apply."[20] White civilians and politicians also asked more specific questions about Filipinos' rights in the metropole: Could Filipinos could be taxed for residence in California? Did they have rights to fish and hunt under Alaskan game law? Could they practice law? Could they naturalize? Filipinos also asked these very questions of themselves.

The BIA's responses reveal Filipinos' patchwork assemblage of rights. Filipinos were not subject to alien poll taxes since they were not aliens. Likewise, because they were not aliens, they could fish and hunt. Whether Filipinos could practice law depended on state law. In California, for example, one had to be a citizen, and therefore, although they were not aliens, Filipinos could not practice law. Finally—although according to nationality laws, only white and people of African descent were eligible for naturalization—the BIA noted that naturalization depended on the judge. Filipinos in the military, however, could naturalize.[21] Filipinos' rights were not only decided on a discretionary basis, but they were inconsistent and depended on whether existing laws extended rights based on citizenship or excluded them based on alienage.

Nativists thus faced a two-fold problem of lack of consistency in the federal classification of Filipinos and of the presence of Filipinos in the metropole. To remedy the situation, nativists and labor lobbies in California and Washington pressured the U.S. federal government to clarify Filipinos' status and bar their entry to the metropolitan United States. As Rick Baldoz notes, "nativist leaders wielded heavy sway over immigration and nationality policy and played a leading role in framing public debate about the 'Filipino problem.' . . . [T]hey were treated as legitimate authorities acting on behalf of public interest."[22] The most vocal opponents of Filipinos in the United States were not white farm laborers, who were few and worked with different crops,[23] but industrial labor unions. The Washington State Federation wrote that Filipinos "represent cheap and irresponsible labor of a type that cannot be assimilated, and as such they threaten American standards or wages and living conditions."[24] The Federation of Labor believed that Filipinos' inability to assimilate threatened the material wealth of white workers. Filipinos, however, were generally excluded from skilled or industrial work. They competed mostly with Mexican, East and South Asian, and Black laborers, and sometimes white women, in agriculture and service work. Nevertheless, white labor unions regularly referred to Filipinos as "invaders" who threatened white men's jobs.[25]

SOLVING THE FILIPINO PROBLEM

In the halls of Congress, legislators allied with West Coast labor invoked vulgar racial ideas as they proposed, debated, and passed exclusionary legislation. When attempts to exclude Filipinos by reclassifying them as aliens failed (see Table 4.1), legislators turned to another strategy—calling for Philippine independence. In practice, immigration restriction is not only a matter of labor policy but also a question of sovereignty.[26] Setting the colony on a path toward independence brought with it the prospect of classifying not only the Philippine territory as foreign but also treating the people as racialized

TABLE 4.1.   Filipinos' Citizenship Status, 1917–1940

PROPOSED LEGISLATION	FILIPINOS' (PROPOSED) CITIZENSHIP STATUS	PASSED
1917 Immigration Act	Nationals	Yes
1924 Immigration Act	Nationals	Yes
1928 Welch Bill	Aliens	No
1930 Welch Bill	Aliens	No
1930 Hawes and Cutting Bill	Nationals (no change)	No
1931 Crail Bill	Aliens	No
1932 Hare Bill	Aliens	Yes (combined with below)
1932 Hawes–Cutting Bill	Aliens	Yes
1934 Tydings–McDuffie Act	Aliens	Yes
1935 Filipino Repatriation	Aliens according to Tydings–McDuffie and thus deportable	Yes
1940 Alien Registration Act	Aliens	Yes

outsiders. State actors braided domestic demographic management with foreign (imperial) relations. The possibility of Philippine independence gave new life to arguments about Filipinos' lack of racial fitness. Relying on claims of dependency, disease, immorality, and Asian ineligibility, legislators could thus cast Filipinos as Asian outsiders to whom the United States had no responsibility. By relying on vulgar racist arguments to restrict migration and naturalization, nativist legislators hid the imperial relationship of the United States with the Philippines and Filipinos.

Failed Attempts at Exclusion: The Welch Bills

Prior to the hearings for Philippine independence, in the early 1920s, labor lobbyists and nativist legislators expressed concerned about the growing number of Filipinos who had been encouraged to migrate to the United States. With the support of the attorney general of California, the California State Federation for Labor, and the California Joint Immigration Committee, Representative Richard Welch (R-CA) introduced two bills to declare Filipinos aliens in 1928 and 1930. Those who supported the bills had previously advocated for Japanese exclusion, suggesting that West Coast labor saw Filipinos as an Asian threat similar to the Japanese.[27] While Californian state actors and labor organizations supported Filipino exclusion, Filipino legislators and the War Department opposed the legislation. Filipino legislators had no interest in curbing Filipino migration to the United States at its source. The War Department, more concerned with imperial relations than U.S. Congress was, advised that legislative attempts to limit Filipino migration could lead to protest and resentment in the archipelago. Although the War Department opposed exclusion, opinions were not uniform. Even chiefs of the BIA held different opinions. Major General Frank McIntyre, who led the BIA from 1912 to 1929 under the Wilson, Harding, and Coolidge administrations, hoped that "without too much publicity or too much government regulation everything possible should be done in the Islands to limit the flow of Labor to Hawai'i and to the Pacific Coast."[28] Under McIntyre's successor, Brigadier General Francis L. Parker, who oversaw the BIA from 1929 to 1933 under Hoover's administration, the BIA more explicitly discounted nativist claims that Filipinos were a menace. Instead, the agency referred to these arguments as "unjustified or exaggerated" and "the nature of propaganda."[29]

These so-called Welch bills did not pass in part because, according to the 1917 and 1924 Immigration Acts, Filipinos—unlike others from Asia—were not aliens. Citing *Gonzales v. Williams*, the War Department's Judge Advocate General E. A. Kreger noted in a letter to BIA Chief Francis Parker that the category of alien could not apply to "citizens of the islands under the jurisdiction of the United States."[30] Kreger also argued that it was unconstitutional for Congress to exclude Filipinos from migration. He noted that "immigration laws of the United States, in terms and by judicial construction, relate to persons owing allegiance to a foreign government. They do not apply to the citizens owing permanent allegiance to this country."[31] He continued that "it would seem to be questionable how far the Congress may restrict the liberty of movement of the citizens of those Islands." BIA Chief Parker also objected to Congressional attempts to exclude Filipinos on the grounds that exclusion would go against "just and fair treatment for those owing allegiance to, and under the protection of, the United States."[32]

Efforts of nativists to bar Filipinos from entry to the United States fell short because of the colonial relationship between the United States and the Philippines. Nevertheless, in the Welch bills, nativists attempted to police the racial boundaries of the United States. Their concerns about the assimilability and morality of Filipinos shaped their support of Philippine independence and the Congressional classification of Filipinos as alien.

Reclassifying the Philippine Territory: The Philippine Independence Acts
Just five years after the Welch bills, nativists succeeded in excluding Filipinos from migration and settlement in the United States by tying concerns over Filipinos' racial status to legislation about the geopolitical relationship between the United States and its colony. They passed the 1934 Tydings–McDuffie Act, creating a pathway to Philippine independence. By claiming the Philippines would become its own independent nation, the United States could now deport and exclude people like Ambrocio Aclang. After the years of political debate about the United States' relationship to the Philippines and Filipinos, the act itself reflected Congress's declining support for formal empire in the Philippines. The main stated purpose of the act was to promise and define terms of independence for the Philippines after a ten-year period as a Commonwealth. By the terms of the act, the Philippines, though still a colony, "shall be considered a separate country" and "citizens of the Philippine Islands, who are

not citizens of the United States shall be considered as if they are aliens."[33]
Whereas in 1902, Congress debated but did not conclusively settle what being
a citizen of a territory without sovereignty meant, in the 1930s, Congress decided Filipinos were indeed aliens.

The Tydings–McDuffie Act was the outcome of years of debate over the imperial relationship, Philippine independence, and concerns about Asian migration. On January 6, 1930, Senators Harry Bartow Hawes (D-MO) and Bronson
Murray Cutting (R-NM) introduced S. 3822 to provide for the withdrawal of
sovereignty of the United States over the Philippine Islands and for their independence. The original version of the bill, which did not propose changing the
status of Filipinos to aliens, did not advance. On December 11, 1931, Representative Joseph Steele Crail (R-CA) introduced H.R. 5462 for Philippine independence by July 4, 1933. The bill also stated that Filipinos would become subject
to "the laws of the country excluding from immigration other Asiatic peoples
ineligible for citizenship."[34] Crail cited the U.S. revolution against Britain and
Filipinos' own struggle for independence as a rationale. Crail's bill did not gain
support, but a month later, on January 8, 1932, Representative Butler B. Hare
(D-SC) introduced what came to be known as the Hare–Hawes–Cutting Bill.
In his support of Hare's bill, Crail acknowledged "love of country" as a basis for
granting "no equivocal or uncertain" independence to the Philippines. Crail
also said that an important part of the bill was "the provision that Filipinos
shall be excluded from migration to the United States" and that this exclusion
was "vitally important" to U.S. welfare.[35] On January 26, 1932, Senators Hawes
and Cutting introduced a new Philippine Independence Bill into the Senate.

Attempts to exclude Filipinos from migration to the United States were
not solely the work of nativist legislators, however. For example, on February
16, 1932, BIA Chief Brigadier General Francis Parker phoned Judge Advocate
General of the Army Blanton Winship to ask if Philippine independence would
mean that Congress had the power to limit immigration from the Philippines.
Winship—who would later serve as governor general of Puerto Rico in 1934—
replied with a memorandum in which he reviewed U.S. constitutional law on
the relationship of the Philippines to the United States. Based on decisions from
Fourteen Diamond Rings, Dorr, and other *Insular Cases*, Winship affirmed that
"Congress has ample power, under the Constitution, to limit immigration
from the Philippine Islands to the continental United States."[36] Constitutional
law enabled nativists to reclassify Filipinos and limit their immigration.

The Philippine Independence Act was also the work of the Filipino elite. Even before the United States arrived in the archipelago, Filipinos were fighting for independence. And their struggles continued throughout U.S. rule. The ambiguous provisions that U.S. Congress made for eventual Philippine sovereignty created opportunities for Filipino politicians to call for independence. Although there was no clear timeline, the 1902 Organic Act and the 1916 Jones Act both contained language about eventual Philippine independence. Sergio Osmeña and Manuel Roxas, two prominent Filipino politicians who would become the first vice president of the Philippine Commonwealth and first president of the Third Philippine Republic (founded in 1946) respectively, helped negotiate the Philippine Independence Act. In a hearing in the U.S. House of Representatives, Osmeña testified that Filipinos deeply desired independence:

> Our desire for independence is age-long. It is an informed, intense, and sincere desire. It has been attested in the course of our unhappy history throughout our many struggles for freedom against Spain. It comes to us from our forebears. It will go down to our children and those who come after them.[37]

For Roxas and Osmeña, Philippine national sovereignty meant territorial independence or exclusion from the U.S. "nation." Through the combined efforts of Filipinos and nativists in U.S. government, in 1933, Congress passed the first Philippine Independence Bill, the Hare–Hawes–Cutting Act. This bill promised independence to the Philippines after a ten-year trial period as a Commonwealth.

When the act came to President Hoover, he consulted with members of his cabinet, including the secretaries of commerce, agriculture, war, and state. Secretary of Commerce Roy Chaplin warned that independence might harm the Philippine economy. Secretary of Agriculture Arthur Hyde had nothing to say about the conditions in the Philippines, focusing instead on how future independence did not help American farmers in the immediate future. Secretary of War Patrick Hurley opposed the act, arguing that the United States still had obligations and work to do in the Philippines. Finally, Secretary of State Henry Stimson—who was formerly governor general of the Philippines from 1927 to 1929 and secretary of war under Taft from 1911 to 1913—emphasized the importance of keeping the Philippines for "political, social, economic, and spiritual" reasons.[38] He did not recommend a timeline for independence but instead thought the United States could permanently keep the Philippines. While he did not intend to follow Stimson's recommendation, Hoover expressed his concern that granting independence to the Philippines at this point would destabilize geopolitics in Asia.[39] He thus vetoed the bill, publicly arguing that it threatened "liberty and freedom."[40] Congress passed the act over Hoover's veto.

Just as U.S. federal state actors debated Philippine independence, so too did Filipino politicians struggle to reach consensus. Although U.S. Congress passed the act, the Philippine Legislature still needed to approve it. Whereas nativism and geostrategy shaped U.S. debates, in the Philippines, politicians debated the scope of the soon-to-be Philippine Commonwealth's sovereign powers. These debates were in many ways performances to garner control over who could speak for the Philippine people and represent the Philippines to the United States. When the Hare–Hawes–Cutting Act arrived for approval to the Philippine Legislature, Manuel Quezon, then president of the Philippine Senate, challenged Osmeña for control over the nationalist party. Quezon wanted to be the one to bring independence to the Philippines, and he publicly spoke out against the act, forming a mission to discredit it. The Philippine Legislature rejected the Hare–Hawes–Cutting Act, partly because of Quezon's public dismissal and organizing efforts. Quezon then traveled to Washington to negotiate a new deal known as the Tydings–McDuffie Act. On March 24, Congress passed the Tydings–McDuffie Act, which was then approved by the Philippine Legislature on May 1, 1934. Although the 1934 Tydings–McDuffie Act was almost identical to the earlier Hare–Hawes–Cutting Act, Quezon succeeded in his campaign for political authority.[41] Eighteen months later, on November 15, 1935, he was inaugurated as the first president of the Philippine Commonwealth.

Because of Filipino political battles, economic concerns stemming from the Great Depression, and racialized fears about immigration and labor competition, the Tydings–McDuffie Act became law. Importantly, although Congress set the Philippines on a path to independence, the United States did not relinquish sovereignty. Through negotiations over the Philippine Independence Act, U.S. nativists secured a new avenue to pursue their exclusionary aims. Paradoxically, nativists could ignore the colonial status of Filipinos and gain traction for their exclusionary aims because of a law about the colonial relationship between the United States and the Philippines. Prior to this point, colonial status constrained nativists' goals. The colonial relationship was flexible, but it did not enable all classifications. Law constrained even racist

legislators. With forthcoming independence and projected change in the political status of the Philippine territory, however, nativists had surprisingly
firm ground on which to argue for racial exclusion.

Deporting Filipinos: The Repatriation Acts
Racial arguments for exclusion gained even more traction after the Philippine
Independence Act, persisting in debates over repatriation to the Philippines.
After Congress reclassified the Philippines as its own country and limited Filipino migration to the United States, Representative Welch—whose exclusion
acts failed in the late 1920s—proposed the 1935 Filipino Repatriation Act, which
passed on July 10. By this act and the subsequent extensions in 1936, 1937, and
1939, U.S. Congress attempted to deport Filipinos like Ambrocio B. Aclang.[42]

By funding the outmigration of Filipinos already living in the metropole,
the repatriation programs sought to alleviate the racial threat posed by Filipinos. The 1935 Repatriation Act read, "Any native Filipino residing in any State or
the District of Columbia on the effective date of this Act, who desires to return
to the Philippine Islands, may apply to the Secretary of Labor." The secretary of
labor would then approve the application, and the United States would pay for
transportation. Notably, "no Filipino who receives the benefits of this Act shall
be entitled to return to the continental United States," except by the provisions
of the Philippine Independence Act (meaning that only fifty per year could
come and they had to have already been in the United States before 1934). The
repatriation program was voluntary, and Congress referred to the payment for
"emigration" as "benefits," as in social welfare benefits.[43] Congress charged bureaucrats from the INS with monitoring the entry and deportation of Filipinos.

As members of Congress debated and passed these acts, Filipino elites
registered their concerns about racial discrimination in the United States.
In hearings over repatriation, for example, the two resident commissioners
of the Philippines—non-voting members of the U.S. House of Representatives—testified.[44] One commissioner, Pedro Guevara, claimed that Filipinos
had "unfortunate experiences" and suffered "distress" in the United States.
Commissioner Francisco Delgado, when asked why Filipinos did not become
citizens of the United States, cited racial discrimination. He noted that Filipinos "are not allowed to become citizens, I am sorry to say, because of racial
reasons. Some states have even gone so far as to apply other restrictions and
discriminatory measures." He continued, suggesting that "if many Filipinos

have not become citizens of the United States it is mainly due to the fact that they have not had the opportunity or because they were ruled ineligible."[45] While the commissioners acknowledged that Filipinos in the United States experienced hardship and racial discrimination, they also supported Filipino migration to the United States. They hoped that Filipinos who were in the metropole could help bolster the Philippine economy.

Registering Filipinos as Alien: The Alien Registration Act
After the Philippine Independence Act and the Repatriation acts, U.S. Congress considered Filipinos aliens for the purposes of migration. They were not aliens in all senses of the term, however. In the 1940 Alien Registration Act (or Smith Act) introduced by Representative Howard Smith (D-VA), Congress also classified Filipinos as aliens for wartime registration of noncitizens. The act did not consider the Philippines part of the United States: "the term 'United States,' when used in a geographical sense means the States, the Territories of Alaska and Hawai'i, the District of Columbia, Puerto Rico, and the Virgin Islands."[46] Congress required that any alien residing in the United States register before a federal court official. The law barely discussed the definition of the Philippines and Filipinos. This is likely because this definition of Filipinos was already consistent with the 1934 Tydings–McDuffie Act that granted the Philippines status as a Commonwealth and made Filipinos aliens for the purposes of migration.

The 1940 Alien Registration Act defined an alien as any person "who is not (1) a native-born or naturalized citizen of the United States, (2) a citizen of an island under the jurisdiction of the United States, or (3) an accredited official of a foreign government or a guest or a member of the family or staff of such an official."[47] Compare this to the definition of alien in the Tydings–McDuffie Act, which referred to the 1924 Immigration Act:

> The term "alien" includes any individual not a native-born or naturalized citizen of the United States, but this definition shall not be held to include Indians of the United States not taxed, noncitizens of the islands under the jurisdiction of the United States.[48]

Both the Tydings–McDuffie Act and the 1940 Alien Registration Act defined Filipinos as alien. Although the Philippines remained under U.S. sovereignty and Filipinos remained islanders under U.S. jurisdiction, the 1940 act nevertheless defined them as alien. Congress did not take Filipinos' allegiance as given, including them hence in the registration of aliens.

On the ground, Americans and Filipinos remained confused about Filipinos' status. Thomas Tabanda, for example, wrote Ruth Hampton, assistant director of the Division of Territories and Island Possessions (formerly the BIA). In his letter, he confirmed he had registered under the Alien Registration Act, but the "gentleman in charge of registration at a local New York Post Office" told him that because Filipinos were "under the U.S. flag, he did not believe that they were required to register, especially in the case of those of them who have been in the armed forces." He underscored that, while he and all Filipinos he knew registered, this situation highlighted "how some honest misapprehensions might have taken place."[49]

Even as legislators did not consider that Filipinos owed allegiance to the United States, colonial administrators reassured Filipinos that their loyalty was not in question. In letters to Tabanda and other Filipinos, Hampton comforted them, saying that "although it is quite probable that many Filipinos have received inaccurate information," she did not imagine that there would be "any severe penalties."[50] At the same time, she wrote that the Alien Registration Act might have considered Filipinos aliens but did not suggest that "Filipinos are considered aliens for all other purposes." Rather, she underscored that the U.S. government valued the "the devotion and loyalty of Filipinos to the United States."[51] U.S. officials in charge of colonial rule continued to subscribe to the flexibility of Filipinos' colonial status even as Congress reclassified Filipinos as aliens.

ENDURING AMBIGUITY

Even as members of Congress defined Filipinos as racial outsiders, they perpetuated the ambiguities of colonial classification. In theory, through the Tydings–McDuffie Act, Congress could completely bar Filipinos from migration. This, however, did not happen. Congress elected to allow for fifty Filipinos to migrate a year. This was a middle ground between the complete exclusion of Asian migrants and the minimum number of migrants (one hundred) that could be admitted from southern and eastern European countries. How Congress arrived at the number fifty reflects competing ideas about Filipino colonial membership and demonstrates that Filipinos still occupied an ambiguous status as aliens (while still colonial subjects) that was between Asian and non-Asian.

The original Hawes–Cutting Bill proposed in the Senate on January 26, 1932, did not place a quota on Filipino immigrants to the continental United States but instead treated them as immigrants from most countries in the Western Hemisphere. At the same time, however, it stipulated that immigrants from the Philippines could not exceed one hundred per year.[52] On January 19, 1932, Senator Hiram Bingham (R-CT), chairman of the Committee on Territories and Insular Affairs, wrote the secretary of war asking for his opinion on bills for Philippine independence. In earlier amendments to the 1924 Immigration Act proposed by Senator William J. Harris (D-GA) and introduced by Senator Samuel Shortridge (R-CA) and Senator Clarence Dill (D-WA),[53] Senator Bingham opposed quotas for Filipino migrants.[54] On the matter of quotas, Secretary Hurley recommended that "no restriction of Filipino immigration to the United States, based on racial grounds, be imposed." He also noted, however, that the Philippine Legislative Mission (made up of Roxas and Osmeña) would likely not oppose quotas on Filipino migration.[55]

The system of admitting migrants by quotas only applied to European immigrants since, at the time, migrants from the Asian region were barred from migrating. The 1924 Immigration Act (or Johnson–Reed Act) instituted a 2 percent quota for European migrants based on the 1890 Census, with a minimum quota of 100 a year. As David Scott FitzGerald and David Cook-Martín note, this had the effect of limiting unwanted Southern and Eastern European migrants.[56] A BIA memo from January 29, 1932, stated that in 1920 there were approximately 11,300 Filipinos in the United States, and, according to these regulations, if a quota were imposed for Filipino immigrants, it would be 19, which was less than the 100 minimum established in the 1924 Johnson–Reed Act. This math is incorrect, however, as the number should have been 226 (11,300*.02). The memo's author speculated that the Hawes–Cutting Bill put Filipinos on a non-quota basis because they feared that the number of Filipinos admissible to the United States would exceed the minimum of 100.[57] And if not for the BIA's erroneous calculation, it would have. The historical record does not show others' calculations, but perhaps someone realized that there would have been more than 100 Filipinos eligible for admission each year.

While the Hawes–Cutting Bill proposed a maximum of 100 Filipinos admitted per year, there were other proposals. For example, Senator Arthur

Vandenberg (R-MI) proposed a quota based on 90 percent of the Filipino population residing in the United States in 1931, which would have amounted to 10,170 people, far above the minimum of 100. After five years, Vandenberg suggested lowering the quota to 80 percent, and in ten years it could be adjusted to anywhere between 5 and 60 percent. At minimum, this would have amounted to 565 Filipinos a year. In his bill, Vandenberg gave preference to Filipinos as U.S. colonial subjects. The bill, however, did not advance in committee or to the floor of the Senate.[58]

Meanwhile, in the House the Hare Bill did not originally propose regulations on immigration. In hearings over the Hare Bill, Roxas testified that Filipinos "should not be classed as aliens ineligible for citizenship." Instead, he suggested that, as proposed in the Hawes–Cutting Bill, Filipinos "could be classed as non-quota immigrants, similar to the present status of the peoples of the Western Hemisphere."[59] The next day, he continued, "exclusion would not be our preference," and that the Philippine Delegation would, pending complete independence, accept a reduced quota for migration, which he suggested might be at least 100 people per year.[60] On January 29, Sergio Osmeña introduced amendments to the Committee on Insular Affairs in the House of Representatives, including sections on immigration in which Filipinos would be considered non-quota immigrants not exceeding 100 per year. The March 15 version of the Hare Bill included a section on migration stipulating that Filipinos would be considered aliens and shall have a quota of fifty per year.[61] A few months later, in the Senate, Senator Shortridge (R-CA) also suggested that Congress limit Filipino migration to a quota of fifty people per year.[62] Fifty was more than other Asians were allowed in a year (zero), but also less than the minimum 100-person quota allowed by INS for non-Asian countries.

Similarly, in the debates over the 1935 Repatriation Act—which sought to deport Filipinos living in the United States—the Philippine resident commissioners and members of the House of Representatives acknowledged the confusing status of Filipinos. Both the chairman of the Committee and Resident Commissioner Guevara called Filipinos "quasi aliens" of the United States.[63] On the one hand, in this period, because Congress reclassified Filipinos as foreign aliens in the 1934 Tydings–McDuffie Act, Congress could mobilize Filipinos' "foreignness" to repatriate them. Doing so would help address and minimize nativist concerns about Filipino labor competition and racial threat. And yet, by the same token, Congress still curiously classified Filipinos as aliens owing allegiance. While formally classified as alien, in practice, Filipinos continued to occupy an ambiguous position in the United States.

U.S. state actors acknowledged the confounding nature of Filipino alienage to the United States. In 1939, Senator Tydings proposed amendments to the Philippine Independence Act of 1934. While the main purpose of the amendments was to remedy trade arrangements and ensure economic and political stability in U.S.–Philippine relations, he also addressed the citizenship status of Filipinos, noting discrepancies in the classification and treatment of Filipinos. On the one hand, "because the Tydings–McDuffie Act specifically provides that Filipinos, in immigration matters, are to be considered as if they are aliens, and because Filipinos are not citizens of the United States," Tydings remarked that "the idea has arisen in some quarters of the United States that Filipinos are aliens in every sense of the word." He noted Filipinos owe allegiance to the United States and that Filipinos are not aliens, and he sought to clarify in the bill that "Filipinos in the United States shall continue to enjoy until July 4, 1946, the rights and privileges which they enjoyed when the Commonwealth Government was inaugurated."[64] The flexibility of the colonial relationship enabled Filipinos to be aliens, owe allegiance, and have the guarantee of some rights and privileges. All this was true even while nativists sought to exclude Filipinos from the metropolitan boundaries of the United States.

LOGICS OF EXCLUSION

From the late 1920s until 1940, nativist legislators and friends of U.S. labor attempted to secure the exclusion of Filipinos from the U.S. metropole. Nativists feared Filipinos were likely to become dependents. They claimed Filipinos carried diseases and degraded the morals of white people. In these ways, Filipinos were like previous waves of Asian migrants. Nativists argued that the U.S. Congress needed to exclude Filipinos from the United States.

Risks of Filipino Dependency

Legislators relied on ideas of Filipino dependency as incompatible with citizenship or even residency in the United States. They constructed Filipinos as foreign (alien) wards of the state who were distressed and no longer wanted to live in the United States. For example, the INS Board, Labor Department administrators, and nativist members of Congress saw Filipinos like Aclang as public charges. This was not entirely false. As Casiano Coloma notes, "In 1933, approximately twelve thousand Filipinos lived in the County of Los Angeles alone and 75 per cent [*sic*] of them were unemployed."[65] Motivated by concerns about domestic unemployment, Secretary of Labor Frances Perkins and Deputy Superintendent of Los Angeles County Rex Thomson suggested that the plan to return Mexicans to Mexico had been successful and could serve as a model for Filipino repatriation.[66] The Filipino Repatriation Act could both address growing unemployment after the Depression and nativist goals of exclusionary white citizenship.

Although the administrative records of the repatriation program were destroyed,[67] INS deportation hearings demonstrate the ongoing concerns about Filipinos who remained in the United States after the Tydings–McDuffie Act. Echoing the sentiments of nativist lawmakers, one INS case inspector argued that given the poor economic situation of the United States, Filipinos were likely to become dependents of the U.S. state. Many of them, he noted, were already on relief rolls and should therefore be deported.[68] In another deportation hearing, the chairman of the INS inquiry board addressed Antonio Crispolo, asking, "There are many Filipinos now in California who are unemployed and public charges. Isn't it likely that you also will become a public charge?" Crispolo reported it was not likely, as he was promised a job with room and board.[69] Although Crispolo appealed to stay in the United States, the INS denied him entry because now he was an alien. The board gave Crispolo thirty days to report for deportation. Perhaps unsurprisingly, he did not appear. As of March 7, 1946, Crispolo and sixteen other Filipinos evaded the efforts of the INS to locate them.[70]

In Congressional hearings over repatriation, legislators raised concerns about employment prospects and the possibility that Filipinos would become indigents. Drawing attention to struggles of Filipinos in Chicago, Representative Adolph J. Sabath (D-IL) referred to Filipinos as "unfortunate" but "splendid young men who, due to existing conditions, are out of employment." Owing to their condition, he was "fearful" that they would engage in nefarious activities.[71] Although Representative Dickstein (D-NY), Chairman of the House Committee for Immigration and Naturalization, had objected to Welch's 1928 and 1929 legislation, he also supported repatriation. He characterized Filipinos as unemployed dependents who relied on Congressional support. While not explicitly referencing logics of racial exclusion, he complained about Filipino unemployment, remarking:

> [Filipinos] are stranded; they walk from place to place trying to find a job, some even find themselves in jails. . . .These people have been spread around the country without general sympathy of the local communities and they have to depend upon whatever the Congress of the United States allocates to charity for their benefit.[72]

Dickstein argued it would be good for the United States to "get 40,000 Filipinos off the relief rolls of the communities of California, New York City, and Chicago."[73] By classifying Filipinos as alien and repatriating them, the U.S. government could not only expel Filipinos from the country but could also limit associated welfare expenditures.

Filipinos as Diseased

As they worked to exclude Filipinos from the metropolitan United States, U.S. labor leaders and nativist legislators not only claimed that Filipinos were likely dependents, but they also leveraged racialized concerns about disease.[74] If Filipinos were sickly, then they were even more likely to end up on welfare rolls. U.S. legislators' concerns about Filipinos as disease carriers appear to originate from the American Federation of Labor. On January 29, 1930, W. C. Hushing, the legislative representative for the AFL, stated that "for many years the American Federation of Labor favored independence of the Philippines." Citing the 1929 AFL convention report, he justified support for independence by pointing out that Filipino migrants brought disease to the United States. The report noted that "great numbers rushed to the boats to come to the United States. Scores of them died on the way from spinal meningitis and other diseases."[75]

Several months later, Senator Harris (D-GA) introduced a bill to amend the 1924 Immigration Act. Although the proposed bill did not discuss Filipino migration, Senator Clarence Dill (D-WA) raised concern about Filipinos carrying spinal meningitis to the United States. He stated, "We find that thousands of them come afflicted with spinal meningitis and it has taxed the efforts of our health officials to limit or prevent those who were actually afflicted with that disease coming into the country at all." Even if they were "not yet afflicted" Dill believed Filipinos were "carriers of spinal meningitis," who risked infecting "ordinary" Americans. Additionally, Dill underscored that he and West Coast legislators better understood the problem than their colleagues who did not have to deal with "the enormous number of Filipinos who have been coming to our Pacific coast cities."[76] Therefore, Dill supported limiting Filipino migration.

Although no one in Congress seemed to contest the arguments by the AFL and Dill, the chief of the BIA worked to investigate and discount these remarks. On April 23, 1930, BIA Chief Francis Parker wrote Senator Hiram Bingham (R-CT) about Senator Dill's remarks, calling them "allegations." He also transmitted information he gathered from the surgeon general in April 1929. Parker underscored that "it is not altogether clear that immigration from the Philippines is the vector of this disease."[77] On the same day, Parker also wrote the surgeon general asking for updated information to evaluate the "alleged number of Filipinos afflicted with spinal meningitis."[78] The surgeon general replied, stating that last year, investigations "did not show that Filipino immigration was a material contribution causative factor" to the increased prevalence of the disease. The surgeon general clarified that the cause of high rates of meningitis among other arrivals from Asia "was due to the crowded and unsanitary condition under which such steerage passengers were carried." The United States, the surgeon general claimed, neglected sanitation in navigation. And although he warned that Filipinos are "unusually susceptible when exposed to respiratory types of infections," he also underscored that this was not a serious health issue facing quarantine and public health officials.[79] In other words, the surgeon general and the chief of the BIA, while acknowledging that some Filipinos fell sick aboard ships to the United States, did not support nativist claims that Filipinos carried disease and should be excluded.

Filipinos as Immoral Influences

As they argued for exclusion, U.S. labor leaders and legislators not only leveraged racialized concerns about disease but also raised alarms about Filipino immorality. As in the Jim Crow South and with migrations of Chinese and Japanese laborers to the West Coast, white politicians argued against Filipino migration in gendered terms. In California between 1920 and 1929, 93 percent of migrants identified as male. Nearly 80 percent of the Filipino migrant population was between sixteen and thirty years old. And 77 percent were single.[80] As Ngai notes, "By the late 1920s, the most common complaint against Filipinos, in addition to their alleged displacement of white labor, was that they fancied white women."[81] White politicians constructed Filipino men as a threat in relation to the chastity of white women and the potential contagion they posed to other young white people. Popular and scholarly accounts of taxi dance halls—places where men paid to dance with young women—also fueled concern about Filipino migration.[82] Scholars of the time likewise wrote about Filipinos' lack of a normal family and social life.[83] Sociologist Emory Bogardus—who trained at the University of Chicago, and founded the sociology department at the University of Southern California—wrote that "this disproportion between the sexes of Filipino immigrants leads to special problems."[84] He also commented that "the dance hall situation with nine white girls dancing with Filipino youth was highly inflammatory. The mores had been defied."[85] Together with earlier racial portrayals of Filipinos as savage and childlike, male-dominated labor migration concerned white Americans.

In 1927, both the California and Washington State Federations of Labor pressured their members of Congress to bar Filipinos from the United States. They characterized Filipinos as "immoral" influences that would degrade "American institutions and standards."[86] Representative Ralph Horr (R-WA) argued that Seattle was "getting a lower type of Filipino." He denounced Filipinos' lack of morality and suggested it could result from "white people," who "in all probability have spoiled the Filipinos." In addition to characterizing Filipinos as children, Horr thought Filipino labor threatened the moral standing of white women and children, noting that Filipinos "aligned themselves with people of extremely low morals, particularly of the feminine sex" and that their presence in school meant white "youngsters were being debauched."[87] Horr used his racial arguments to support Philippine independence as a means of exclusion.

Reflecting on the immorality of Filipino laborers in the United States, Representative Welch compared Filipinos to the Japanese, saying that while Japanese male laborers brought their families with them, "those fellows [Filipinos] do not." Vaguely referencing the threat of miscegenation, Welch added that "there is a social condition which has developed on the West Coast which I would rather not go into, gentlemen, but leave it for your imagination."[88] Welch expressed concern for Filipino labor competition and said this could lead to the "degradation" of white society. While he may not have accomplished the reclassification of Filipinos as alien prior to the Tydings–McDuffie

Act, Welch used his racial arguments about citizenship to support the deportation and repatriation of Filipinos after the fact. It is important to mention that, while vocal, Welch was not alone in his concerns. As previously noted, Congress renewed acts for Filipino repatriation four separate times.

The Asian Ineligibility of Filipinos

As politicians continued to debate the status of the Philippines and Filipinos in the post–World War I era, they made exclusionary arguments citing not only dependency, disease, and immoral behavior but also racial ineligibility. This claim that Filipinos were racially ineligible for membership in the United States relied on lumping them with people classified as Asian. By today's commonsense knowledge on racial classification, it might seem logical that legislators saw Filipinos as Asian, but this was an open question in the early and mid-1900s. Indeed, as Chapter 2 showed, in the early years of U.S. empire in the Philippines, the racial classification of Filipinos was not clear. U.S. elites, academics, and politicians puzzled over what kind of people Filipinos were.

Comparisons to known Asian populations in the 1920s and 1930s echoed those made by West Coast nativists when the United States first acquired the archipelago. For example, a representative of the American Federation of Labor testified that the AFL's support for Philippine independence dated back to 1898: "We believe that they should be given their independence and be barred from this country the same as any other race that can not [sic] become citizens."[89] Here, the AFL representative referred to Asians as those barred from migrating to the United States. In 1936, Representative Welch relied on the idea that Filipinos were Asians and therefore excluded from the United States. He asserted: "the Filipino was an Asiatic and Asiatics under our exclusion law are not permitted to become citizens of this country." Representative Welch continued: "They do not make good citizens as a rule . . . we have some undesirables here that we cannot get rid of, but they are not eligible to citizenship." And then he suggested that anti-miscegenation laws were one reason to not permit Filipino migration and settlement, saying, "It is not intended to mix the blood of Asiatics with the blood of Caucasians. That is not permitted in California."[90] In other words, Welch referenced Filipinos' racial unsuitability and presumed racial difference from white people as grounds for exclusion.

People of that time understood the illogic of excluding Filipinos from the U.S. due to their Asian heritage. For one, even if they were classified as alien for the purposes of migration, Filipinos were colonial subjects of the United States. During the testimony of Roxas on Philippine independence, Representatives Harold Knutson (R-MN) and Welch repeatedly interrupted Roxas, complaining about Filipino settlement in the United States. Welch asked, if the Philippine Independence Act passed, would the delegation "be willing that the United States immigration laws apply?" Here, Welch referred to preexisting Asian exclusion, hoping that independence would expand Asian exclusion to Filipinos. Roxas responded that if the Philippines did not have independence, then Filipinos "should not be classified as aliens ineligible to American citizenship." He added, "Filipinos will never understand why the United States leaves its doors open to immigrants from Canada, Cuba, Mexico, and the South American countries, which are foreign to the United States, if she should shut off the people of the Philippine Islands while they are a part of the United States." Roxas also cited migration laws in other empires, underscoring the unique exclusion that the United States was attempting to apply to Filipinos. He remarked, "I found that in the whole history of colonization no country has ever imposed restrictions on the freedom of immigration of peoples of the colonies to the mother country." Even "England does not prevent any of her subjects from entering Great Britain," he noted. Roxas ceded, however, that if the United States was going to exclude Filipinos, then they ought to do so "on economic rather than racial grounds." To this, Knutson and Welch affirmed that the reasons for excluding Filipinos from migration would indeed be economic, ensuring that Roxas and the delegation would not object.[91] If one merely reads the Philippine Independence Act, these racial motivations are absent. The justifications for the Repatriation Act did largely happen in economic terms, even as the aforementioned arguments about dependency and immorality were both racialized and gendered.

Even if nativists in the House could reclassify Filipinos as alien through Philippine independence, nativists still had concerns about the future racial makeup of the United States. For example, would children of Filipino descent become citizens? Unfortunately for these nativist politicians, the Fourteenth Amendment guaranteed the right of citizenship to all non–Native Americans born in the United States, regardless of race. To these legislators, as with their counterparts over three decades prior, mitigating the threat of a growing Asian (in this case Filipino) American population was only possible by limiting migration and settlement. Senator Samuel Shortridge (R-CA) summarized the issue: "In the case of any race, the parents being ineligible to citizenship, their children born here are, under the Constitution, citizens." He continued, "That is one reason why I and many others have opposed the coming to this country of races not eligible to citizenship."[92] As Congress had done for other Asians, legislators like Shortridge advocated for making Filipinos univocally and unambiguously aliens ineligible for citizenship. Restricting migration would help limit the citizenship of children of Filipinos.

Such exclusionary thinking based on race persisted through the early 1940s, even after Congress reclassified Filipinos as aliens. Legislators opposed bills for Filipino naturalization, arguing instead that the U.S. government should not only exclude Filipinos from migration and deport them but also make them ineligible for citizenship. Legislators and lobbyists claimed that the United States was intended only for white people, that Asians were unassimilable, and that Filipinos should not be allowed to naturalize. If Congress gave Filipinos the right to naturalize, it could create a precedent by which other Asians could also become eligible for U.S. citizenship. Representative Welch, for example, cautioned, "If this bill [for Filipino naturalization] should by chance become law it is sure to be followed by a demand on the part of the Chinese, Japanese, and other races to be granted the same privilege."[93] Welch was not alone in these concerns. Representative Samuel Dickstein (D-NY) saw the growing ethnoracial diversity of the U.S. population as a problem. He noted that "some day we will have to clean house. We have all sorts of races and people in this country which we cannot support. And they are just a population, technically, without a country, and without any status at all, and are just known as an alien population."[94] Although Dickstein acknowledged the peculiar situation of Filipinos, he was against creating opportunities for them to gain membership as citizens of the United States.

Both nativist legislators and labor leaders and opposed granting Filipinos the right to naturalize. They believed that the United States country was a white nation. Paul Scharrenberg, the legislative representative for the American Federation of Labor, also advocated for preserving a white nation. He cited the "American tradition," in which "the founding fathers of our republic passed the first naturalization law, and they laid down the basis, which has been maintained ever since." According to this tradition, Scharrenberg reminded the House Committee on Immigration and Naturalization, "naturalization should be restricted to free white-born people."[95] Drawing on notions of racial eligibility, immorality, and dependency, U.S. lobbyists and state actors ignored the forcible inclusion of Filipinos into the United States, treating instead them as unwanted aliens who should be excluded. These arguments for Filipino exclusion from migration, settlement, and naturalization hid colonial ties.

FILIPINOS AS VICTIMS OF EXPLOITATION

While nativists succeeded in excluding Filipinos from the metropolitan United States, others argued that the U.S. treatment of Filipinos was discriminatory. Advocates for Filipino naturalization cited the confusing status of Filipinos as a source of their exploitation in the metropole. Their acknowledgment of the United States' mistreatment of Filipinos represents a path not taken. At the same time, of the many ways that U.S. state actors could have classified and treated Filipinos, no one questioned whether Filipinos were racial others. The perception of Filipinos as a race by both nativists and advocates of inclusion reveals how—whether for or against exclusion—U.S. state actors hid empire at home. They cemented the commonsense notion that Filipinos were a race and that if redress were to occur, it would happen in terms of racial equity rather than by rectifying the colonial relationship.

Against the nativist tide, Vito Marcantonio—a representative from New York, who was originally a progressive, pro–New Deal Republican but in 1937 switched to the American Labor Party—introduced bills to naturalize Filipinos.[96] When introducing his first bill in 1940, Marcantonio referred to the unclear and confusing status of Filipinos as "rather anomalous." He described the contradictory expectations that Filipinos be "subject to all the duties and requirements of any citizen of the United States," and yet "not entitled to any of the rights thereunder."[97] Marcantonio claimed that Filipinos, because of their lack of citizenship, were at a higher risk of exploitation. "Of course," he said, "they are victims of labor exploitation in this country absolutely because of the fact that certain people are interested in exploiting labor that they want to deprive them as much as possible of citizenship."[98] Resident Commissioner of the Philippines Joaquin Elizalde also cited Filipinos' peculiar situation, noting that the bill "again brings to light the tragic situation of these Filipinos. They are practically men without a country."[99] In his statements, Elizalde emphasized that Filipinos owe allegiance to the United States, which differentiates them from all other Asians: "They are definitely under the American flag and have a peculiar status, which I believe should give them, certainly if not a right, at least a certain advantage over others."[100] Due to Filipinos' ambiguous situation under U.S. sovereignty, some believed they should have the right to naturalize.

Inclusionary arguments based on colonial status did not gain traction, demonstrating how U.S. state actors increasingly saw Filipinos in the United States in light of their racial difference. Even advocates for Filipino naturalization spoke less in terms of Filipinos' colonial status. Instead, they primarily made their arguments in polite racial terms and characterized the unequal treatment of Filipinos as a domestic racial problem. While recognizing the ambiguity of Filipinos' position in the United States, Marcantonio also justified his bills for Filipino naturalization as efforts to address the racial discrimination faced by Filipinos in the United States. It was not only nativists that racialized Filipinos. Marcantonio spoke of Filipinos as a racial group. He saw his bills as "correcting a gross injustice against these people, an injustice which in the United States exists solely, and let us be frank about it, because of their race and because of the prejudice existing against that race." Most in Congress ignored the racial prejudice against Filipinos. Marcantonio, however, was fervent in arguing so: "When a person is deprived of his citizenship because of his race or color, I believe, certainly, he becomes an underdog because he is discriminated against." In other words, Marcantonio argued that Filipinos should have rights because racial discrimination was wrong.

After his first bill stalled in committee and failed to go to the floor, Marcantonio continued to argue for Filipinos' rights by appealing to racial equality. He proposed a pathway to including Filipinos in the U.S. nation in a new January 1941 bill. The House Committee on Immigration and Naturalization held hearings in January 1942, and Marcantonio again argued that excluding Filipinos from the right to naturalize was racial discrimination. This time, with the United States well into the war, Marcantonio explicitly referenced Japan and Germany to persuade his fellow representatives that the United States should live up to democratic ideals. He stated, "I cannot find any valid argument under our democratic system of government that justifies the placing of a discriminatory ban against any racial group." Such discrimination, was, in his opinion, "incompatible with the keynote of this war as enunciated by the President of the United States in his address to Congress." He continued, "further than that, the discriminatory ban carrying out a hitleristic [*sic*] process of Hitler racial theory."[101] Marcantonio appealed to the idea that the United States was a democratic nation state, rather than an empire state. He also used the wartime concerns of his fellow representatives in his argument, claiming that if Congress would pass the bill allowing Filipino naturalization, then this would deal "a death blow to Japanese propaganda in the Far East."[102] As he called out the hypocrisy in the United States' condemnation of Hitler and the Japanese empire while they maintained racial exclusion in the metropole, Marcantonio also framed Filipinos as racial outsiders rather than colonized people.

Filipinos in the United States similarly leveraged ideas of racial difference and the fact of racial discrimination as they argued for the right to naturalize. They appealed to ideals of democracy and equal rights promised by the U.S. Constitution. These Filipinos spoke of their desire to be members of a country they loved and had lived in for decades. Nick Young, a member of an AFL chapter (though not a member of AFL leadership), testified on the discriminatory exclusion of Filipino people from naturalization, arguing that exclusion did not fit with the United States' principles. Although he acknowledged that some in the United States were determined "to keep America 'white,'" Young cited the Fourteenth Amendment and argued that discriminating based on race "is a crime against the Bill of Rights, it is a crime committed against the Constitution of this country, because it is a violation of the very spirit of this present law." Like Marcantonio, Young also argued that discrimination was "the principle of Hitler, and the Axis powers," and not of the United States.[103] Young and Marcantonio argued for rights and inclusion based on democratic principles, reflecting what was legally possible. In a country in which the Court ambiguously defined colonial places and people and legislators acted with discretion, arguing for greater equality for colonized people was a harder task. Young and Marcantonio could, at least, appeal to the ideals of the U.S. Constitution—specifically the Fourteenth Amendment.

While most members of Congress did not share Young and Marcantonio's concerns about Japan and Germany, their geopolitical concerns about the rise of fascism would become important five years later, as discussed in the next chapter and Part III of this book. Marcantonio's stance on inclusionary citizenship based on racial equality seemed to damn him and his bills.

Even those who argued for increased rights and equality—noble efforts as they might have been—made their arguments in terms of Filipinos' racial status. Members of the committee were not in favor of blanket citizenship, but as the next chapter shows, they would create possibilities for certain Filipinos to naturalize. They rarely appealed to Filipinos' status as colonial subjects, reflecting again that discussion of empire at home was muted.

CONCLUSION

Owing to the flexible legal and administrative structure that U.S. state actors created in the early 1900s, in the 1920s and 1930s, nativist legislators could leverage vulgar racial concerns to exclude Filipinos from migration, settlement, and naturalization in the United States. As Congress passed exclusionary laws, they often ignored the facts of U.S. empire and Filipinos' ambiguous membership in the United States. Instead, with persistent efforts by nativists, Congress treated Filipinos as Asian aliens. Re-envisioning Filipinos' status as racialized outsiders also relied on the reclassification of the Philippine territory as a soon-to-be foreign nation. Nativists coupled their desires for exclusion to the promise of Philippine independence.

In the debates over the 1934 Philippine Independence Act, Filipino elites, West Coast labor, and nativist members of Congress relied on two definitions of citizenship—one based on territorial sovereignty and another on racial eligibility. These are different but not mutually exclusive ideas of belonging and how to define what (where) and who constitutes the United States. Members of Congress brought concerns over dependency, disease, and morality to bear on legislation about Filipinos migrating and living in the metropole. In relation to naturalization, nativist members of Congress explicitly argued that the United States was a white nation, and Filipinos posed a threat to this integrity. Metropolitan law limited the rights of overseas subjects who might threaten white norms at home in the metropole. From 1934 until 1940, Congress primarily classified Filipinos and the Philippines as foreign to the United States for the purposes of migration, residency, and naturalization. In doing so, they excluded and sought to deport people like Ambrocio Aclang.

Even as Congress hid empire at home and excluded Filipinos from the metropole, the U.S. racial-imperial grammar was flexible. Ambiguous classification persisted. Thus, there were possibilities for Filipino inclusion.

The arguments by people like Marcantonio never gained much traction, but arguments based on Filipino loyalty evidenced by military service did. As the following chapter details, the difference in U.S. state actors' understanding of Filipinos can be attributed both to geography—whether they were in the metropole or the colony—and to shifting geopolitical priorities as World War II arrived on U.S. shores.

FIVE HIDING RACE
ABROAD, 1934–1941

On June 15, 1942, in La Union, Philippines, Samuel Molina took an oath of allegiance and was sworn into the United States Armed Forces. His records with the Office of the Adjutant General of the United States Army show he was a member of the 121st Infantry of the United States Armed Forces in the Philippines in North Luzon. He was on active duty from June 15, 1942, through June 10, 1946, during which the Japanese held him as a prisoner of war for two and a half months.[1] Under a provision of the same 1934 Tydings–McDuffie Act that reclassified Filipinos as alien, the U.S. military inducted at least 200,000 Filipino veterans like Molina.[2] Congress and other U.S. state actors recognized Filipinos' service and saw these veterans as loyally defending the United States.

The disparity in how U.S. politicians treated Molina and Ambrocio Aclang, who was discussed in Chapter 4, reflects different approaches to empire that coexisted during the 1920s through 1940s. One the one hand, the free migration of Filipinos into the metropolitan United States raised questions about how U.S. geographic boundaries corresponded with exclusionary demographic definitions of the nation. In response, metropolitan law limited the rights of overseas subjects like Aclang who might threaten white norms at home in the metropole. Racial concerns were salient for questions of migration and settlement. U.S. state actors saw Filipinos less as colonial subjects and increasingly racialized them as Asians, a population that was already excluded from the United States.

On the other hand, the looming threat of war raised questions about the United States' place in global affairs and its treatment of colonial territories and people abroad. As discussed in Chapter 2, in the early 1900s, U.S. state actors racialized Filipinos who served in the U.S. military (the Philippine Scouts) as uncivilized savages or "little brown brothers." At the same time, they were included in the military, rewarded for their service, and held up as examples of the civilizing potential of the U.S. colonial project. Now, in the late 1930s and early 1940s, with Filipinos excluded from the metropole and in response to a new Pacific threat, U.S. state actors no longer spoke of their overseas subjects in belittling terms. Instead, metropolitan law included the Philippine territory and select Filipino subjects who exhibited loyalty and martial sacrifice. This reflects how, in World War II, U.S. state actors no longer used vulgar racial arguments to talk about their colony or colonial subjects. Rather, to serve U.S. interests abroad, the idea that Filipinos were loyal subjects under U.S. rule rose to the fore. War-making led politicians across both sides of the aisle to reconsider the boundaries of belonging and talk about Filipinos in "polite" rather than "vulgar" racial terms.

Japanese imperial war-making and attacks on Hawai'i and the Philippines catalyzed a shift in legislators' approach to global affairs. As World War II drew closer to U.S. shores—and Japan's expansion in Asia and the Pacific threatened U.S. interests and security—the discourse on and policies toward Filipinos shifted. Isolationism waned and, with it, explicit nativist arguments for the exclusion of Filipinos. Increasingly, both Democratic and Republican state actors saw the geopolitical benefit of including the Philippines in the United States' strategy abroad. Japan's attacks on U.S. territories on December 7, 1941, cemented their consensus. The threat of another racial outsider, the Japanese, and the geopolitical importance of the Philippines in the war catalyzed changes in the racial vocabulary of U.S. empire. U.S. state actors did not deny the importance of the Philippine territory to U.S. interests. As Filipinos helped meet needs abroad, state actors hid their explicit racial characterizations. They made race inevident by speaking of Filipinos as loyal troops whose service was important to the war effort. Laws that hid race in the colony helped the United States frame Filipinos as important allies and build a military form of informal empire that would become important after World War II (and which I discuss in Part III of the book).

In this chapter, I first discuss U.S. state actors' shifting stance on isolation. After detailing how Congress initially was reluctant to involve the United States in European and Asian wars, I provide an overview of wartime legislation related to neutrality and the geostrategic role of the Philippines. I discuss isolationist and nativist legislators' opposition to the war and incorporating the Philippine territory in U.S. military strategy. I then turn to detailing the justifications for war and including the Philippines in U.S. geostrategy. U.S. legislators came to believe that both the Philippine territory and Filipinos were critical to the U.S. war effort. In exchange for their service, the United States promised citizenship and social welfare benefits to loyal Filipinos. Despite the inclusionary possibilities offered to Filipinos who served in the military, ambiguity persisted.

THE CHANGING TIDE ON ISOLATION

Conflicts over whether the United States would intervene in European and Asian wars eventually gave way to consensus on the geopolitical importance of the Philippines and the place of Filipinos in the wartime effort. The memory of World War I meant many in the United States were wary of conflicts in Europe and Asia and wanted to avoid intervention. As in the late 1800s, U.S. state actors, especially those involved in domestic affairs, were more reticent about war and less concerned with U.S. global hegemony. During the early years of the 1930s, as Germany invaded Europe and Japan invaded Asia, Democrats in Congress proposed a series of Neutrality Acts designed to limit U.S. involvement in a global war.[3] These acts, the first of which passed in 1935, prohibited the sale and export of arms and war supplies to countries at war. The laws also forbade U.S. citizens from traveling or transporting goods on "belligerent ships."

Meanwhile, the 1934 Philippine Independence Act reshaped dynamics in Asia and the Pacific. Dutch and British imperialists, Australians, and Chinese nationalists worried that forthcoming Philippine independence could create a power vacuum and strengthen Japan's geopolitical position. Anti-colonial nationalist leaders in Indonesia looked with hope to the Philippines, citing it as a potential model for their own calls for decolonization. In the Philippines, Spanish elite aligned themselves with General Francisco Franco's fascist

Falangist Movement in Spain. As colonial administrators worried about illiberal and undemocratic threats, they also grew concerned about the possibility of Japan taking over the islands.[4]

Although they initially avoided military action and promised neutrality in the Philippines, the Japanese empire looked to expand beyond Korea, Taiwan, and Manchuria. Wars in China foretold the threat to the Philippines. In the 1930s, however, the Japanese government pursued softer forms of influence. They supported Japanese emigration to the Philippine province of Davao, as well as the region's economic development. They sought allies in the Philippine government to protect Japanese interests. Filipino political elite were divided. Some supported Japan and received financial benefits in return. Others warned that Japan would subject the Philippines to "economic vassalage" and that the Philippines needed to tie themselves to the United States for protection.[5] Quezon equivocated. He neither pushed out the Japanese nor endorsed their influence.[6]

As Quezon worked to maintain his power amidst the competing influence of Japan and the United States, U.S. colonial and military officials supported increased U.S. intervention in Asia. For example, J. Weldon Jones—who served as the financial advisor to the high commissioner and later the acting high commissioner to the Philippines between 1934 and 1940—argued that foreign and domestic affairs were linked. In 1936, even before the events of World War II, he argued for greater U.S. intervention. Jones asserted that the "world had been rapidly diminishing in size," thus "intricately binding the relationships of national groups." He saw a special place for his country, stating that the United States "holds an enviable place," but that "hermitage" should not be the direction, as it contradicted the United States' "inherent philosophy and cultural pride." Moreover, Jones queried, "would seclusion be in harmony with America's contribution of the past 160 years to this thing called civilization? I do not think so." He suggested that the United States, with "its preeminent position of power and prestige," "its record to use that power without abuse and without offense," and "its moral traditions," ought to "assume some responsibilities not heretofore emphasized." Like imperialists of the early 1900s, Jones argued that because of its moral superiority, the United States should take on a more interventionist stance in war and in economic affairs.[7]

In 1939, as Japan prepared to take Hainan and the Spratly Islands west of the Philippines, U.S. military and colonial officials underscored the centrality of the Philippines to U.S. global strategy. The navy hoped Congress would approve $5 million for a naval station in Guåhan.[8] General Douglas MacArthur also argued that this base would be important to block Japanese efforts. Jones again advocated for U.S. intervention and spoke of the Philippines as a model of U.S. partnership in a global era.[9] He stated, "Almost for the first time in history conflicting interests in Europe reverberate in Asia and events in Asia bear more than indirectly upon European policy. In truth, oceans disappear, and continental borders become obsolete. We grow up in a lone hemisphere and hesitate to believe that our neighbors to the East and West are amazingly near and real." He asked, "What of America in this drama?" Before many U.S. state actors committed to the imperialist vision of U.S. internationalism, Jones answered that isolationism was not a viable option for the United States. As part of his vision for the United States, Jones also asked, "What of the Philippines?" He answered, "The relationship between the United States and the Philippines is unique in world history. The Islands, alone in the Orient, are in possession of the two most powerful ideas engendered by man—Christianity and Democracy. And today the Philippines are a part of America." Thus, he claimed that when it came to U.S. hegemony, "the role of the Philippines is by no means inconsequential." The Philippines served to "interpret Christianity, Democracy, and the American way of life to the Orient." Thus, to secure U.S. global influence, Jones argued that the United States must maintain its relationship with the Philippines. Together, the United States and the Philippines defend the "Fort of Democracy," which he claimed was built on the foundation of "economic security and social peace."[10] Nevertheless, in 1939, there was only minimal support for U.S. foreign intervention.

As European and Asian wars dragged on, more members of the U.S. executive supported intervention.[11] Unlike many of his Democratic colleagues in Congress, newly reelected President Franklin D. Roosevelt advocated for ending the U.S. policy of neutrality so that the United States could support the Allies in Europe. Like Woodrow Wilson before him, Roosevelt favored more U.S. involvement in global affairs. He went further than Wilson, however. Even before the United States entered World War II as an Allied power, he critiqued neutrality. In a speech to Congress, he stated that neutrality "may actually give aid to an aggressor and deny it to the victim." He urged legislators to repeal neutrality and the embargo on trade with countries at war, arguing that his proposal made for "sounder international practice" for "peaceful relations." Roosevelt, like J. Weldon Jones, emphasized the connections between global and domestic affairs, stating that "any war anywhere necessarily hurts

American security and American prosperity," and that war "retards the progress of morality and religion and impairs the security of civilization itself."¹²
As Germany conquered more territory in Europe, Roosevelt continued to
push legislators toward intervention, which he framed as a matter not of war,
but of "national security."¹³ Referring to U.S. support of Great Britain, he called
the United States an "arsenal of democracy" against Nazi Germany's intention
"to dominate all life and thought in their own country, but also to enslave the
whole of Europe, and then to use the resources of Europe to dominate the
rest of the world." Roosevelt warned of threats not only in Europe but also
in Asia, saying, "It is a matter of most vital concern to us that European and
Asiatic war-makers should not gain control of the oceans which lead to this
hemisphere."¹⁴ The threat of war provided occasion for Roosevelt to articulate
his vision for the United States' place in the world.

In his pleas to end isolation, Roosevelt argued that the United States could
not avoid the affairs of the world. The Monroe Doctrine had become irrele-
vant. The world was much smaller now. No longer could the United States only
manage its affairs in the Western Hemisphere. Like imperialists of the late
1800s and early 1900s, Roosevelt referenced U.S. and British shared interests,
asking, "Does anyone seriously believe that we need to fear attack anywhere in
the Americas while a free Britain remains our most powerful naval neighbor in
the Atlantic? Does anyone seriously believe, on the other hand, that we could
rest easy if the Axis powers were our neighbors there?" If Britain were to lose,
Roosevelt implored, the Axis powers would spread not only across Europe, Asia,
Africa, and Australasia but also to the Americas, threatening the U.S. way of
life. Roosevelt, unlike many of his Democratic colleagues in Congress, pushed
for a greater and expanded role for the United States in the world.

Under pressure from Roosevelt, Congress ended the U.S. policy of neutrality on March 11, 1941, with the Lend-Lease Act, passing in the House with
260 yeas, 165 nays, and 6 not voting and in the Senate with 60 yeas, 31 nays,
and 4 not voting.¹⁵ Whereas 55 percent of Congress supported neutrality in
the 1939 Neutrality Act,¹⁶ now 60 percent of Congress favored supporting the
Allied war effort. In this act, which laid the foundation for economic and
military cooperation, Congress empowered the president, when "in the interest of national defense," to approve the manufacture, sale, transfer, lease, or
lend of ammunition and other supplies to Europe.¹⁷ The United States would
now allow for the deferral of payment on wartime supplies. Both the United

Kingdom and China took advantage of U.S. support, thus linking the United States to wars in both Europe and Asia.

While Japan had not yet invaded the Philippines, tensions in the region rose. Japanese diplomats offered to stay out of the Philippines if the United States would allow for Japanese immigration and business development in the archipelago. U.S. negotiators, however, did not agree to these terms, noting that there were technically no laws restricting the Japanese. In July 1941, when Japan invaded northern French Indochina's (present-day Vietnam) naval and air bases, the United States responded by freezing Japanese assets and placing an embargo on oil. Secretary of War Henry Stimson and Army Chief of Staff George C. Marshall, concerned about the Japanese threat in the Pacific, advocated for Douglas MacArthur to step in. On July 25, 1941, MacArthur gained command of the United States Armed Forces in the Far East (USAFFE) and added thirteen thousand U.S. military personnel to the islands. In November, the Japanese military made plans to invade the Philippines.[18]

Even as the military prepared for war and Roosevelt convinced Congress to support the Allied war effort, it was not until Japan attacked Pearl Harbor and the Philippines on December 7, 1941, that U.S. legislators agreed on intervention.[19] As the victims of attack, interventionist and formerly isolationist legislators argued that the United States could not remain idle, but must go to war. The next day, Congress, with 399 yeas, 1 nay, and 41 not voting in the House and 82 yeas, 0 nays, and 13 not voting in the Senate,[20] declared war on Japan. Japan's assault on Pearl Harbor and the Philippines unsettled U.S. isolationism, its position on Asia, and its relationship to Filipinos. As they made war, U.S. state actors considered what locations were strategic, what sites needed protection, which boundaries would be respected, and where the United States would intervene. Facing another global war, the United States considered who and what was worth protecting and who could do that work. The Philippines and Filipino people became key to U.S. war strategy, and the United States changed the terms of its racial-imperial grammar.

WARTIME LEGISLATION AND THE PHILIPPINES

The aforementioned debates over neutrality and intervention were not only about the place of the United States in the world but also about the relationship of the Philippine territory to the United States. As journalist Hanson Baldwin summarized:

We must first define what we are prepared to defend, and we must know, second, against whom we are to defend it. Neither task is easy. For no definition of defense will every satisfy all of the vocal pressure groups of this country. . . .Nor is it easy to delimit our vital areas. Are the East Indies, for instance, with their supplies of rubber and tin—strategic raw materials which we lack—vital to us? And should we build up a defense organization capable of defending the Philippines, even though we are now legally committed to withdrawal from those islands in 1946?[21]

Baldwin asked if the Monroe Doctrine, which he characterized as "the most firmly rooted foreign policy in our history," would determine U.S. strategy or if "hemisphere defense" would mean expanding the geographic scope of U.S. intervention.[22] In other words, what would it mean to defend the Western Hemisphere? Would such a strategy include the Philippines? Although more politicians realized the importance of the Philippines after the attack on Pearl Harbor, they had not yet settled these questions in the years preceding Japan's invasion of U.S. territories.

Below, I chart these transformations and the growing support for including the Philippines in U.S. wartime strategy. In the 1930s and 1940s, U.S. legislation about the war, the military, and the Philippines reflected shifts toward global intervention. The war was one avenue through which U.S. actors reconceived their relationship with the Philippines in ways that were not explicitly racial. In the 1930s, just as most U.S. state actors were against intervention prior to the Japanese attack on Pearl Harbor, neither were they sure of the geostrategic importance of the Philippines. For example, in 1934, President Roosevelt argued that the United States need not maintain bases in the Philippines.[23] Nevertheless, the United States still had claim to the islands. Under the 1934 Tydings–McDuffie Act, the United States had "the right to intervene for the preservation of the government of the Commonwealth of the Philippine Islands and for the maintenance of the government . . .for the protection of life, property, and individual liberty."[24] And the president of the United States had the right to call into service the Armed Forces of the Philippines. Even as the 1934 Tydings–McDuffie Act prepared the Philippines for independence, U.S. state actors continued to define the Philippine territory as domestic to the United States.

As their positions shifted from isolation to neutrality to intervention, U.S. state actors also reconsidered the place of the Philippines in U.S. war mobilization. In 1940, Philippine Resident Commissioner Joaquin Elizalde reported that Roosevelt also requested that Congress consider two bills for national defense.[25] One—76 S.J. Res 286, introduced by Senator Morris Sheppard (D-TX), chair of the Military Affairs Committee—would allow the U.S. president to call the U.S. National Guard and Army to service in the Western Hemisphere and U.S. possessions, including the Philippines.[26] The other concerned the Selective Service and would exclude the Philippines from the territorial definition of the United States.[27] After receiving Elizalde's memo, President of the Philippine Commonwealth Manuel Quezon wrote President Roosevelt expressing concern about the vulnerability of the Philippines during the coming war. The secretaries of the interior and of war shared his strategic concern. Roosevelt replied that he believed it "important not to leave the islands at this time."[28] In other words, the growing likelihood of war catalyzed a shift in considerations of the Philippines' geostrategic importance.

In the 1930s and 1940s, then, even as some remained committed to neutrality and doubted the importance of the Philippines, the U.S. Congress passed acts that affirmed U.S. territorial sovereignty over the archipelago, as shown in the table below. Through a conversation that evolved over these acts, opposition to including the Philippines in U.S. global strategy eventually turned into

TABLE 5.1. Geopolitical- and War-related Legislation and Classification of Philippine Territory 1934–1941

	ISSUE	TERRITORIAL CLASSIFICATION OF THE PHILIPPINES IN THE ACT
1934 Tydings–McDuffie Act	Ten-year trial period toward independence	Commonwealth
1939 Neutrality Act	Security and peace of the United States	United States includes the Philippines
1940 Common Defense Act	Order U.S. military into service	United States includes the Philippines
1940 Selective Service Act	Military draft	United States includes the Philippines
1941 Declaration of War Against Japan	Declaring that a state of war exists between the Imperial Government of Japan and the United States	N/A

growing consensus for defining the Philippines as part of the United States. Below, I discuss opposition and the growing consensus. Notably, whether U.S. state actors opposed or supported intervention, they rarely spoke about the Philippines in demeaning racial terms as they did in the early 1900s. The 1934 Tydings–McDuffie Act, discussed in the previous chapter, helped settle racial concerns about the migration and incorporation of Filipinos. Because Filipinos no longer posed a demographic threat to the nation, characterizations of Filipinos as loyal subjects could now rise to the fore.

OPPOSITION TO INCLUDING THE PHILIPPINES IN U.S. GEOSTRATEGY

The 1934 classification of the Philippines as a Commonwealth on the path to independence and Filipinos as aliens helped U.S. state actors decouple questions about the Filipino people from questions about the Philippine territory. At first, however, nativist legislators' successful exclusion of Filipinos from the metropole did not warm them to the possibility of including the Philippines in geographic definitions of the United States. Their opposition took three forms. First, like Senators Royal Copeland and Millard Tydings in the introduction to Part II, legislators were simply confused about the relationship of the Philippines to the United States. They were not sure if the Philippines was part of the United States. Second, some U.S. legislators argued the Philippines would soon be independent and should be excluded from U.S. policy. Third, legislators argued that U.S. global intervention was tyrannical and anti-democratic.

Owing to ambiguous legal classifications, many U.S. state actors did not understand if the Philippines was foreign or domestic to the United States. Confused, they questioned the inclusion of the Philippines in U.S. war and miliary defense strategies. In hearings for the 1940 Common Defense Act, Senator Edwin Johnson (D-CO) questioned General George C. Marshall, army chief of staff, about why the proposed bill "doesn't confine the training to the continental United States and the Territories of the United States," asking "why it goes more or less into foreign land, the Philippine Islands." The Philippines was still domestic to the United States, yet this question represents long-standing nativist-isolationist thinking about the Philippines. The general replied it was important for the U.S. military to serve in places outside the continental boundaries of the United States, reflecting the more global orientation of U.S. military strategy of the time. When the general's answer did not reference the Philippines specifically, Senator Johnson pressed, "Do you think the Philippine Islands are necessary to this bill?" Marshall replied that while he did not have a specific thought or plan to send the National Guard to the Philippines, he thought it would be "a short-sighted policy" to "take one of our possessions and eliminate that and leave other possessions in the law."[29] Johnson continued, confused, "The Philippines are not a possession, are they?" While Marshall replied that "maybe they are not a possession," he also said, "they are a grave responsibility."[30] Of course, the Philippines was still a U.S. colony.

Senator Johnson was not alone in his confusion about the territorial status of the Philippines. Senator Henry F. Ashurst (D-AZ) also stated, "I have heard it argued that the Philippine Islands are a part of the Western Hemisphere." Ridiculing this, Ashurst suggested that someone needed to clarify international law and what exactly was meant by the Western Hemisphere. Senator Guy M. Gillette (D-IA) chimed in, noting that whether Congress defined what the "Western Hemisphere meant," the Philippines was a possession or a territory under the sovereignty of the United States. Thus, it was "not contained within what we usually, in common parlance consider the Western Hemisphere." The same was true, Gillette noted, for the Sāmoan Islands, Guåhan, and the Midway Islands.[31] Thus, although the Philippines was undeniably far away, Gillette suggested that its status as a U.S. territory challenged the relevance of these geographic designations for envisioning a U.S. global strategy.

While some legislators were merely confused, others actively argued that the Philippines should not be considered part of the United States. Based on forthcoming Philippine independence, promised in the 1934 Tydings–Mc-Duffie Act, Representative Karl Stefan (R-NE) argued that the United States should end military operations in the Philippines as they were expensive and would delay Philippine independence. In 1936, he downplayed the threat of a Pacific war, stating "that the Japanese scare is one which has been overdone by the anti-independence advocates and that it will be many, many years before Japan, with its hands full of the Russian menace in China, can turn its eyes to the acquisition of the Philippines." He argued that continued U.S. presence Philippines would only bring war to the United States. Thus, rather than retain the islands, the United States should get rid of them and maintain a more isolationist stance.[32]

In addition to expressing confusion about the status of the Philippines and opposition to including the soon-to-be independent Philippines in definitions of the United States, legislators argued that the United States should avoid preempting attacks by foreign countries and pay more attention to domestic issues. Against imperialism, they remained committed to isolationism. In debates over national defense, Representative Pierce (D-OR) argued in favor of isolation to protect the U.S. way of life. Even considering that "Germany will have life or death rule over nearly half a billion people," and that "Japan dominates the Orient," Pierce believed that the United States should not consider interests in the Philippines. He continued, "It was a very unfortunate venture when the United States entered upon the imperialistic policy which forced us to be interested in the Orient." He warned that the Philippines "invites trouble and involves great expense and difficulty." Instead, to ensure the survival of U.S. democracy, Pierce argued against preemption, suggesting that the United States should not prepare for a global war against "the Hitler war machine," but should only defend itself. "We have all the food we need. We have all the genius we require," he argued. Yet, even as Pierce argued for an "isolated America," he also proposed an extraterritorial line of defense. Calling upon the Monroe Doctrine, he stated, "We must, at least, throw a ring of steel around every island in the Caribbean Sea, the northern part of South America, the Panama Canal, Central America, Mexico, and Canada. The Hawaiian Islands are a part of the United States."[33] While many legislators, like Pierce, were not wholly opposed to U.S. foreign intervention and empire, the Philippines was simply too far or foreign to conceive of protecting and including in U.S. global strategy.

Legislators not only argued against preemption on the grounds of U.S. self-sufficiency but also claimed that intervention was anti-American. On August 5, 1940, Senator Alva B. Adams (D-CO) proposed an amendment to prohibit the U.S. president from sending the National Guard to anywhere in the Western Hemisphere, limiting it to the continental United States or its possessions. Senators continued to object to including the Philippine Islands, arguing that domestic interests were more important than foreign ones. Senator Walter F. George (D-GA) raised alarm that the government could send the National Guard "to possessions of the United States and to the Philippine Islands in the very doorway of a conflagration which has arisen in the east." Calling upon Democrats' commitments, he implored, "What does a party declaration mean when it says 'we are against war; we will not send American men to fight in the battles of any other nation beyond the seas,' when here, before the ink is dry upon that platform, we are asked to send the guard without opportunity of its members to give assent—men who have enlisted in their local communities largely for the protection of local interests, the old idea of the militia—into the Army of the United States, and anywhere in the Western Hemisphere?" Questioning the logic of the Monroe Doctrine, Senator George continued: "The strange doctrine has arisen in this country that we must send our soldiers outside to take up a defensive position for the United States. Mr. President, there is no logic or reason in that position." Sending the National Guard outside national borders, George argued, was "the doctrine of militarism . . . of tyranny . . . of dictatorships," and "not the doctrine of democracy."[34] Like Pierce, George equated extraterritorial use of the military with tyranny and empire. Explicit opposition to intervention, projections of Philippine independence, and confusion about the relationship of the United States to the Philippine territory informed legislators' arguments for the exclusion of the Philippines from U.S. global strategy.

GROWING CONSENSUS ON U.S. INTEREST IN THE PHILIPPINES

From the early days of U.S. empire in the Philippines, U.S. colonial officials and members of the executive branch, desiring economic and political influence in Asia, saw the Philippines as a stepping stone. In the 1930s, despite nativists' and isolationists' apprehensions, imperialists continued to argue for global intervention. Their justifications took three forms. First, imperialists continued to argue for the geostrategic importance of protecting U.S. colonies. They identified a new threat in the Pacific: the Japanese. Second, imperialists tied U.S. military and geostrategic priorities to U.S. economic interests in Asia. Third, when Japan attacked U.S. territories on December 7, 1941, formerly isolationist U.S. state actors joined their interventionist and imperialist counterparts, uniting around a new enemy. Politicians on both sides argued they must defend U.S. civilization from a pagan race. Racial-civilizational arguments, again, motivated and justified global war. This time, however, the enemy was not Filipino but Japanese.

Geostrategy

Imperial and military officials long supported the defense of the Philippine archipelago as part of securing the United States' strategic position in the world. In May 1933, J. Weldon Jones, financial advisor to the governor general of the Philippines, prepared a memo on the Defense Force for the Philippine Commonwealth. In it, he stated that "it is imperative that the Commonwealth must have at its disposal, at all times, a sufficient force, absolutely reliable, thoroughly disciplined, well trained and able to enforce the authority of the Commonwealth and to suppress, without delay, any movement that might disturb or endanger peace and order or endanger lives or property of the people."[35] Secretary of State Henry Stimson—once secretary of war for President Taft from 1911 to 1913 and governor general of the Philippines from 1927 to 1929— likewise argued that the Philippines was an important "base for American influence—political, social, economic, and spiritual." The Philippines, he claimed, was "the new basis of equilibrium in the Far East which America's presence has created."[36] General Douglas MacArthur tied years of U.S. imperialism in the Philippines to the latter's importance to U.S. interests. He stated, "Of all western nations none is more fortunate in the location and character of its contact with the Far East than is the United States in its position in the Philippine Islands."[37] Even before the United States entered World War II, military officials used strategic interests in Asia to justify U.S. claim to the Philippines. They prepared to protect the Philippines from invasion.

For imperial and military actors, U.S. action in the Philippines was an extension of U.S. western hemispheric hegemony. In 1940, Representative Walter G. Andrews (R-NY) asked Stimson—who was now serving as secretary of war—about the War Department's approach to defense. Unlike isolationists who opposed sending the National Guard outside U.S. continental borders, Stimson cited the Monroe Doctrine as evidence of the need to keep war at bay. Although he believed defending some U.S. territories, like the Panama Canal, was more urgent, he also referenced his time as governor general of the Philippines as demonstrating to him the importance of a global approach to defense. He continued, "There are places all along the coast of South America where the same principle applies. There are plenty of possessions in the Pacific Ocean, which we do not think very much about when we sit here in the East. But they are there, and they have got to be defended."[38] In short, military leadership and colonial officials did not sharply distinguish between the Western Hemisphere and Asia. The Philippines was important to U.S. global strategy.

It was not only colonial officials, however, that supported including the Philippines in U.S. global strategy. Even with the resistance to global intervention discussed above, some legislators, Democrats included, pushed for an end to neutrality, citing the strategic importance of the Philippines. For example, in 1936, during a session of the House of Representatives, legislators discussed the wars in Europe and Asia, neutrality, protectionism, and economic depression. Representative Byron B. Harlan (D-OH) raised concerns about the U.S. strategy of isolationism as wars raged on in Europe and Asia. He critiqued his colleagues, who believed in both maintaining economic isolation (through tariff walls) and that economic measures could secure peace. He drew out the hypocrisy of his isolationist colleagues, characterizing their arguments as akin to saying: "'we will not drop bombs on your cities . . .but we do insist on the privilege of starving you and your children.'" Referring to the resulting economic depression facing the world, Harlan asked, "Can anyone expect the world to remain in peace under these conditions? Can anyone expect Japan, Germany, and Italy, and other nations similarly situated to do anything else than bide their time to strike?" He argued that while the United States may be sufficiently armed to "frighten away attacks," that "some of our weaker neighbors—the Philippines or Cuba—will be victim, and from there on is a short step." Harlan saw U.S. possessions as an easy entry through which hostile empires could threaten the United States.[39] Five years later, Representative Harlan's predictions played out. Japan attacked Pearl Harbor on December 7, 1941, and hours later invaded the Philippines.

As the threat of war drew closer, military officials again underscored the importance of the Philippines for geopolitical military strategy. On November 27, 1941, ten days before Japan attacked Pearl Harbor, Chief of Naval Operations Harold Rainsford Stark wrote a memo for President Roosevelt urging for reinforcements in Asia. Stark wrote that although "considerable Navy and Army reinforcements have been rushed to the Philippines," "the desirable strength has not yet been reached." Ominously, he noted that ground forces should set sail from the United States to the Philippines on December 8, 1941, "before hostilities commence," which ended up being the day that Japan attacked Manila. At the same time, Stark favored delaying military action. He argued that "the longer the delay, the more positive becomes the assurance of retention of these Islands as a naval and air base." In other words, from the navy's perspective, military action was likely but should be avoided. The United States should only act defensively. Doing so would increase the likelihood of keeping the Philippine territory, which Stark saw as important for transporting supplies and aid to Russia and China.

Economic Stability

Those in favor of intervention and including the Philippines in definitions of the United States not only emphasized the geostrategic importance of the archipelago but also argued that geostrategy and economic gains went hand in hand. A political scientist and lawyer by training, Francis B. Sayre underscored both the economic and strategic importance of the Philippines. Sayre, assistant secretary of state and chairman of the Interdepartmental Committee on Philippine Affairs, was also Woodrow Wilson's son-in-law. Although he was a Democrat who believed that the United States should prepare the Philippines for independence, he also argued that the United States needed to support the emerging republic. In 1939, Franklin D. Roosevelt appointed Sayre as high commissioner of the Philippines. In a hearing on economic adjustments to the 1934 Tydings–McDuffie Act, Senator Arthur Vandenberg (R-MI) asked Sayre when the U.S. obligation to the Philippines would cease: "is there ever any finality to it?" Sayre responded that letting go of the Philippines would not only "bring disaster to their economy," but also would create a "very grave" situation that would jeopardize U.S. economic and political interests in the "Far East." Sayre also noted that the United States has "controlled the destinies of the Philippines for 40 years," and "passed laws which had the effect of making the Philippine economy dependent upon our own economy." Thus, in addition to protecting U.S. interests in Asia, Sayre argued that the United States is "under very real obligations of a moral nature to the Philippines."[40]

While it is perhaps unsurprising that a U.S. colonial official would seek to protect U.S. interests in the Philippines, members of Congress also raised concerns about U.S. interests. As concerns about Japan became more serious, in hearings over the 1939 Neutrality Act, Representative John G. Alexander (R-MN) considered the inevitability of the coming war. He was especially concerned with U.S.–Asia relations, stating that "in the Orient—the Far East, the United States needs to watch our step, not only because of our interest in China, but also because of our interest and stake in the Philippines."

Alexander emphasized that wartime legislation must deal with Asian issues, including Japanese interest in the Philippines, where the United States already had $840,000,000 of investments and where U.S. "sovereignty over those very rich islands . . . is to continue until 1946."[41] At least for the time being, Alexander favored protecting the Philippines because it meant protecting U.S. interests.

A year later, in debates over the Selective Service Act, Representative Charles I. Faddis (D-PA) also cited U.S. material interests in the islands as grounds for including the Philippines in the territorial definition of the United States. Acknowledging the changing status of the Philippines, he stated, "although it is true that, under the terms of existing law, the Philippine Islands will be granted their independence in 1946, at the present time we have certain national interests in the Philippine Islands, including a great deal of Government property. These interests require protection."[42] After Japan attacked the Philippines, more state actors adopted this position. In hearings over the Declaration of War with Japan, Senator Mead (D-NY), for example, drew attention to U.S. interests in the Philippines. He stated that Japan was a "growing menace to our safety and security in the Pacific. Our trade and commerce, in fact, our right to the freedom of seas, has for some time been threatened by the militarist of Tokyo. Our strategic materials, vital commodities, and normal exchange of commerce, have been placed in jeopardy." He continued, stating that "the future of the Philippines has been jeopardized." Mead argued that the United States should go to war against Japan to "apply American force in the cause of justice, decency, and our own security."[43]

Prior to Japan's attacks, there was little support for war, and with that few legislators saw the importance of including the Philippines in U.S. global strategy. After, however, even former skeptics changed their tune. For example, although imperialists had long worried about Japan, Representative Lewis Thill (R-WI) characterized Japanese hostilities as "without warning." He cited the attacks on Hawai'i, the Philippines, and Guåhan, saying "all this means war. Insane, catastrophic war." And "since it is Japan's avowed intention to fight us," he said, "we must fight back."[44] Representative Martin L. Sweeney (D-OH) noted the tide change on intervention: "Just as I felt for the past 2 years that over 80 percent of our people were opposed to being involved in the blood business of Europe and Asia without just cause, I feel at this very hour that the same 80 percent of our people are united in full support of war resolution against the Imperial Government of Japan." He continued, "Interventionists and noninterventionists alike are now brothers in a common cause." For non- or anti-interventionists like Sweeney, the Japanese invasion provided "every justification" for war, as the United States was now tasked with "protecting our honor."[45] The newfound consensus hinged not only on concerns over geo-strategy or economic interests but also on ideas of racial difference.

A New Racial Threat

After December 7, 1941, as the importance of the Philippines became undeni-able, nativists and isolationists found a new racial enemy and thus joined their interventionist counterparts. In Congressional debates over the declaration of war with Japan, legislators spoke of war with Japan in strikingly similar terms to how imperialists argued for the war with Spain and rule over the Philip-pines forty years earlier. Representative Sweeney characterized U.S. entrance into war with Japan as one led by "Divine Providence," in which the United States would "speak for poor and distressed people of the earth." He argued that Japan threatened the United States' benevolent global mission, stating, "Our continuation as a world power should not be bound up with the role of a bully to crush the weak and oppressed, but, on the contrary, should be sus-tained by example and assistance in encouraging the many and varied races of the human family to emulate our way of life."[46] While Sweeney spoke of the United States' divine mission much like early imperialists of the late 1800s, others defined the United States as a Christian and therefore civilized nation in opposition to the Japanese. Representative John Elliot Rankin (D-MS), for example, stated that "history reveals no act of aggression and mass murder as dastardly, as cowardly, or as contemptible as the attack made by pagan, godless Japan on the United States and the Christian people of the island of Hawai'i on yesterday."[47]

In the United States' renewed Christian civilizing mission, Filipinos were no longer the savage, brown antithesis to white Anglo-Saxon Americans. The new enemy was the Japanese. Representative Homer D. Angell (R-OR), for example, argued for war with Japan, stating, "No one will halt or hesitate until these brown devils from over the seas have been crushed to earth and civiliza-tion saved from the ravages concocted by the diseased minds in control of this treacherous nation."[48] Representative Adolph Joachim Sabath (D-IL)—who raised concern about Filipinos' dependent status in 1933—now admonished those who favored isolation. Sabath also warned of a racial threat, albeit in different terms. He stated, "Some Members of Congress and certain sections of the press have permitted themselves to be influenced or blinded, and have refused to see clearly the danger which was confronting our country. Only the shock of an actual attack by these little yellow rats has finally opened their eyes."[49] Similarly, Representative James E. Van Zandt (R-PA) justified war with Japan in 1920s racial exclusionary terminology, stating: "Let us at once declare war on the Empire of Japan and all other nations who are aiding and abetting this yellow peril to the American way of life that has already murdered in cold blood our own fellow Americans."[50] Representative Charles A. Plumley (R-VT, at large) explicitly justified the war in terms of U.S. logics of racial exclusion, stating "the diabolically infamous treachery of the Japanese brands the race as never to have been and not now entitled to be trusted or treated as civilized. It confirms the judgement and wisdom of our forebears, who would and did exclude them from citizenship." Plumley extended arguments of Asian exclusion discussed in Chapter 4 to a global war, arguing that the Japanese were both uncivilized and untrustworthy. Speaking on the declaration of war, he continued, "We go forward today on the road to freedom and unity at whatever cost or else backward, as we submit to Hitlerism, paganism, and serfdom. A vote against this resolution is a vote to put us all in chains."[51] The Japanese were not only a clear geopolitical enemy but also a racial outsider around which U.S. state actors could unite.

Although nativists had excluded Filipinos from the metropole as Asian aliens, in the realm of geopolitics, interventionist state actors did not talk about them in denigrating racial terms. Instead, they slowly gained ground in arguing for the advantages of maintaining sovereignty over the Philippines. Their claims for territorial inclusion did not rely on the language of Filipinos' racial inferiority as it had in the early 1900s, but on a wartime threat and on the racialization of the Japanese as the enemy outsider. In fact, the territorial inclusion of the Philippines in World War II strategy was facilitated by how, in 1934, nativists excluded Filipinos from the metropole. Under the Tydings–McDuffie Act, the Philippine territory could be domestic to the United States, but the people could remain foreign from the metropolitan boundaries.

Freed from nativist opposition, interventionist and imperialist state actors made material and geopolitical arguments for including the Philippines in the territorial definitions of the United States. These claims were important because they rearticulated the importance of the territories like the Philippines in the United States' global strategy. In this period, U.S. state actors who were concerned with protecting U.S. interests in the Pacific worked to convince their skeptical counterparts that the Philippines was important to the United States' wartime and global policy. It was not until U.S. state actors saw a clear external threat, however, that they united around war and the importance of the Philippine Islands.

FILIPINOS IN THE U.S. MILITARY

Arguments for the strategic inclusion of the Philippines extended to military recruitment and remuneration. Leading up to and through World War II, state actors concerned with U.S. foreign affairs and geopolitics not only defined U.S. territorial reach to include the Philippines as a strategic site, but also created opportunities for inclusion and provided new rights to select Filipinos. In exchange for military service, U.S. state actors gave Filipinos opportunities to naturalize and claim social welfare benefits promised to all other veterans, regardless of colonial or racial classification. The geostrategic and economic importance of the Philippine territory and racial antagonism toward the Japanese eclipsed arguments about the racial fitness of Filipinos.

At first glance, it might seem odd that legislators discussed Filipinos—as non-U.S. citizens—in debates over U.S. wartime policy. After all, Chapter 4 showed that legislators concerned with maintaining white hegemony at home racialized Filipinos as Asian outsiders. Nevertheless, in law and formal debates over military service and inclusion and against a new outsider, U.S. state actors racialized Filipino servicepeople as good and loyal subjects. It might seem odder still that Filipinos could be included in the U.S. military, but this reflects a broader orientation toward the military in the United States that—on its surface—prioritized service and loyalty over racial classification. Whereas other countries have systems of common welfare for all citizens, the United States has historically distinguished between civilians and soldiers, suggesting that members of the military, whether citizens, aliens, or nationals, deserve special rights. After the Revolutionary War, foreign German and Irish nationals serving in General Washington's forces could naturalize. In both the War of 1812 and the first U.S. invasion of Mexico in 1846 (the Mexican–American War), European foreign nationals who were residents of the United States enlisted and served in the army. During the Civil War, the Union Army recruited immigrants from Europe, and in 1862, Congress passed legisla-tion granting foreigners serving in the U.S. military the right to expedited naturalization.

Asian aliens have also served in the U.S. military and eventually gained naturalization rights through their service. After World War I, local natural-ization officers, judges, and U.S. Supreme Court justices, keeping with nativist sentiment of the time, held that Asian origin was a bar to naturalization for veterans. Although the Alien Naturalization Act of May 9, 1918, granted an ex-pedited path to naturalization to "any native-born Filipino" and to *"any alien or any Porto Rican [sic]"* (italics added) after three years of service, in 1923 and 1925, the Supreme Court held that Asian aliens were not eligible for citizenship in exchange for military service.[52] This changed a decade later when, in 1935, Congress passed the Nye-Lea Act, guaranteeing all alien veterans the right of naturalization. The U.S. government upheld that loyalty, and martial sacrifice would trump national origin or race when it came to eligibility for citizenship.[53]

Whereas the history of Asian veteran naturalization was fraught until 1935, even prior to the passing of the Nye-Lea Act, Filipinos were *not* excluded from the right of naturalization and military benefits due to their race or na-tionality (see Table 5.2). Quite the contrary—their status as Filipinos granted them an expedited path to naturalization, again suggesting that their martial sacrifice was grounds for inclusion. As discussed in Chapter 2, since the early days of U.S. rule in the Philippines, Filipinos have served in the U.S. mili-tary and been rewarded for their service. In 1901, the United States recruited Filipinos to fight on the U.S. side in the Spanish–American and Philippine–American Wars. Known as the Philippine Scouts, these Filipinos were con-sidered part of the U.S. Army.[54] The special mention of Filipinos and Puerto Ricans in the Alien Naturalization Act of May 9, 1918, demonstrates that the United States treated colonial subjects in the U.S. military differently than Asian aliens ineligible for citizenship.[55] As Rick Baldoz notes, "The political exigencies of World War I forced American policymakers to address the status of noncitizen nationals in a more unequivocal way."[56] The 1920s U.S. Supreme Court also noted the exceptions for Filipinos. In *Toyota v. United States* (1925), when the Court ruled that the May 9, 1918, act was *not* intended to include any alien, they also upheld a separate clause of the Alien Naturalization Act, ar-guing that Filipinos could naturalize as colonial subjects (or nationals) of the United States. In short, the United States provided opportunities for Filipinos to become citizens even when racial bars against Asian naturalization existed.

TABLE 5.2. U.S. Acts Related to Veteran Status and Rights of Filipinos

ACT/DECISION	TERMS OF ACT RELATED TO FILIPINO MILITARY	STATUS OF FILIPINOS
1902	Old Scouts rewarded with social welfare benefits and pensions	Filipinos eligible for social welfare benefits
Act of May 9, 1918	For the naturalization of World War I soldiers	Nationals eligible for naturalization through military service
Toyota v. United States (1925)	Court case ruling that Asian origin trumps military service in exchange for right to naturalize, except in the case of Filipinos	Filipinos eligible for naturalization through military service owing to above act
1934 Tydings–McDuffie Act	Contains a provision by which the U.S. president can call to service the Philippine Army	Aliens
1940 Selective Service Act	Military draft	Nationals
1940 Nationality Act	Naturalization of aliens	Aliens, eligible for naturalization with military service (with terms expanded for Filipinos)
1941 Executive Order	Roosevelt calls the Philippine Commonwealth Army to service under the U.S. Armed Forces in the Far East	
1942 Second War Powers Act	For the expedited naturalization of noncitizens	Noncitizens, eligible for naturalization through military service
1944 Servicemen's Readjustment Act (G.I. Bill)	To provide federal government aid for the readjustment in civilian life of returning World War II veterans	Veterans eligible for benefits

During World War II, in the exigencies of war, U.S. state actors again affirmed expansive terms of inclusion in exchange for military service. Under the well-known 1944 G.I. Bill, Congress promised all those who served in the U.S. military—citizens, nationals, and aliens alike—social welfare benefits including job training, educational opportunities, home ownership loans,

insurance, and medical care. Aliens and nationals were also eligible for expedited naturalization. In part, the opportunity to gain citizenship through
martial sacrifice is based on the idea that risking one's life demonstrates loyalty to the nation. And war is a time when state actors reinforce the norm of
martial rights.[57] The inclusion of colonial subjects and foreign nationals in the
U.S. military has contributed to the idea that the military is a site of racial
equality or at least race neutrality.[58] Providing noncitizens with a pathway to
citizenship and certain rights and benefits—on its surface—represents a way
of thinking about the nation in more inclusionary terms. In light of their newfound consensus on U.S. global strategy, state actors applied these logics to
Filipinos, creating pathways for their enlistment, naturalization, and social
inclusion. Legislators, administrators, and military officials justified Filipino
inclusion in terms of allegiance, loyalty, U.S. obligation, and equality. In what
follows, I discuss the inclusion of Filipino veterans as part of U.S. global wartime strategy.

Incorporating Filipino Servicepeople

At the time of World War II, there were five classes of Filipino veterans. The
United States military organized and recruited four of them in the Philippines: the Old Scouts, the Philippine Commonwealth Army (which became
USAFFE), the guerrillas, and the New Scouts. The Old Scouts, the unit that
served for the United States in the Spanish–American and Philippine–American Wars, were composed of about 12,000 individuals. During World War II
there were over 200,000 Filipino servicepeople, an over fifteenfold increase
of Filipinos serving in the U.S. military up to that point. In 1935, President
of the Philippine Commonwealth Manuel Quezon asked U.S. Army General
Douglas MacArthur to organize the Philippine Commonwealth Army (PCA).
The PCA grew to approximately 120,000 individuals in the years preceding
World War II. On July 6, 1941, under a provision of the 1934 Tydings–McDuffie
Act, President Roosevelt issued an executive order formally incorporating the
PCA into the U.S. military as the United States Armed Forces in the Far East
(USAFFE).[59] The majority of Filipino World War II veterans were members of
this military body.

In addition to the Old Scouts and the PCA, recognized guerrillas served
on behalf of the United States in World War II and were, by order of the
Philippine Commonwealth president, incorporated into USAFFE. The

U.S. Department of Veterans Affairs (VA) recognized guerrillas as those who "served in resistance units recognized by and cooperating with U.S. Forces during the period of April 20, 1942, to June 30, 1946."[60] There remain veterans who claim to have served as guerrillas but whose service has never been recognized by the U.S. government.[61] Finally, in the Philippines, the U.S. Army recruited the New Scouts after October 6, 1945.[62] Together the last two classes of veterans—the guerrillas and the New Scouts—were composed of about 70,000 individuals.[63]

The fifth group of Filipino soldiers was known as the "First and Second Fil."[64] After Japan invaded U.S. territories, Filipino community leaders proposed a volunteer battalion, which, as Christopher Capozzola notes, "would demonstrate Filipinos' patriotism to Americans."[65] Unlike their counterparts in the Philippine territory, the First and Second Fil enlisted in the Regular Army of the United States. Organized in April and October of 1942, they mostly trained in California until 1944, when they left the metropolitan United States for the Pacific. They fought in New Guinea until February 1945 and then transferred to the Philippines.[66] Both in the metropole and colony, Filipinos formed an important part of the U.S. wartime efforts against the Japanese.

During the war, Congress, the War Department, and the VA affirmed the incorporation of Filipino units, suggesting that U.S. state actors saw Filipino servicepeople as a vital part of the war effort. For example, U.S. Congress passed the 1942 Second War Powers Act,[67] which provided for the expedited naturalization of noncitizens.[68] That same year, on April 27, the attorney general, Francis Biddle, wrote the administrator of Veterans Affairs, stating that military forces of the Philippine Commonwealth were considered to be in the active service of the United States and thus were eligible for insurance associated with their service under the National Service Life Insurance Act of 1940.[69] Biddle emphasized, "It seems clear that personnel of the organized military forces" of the Philippines were in active service and that in his opinion they were entitled to insurance.[70] Memos from Secretary of War Robert Patterson also suggest that, as of 1944, the War Department considered Filipinos eligible for military benefits. On October 28, 1944, President of the Philippine Commonwealth Sergio Osmeña formally recognized the guerrillas in Executive Order No. 21, inducting recognized and qualified individuals into the Commonwealth Army—considered part of the U.S. Armed Forces. The War Department recognized this order.[71] And in September 1945, the VA stated that

Filipino veterans were eligible for the same benefits as American soldiers.[72] After the war, state actors continued to affirm the inclusion of Filipino military personnel. On December 4, 1945, the commissioner of the Immigration and Naturalization Service, Ugo Carusi, highlighted that the Second War Powers Act gave rights and benefits to members of the organized military forces of the Philippine government. He also noted the U.S. attorney general approved this.[73] Through World War II, support for the inclusion of Filipinos in the U.S. military grew. Not only did members of Congress and state bureaucrats advocate for Filipino military service and expedited naturalization, but they also made promises of social citizenship, namely in the form of welfare benefits.

Justifying Filipino Military Inclusion
These inclusionary classifications of both the Philippine territory and Filipino servicepeople sharply contrast with the discussions of Filipinos in the U.S. metropole covered in Chapter 4. Rather than excluding Filipinos based on their alleged dependency, disease, or immorality, or by classifying them as Asian aliens, U.S. state actors instead invoked notions of allegiance, loyalty, U.S. obligation, and equality to create pathways for including Filipinos.

Filipinos were included because of U.S. sovereignty over the Philippines and the U.S. executive's control of the Philippine military. The 1934 Tydings–McDuffie Act, the 1940 Selective Service Act, and Roosevelt's call to service in 1941 all affirmed that Filipinos owed allegiance to the United States. Roosevelt's 1941 order stated that all officers of the Philippine Commonwealth government must "recognize and accept the supreme authority of" and "maintain true faith and allegiance to the United States."[74] The Philippines was under the U.S. flag and Filipinos owed allegiance. As Richard R. Ely, special assistant to the United States high commissioner, noted, "the Philippine Scouts have always been purely a Federal organization over which the Philippine government never had any control whatsoever." He continued, "The people of the Philippines are still under American sovereignty."[75]

The U.S. government demanded allegiance, and in these decisions and proclamations over Filipino service in the U.S. military, members of Congress and administrators increasingly drew on ideas of loyalty as a rationale for at least partially including veterans like Samuel Molina. Dating back to nativist attempts to exclude Filipinos from migrating to the United States, a few state actors cited Filipino loyalty. For example, the governor general of the Philippines from 1929 to 1932, Dwight Davis, opposed the 1930 Welch Bill, noting that not only did Filipinos owe allegiance to the United States, but they also "have frequently displayed their loyalty to the United States." Overlooking Filipinos' loyalty and excluding them from migration would "be most harmful," and "might cause serious embarrassment" to his administration.[76] Representative Marcantonio, who also made arguments for inclusion based on equality and anti-discrimination, referred to Filipino friendship to the United States and "the loyalty of the people in the Philippine Islands." For Marcantonio, both friendship and loyalty were reasons to pass legislation for Filipino naturalization.[77] As discussed in Chapter 4, Marcantonio's loyalty-based arguments for wholesale Filipino naturalization failed.

As the United States moved away from isolation, however, state actors increasingly adopted inclusionary language when speaking specifically of Filipino military personnel. For example, in 1940, Senator William H. King (D-UT) supported Filipino veterans' naturalization in exchange for military service. He even adopted Marcantonio's arguments about discrimination, stating that "regardless of their loyal service to the Government, [Filipinos] are discriminated against and are denied the opportunity of becoming American citizens."[78] While legislators were not moved by anti-discrimination arguments about Filipino workers in the United States, they were more open to this line of reasoning about a specific group of Filipinos: veterans. To King, Filipinos who demonstrated martial sacrifice should not be "cast out."

As the war continued, bureaucrats also argued that the United States had a colonial obligation to Filipinos: they were owed rights in exchange for their loyal service. For example, when asked about the U.S. defensive strategy in its territories in 1940, U.S. Secretary of War Stimson spoke of Filipinos. He cited U.S. colonial obligation; the United States had "certain duties as a nation," doing "work in civilization" "in those far-off islands." From his personal experience, Stimson testified that Filipinos "love and depend on the United States." And despite "their most enthusiastic moments of desire for independence," Filipinos always "in the back of their minds counted on the great defense which they had in having a friend in the United States." On these grounds, Stimson added that the United States should honor the reciprocal commitment of rights in exchange for service. Referencing the coming war with Japan, he continued, "It would be a bitter dose to me to realize the condition and the feeling of that trusting people if they were left alone by us to face what now seems to be quite possible in their neighborhood."[79] While he did not explicitly talk about their citizenship, Stimson invoked notions of Filipinos' loyalty and the United States' colonial obligation to protect them in the coming war.

The military leadership also affirmed Filipino veterans' right to an expedited path to naturalization and military benefits. General MacArthur justified the inclusion of Filipinos in terms of equality when, in 1942, he announced: "War is the great equalizer of men. Every member of my command shall receive equal pay and allowances based on the U.S. Army pay scale, regardless of nationality."[80] Lieutenant-Colonel William E. Carpenter of the War Department also testified in Congressional hearings regarding the Second War Powers Act of 1942, saying "that any man who is inducted into the service and conducts himself well in the service and performs the duties of a soldier and bears arms in defense of this country, should be entitled to whatever process Congress designates to become a citizen, as long as he has served honorably."[81] In other words, the military establishment was in favor of citizenship for aliens or noncitizens who showed their loyalty through service.

In sum, the war presented soldiering needs, and U.S. state actors saw Filipinos as vital to U.S. strategy in the Pacific. As World War II drew closer, U.S. state actors argued both for the strategic inclusion of the Philippine territory and of Filipino military personnel. Even with ongoing racist policy in the metropole and colony, when speaking about Filipinos in the U.S. military, legislators and bureaucrats did not rely on explicitly vulgar racial language. Instead, considering geostrategic aims, U.S. state actors spoke of allegiance, loyalty, colonial obligation, and equality. They affirmed rights in exchange for service.

ENDURING AMBIGUITY

Even as many U.S. state actors saw Filipinos as loyal and vital to the war effort, members of Congress remained confused about Filipinos' status in the U.S. empire. The conditions that led to the formation of the First and Second Filipino Infantry Regiments reflect this persistence. In 1940, Filipinos' civil status was ambiguous. Whether they would be drafted into the United States military was unclear. According to the 1940 Selective Service Act, Filipinos were essentially classified as nationals, akin to their pre-1934 status. The bill read: "it shall be the duty of every male citizen of the United States, and of every male alien residing in the United States . . . to present himself for and submit to registration" for the training of the armed forces of the United States. For this purpose, "United States when used in a geographical sense, shall be deemed to mean the several States, the District of Columbia, Alaska, Hawai'i, and Puerto Rico." Because the act did not include the Philippines in the definition of the United States, Filipinos were not considered citizens. While Filipinos were not citizens, whether Filipinos were aliens was also unclear. Because the act only specified service for U.S. citizens and aliens, the act omitted consideration of whether Filipinos could be inducted into the U.S. military.

After the Japanese attacked U.S. territories, however, Congress passed a special amendment to the act on December 20, 1941. In it, they authorized military service by "every male citizen of the United States, and of every other male person residing in the United States." Other male persons included citizens and subjects of the United States and neutral countries.[82] Because the amendment allowed for the induction of any resident, including subjects of the United States, Filipinos could now serve in the U.S. military. Nevertheless, even as Congress authorized the service of Filipinos, they did not clarify their citizenship status. As Baldoz notes, this amendment suggests that Filipinos were *not* citizens of the United States but classified as something else. And on January 3, 1942, the Selective Service System issued a directive stating that "all registrants who are citizens of the Philippine Commonwealth are deemed nationals of the United States and shall be reclassified in the same manner as citizens of the United States."[83] Thus, by the aforementioned 1940 Selective Service Act, Filipinos were not considered citizens or aliens, but again nationals akin to their pre-1934 status. Regardless, either as nationals or aliens under the 1934 Tydings–McDuffie Act, Filipinos already owed allegiance to the United States. This clarification of the 1940 Selective Service Act—in which Filipinos were nationals treated as citizens who could serve in the U.S. military—led to the formation of the First and Second Fil in the United States.

While Filipinos could serve and gain expanded rights as veterans, they were not quite foreign and not quite domestic. Belonging was contingent on military service. Some Filipinos in the Philippines had served in the U.S. military since 1901, while others served a colonial army belonging to the United States. At the same time, although Filipinos in the United States were not explicitly included as members of the United States by the 1940 Selective Service Act, their status as nationals suggested that martial service trumped racial ineligibility for naturalization. By calling the Philippine Army to service in 1941 and issuing a special statement to ensure the enrollment of Filipinos in the United States into the U.S. military, President Roosevelt and the Selective Service System demonstrated the U.S. interest in taking advantage of all people who could fight on behalf of the United States in World War II.

CONCLUSION

In response to Japanese imperial war-making, U.S. state actors reached consensus about geostrategy. As they made war and saw the importance of the Pacific theatre of World War II, U.S. politicians characterized the Philippines and Filipinos in new terms—as a place and people important to the war effort. The war dampened isolationists' concerns and changed politicians' vocabulary for speaking about their colonial subjects. Rather than migrating Asian aliens who threatened white norms at home, Filipinos were loyal military personnel important to the defense of U.S. interests abroad. Legislators and administrations leveraged geopolitical security concerns to create expansive opportunities for Filipino veterans' membership in the United States. War provided the opportunity for U.S. state actors to reconceive of their relationship to the Philippines. The need to protect the United States' interests catalyzed U.S. state actors' reframing of Filipinos as allies.

Including the Philippine territory in strategic definitions of the United States and emphasizing rights in exchange for military service stand in contrast to the vulgar, explicitly racist, and exclusionary understandings of Japanese and of Filipinos in earlier periods. The incorporation of Filipinos was no longer framed as a mission of racial uplift of civilization nor as a racial threat to avoid but in terms of wartime strategy and need. In the years leading up to and following the United States' entrance into World War II, U.S. state actors increasingly married ideas of Filipinos as loyal military personnel with geopolitical interests in the Pacific. In this way, the terms of racial-imperial rule became less about racist exclusion and more about military and strategic opportunities.

This part of the book—Chapters 4 and 5—addressed a crucial period in which the United States reworked its relationship to empire. U.S. state actors took advantage of the flexible colonial relationship to bifurcate the domestic and foreign aspects of imperial rule. They relied on vulgar racial arguments when it came to domestic affairs. At the same time, they decoupled these racial claims from foreign affairs, politely reframing Filipinos as loyal subjects. The 1934 Tydings–McDuffie Act enabled state actors to hide both empire at home and race abroad (See Figure 5.1).

By the terms of the act, the Philippines, though still a colony, "shall be considered a separate country," and "citizens of the Philippine Islands, who are not citizens of the United States shall be considered as if they are aliens" for the purposes of migration. Congress changed the thirty-year precedent of classifying Filipinos as nationals who could freely migrate without oversight by the INS. In the metropole, Filipinos were cast as Asian foreigners rather than colonial subjects. On these grounds, Filipinos were barred from migration and settlement in the United States.

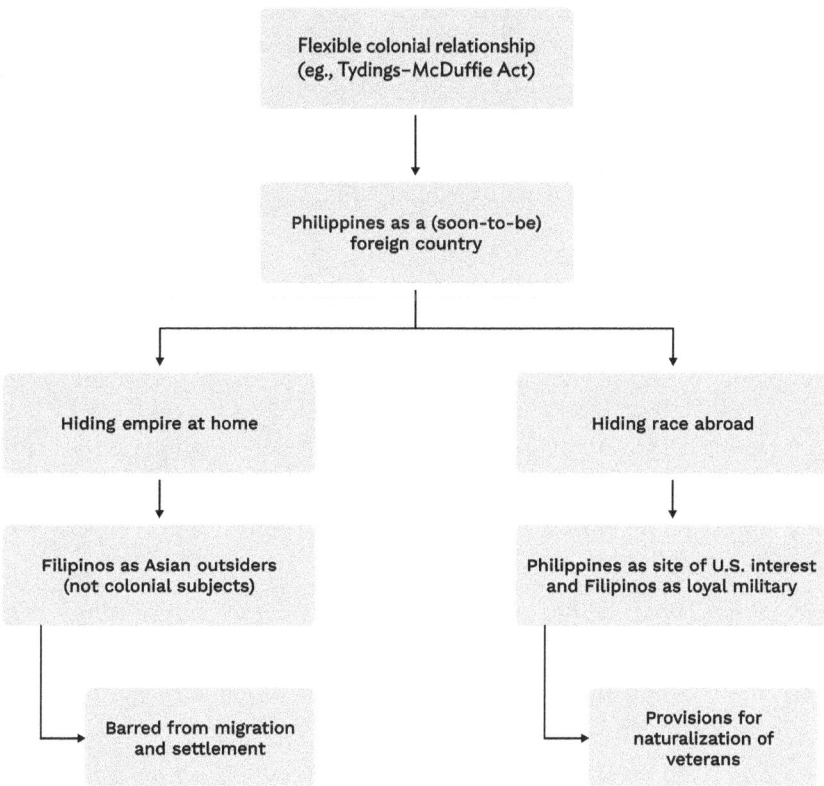

FIGURE 5.1.   Bifurcating Rule

The United States did not relinquish sovereignty abroad, however. Congress maintained the right of the United States to intervene in the islands to protect U.S. interests and stated that citizens of the Philippine Commonwealth owed allegiance to the United States. A provision of the act allowed the president to call the military forces of the Philippine Commonwealth to service. When it came to U.S. actions outside the metropole, the Philippines and Filipinos remained important to the empire. U.S. state actors increasingly discussed the geostrategic importance of the Philippines. Filipinos who served in the U.S. military were heralded for their loyalty to the United States, no longer excluded on the basis of their race or portrayed as savage children in need of training by Anglo-Saxon fathers. They had become allies in war. The United States was able to accomplish racial exclusion at home by denying colonial obligation and could continue to do empire abroad by wiping justifications clean of race.

PART THREE

DISGUISING EMPIRE, 1943–1947

From 1898 to 1946, U.S. state actors made war. Grappling with more than military spending, recruitment, or body counts, war raised questions about how to define the nation's boundaries. State actors wrestled with conflicting visions for white hegemony. This book started with how, in going to war with Spain, U.S. state actors embarked on a project of overseas empire and lay new foundations for racial-imperial rule. As discussed in Part I, they redefined constitutional law and restructured the scope of state administration in ways that enabled the separation of foreign and domestic aspects of rule. Part II showed how U.S. nativist legislators hid empire at home and U.S. imperialists hid race abroad. Racial exclusion of colonial subjects from the U.S. metropole and participation in a global war brought U.S. federal state actors together in ways that were previously not possible.

This book ends with how, at the conclusion of World War II, U.S. state actors disguised U.S.–Philippine imperial relations in new terms. World War II raised new anxieties and threats that informed how U.S. state actors defined themselves and their relation to the Philippines. In 1898, imperial war-making with Spain animated debates over the Philippine Question, of whether to incorporate new racially inferior people. In the early years of rule, war and colonial conquest divided imperialists and nativist-isolationists.

Although in 1946 U.S. state actors faced similar questions about the future relationship between the United States and the Philippines, the war and a shared perception of new global threats united the formerly divided camps. U.S. state actors again confronted two questions. First, what would be the relationship of the United States to their soon-to-be former colonial subjects? Second, what would be the relationship of the United States to the new Philippine state "abroad"?

As they answered these questions, U.S. politicians considered their positions on racial equality at home, the future of imperial rule, and extraterritorial influence. Chapter 6 addresses the first question, showing how U.S. state actors, once divided over the place of Filipinos in the U.S. nation, created limited and symbolic pathways for Filipino naturalization. Although they attempted to signal that the United States renounced racial exclusion, Republicans and Democrats—no longer sharply divided by nativist, isolationist, and imperialist interests—relied on the construction of Filipinos as (Asian) outsiders and abandoned the arguments that the United States owed colonial subjects rights for their military service. When it came to policing the demographic boundaries of the United States, Filipinos were no longer considered "foreign in a domestic sense," but Congress reclassified them as unequivocally alien. For the Filipino people who might migrate to the United States, U.S. state actors construed rights as unnecessary aid.

Whereas U.S. state actors cast Filipinos as foreigners to whom they owed nothing, when it came to the Philippine territory, they secured imperial policies. Chapter 7 answers the second question, showing how through economic and military arrangements—built during decades of formal racial-imperial rule—U.S. state actors maintained economic and political influence in the Philippines. World War II showed formerly nativist-isolationist state actors that they could not ignore the world beyond the United States' metropolitan borders. They joined their imperialist counterparts in seeing the geostrategic importance of the Philippines. They disguised the civilizing project of formal empire as foreign aid. While explicitly vulgar racial arguments disappeared from the discussion of Filipinos abroad, imperial relations between the United States and the Philippines relied on earlier polite racial logics of tutelage. Recognizing Filipinos' loyalty during the war, legislators and administrators argued that the United States must help the new nation. Empire became economic and military aid.

These two chapters demonstrate how U.S. state actors came together across ideological and partisan divides to change the terms of rule without upsetting the foundational racial-imperial grammar. At the end of World War II and in the years leading up to the Cold War, U.S. state actors on both sides of the aisle used polite racism to justify extraterritorial control over the Philippines, even as they excluded Filipinos from the metropole. Building on the bifurcation of the foreign and domestic aspects of rule discussed in Part II, state actors disguised U.S.–Philippine relations in terms that evaded explicit reference to hierarchy. They framed empire as a partnership between allied republics. By changing the terms used to describe U.S.–Philippine relations, U.S. federal state actors engaged in political theatre, allowing for the symbolic naturalization of Filipinos and the ostensible decolonization of the Philippines. Against accusations that the United States was an illiberal racist state, disguising imperial relations allowed the United States to make empty promises and reinscribe the global color line without referencing racial or imperial rule.

Before turning to the chapters, I first review key background events that shaped how U.S. state actors refashioned their empire in 1946. Confronted with the contradictions between U.S. wartime propaganda and racial inequality at home, growing concerns about communism in Asia, and worldwide calls for decolonization, U.S. state actors realized the untenability of the old terms of racial-imperial rule. With explicit nativists pacified and in agreement about the necessity of global intervention, Democrats and Republicans turned to a new vocabulary. Rather than managing the exclusion of nonwhite people within U.S. metropolitan borders, they now spoke of managing the threats that communists and anti-colonial resistance posed to democracy and foreign affairs. As U.S. state actors confronted these questions, they changed the terms without upsetting the deep grammar of racial-imperial rule.

RACIAL PROPAGANDA AND INEQUALITY IN WORLD WAR II

U.S. state actors united around an external threat in World War II. In doing so, they agreed that the United States should defend itself against a new racialized enemy on the global stage. It was not only U.S. legislators' vulgar racialization of the Japanese that made World War II a race war, however. The war was one of empires struggling to expand extraterritorial control.[1] In making war, both

Axis and Allied powers saw the war as one of national survival against internal racialized others and superpowers threatening their economy, culture, and politics.[2] It was also a war over moral authority, as in which country had the best vision for modern advancement. Whereas Japan claimed it united Asia, the Allies and the United States presented themselves as defending the world against tyranny, fascism, and oppression.[3] U.S. state actors treated Nazi racism and Japanese imperialism as foils against which they distinguished their global interventions. Facing assaults to their reputation, U.S. state actors again addressed questions of race and membership.

As discussed in Chapter 5, U.S. federal state actors argued that, by going to war, they were fighting against the spread of Japanese tyrannical, imperial rule in Asia and the Pacific. After Japan attacked the Philippines on December 8, 1941, General Douglas MacArthur led the defense of the Philippines with few reinforcements. Facing dire conditions, on March 11, 1942, three weeks after the evacuation of Philippine Commonwealth President Manuel Quezon and Vice President Sergio Osmeña, MacArthur left the Philippines for Australia. On April 9, 1942, nearly 76,000 Filipino and U.S. soldiers surrendered after months of defending Bataan. The Japanese Army led them on the Bataan Death March to Camp O'Donnell. First, they walked sixty-six miles to San Fernando, where the Japanese Army packed Filipino and U.S. soldiers into train cars to walk another eight miles. An estimated 7,000 to 10,000 died before arriving, and another 18,000 soldiers died from starvation, abuse, and torture at the camp.[4]

Japan's occupation of the Philippines brought more than wartime horrors; to turn Asia against the United States, the Japanese empire promised independence to the Philippines. In October 1943, where the United States once had a colony, Japan established an ostensibly independent Philippine republic. José Laurel became the president of the Second Philippine Republic and declared his anti-U.S. sentiments, saying, "Because I like my country to be free, I do not like America to come back." Criticizing the U.S. program of benevolent assimilation, he wrote in the *Manila Tribune* that "we are wearying with the pretensions of the 'white man's burden,' which more often than not has only served to cloak exploitations of weaker peoples."[5] Through his puppet presidency, the Japanese Empire portrayed their war-making as a racial project of Asian unification against U.S. and European colonizers.

Faced with Japanese violence and propaganda, Philippine and U.S. state actors bolstered their claims that Japan was a ruthless enemy and that the United States fought for democracy and Filipino freedom. Former ambassador to Japan Joseph Grew argued that Japan was "utterly ruthless, utterly cruel, and utterly blind to any of the values which make up our civilization."[6] As the Philippines remained under Japanese imperial rule, the exiled Philippine Commonwealth created the war poster below, which depicts a wounded Filipino soldier holding a Philippine flag and a grenade (see Figure PIII.1). In September 1944, the U.S. Office of War Information (OWI) produced booklets highlighting Asian service in the U.S. military, including one titled "Filipinos in the War." In these pamphlets, the OWI highlighted that the United States was "a peace-loving democratic nation," committed "to the soundness of the democratic process." The United States, the OWI claimed, was "especially concerned with the progress of the Philippines."[7] After the Second Philippine Republic declared war on the United States on September 22, 1944, General MacArthur returned to the Philippines. On October 20, MacArthur began the campaign of "liberation," re-taking the Philippine colony for the United States. And, as Chapter 7 will show, U.S. state actors continued to argue that U.S. intervention was in defense of both democracy and racial equality.

That U.S. state actors espoused their democratic values in the face of foreign threats did not mean that they became more egalitarian at home. Jim Crow statutes persisted, as did racial barriers to Asian migration and naturalization. The U.S. government's treatment of Asian and other nonwhite populations was in tension with the expressed goals of U.S. foreign policy. Social scientist Gunnar Myrdal noted that Nazi propaganda drew attention to the U.S. treatment of Black Americans and that racial segregation in the United States could threaten the U.S. war effort.[8] Meanwhile, as Japan invaded more of Asia and the Pacific, its leaders launched propaganda campaigns, decrying U.S. and European colonialism and the unequal treatment of Asians. In the case against the United States, Japan drew attention to the U.S. exclusion of the Chinese and other Asians. In opposition to U.S. practices of Asian exclusion, Japan espoused a pan-Asian ideology and argued that, under its imperial control as the Greater East Asia Co-Prosperity Sphere, Japan would liberate Asian territories from Western domination.[9] Secretary of War Henry Stimson and General George Marshall believed that Japan's propaganda agitated Black

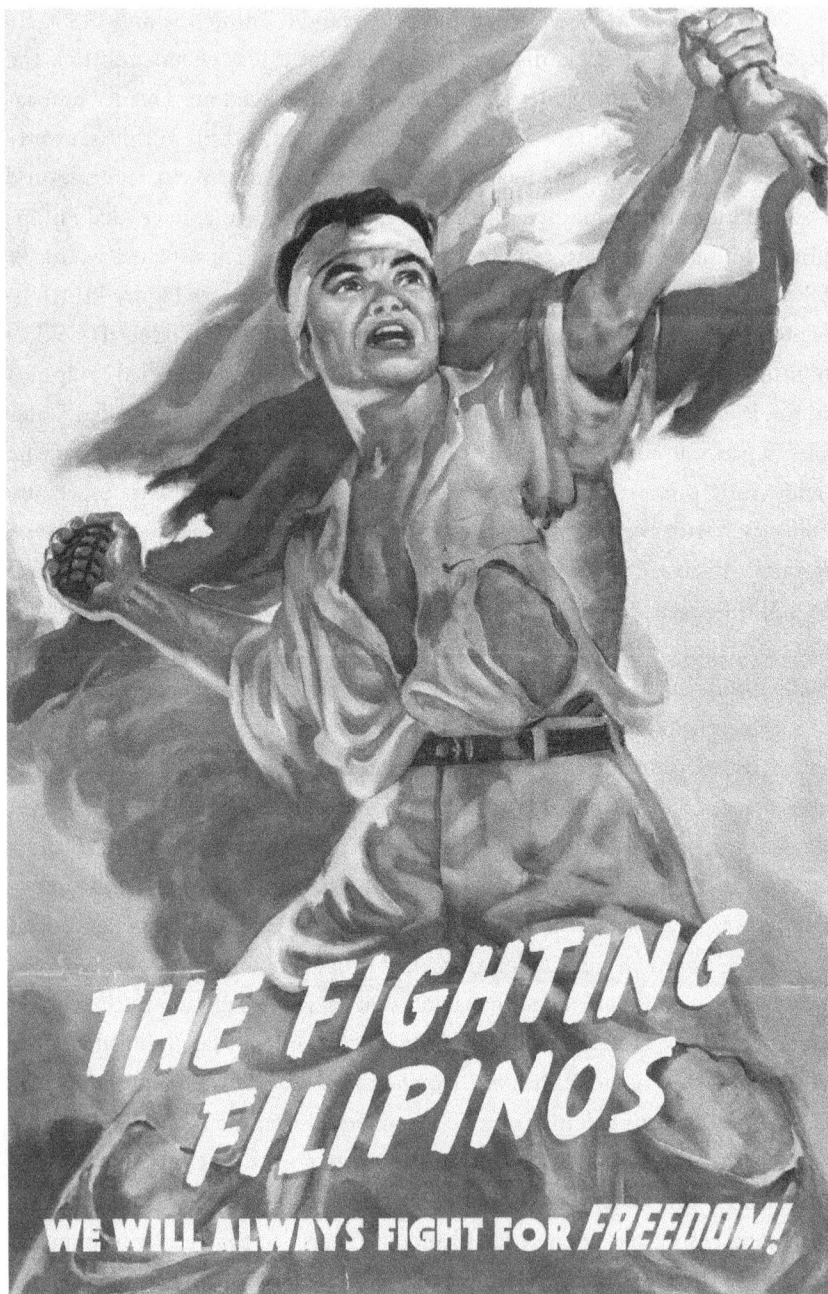

FIGURE PIII.1.   The Fighting Filipinos: We will always fight for freedom! Source: Office of Special Services, Commonwealth of the Philippines, Washington, D.C., 1943, World War Poster Collection, University of Minnesota Libraries.

Americans to fight for equality.[10] Japan's propaganda was not wrong. After all, many in the United States continued to support Asian exclusion (especially members of Congress from Western and Southern states, the American Federation of Labor, the American Legion, and the Veterans of Foreign Wars).[11] Not only did members of the public and Congress testify against repealing Chinese exclusion, citing the threat of Asian hordes, the U.S. executive branch under President Roosevelt incarcerated Japanese Americans in the name of a "wartime emergency."[12]

While war-making shone an unwanted light on the United States' practices of racial exclusion and subordination, members of the public advocated for greater inclusion. Against anti-Asian policies and in response to wartime racial propaganda, U.S. intellectuals, the Congress of Industrial Organizations, the Federal Council of Churches, and others denounced the United States' racial policies, especially toward other Asians who were fighting alongside the Allies.[13] Asian elites and Asian American communities lobbied for repealing Chinese and other Asian exclusion laws. Often, their political activism relied on coalition-building across ethnic and racial lines as well as tying their struggles to independence and anti-colonial activism in their homelands. Their efforts gained more traction in earlier periods, in part because wartime labor shortages encouraged employers, especially defense industries, to hire Chinese Americans.[14] After China joined the Allied Forces, private citizens—including missionaries and businesspeople interested in trade ventures and investment in Asia—increasingly spoke against U.S. exclusion of Chinese migration and naturalization.[15] Perhaps most famously, Soong May-Lin, better known as Madame Chiang Kai-Shek, visited the United States in 1943 and publicized the Chinese war effort, stirring the sentiments of U.S. elite. Author Pearl S. Buck, her spouse Richard J. Walsh, *Time* and *Life* publisher Henry Luce, and Roger Baldwin of the American Civil Liberties Union also wrote to support equality for the Chinese. In a public speech in 1942, Buck said that "prejudice is the most vulnerable term in our American democracy," adding that the United States could only win the war by "convincing our colored allies—who are most of our allies—that we are not fighting for ourselves as continuing superior over colored peoples."[16] For people like Buck, the war presented an opportunity to think differently about the United States' strategic needs and its position in the world.

As they made war, U.S. officials especially concerned with overseas affairs also argued for the end of Chinese exclusion. Citing the discrimination against Chinese people, they distinguished among different Asians.[17] In a letter to

Congress, President Roosevelt wrote: "I regard this legislation as important in the cause of winning the war and of establishing a secure peace. China is our ally." He went on, "By the repeal of the Chinese Exclusion Laws, we can correct a historic mistake and silence the distorted Japanese propaganda."[18] Even Representative Samuel Dickstein (D-NY), chairman of the Committee on Immigration and Naturalization, spoke in favor of repealing Chinese exclusion. He said that it would be "a simple matter of justice" and serve as "recognition of the heroic resistance of China against our common enemy."[19] On June 29, 1943, Representative Warren Magnuson (D-WA) introduced a bill to repeal the Chinese Exclusion Acts. And on December 17, 1943, the U.S. Congress passed the Magnuson Act.

The fact that West Coast and formerly nativist legislators supported an end to Chinese exclusion reflects how, in response to concerns about the United States' geopolitical position, U.S. state actors adjusted policies aimed at shaping U.S. demography.[20] The most important consequence of how U.S. state actors addressed their global concerns was that they distinguished between what they saw as good, friendly Asians (the Chinese) and bad, enemy Asians (the Japanese).[21] This distinction between "good" and "bad" Asians would transform as World War II ended. With the rising threat of communism, anti-imperial communists became the new bad Asians.

NEW THREATS TO WHITE HEGEMONY

As U.S. state actors considered their relationship to nonwhite people both within and outside the U.S. metropolitan borders, they also wrestled with the obstacles that communism and calls for decolonization posed to reaching their geostrategic goals. Communism, as an alternative political and economic system to U.S. capitalism, promised to reconfigure the global order. U.S. state actors saw communism and anti-colonial nationalism as political threats to capitalism and imperialism. Communism offered an alternative to racial-imperial rule in which poor, colonized, and nonwhite people would rise against their elite, white, and metropolitan rulers. Fearing the loss of white hegemony, U.S. state actors united in the fight against communism.

Communism, however, was not a new concern. Dating back to the Spanish–American War, U.S. state actors were consumed by threats of revolution, radicals, and sedition. In response, they passed restrictive immigration laws,

engaged in counterinsurgency, and expanded their influence in the archipelago and in Asia. Although the pre–World War II counterrevolutionary campaigns were much smaller in scale than what rose post–World War II, they
proved to be useful for extending U.S. oversight of the islands and influence in
the world more widely. As Colleen Woods notes, "During the 1920s and 1930s,
discussions of Bolshevism, imperialism, and the potential for both to destabilize domestic and global racial orders frequented debates over the character,
purpose, and direction of the United States' role in the world." In these years of
colonial rule, the United States surveilled suspected revolutionary anarchists
and communists in the Philippines and "used sedition laws to prevent the
circulation of communist literature and curtail the growth of communist parties."[22] Counterinsurgency campaigns were aimed at maintaining both U.S.
control and elite Filipinos' economic and political positions, which would, in
turn, bolster American influence and security aims.

During World War II, in light of what they considered a more pressing
external threat, U.S. colonial officials temporarily paused anti-communist
campaigns. Filipinos of all classes united against the Japanese invasion of the
Philippines. And after Japan captured U.S. and Filipino soldiers at Bataan,
guerrilla resistance rose in their place, and the guerrillas were formally incorporated into the U.S. military, as discussed in Chapter 5.[23] Some of the
guerrilla groups, like the Hukbalahap (*Hukbo ng Bayan Laban sa Hapon*, the
People's Army against the Japanese), or Huks for short, came from peasant
communities and organized for socialism and communism. Initially, the
United States and the Huks cooperated against the Japanese despite their different political aims.[24] After the war, however, U.S. antagonism toward the
Huks rose. U.S. and Filipino politicians and military officials argued that the
Huks were violent, communist threats to the emerging Philippine nation and
to U.S. international security.[25] Communism was not the only perceived threat
in the islands, but identification and prosecution of Japanese collaboration-
ists waned at the urging of the Departments of State and Interior.[26] U.S. state
actors and Filipino elite prioritized anti-communist efforts, reflecting greater
concern for threats to U.S. capitalist and imperial influence than for a collaboration with the wartime enemy.

During World War II, as the Allies claimed they fought against the tyranny and oppression of the Axis powers, more anti-colonial nationalist leaders
emerged and called for an end to empire. Japan granted nominal independence

to the Philippines, hoping to garner the support of Asian anti-colonial nationalists. Intellectuals from the colonies traveled the world and studied in
the metropole. Ho Chi Minh, Sukarno, Mohandas Gandhi, W.E.B. Du Bois,
and Aimé Césaire—to name only a few—advocated for nationalist and pan-
nationalist movements.[27] Global anti-colonial calls gained a place on the global
stage. David Scott FitzGerald and David Cook-Martín note that "countries of
immigration," like the United States, "could afford to ignore the reactions of
colonized people and weak states prior to World War II." After the war, however, "decolonization and the formation of world institutions such as the United
Nations suddenly made the views of post-colonial governments matter."[28]

As World War II ended, U.S. state actors' concerns about colonized people
rising against them grew. Given the history of nativism and isolation in the
United States, one might expect anti-colonial agitation and the promise of
Philippine independence to bring about the end of U.S. influence in the Philippines. This, however, is not what happened. Faced with rising communist and
anti-colonial resistance in the world, U.S. state actors worked to secure their
influence and reinscribe the global color line to combat the threat of nonwhite
people rising against white rule. As they espoused anti-communist rhetoric,
U.S. state actors remained committed to white supremacy and believed that
communist and peasant resistance was aimed at "expelling whites," as Woods
shows.[29] Formerly interventionist politicians acknowledged that formal "colonialism could not last much longer in the face of mounting worldwide resistance."[30] They did not, however, want to abandon their hegemony.

Whereas in the late 1800s and early 1900s, only a few (but powerful) U.S.
actors supported global intervention, now, both Republicans and Democrats
argued for combatting communism abroad. The fight against communism
was not only a question of political economy but also of preserving the racial
order at home and the colonial order abroad. U.S. state actors united to preserve white hegemony through a worldwide capitalist system with the United
States at the helm. The United States would build allies through foreign aid
and diplomacy.[31] United in their vision for U.S. global intervention, state
actors concealed racial-imperial rule and disguised it as a struggle of democracy against communism.

The first four decades of U.S. rule in the Philippines were a battle between
those concerned with maintaining white hegemony at home and those who

saw possibilities of expanding it abroad. At the close of World War II, however, U.S. state actors reached a consensus about the United States' place in the world and the place of Filipinos in the United States. Making war against Japan and communists globally shaped how the United States treated allied Asian nationals. No longer savages or moral threats to the United States, U.S. state actors now defined Filipinos abroad as "good" Asians in the post-war era.[32] Anti-communism and the symbolic liberalization of immigration policy worked together as the U.S. claimed to be a democratic and inclusive world power. Through formal decolonization of the Philippines, lifting immigration restrictions, and foreign policymaking, U.S. state actors sought to manage their position in the new postcolonial world. They claimed they embarked on a new type of global intervention. Of course, claims of novelty were not new, but in the post–World War II era, U.S. state actors no longer argued for foreign intervention in explicitly vulgar racial or imperial terms. This last part of the book charts how, although the Philippines gained its independence, decolonization of the Philippines cemented a "polite" racial-imperial approach to overseas rule.

TABLE PIII.1.   Timeline of Key Events in Chapters 6 and 7

	DATE	EVENT
1943	December 17	Magnuson Act enacted
1944	June 22	G.I. Bill enacted
	July 29	Act declaring the policy of the Congress with respect to the independence of the Philippine Islands, and for other purposes enacted
1945	May 14	Truman and Osmeña sign preliminary agreement on U.S. bases
	September 2	World War II ends
1946	February 18	Rescission Act enacted
	April 30	Philippine Trade Act and Philippine Rehabilitation Act enacted
	June 26	Philippine Military Assistance Act enacted
	July 2	Luce–Celler Act enacted
	July 4	Philippine independence
1947	March 14	United States and the Philippines sign Military Bases Agreement

SIX   NATIVISM AS LIBERAL INCLUSION, 1945–1946

In 1977, Samuel Molina wrote Senator Daniel K. Inouye (D-Hawai'i), sharing records of his U.S. military service during World War II and thanking Inouye for his support of Filipino veterans. Molina disputed the U.S. adjutant general's decision about his military service. The adjutant general claimed that Molina's service from June 15, 1942, to June 10, 1946, was not for the U.S. Army, but the Philippine Army. Therefore, the adjutant general "cancelled payments for longevity pay, allowances, and other benefits derived from" his service. As proof of his service to the U.S. Army, Molina attached the oath of allegiance he made on June 15, 1942, to his letter.

Despite the historical momentum, detailed in Chapter 5, that Filipino veterans like Samuel Molina would be eligible for the benefits provided under the 1944 G.I. Bill, the U.S. Congress reclassified him and over 200,000 other veterans as having not served in active duty. The First Supplemental Surplus Appropriation Rescission Act of 1946, more commonly referred to as the Rescission Act, not only reclassified Filipino veterans but did so for the purposes of denying them military benefits and an expedited path to naturalization. The 1946 act read that

> service . . .in the organized military forces of the government of the Commonwealth of the Philippines, while such forces were in the service of the

Armed Forces of the United States . . .shall not be deemed to have been active military, naval, or air service for the purposes of any law of the United States conferring rights, privileges, or benefits.[1]

Congress reclassified Filipino veterans who had served in an army under the command of the U.S. military as having not served in or for the U.S. military. Filipino military personnel had no claim to the benefits promised to them. For Filipino veterans of World War II, martial eligibility for citizenship—based on sacrifice, loyalty, and allegiance—proved fragile.

After World War II and in the months leading up to Philippine independence, the U.S. Congress not only revoked the path to inclusion for Filipino veterans, but they also formally ended restrictions to Philippine naturalization in the United States. In other words, Congress reversed both the special treatment for Filipino military discussed in Chapter 5 and restrictions to naturalization discussed in Chapter 4. On July 2, 1946, two days before Philippine independence, President Truman signed the Luce–Celler Act, providing for the naturalization of Filipinos. As he signed it, two Filipinos—Antonio Gonzalez (president of the Philippine Inter Community of the Western States) and Juan Dionisio (director of the Philippine Resident Commissioner's Office of the Pacific Coast)—were among those who stood behind Truman. The Luce–Celler Act, sponsored by one Democrat and one Republican representative, simplified the U.S. stance on Filipino migration, settlement, and naturalization in the metropole.

When viewed in light of prior restrictions to Filipino migration and naturalization under the 1934 Tydings–McDuffie Act, allowing for Filipino naturalization seems like a break with the U.S. racial-imperial grammar. Prior to 1946, only Filipinos who were in the United States before 1934 and those who served in the U.S. military were eligible for naturalization. By the terms of the newly approved Luce–Celler Act, however, Congress considered Filipinos—regardless of military status—as eligible for naturalization. The actual act did not specify the number of Filipinos that could naturalize, but as part of Philippine independence, on July 4, 1946, Truman set an immigration quota for one hundred Filipinos a year, doubling the fifty-person quota in the 1934 Tydings–McDuffie Act.[2] On its surface, the Luce–Celler Act appears to be a liberal, post–World War II reform.

FIGURE 6.1.   President Harry S. Truman (seated) signs a bill regarding immigration and naturalization for Filipinos and East Indians in the Oval Office of the White House. Standing behind President Truman are (left to right): Representative John Lesinski of Michigan; Antonio Gonzales, president of the Philippine Inter Community of the Western States; J. C. Dionisio; Joseph R. Farrington, delegate from Hawai'i Representative Emanuel Celler from New York; M.O.A. Baig, first secretary of the Indian Agency General; J. J. Singh, President, India League of America; Dr. Anup Singh, Secretary, National Committee for India's Freedom; and Leonides S. Virata, Executive Officer, Resident Commissioner for the Philippines. Source: Accession Number 59-1215, Truman Library, Independence, MO.

Considering the rights Filipinos once had in the metropole, however, the Luce–Celler Act excluded the vast majority of Filipinos from migrating and gaining the rights of citizens. At the end of World War II, there were approximately 150,000 Filipinos in the United States and Hawai'i.[3] Prior to the Rescission Act, approximately 200,000 veterans were eligible for migration and naturalization, but now only one hundred Filipinos a year could migrate and naturalize. The Luce–Celler Act also treated Filipinos like Asian nationals rather than as U.S. colonial subjects. During World War II, Congress equivocated between classifying Filipinos as citizens, nationals, and aliens. Now, Congress decided Filipinos were univocally alien. Veterans like Molina lost their rights.[4] This is not to suggest that the situation for Filipinos was better in earlier years of empire. Rather, the shift in administrative classification draws attention to how, on the verge of Philippine independence, U.S. state actors changed the terms of rule but not its foundational grammar. They reconfigured and concealed their approaches to nativist exclusion.

Over decades of state formation—during which justices institutionalized ambiguity and legislators and administrators bifurcated the foreign and domestic aspects of rule—the United States determined how it would treat and classify Filipino people. Demobilization from World War II and preparations for decolonization reanimated demographic questions. What was the place of Filipinos in the metropolitan United States? The bipartisan support of both the Rescission and Luce–Celler Acts suggests that nativism won at home. Although Democrats abandoned explicit exclusion based on race and joined Republicans in lauding Filipinos for their loyalty to the United States, loyalty became an empty invocation. Legislators made merely symbolic nods to Filipinos' service in the war. While they made public gestures toward racial equality, Democrats and nativists in the legislative branch continued to see Filipinos as Asian outsiders to whom the United States owed nothing. With independence forthcoming, U.S. state actors redefined U.S.–Philippine relations in terms that erased colonial obligation. Both U.S. bureaucrats and legislators prioritized Philippine independence over the mutual obligations of service and rights, recasting the latter as unnecessary aid. Focusing on independence enabled state actors to unite under one approach to maintaining white hegemony. Building on the classification of Filipinos as aliens, legislators emphasized Filipinos' status as non-U.S. citizens. If Filipinos were not citizens, then, state actors argued, granting rights to them was unnecessary aid for an already overburdened U.S. government. Thus, the United States could accomplish nativist exclusion without explicitly naming race.

Avoiding mention of race helped legislators manage concerns about the United States' global reputation. While one might expect those in favor of naturalization for Filipinos to express progressive and anti-discriminatory ideologies, they made only tempered arguments for Filipino naturalization, referring to how a global race war and communism threatened the United

States. Legislators on both sides of the aisle, however, continued to express racial fears in debates. They not only worried about Filipinos in the United States, but they also believed that formerly colonized subjects of the world could turn against them. With independence on the horizon, U.S. state actors could remain committed to nativist exclusion. Under the guise of opening immigration, legislators attempted to respond to calls for decolonization and accusations of racism.

In this chapter, I first provide an overview of how Congress debated and passed the Rescission and Luce–Celler Acts. I discuss the terms of both acts and how they impacted Filipinos' potential rights in the metropole. Although Democrats and Republicans alike lauded Filipino loyalty, I show how these were merely symbolic gestures. U.S. legislators neither abandoned their racist opinions of Filipinos nor did they materially reward Filipinos for their service. Instead, they excluded soon-to-be former colonial subjects from the metropolitan United States. After showing how they changed the terms in which they spoke of both the Philippines and its people, I discuss how U.S. legislators used naturalization to counter both wartime anti-U.S. propaganda and perceived threats of a global race war and communist uprisings.

RIGHTS, NATURALIZATION, AND PHILIPPINE INDEPENDENCE

As the set date for Philippine independence neared, U.S. state actors faced questions about what the United States' relationship would be to its soon-to-be former colony. The Philippines played an important role in World War II. Filipino military personnel had loyally served, and the U.S. government had promised them rights in exchange for their service. At the same time, legislators and administrators worked to recover from the war, setting the terms for both the post-war metropolitan United States and its relationship to the world at large. When it came to considering the place of Filipino people in the United States, both administrators and legislators held to exclusionary impulses. Given the historical momentum and support for Filipino naturalization in exchange for loyal service, how Congress revoked these rights in the Rescission Act presents a puzzle. Considering the durable rights for soldiers discussed in Chapter 5, what happened to Filipinos seems aberrant. In light of the long history of administrative reclassifications of Filipinos as U.S. colonial subjects, however, the revocation of military benefits in exchange for service is less surprising. Similarly, the Luce–Celler Act seems like a departure from the efforts of persistent nativists to exclude Filipinos, which they finally accomplished through the 1934 Tydings–McDuffie Act. Given what it actually specified, however, the Luce–Celler Act was but a continuation of exclusionary momentum reformulated in light of new post-war global exigencies. Before discussing how administrators and legislators justified these two acts, I detail how Congress passed them.

Terminating Military Rights: The 1946 Rescission Act
As the war ended and the United States considered pending Philippine independence, members of the executive and legislative branches reevaluated the United States' obligations to Filipinos. As in the previous decades of rule, Democratic legislators and administrators responsible for what they saw as domestic and demographic questions tended to favor an end to colonial obligations. Although their numbers had dwindled since the early days of U.S. empire in the Philippines and through the project of Filipinization discussed in Part II, colonial officials in the executive branch and the Philippines argued for maintaining the colonial relationship. The promise of independence, however, gave them little ground for negotiation.

The first documented events to trigger a conversation about Filipino veterans' rights occurred in August 1945. Months before Congress considered the Rescission Act, Senator Carl Hayden (D-AZ) gathered information about enlistment, pay, and benefits for Filipino veterans. On August 27, 1945, Hayden wrote General Omar Bradley, administrator of Veterans Affairs, asking about

TABLE 6.1. U.S. Acts Related to the Naturalization and Rights of Filipinos

ACT OF U.S. CONGRESS	RELEVANT PROVISIONS	JUSTIFICATIONS
1946 Rescission Act	Filipinos who served in the Philippines during World War II reclassified as having not served in active duty, thus making them ineligible for any rights or benefits associated with their military service	Forthcoming independence Filipinos as noncitizens Unnecessary Foreign Aid
1946 Luce–Celler Act	Allows for the naturalization of Filipinos in the United States	Counterpropaganda

the obligations of the United States to Filipino veterans. He wanted to know the cost of awarding benefits, how many Filipinos had received them, if they were paid on a dollar or peso basis, and the effect of "complete independence" on benefits.[5] A month later, Hayden phoned Richard Ely, executive assistant to the high commissioner of the Philippines, inquiring about the pay of the Philippine Army and raising questions about the G.I. Bill.

As Hayden sought information about the rights of and remuneration for Filipino veterans, the executive branch also considered its future relationship to the Philippines. Administrators concerned with domestic matters, including the federal budget, favored more restrictions for Filipinos, while those concerned with international affairs advocated for continuity in U.S.–Philippine relations. In October 1945, President Harry Truman sent letters to eleven heads of state agencies, including the secretaries of War and the Treasury, the administrator of Veterans Affairs (VA), the U.S. high commissioner to the Philippines, and the attorney general. In his letters, Truman asked administrators for reports on the Philippine economy, trade, currency, politics, law enforcement, and military activities, and requested they propose plans for Philippine rehabilitation and independence.[6] Specifically regarding veterans, Truman asked the VA to "make a careful analysis of all phases of past and current benefits payable in the Philippine Islands to American and Filipino veterans" with "recommendations for any new legislation."[7]

Four months later in February 1946, after the first version of the bill was vetoed for reasons unrelated to Filipino veterans, Congress passed the Rescission Act.[8] It was the first major post-war budget bill. Containing only a paragraph on Filipino veterans, the act declared retroactively that the military service of the Philippine Commonwealth Army (which later became USAFFE), the guerrillas, and the New Scouts would not be considered service for the United States. Like with the Spooner Amendment to the 1901 budget bill discussed in Chapter 3, the Senate Appropriations Committee attached a rider related to Philippine affairs in a committee meeting before sending it to the floor for approval. Attaching a short paragraph to a large budget bill made it more likely to pass, as Congress was unlikely to stall decisions on the government's budget for the next year.

In the Senate Appropriations Committee meetings, most discussion of Filipino veterans happened off the record. On the record, however, Senators Kenneth McKellar (D-TN), Joseph Ball (R-MN), and Hayden of the

Appropriations Committee stated concerns about the appropriation for the Philippine Army. At this point in the meeting, Hayden, who had previously inquired into the eligibility of Filipino veterans for benefits, asked to go off the record. What happened in the off-the-record portion of the meeting is, of course, unknown. Perhaps prior to the Tydings–McDuffie Act and to World War II, Congress would have more outwardly debated this revocation. Indeed, the history discussed in Part II of this book suggests this. Now, however, with the war won and Philippine independence on the horizon, few protested the Rescission Act before it passed. High Commissioner of the Philippines Paul McNutt even noted that few knew Congress reclassified Filipino veterans in this manner.

As they prepared for independence, Philippine politicians also considered benefits for Filipino veterans. On November 25, 1945, after Truman vetoed the first version of the Rescission Act, Resident Commissioner of the Philippines Carlos Romulo reported to President Osmeña that he spoke with Senator McKellar, then chair of the Senate Appropriations Committee, about war damage payments for the Philippines and the G.I. Bill. Romulo hoped the Senate would continue to consider Filipino veterans as eligible for the G.I. Bill. Romulo recounted to Osmeña that McKellar told him, "The sense of the committee was against such action and that he [McKellar] could not see his way clear to recommending favorable action" on Filipino eligibility for military benefits. Attempting to secure the rights and benefits for Filipino veterans, Romulo spoke again with Senator Hayden and with the secretary of war, Robert Patterson. Romulo asked if, as part of the First Supplemental Surplus Appropriation Rescission Act of 1946, Congress could allocate some money to the Philippine Army for life insurance and military benefits. Romulo thought that this money could offset McKellar and the Appropriation Committee's interpretation that Filipinos were not eligible for benefits under the G.I. Bill.[9] Although Romulo knew that this would come with a reclassification of Filipino veterans, it remains unclear why Romulo would accept—or seemingly not find problematic—this recommendation of the Appropriations Committee.

By the terms of the act, Filipino veterans received only service-connected disability compensation, contract National Service Life Insurance, and hospital and outpatient treatment for service-connected disabilities, all paid at only half the rate for other veterans. Also unlike other veterans, Filipino veterans did not receive non-service-connected disability or death pensions, vocational rehabilitation and education, and VA medical care.[10] Families of Filipino veterans could still claim life insurance and pensions for disability or death to be paid at a rate of one Philippine peso per U.S. dollar. Since, at the time, the Philippine peso was valued at half the price of the dollar, they effectively received half the compensation (see Table 6.2).

TABLE **6.2.** Benefits Available to Filipino Veterans, Compared to Eligibility Rules.

	EXCLUSIVE TO U.S. CITIZEN?	EXCLUSIVE TO U.S. TERRITORY?	OLD SCOUTS	OTHER FILIPINO VETS
Pension	X	X	✓	½ rate
Insurance	X	X	✓	½ rate
Insurance premium guaranty	X	✓	✓	X
Retirement	X	X	✓	X
Outpatient treatment, appliances, etc.	X	X	✓	½ rate
Burial allowances	X	X	✓	X
Vocational rehabilitation, education, or training	X	✓	✓	X
Guaranty of loans for purchases of homes, farms, or business	X	✓	✓	X
Readjustment allowances	X	✓	✓	X
Hospital and domiciliary care	X	✓	✓	X
Non-service connected disability compensation	X	X	✓	X
Death pension	X	X	✓	X

Sources: Servicemen's Readjustment Act of 1944, 78 S. 1767, 58 Stat. 294, Chap: 268 (1944); Omar N. Bradley to Harry S. Truman. October 31, 1945. WHCF: OF 1055; Truman Papers, Truman Library, Independence, MO.; United States Retraining and Reemployment Administration. 1944. Your Rights and Benefits: A Handy Guide for Veterans of the Armed Forces and Their Dependents. Washington, D.C.: Office of War Mobilization.

Despite the actions of the legislative branch, some members of the executive branch considered extending aid to Filipino veterans. When President Truman signed the act, he also set up an Interdepartmental Committee on Philippine Veterans Affairs, to be staffed by Secretary of War Robert Patterson, VA Administrator Omar Bradley, and U.S. High Commissioner to the Philippines Paul McNutt. Truman requested they provide a study "of a program of benefits for Philippine Army veterans, following in general along the lines of our G.I. Bill of Rights benefits, but adapted to the special conditions found in the Philippines."[11] Truman differentiated the Philippines from the United States, suggesting that he believed that people in the metropole could be treated differently from those in the colony.

The act cemented differential treatment. Although Omar Bradley, writing for the committee, conceded that Filipinos could receive certain benefits, he did not suggest (re)extending the G.I. Bill to the Philippines. Instead, he recommended easing the restrictions on confirming service for disability and death pensions, which the 1946 Rescission Act already had. He also advocated for hospitalization and medical treatment at the expense of the U.S. government, provisions for burial allowances, and a U.S. flag for burial.[12] The option to be buried with a U.S. flag suggests a partial acknowledgment of Filipino service for the United States, albeit one that was only rewarded after death. Thus, it was with little fanfare that Congress, with the help of the administrator of Veterans Affairs, reclassified Filipino veterans as having not served in active duty, making them ineligible for the expedited path to naturalization and social welfare benefits promised to them prior to and during World War II. In the post-war era, the United States would owe nothing to loyal Filipino veterans.

Limiting Naturalization: The Luce–Celler Act
While forthcoming independence prompted U.S. state actors to break promises to Filipino veterans, it also raised questions about the eligibility of all Filipinos to migrate to and naturalize in the United States. For the past twelve years, from 1934 to 1946, Congress classified Filipinos as aliens for the purposes of migration, treating them more like excluded Asians than colonial subjects. As discussed in Chapter 4, in 1934, nativist legislators took advantage of plans for Philippine independence to exclude Filipinos. Congress also specified that when the United States eventually withdrew sovereignty, "the immigration laws of the United States (including all the provisions thereof relating to persons ineligible to citizenship) shall apply to persons who were

born in the Philippine Islands to the same extent as with other foreign coun-
tries."[13] Which foreign countries Congress referred to, however, was not clear.
After all, as Chapter 4 showed, Filipinos were treated in a way that was not
the same as either Asians or Southeastern Europeans. According to the 1934
Tydings–McDuffie Act, which set the terms for independence in 1946, Con-
gress considered Filipinos aliens. Although fifty Filipinos could migrate to the
United States each year, whether they would be eligible for naturalization after
Philippine independence remained an open question.

On the heels of the 1943 Magnuson Act, which lifted Chinese exclusion
and allowed for the migration and naturalization of Chinese people, legislators considered possibilities for Filipino naturalization. In November 1944,
the House Committee on Immigration and Naturalization considered six
bills for Filipino naturalization proposed by Representatives Marcantonio
(American Labor–NY), Joseph Farrington (Nonvoting R-HI), Norris Poulson
(R-CA), Jennings Randolph (D-WV), Harry Sheppard (D-CA), and Dan R.
McGehee (D-MS).[14] Whereas in the early 1940s, most West Coast and Southern representatives opposed Filipino naturalization, now either Californians
or Southerners proposed two-thirds of the bills for naturalization. Alone, this
suggests a changing tide on immigration and naturalization restriction. At
the same time, legislators proposed these bills after the exclusionary precedent
set by the 1934 Tydings–McDuffie Act, by which the Philippines would soon be
independent. No longer did nativist politicians worry about the legal inclusion
of Filipinos as U.S. colonial subjects. Likewise, after the 1943 Magnuson Act—
which created a symbolic opening to Asian migration—neither did legislators
think that the immigration and naturalization of one hundred Chinese or
Filipino individuals a year would pose as big a risk to the United States as the
external threats on the global stage.

The bills proposed in 1944 varied in the scope to which Filipinos would
be eligible for naturalization, ranging from more liberal measures for the
naturalization of any Filipino to more restrictive ones that provided only for
Filipinos who were veterans of World War I. On the one hand, Marcantonio, Farrington, Randolph, and McGehee proposed the more liberal bills. U.S.
representatives from colonial territories connected the concerns of racial inequality faced by the Chinese to the status of Filipinos, suggesting that the
naturalization provisions for the Chinese could be a model for Filipinos. For
example, as the House delegate from the Territory of Hawai'i, Farrington

noted that "all through the debate on the Chinese exclusion enormous emphasis was given to the treating [*sic*] of the Chinese people on the basis of equality." Regarding the 100,000 Filipinos in the United States, many of whom "can
not [*sic*] become naturalized," Farrington thought that "some of the same considerations" prevailed.[15] Resident Commissioner of the Philippines Joaquin
M. Elizalde also referenced the Magnuson Act for Chinese naturalization as
opening a pathway for Filipino naturalization.[16] On the other hand, the two
representatives from California, Sheppard and Poulson, wrote bills that only
gave special rights to those who had served in the military. In other words,
even as legislators from states that historically favored restriction became
more liberal in their stance on Filipino migration, they remained more exclusionary than other members of Congress. And even while some favored martial citizenship over more inclusionary possibilities, no legislator at the time
created pathways to inclusion for Filipino veterans of World War II. Despite
the number of proposals, the House did not vote on the issue before Congress
closed for the year.

On January 4, 1945, McGehee reintroduced his bill. As a Southern Democrat
who opposed the naturalization of other Asians, it is unclear why McGehee
supported Filipino naturalization. Jane Hong suggests that McGehee may have
taken a personal interest in the islands after attending the 1935 inauguration of
the Philippine Commonwealth and participating in a 1944 to 1946 Congressional
Rehabilitation Commission delegation to the Philippines.[17] McGehee's bill proposed to amend Section 303 of the 1940 Nationality Act to read:

> The right to become a naturalized citizen under the provisions of this Act
> shall extend only to white persons, persons of African nativity or descent,
> and the descendants of races indigenous to the Western Hemisphere, and
> Chinese persons or persons of Chinese descent, and Filipino persons or
> persons of Filipino descent.[18]

The bill also amended Section 324, pertaining to the naturalization of people
who served in the U.S. Armed Forces. The original 1940 act read: "A person,
including a native-born Filipino, who has served honorably at any time."[19]
The new bill struck out the words, including "a native-born Filipino," so that
Filipinos would no longer be a separate clause. There was widespread support from administrative offices, including the Departments of the Interior,
State, and Justice; the Immigration and Naturalization Service; the Attorney

General; and the Bureau of the Budget, for the bill, and it passed in the House by voice vote and with no debate on April 17, 1945.[20]

In the same way that calls for racial equity and preparations for Philippine independence catalyzed a reevaluation of Filipinos' status, so too did anti-colonial nationalist movements in India prompt U.S. legislators to reconsider the eligibility of their ally's colonial subjects.[21] After McGehee's bill for Filipino naturalization, the House considered a related bill concerning the naturalization of Asian Indians proposed by Representative Emanuel Celler (D-NY) on June 20, 1945. Representative Clare Boothe Luce (R-CT) also proposed a similar bill for the naturalization of Asian Indians.[22] As Rick Baldoz notes, Asian Indians' political standing "as British imperial subjects paralleled the situation of Filipinos in some important ways. Both populations were called into military service by colonial authorities during the war, and both Indians and Filipinos earned praise from Allied leaders for their valor on the battlefield."[23] Like the McGehee Bill, proposals for Indian naturalization were also part of an attempt to demonstrate that the United States had disavowed exclusionary racism.

Whereas there was little recorded opposition to the bill for Filipino naturalization on the floor of the House, there was especially vehement opposition to the naturalization of Asian Indians. Leo Allen (D-LA), for example, cited concerns about upsetting the U.S. and British alliance. He argued that, as British colonial subjects, Indians could not be treated in the same way as the Chinese. Representative Edward McCowen (R-OH) warned that this would only open the gates to more repeals of Asian exclusion, and John Murdock (D-AZ, at large) argued that the influx of Indians could threaten jobs for returning soldiers.[24] On October 10, 1945, the bill initially failed to pass, with 83 yeas and 207 nays. After attempts to stall the bill—primarily by Southern Democrats including McGehee (the sponsor of the bill for Philippine naturalization)—it passed later that day by voice vote in the House. Yeas and nays were not reported.[25]

Meanwhile, the McGehee Bill for Filipino naturalization, which had passed in the House and had the support of President Truman, faced opposition in the Senate. Although not as pronounced as in the 1920s and 1930s, sectional divides remained. Southern Democrats James Eastland (MS) and Richard Russell (GA) of the Committee on Immigration stalled the bill. Concerned, President Truman considered incorporating Filipino naturalization into a bill for Philippine trade (discussed in the next chapter). Congress, however, did not take this route. Instead, building on the historical precedent of bifurcating foreign and domestic aspects of U.S. imperial rule as discussed in Part II, legislators separated economic and social issues, seeking to include the Philippine territory but exclude the Filipino people.[26] Because both the bills for Indian and Filipino naturalization amended the same section of the 1940 Nationality Act, Senator Ball asked they be combined.[27] In June 1946, the Senate Immigration Committee incorporated the language from the McGehee Bill into the Luce–Celler Bill. The McGehee and Luce–Celler bills passed on June 14, 1946, in the Senate by voice vote.

When viewed in light of prior restrictions to Filipino migration and naturalization, the Luce–Celler Act seems in line with more liberal post–World War II reforms. By the terms of the act, Congress considered Filipinos—regardless of military status—as eligible for naturalization. Even as the 1946 Luce–Celler Act appeared to open immigration to Filipinos, when viewed alongside the history of Asian exclusion, colonial migration, and the 1946 Rescission Act, the act was little more than a symbolic opening that served the United States' geostrategic interests in the post-war era. Prior to the Luce–Celler Act, as U.S. colonial subjects (unlike Asian Indians or Chinese), Filipinos did not face the same restrictions to migration and naturalization. As a result of decades of open migration, as of 1940, there were 83,677 Filipinos in the continental United States.[28] Moreover, the United States recruited Filipinos to serve in the U.S. military. By 1945, there were at least 200,000 Filipino veterans like Samuel Molina who were eligible for naturalization. After Truman signed the Luce–Celler Act, however, a mere one hundred, or 0.05 percent of the veterans that were eligible prior to the Rescission Act, could naturalize.[29] Whereas in World War II, Congress saw Filipino military personnel as more deserving and promised them rights in exchange for loyal service, after the war, the U.S. government broke promises and decoupled loyalty from rights. By lumping Filipinos in with Asian Indians in a bill that was modeled on the naturalization of the Chinese, U.S. state actors both defended against accusations of racism and erased U.S. colonial ties.

In discussions over Filipinos' rights and naturalization, the promise of Philippine independence constrained formerly imperialist and interventionist state actors' arguments for continuing the colonial relationship. Meanwhile, U.S. legislators from historically nativist states and those concerned with white hegemony at home built on the precedent set in the 1934 Tydings–McDuffie Act. Filipinos were aliens. Legislators continued to take restrictive stances and advocate for racial exclusion. Although they spoke of Filipinos' loyalty in the war, state actors did not abandon their vulgar racism. They continued to see Filipinos as inferior outsiders.

EMPTY INVOCATIONS OF LOYALTY

Prior to and during World War II, U.S. state actors in favor of U.S. intervention invoked loyalty to justify special rights for Filipino military personnel. After the war, members of both the executive and legislative branches continued to see Filipinos as loyal, but this loyalty did not translate into rights. Concealing the vocabulary of vulgar racism, state actors adapted the way they spoke about Filipinos to fit the United States' strategic interests. For example, President Truman referred to how Filipinos fought for a "common cause" during the war, and many legislators and administrators subsequently invoked this phrase.[30] Members of the U.S. government also cited Filipinos' loyalty and bravery in the face of the Japanese invasion. A little over a month after the Rescission Act passed, on March 25, 1946, Senator Hayden referenced the "long-standing friendship between the American and the Filipino people," and that he had "no doubt about the intention of the Congress of the United States to recognize the loyalty of the Filipino people during the war with Japan." He continued, saying that Filipinos "remained loyal to the Government of the United States" and that "the active assistance rendered by soldiers of the Philippine army and members of the organized Philippine guerillas greatly facilitated the reoccupation of the islands with material saving of lives of American soldiers and a reduction in the cost of war."[31] Although he never questioned Filipinos' loyalty to the United States, Hayden also worked to revoke rights from Filipino veterans. In the post-war era, U.S. state actors decoupled loyalty from rights.

As U.S. Congress broke its promise, Filipino and U.S. colonial state actors continued to emphasize Filipino loyalty. Although they were unsuccessful in their pleas, they asked the United States to honor its promises to Filipino World War II veterans. In a letter to President Truman, High Commissioner of the Philippines Paul McNutt emphasized that "[benefits for Filipino veterans] cannot be considered a special grant to the Philippines as a nation, but is rather part of our national obligation to all our veterans who served so nobly in this war. . . .The Philippine units, especially the guerillas, saw more desperate combat duty than almost any of our others."[32] McNutt also acknowledged how Filipinos' dedication to the United States served the U.S. goals of expanding democracy: "The loyalty and sacrifice of the Filipinos in the war which was more ours than theirs gave us the opportunity to create an era of good feeling and [an] outpost of Americanism in the Far East." In part because they were loyal, Filipinos were deserving of the promises made to them as faithful dependents. McNutt cited Filipinos' participation on behalf of the United States in World War II and how the United States "failed miserably" in protecting them "from external aggression." Filipinos, however, "have taken it with unusual stoicism, loyalty, and good grace" and were crucial to the war effort, McNutt argued.[33] He not only highlighted Filipinos' allegiance but he also favored an interpretation of colonial policy and responsibility that emphasized U.S. obligation to its subjects in the Commonwealth.

While Congress and the VA revoked Filipino veterans' social welfare benefits and their expedited path to naturalization, Filipinos writ large seemed to gain rights in exchange for loyalty. U.S. legislators invoked loyalty as they justified the symbolic extension of naturalization rights. Representative Bertrand W. Gearhart (R-CA) elevated Filipinos' loyalty as colonial subjects to put them above other Asians, asking "if we should extend this right to enter the United States to the Chinese and to the Hindus and at the same time withhold it from the Filipinos, who have lived under our flag for 47 years and who have been loyal to our country through the war which has just been brought to a victorious conclusion?"[34] Gearhart suggested Filipinos were more loyal and deserving of the right to naturalize. Representative McGehee, sponsor of the bill on Filipino naturalization, argued that Filipinos demonstrated "their loyalty and their desire to fight alongside" the United States.[35] Representative Walter Judd (R-MN) similarly noted that Filipinos "stood by us in one of the finest demonstrations of loyalty the world has ever seen."[36]

In the shifting tide of World War II and Filipinos' service to the United States, even formerly nativist state actors supported Filipino naturalization in exchange for loyalty. In a report to accompany the naturalization bill, Representative John Lesinski, Sr. (D-MI), chair of the Committee on Immigration and Naturalization, wrote that the United States "owes to these people—our own nationals—who have been loyal to us in every respect and who have fought so courageously against a common enemy, the Japanese, the right to become citizens of the United States." He added that the committee hoped the bill for naturalization would be "construed as waiving racial barriers." [37] In a subsequent report, Representative Samuel Dickstein (D-CA) of the Committee on Immigration and Naturalization who had previously supported Filipino repatriation, also noted the "peculiar political status" of Filipinos, citing that they have been nationals of the United States, something between alien and citizen. He copied Lesinski's language about the U.S. duty to Filipinos.[38] Republicans and Democrats both characterized Filipinos as loyal subjects and, on this basis, supported the Luce–Celler Act.

In addition, the secretary of the interior and the directors of the INS and the Congressional Budget Office cited Filipinos' status as nationals and their loyalty to the United States as rationales for granting them the right to naturalize.[39] For example, Secretary of State Edward R. Stettinius wrote Representative Dickstein: "the Filipino people have long shown their attachments to the ideals and principles of the United States." He continued that "they have a long and unbroken record of loyalty. . . .[T]hey have valiantly resisted the invaders of the Philippines and are continuing to do so." He concluded he could think of no reason why Filipinos should not be made eligible for naturalization.[40]

While more state actors thought of Filipinos as loyal and lauded them for their accomplishments, speaking of Filipinos' loyalty did not mean that state actors abandoned their vulgar racism after the war. Invocations of loyalty did not translate to anti-discriminatory or inclusionary practices. In the case of the Luce–Celler Act, legislators spoke in both politely and vulgarly racist terms. Members of the Committee on Immigration and Naturalization complained about Filipinos' nonwhite status and moral standing in the country. When questioning Richard Ely of the Department of the Interior, Representative Dickstein objected to the department's proposal to increase the number of Filipino naturalizations. Echoing his arguments in the 1920s and 1930s, Dickstein stated that under the 1934 Tydings–McDuffie Act, Filipinos "must comply with other requirements of admittance, such as moral turpitude and good character and the like." He continued, "They are ineligible for citizenship," and should not be "subject to the same qualifying provisions as a European."[41] Representative Allen, who had opposed Chinese naturalization, asked of Filipinos, "Have they been law abiding, or do they have trouble in the courts?" His colleague Representative John R. Phillips (R-CA) responded, "Not more than the white people," to which Allen clarified, "Not more than our own people?" Phillips rejoined, "Not more than our own people."[42] Phillips, when pushed by Allen, compared Filipinos' good moral behavior to that of white Americans, suggesting they were no different.

This did not seem to satisfy Allen, however. He turned to question Diosdado Yap (a Filipino living in the United States who testified in front of the House Committee on Immigration and Naturalization) on where Filipinos fit into commonsense racial categories of the time. Allen said he did not know "from what racial stock" Filipinos were. Yap replied that Filipinos had been considered of several "races" of the time—"Mongoloid, Caucassoit [sic], and the Negroid." He stated, however, that Filipinos were of the "Malay" or brown race. But, he concluded, "for American interpretation we [Filipinos] are considered as white men" and not of the "Mongolian" race. Dickstein chimed in, saying he did not understand. When Yap attempted to clarify, saying that Filipinos belong to the brown race, Allen again asked to clarify, "And you do not belong to the Negro race?" Yap said no, and Allen asked again, repeating the question. After Yap again said no, Allen moved on to ask about the connections between Filipinos and Japanese. Allen asked, "Now do not get offended, but what is the racial connection, if any, between the Filipino and the Japanese?" Yap responded, "There is no racial connection whatsoever." Allen seemed incredulous and asked again, "No racial connection?" And Yap answered, "Except that we eat rice and the Japanese eat rice. Racially there is no similarity or connection." Allen asked again, "You have no common origin?" And Yap insisted, "We have no common origin."[43] For Allen, like his predecessors concerned with domestic white hegemony in the early 1900s, it was important to figure out how to classify Filipinos—were they like Black Americans or the enemy Japanese? Yap's reply, on the other hand, reflected the plastic and polyvalent understandings of race at the time.

Limited naturalization may seem to be an improvement from the vulgar racist characterizations of the earlier decades, but loyalty did not translate into expanded rights as expected. In the Rescission Act, Congress broke their promise and excluded Filipinos. In the context of imminent Philippine independence, loyalty became an empty invocation used alongside both the revocation of rights and the greater limitations to immigration and naturalization.

AMBIGUITY AND DISGUISING IMPERIAL RELATIONS

Ambiguity characterized four decades of rule. Prior to the debates over the 1946 Rescission Act, ambiguity helped U.S. state actors disguise the hierarchical nature of U.S.–Philippine relations. As independence drew near, U.S. state actors made symbolic nods to Filipinos' loyalty in war. Under the guise of naturalization and forthcoming independence, they clarified the U.S. classification of Filipinos and excluded them from the metropole. Ambiguity helped the United States abandon its obligation to colonial subjects.

The lack of clarity about Filipino veterans' eligibility stemmed from the U.S. Supreme Court's ambiguous decision in *Downes*. Equivocal definitions and administrative discretion shaped how the United States promised and administered rights to Filipinos. When Senator Hayden inquired into Filipino veterans' rights, colonial administrators could not provide straightforward answers. On October 3, 1945, Executive Assistant to the High Commissioner of the Philippines Richard Ely replied to Hayden's inquiry about Filipino veterans' eligibility for the 1944 G.I. Bill. Ely noted that the definition of the United States in the 1944 G.I. Bill needed clarification. He was not sure whether the Philippines was included. Ely explained that according to the 1916 Jones Act, the United States would include the Philippines only if an act of Congress specified the Philippines. Because the 1944 G.I. Bill did not name the Philippines as part of the United States, it was possible the United States could deny Filipino veterans educational and unemployment benefits. Ely noted, however, that Filipino veterans may still be eligible. If they studied in the United States or if the Philippine Bureau of Education could designate Philippine schools as qualified for providing education, then Filipinos could claim benefits. Ely also noted that the disbursement of educational loans was under the discretion of the administrator of the VA. Ely emphasized that, as a whole, "the extent to which the bill is applicable in the Philippines is so unclear."[44]

At the same time, ambiguity gave state actors the opportunity to revoke the rights of loyal subjects. When it came time to fulfill their promise to Filipinos, U.S. state actors instead obscured their colonial obligations. Within the flexible U.S. racial-imperial grammar, they reimagined the relationship between the United States and the Philippines in new terms that hid the history of colonialism. In light of forthcoming independence, legislators and administrators redefined the United States' relationship to the Philippines and its people. They argued that the Philippines was not a colony, claiming that Filipinos were neither citizens nor entitled to equal treatment by the United States. Instead, legislators and the administrator of the VA cast Filipinos as possible beneficiaries of U.S. assistance. They argued that Filipino veterans' rights were merely cumbersome and expensive foreign aid.

The Philippines as an Independent Country

While Ely emphasized the current unclear status of the Philippines as a U.S. colony, others equivocated less. On October 31, 1945, General Omar Bradley, administrator of Veterans Affairs, replied to Truman's request for recommendations on legislation pertaining to U.S. and Filipino veterans in the Philippines. Unlike Ely's reply to Hayden, Bradley stated that under current laws, Filipinos in active service would be eligible for benefits.[45] Their colonial status was not an issue. Nevertheless, in a section of his memo to Truman titled "Effect of Complete Independence of Philippine Islands Upon Various Types of Benefits Now or Hereafter Awarded to Philippine Nationals," Bradley wrote that after independence, certain benefits "would no longer be available to veterans, or to veterans not American citizens, residing in the Philippine Islands after independence is established." Thus, Bradley suggested that the United States and the Philippines should agree that the soon-to-be independent Philippines would take responsibility for these benefits. Bradley did not make a similar recommendation for any other colonial subjects, such as Puerto Ricans or foreign nationals.[46] Bradley constructed only the Philippines as responsible for its citizens. He took advantage of a change in the boundaries of the United States to reconfigure rights available to Filipinos.

After Congress passed the Rescission Act, U.S. state actors continued to justify limiting rights for Filipinos. In hearings over a Second Supplemental Surplus Appropriation Rescission Act, Senator Hayden wrongly emphasized that the Philippines was, at the time of debate over the First Rescission Act, its own independent country: "It was the view of the [Appropriations] committee that the approximately 200,000 Filipinos who first and last served in that army [USAFFE] did so because they fervently desired freedom for their country and not with the idea of acquiring the right to go to another country," by which Hayden meant the United States. In this view, Filipinos fought to serve their country, which Hayden cast as independent from the United States. The Philippines, however, did not gain its independence until four months after the 1946 Rescission Act.

Filipino Veterans as Noncitizens

Filipinos' unclear status allowed U.S. legislators to revoke their rights. Building on the reclassification of the Philippines as independent, senators also recast Filipinos as noncitizens. This line of reasoning relied on the shifting geopolitical arrangement between metropole and colony. Independence made it easier to think of Filipinos as foreign people to whom the United States had no obligation. Nevertheless, the United States made the same promises of citizenship rights and benefits in exchange for service to citizens, aliens, and colonial subjects alike. When discussing activities of the U.S. Army in Germany, Senator McKellar commented that the United States was "paying them [Filipinos] the same salaries as the Americans. They are not American citizens at all. They are Filipinos." In effect, based on their status as non-U.S. citizens, McKellar argued that Filipinos were not entitled to the rights promised to them. McKellar's interpretation emphasized Filipinos' status as noncitizens over their colonial status. For nearly fifty years, politicians like McKellar relied on this well-established logic that bifurcated colony from metropole, claiming that Filipinos were not deserving of rights. Although the post–World War II era seemed more liberal, these exclusionary logics persisted.

While U.S. logics for exclusion had long endured, it is possible that Filipino politicians, anticipating Philippine independence, did not want Filipino veterans like Samuel Molina to receive benefits and leave the Philippines. In the decision of *Matter of Naturalization of 68 Filipino War Veterans* (1975), in which Filipino veterans claimed their right to naturalize, the U.S. District Court for the Northern District of California wrote that "apparently fearful that large numbers of Filipinos would be naturalized and emigrate to the United States on the eve of independence, an unidentified official of the Philippine Government conveyed to the United States Department of State the Philippine Government's concern that Filipinos who had always been domiciled in the Philippines were being naturalized by Vice Consul Ennis."[47] The same decision notes, "The concern of the Philippine Government was not made a fact of record. Indeed, neither the President of the Philippine Commonwealth nor his Government expressed any official opinion on the subject."[48] After the act passed, Filipino elites remained relatively silent on benefits. Although forthcoming Philippine independence may have affected the decision to revoke military benefits, there is no clear record that Filipino concerns motivated the revocation.[49]

On the contrary, Filipino statesmen did not see Filipino emigration to the United States as incompatible with Philippine independence. Filipino leaders "championed U.S. citizenship legislation so eagerly during World War II: they saw these efforts as part of their preparations for Philippine independence."[50] Politicians like Quezon and Francisco Varona, the labor assistant to the Philippine resident commissioner, argued that Filipino naturalization was a way to strengthen relationships between Filipinos in the United States and the Philippine government. On the one hand, remittances were an important part of the Philippine post-war economy, and securing the citizenship of Filipinos in the United States could help this effort.[51] On the other, Quezon, Romulo, and Osmeña all saw Filipinos in the United States as an important constituency from which to garner support in elections back home.[52] The anticipated change in U.S.–Philippine relations, then, did not motivate Filipino actors to advocate for any changes in Filipino naturalization in the United States.

Rights as Unnecessary Foreign Aid

Because the VA and Congress interpreted U.S. colonial policy in a way that erased the colonial status of the Philippines and Filipinos, U.S. politicians could argue that the expenditure of veterans benefits for Filipinos was too high and cumbersome for the U.S. government. Before Congress passed the Rescission Act, Senator Hayden worried about spending for the Philippine Army and guerrillas. He acknowledged that there "may be sound political reasons for keeping the Philippine Army and the Guerrillas on American pay rolls." At the same time, "if members of either of those organizations are entitled to the full benefits of the existing pension laws and the 'G.I. Bill of Rights,' the American Government has assumed a very large obligation."[53] General Richards of the War Department also confirmed that Senator Hayden did not support making funds available for the Philippine Army.[54]

Other U.S. officials concerned with post-war spending, including the administrator of Veterans Affairs, asserted that the United States had, at best, a charitable duty and, at worst, no obligation to the Philippines. General Bradley of the VA suggested that the United States unburden itself from the financial obligation to "the large number of Filipinos who are serving in the armed forces of the United States during the present war." The "large number of Filipinos," however, amounted to only 1.4 percent of the total number serving in World War II. According to these numbers, the total cost of the Philippine cases was estimated at $3 billion. Bradley offered a second option to Truman, suggesting that if the Philippine government would not take responsibility for these veterans' benefits, the United States could pay nationals of the Philippines on a basis other than the dollar, such as the peso. This could amount to 40 million pesos for seventy-five years, which would be $20 million 1946 dollars.[55] Notably, Bradley's first estimate does not correspond with the amount of the second: $3 billion for the United States over fifty years versus $20 million at the peso rate over seventy-five years. Later, in a letter to Truman, High Commissioner to the Philippines Paul V. McNutt stated that this reduced rate of paying benefits would be acceptable to Filipinos.[56]

McKellar also raised alarm at the potential cost of providing for Filipinos. Likely referring to Bradley's first estimate, McKellar noted that "it is estimated it will cost us before we get through something between two and three billion dollars." He continued, increasing the projected cost of supporting Filipino veterans: "We have to feed them and clothe them and everything else. I don't know whether that is for all time, as long as they live, or not. We haven't got the total yet, but it may cost us 20 billion before we get through. So it is incumbent upon those of us who are Americans and who have a regard, and some of us have the highest regard for the American Government and the American people, to look after their interests."[57] McKellar's budgetary concerns relied not only on imprecise and conflicting estimates from the VA but also on half-truths about the status of the Philippine Army and in effect demoted them to mercenaries fighting for a foreign government. As discussed in Chapter 5, however, Filipinos were sworn in as the Philippine Commonwealth Army under the service of the United States and then called to service by Roosevelt in 1941.

In his letter to President Truman, Bradley emphasized the additional administrative challenges to providing benefits to Filipino veterans. He noted that the VA could not send enough American citizens to U.S. VA hospitals in the Philippines. Bradley argued that there were "impossible burdens," making the VA "physically unable" to provide benefits to Filipino World War II veterans. He told Truman that providing for the Philippine veterans in addition to the nearly twenty million veterans of all wars under the G.I. Bill would be a burden. The VA, however, already had an infrastructure, including offices in the Philippines. And, together with the Department of State, the VA worked to provide benefits in other locations abroad.[58]

Not only did state actors raise alarm that administering benefits to Filipinos would be costly and burdensome, but some also invoked racial logics of dependency to argue that the money was better spent elsewhere. According to Senator Hayden, the U.S. government should adjust for the difference in cost of living and "help the Filipino people to help themselves." Hayden continued, distinguishing between the costs of Philippine rehabilitation and benefits paid "in cash" to Filipino veterans. He stated, "I am sure it is better to spend any equal sum of money, for example, on improving roads and port facilities. What the Filipino veteran needs is steady employment rather than to depend for his living on a monthly payment sent from the United States." Moreover, Hayden claimed that the G.I. Bill was "intended to benefit an American who served in the armed forces and who, upon his discharge from the service, returned to civil life in the United States, where American standards of living prevail."[59] Hayden argued that a Filipino veteran did not need as much as an American. Rather than providing the promised social welfare benefits to Filipinos, he preferred spending for national reconstruction that would put Filipinos to work. Like politicians who argued against Black and Mexican people receiving New Deal–era domestic social welfare benefits,[60] Hayden saw Filipinos as potential (nonwhite) dependents.

Democrats in Congress and the administrator of Veterans Affairs reframed rights as unnecessary foreign aid. They relied on the Philippines' projected independence to revoke benefits and dismantle the rights of Filipino World War II veterans. Anticipating a change in the colonial relationship, they treated colonial subjects as outsider aliens to whom the state owed nothing. They redefined Filipino personnel as non-military. By redefining territorial, civic, and military status, U.S. state actors reframed colonial mutual obligation as an administratively cumbersome expense. At the end of the war and on the verge of Philippine independence, politicians and administrators rethought a core principle of citizenship—mutual obligation—to exclude Filipinos from the metropole.

SYMBOLIC INCLUSION AS COUNTERPROPAGANDA

In addition to invoking Filipino loyalty without material reward and disguising imperial relations, U.S. state actors used naturalization laws to manage the United States' global reputation. As they broke promises to Filipino veterans, they sought to maintain U.S. white hegemony at home and abroad. Legislators believed that the United States' immigration and naturalization law could both limit nonwhite migration and signal that the United States disavowed racism. They hoped that symbolic acts of inclusion would minimize threats of peasant, anti-colonial, and communist uprisings. Legislators worked to translate their vulgar racism to new terms that, on their surface, eschewed racism, secured exclusion from the metropole, and strengthened the United States' geopolitical position in the world.

Although she was a sponsor of the bill, Representative Luce invoked nativist logics for exclusion, which she re-signified as economic rather than racial concerns. Luce said that she "would be the first to protest against people from any nation, of any color, coming here in such numbers, as to lower our living standards and weaken our own culture." She cautioned that Asian migrants "in too great numbers" "may undermine our way of life, our living standards, our form of religion." She qualified her statements, however, as not being based on color or skin discrimination but that "the proper reason for keeping orientals [*sic*] out in great numbers is because of those economic facts, but it is certainly improper to keep them out altogether, simply because they are orientals."[61] Like nativists before her, Luce concealed logics of racial fitness behind economic justifications for exclusion, or in this case, very limited incorporation.

Attempting to assuage her colleagues' fears that allowing for naturalization of one hundred Indians a year (and by extension of Filipinos) would threaten U.S. norms, Luce argued that not all those who sought naturalization from Asia would be Asian. She stated, "The instant bill does not change by one single syllable the number of people who can enter this country under the immigration laws. It merely says that of the quota of 100 persons for India a portion of that number may be filled by native Indians, and that all of it does not have to be filled by European people." Representative Celler supported Luce on this point. He also suggested that the people naturalizing from India might not actually be Indians, but could be "English, Dutch, or French, or other nationals who had been born in India."[62] In other words, Celler and Luce claimed that allowing for migration from India (as well as China and the Philippines) would not mean that masses of Asians would migrate and naturalize in the United States.

In addition to expressing concern over the inclusion of nonwhite people at home, U.S. legislators spoke of both Japan and communism in Asia as racial threats abroad. If the latter were allowed to persist, then the United States could lose influence in the region. Representative Justin L. Johnson (R-CA) hoped that the Luce–Celler Act could help the United States maintain global white supremacy. He stated "that there might be another great war brewing in the future." He recalled, "We can see what Japan tried to do; she tried to build up a greater Asia. Her program was a racial program to build up the black man and the yellow man and unite him against the white man." Although Japan's program failed, Johnson warned that "it is taking root in Java and in Sumatra and Indochina and other places. It is the seed of revolution and war against the white man and against imperialism." Johnson argued that the Luce–Celler Act would help avoid the coming of a "great racial war." He was especially concerned that "the white race constitutes a very small fraction of the people on the earth," noting that "they would have no chance against a billion or two billion black, yellow, and brown men if they were properly armed and industrialized." This would be "the white man's last stand," a "deadly, more bitter, more vicious" war. To avoid a racial war in which white people would surely lose, the United States must "plant the seed of friendship among 450,000,000 people in India, among 400,000,000 people in China, among several hundred million people in the islands out in the Pacific." "By allowing a very small quota to enter our country," he said that the United States can demonstrate "that we are not discriminating against people because of their color, that we have no hostility toward them on account of their race." Representative Johnson continued that U.S. rule of the Philippines was "a model every country that has an imperial system ought to follow."[63]

Even former nativists worried that Japan's propaganda impacted the United States' reputation in Asia and the world. In 1944, Representative Richard J. Welch (D-CA)—who famously opposed Filipino migration, settlement, and naturalization in the 1920s and 1930s—remarked that "the Filipinos themselves, as a whole are good people, but they are highly emotional and are therefore more subject to propaganda influences." He continued, "I refer to the fact that the Japanese are a cunning and resourceful people. It will be recalled that it was only a short time after they overran the Philippine Islands that they were successful in setting up a propaganda government."[64] Through legislation, Representative Welch hoped that the U.S. government could "minimize" these threats to the United States' reputation. Many members of Congress justified the repeal of Filipino exclusion—or the creation of possibilities for inclusion—in relation to global concerns about peace and security.

U.S. legislators' concerns about their reputation were well-founded. Not only had Japanese propaganda raised questions about the United States' commitment to racial equality, so too was communist peasant resistance on the rise in the Philippines. To maintain U.S. influence and combat the rise of communism, legislators argued that the United States should allow for the naturalization of Asians. Representative Noah M. Mason (R-IL) claimed that the United States' reputation and position suffered in Asia. Speaking on Asian Indian naturalization, he stated, "We all know that Stalin is seeking a controlling influence in both Europe and Asia. We all know the effort Stalin is making today, through his Communist agents all over the world, to undermine MacArthur and to weaken Uncle Sam's position Asia." Mason continued, "We must do what we can to offset his efforts" in both China and India.[65] In this light, the Luce–Celler Act was less about opening the United States' borders and more about managing the United States' hegemony against communist threats and Japanese propaganda.

Filipinos suggested that naturalization rights could garner support for the United States in Asia. Diosdado Yap entreated legislators to consider the United States' reputation. Referring to "the Philippine–American experiment," he noted that "many have viewed it as a model for post-war international relations between nations and their colonies." Yap continued, "If that model is to succeed most effectively, certainly the nationals of the Philippines must be allowed to become citizens of America."[66] In short, he argued that allowing Filipinos to become citizens was tied to the U.S. global project of promoting peace and democracy in the post-war era. Yap also drew attention Filipinos' colonial status, explaining that they were also treated in a manner unlike white or Black people in the country. According to Yap, Filipinos' "legal and social status" was "most uncertain."[67] Yap hoped, at this critical juncture of Philippine independence, that Congress would allow their former colonial subjects—many of whom had long been residents of the United States and all of whom owed allegiance to the United States—to naturalize.[68] Yap and others hoped that the ambiguous treatment of Filipinos could come to an end through newly proposed legislation on Filipino naturalization post–World War II.

Philippine Commonwealth President Osmeña also argued that Filipino naturalization could support the United States' reputational goals. He noted that faced with World War II's "conflicting ideologies," as a world leader, the

United States needed to demonstrate "something unequivocal and definite in the direction of freedom." He suggested that "the peoples of Asia, who have been searching for justice and freedom, will find consolation, hope, and encouragement in this noble action of the American people." Osmeña argued that U.S. policy toward the Philippines could show Asia and the Americas "the workability of the principles of the Atlantic Charter and of the good-neighbor policy" and that the United States had "sincerity and good faith" toward other nations.[69]

Concerns of Japanese propaganda, communist uprisings, and global racial war were on the minds of Republican and Democrat legislators alike. Nevertheless, accusations of U.S. racism did not drastically transform legislators' racial thinking. Thus, even as they passed a bill to signal their goodwill to the world, legislators remained committed to racial exclusion and white hegemony. When Congress and President Truman allowed one hundred Filipinos a year to migrate and naturalize, they only signaled a symbolic end to exclusion.

CONCLUSION

In the post–World War II era, U.S. state actors reached a new consensus about the place of Filipinos in the United States. To maintain the United States' geopolitical position, its reputation as supporting democracy abroad, and its long-standing practice of limiting nonwhite admittance to the country, U.S. state actors increasingly spoke of Filipinos in positive terms. Despite lauding Filipinos' loyalty as colonial subjects and in the war, legislators broke the promise to award rights and benefits. They passed a symbolic act for naturalization and disguised the colonial nature of U.S.–Philippine relations behind polite terminology of loyalty. Although still a colony, U.S. state actors cast the Philippines as an independent nation. In this light, Filipinos were foreign aliens. Veterans did not serve in active duty. And promised rights were unnecessary foreign aid. As legislators excluded Filipinos in terms that were not explicitly vulgarly racial, they also hoped to assuage concerns that the United States was racist and illiberal. Toward this end, they used limited naturalization as counterpropaganda. Filipinos who actively served for the United States were, in large numbers, unable to take advantage of the new door opened for only one hundred Filipinos a year. Dismantling rights and providing a limited pathway to naturalization—seemingly contradictory practices—relied on the farce that the Philippines was sovereign.

The loss of veterans' rights and the new right to naturalize are part of how the United States masked its influence over the Philippines without disrupting the foundational structures of racial-imperial rule. As the United States prepared for Philippine independence, it erased its obligations and secured the exclusion of its colonial subjects. As in Chapter 4, hiding empire relied on the forthcoming independence of the Philippines and casting Filipinos as outsiders. The exclusion (or, at best, very limited admittance) of people from the metropolitan United States reflects how metropolitan concerns about race were more salient than commitments to honor loyal service. As they saw immigration, naturalization, and benefits as domestic matters that could reshape the demography of the United States, legislators revoked promises and limited Filipinos' rights.

The treatment of Filipino people stands in stark contrast to the economic and geopolitical arrangements that U.S. state actors struck as they decolonized the Philippines, as documented in the next chapter. When it came to remunerating colonial subjects for their martial service, U.S. Congress and other members of the government decided that the United States owed nothing to these individuals. When it came to maintaining the territory of the Philippines in the United States, however, U.S. Congress kept their promises of economic and geopolitical support. Nearly fifty years after the United States acquired the Philippines, building on institutionalized ambiguity and the bifurcation of foreign and domestic aspects of imperial rule, U.S. state actors secured both racial exclusion and U.S. imperial influence. At home, they decided that Filipinos were undesirable outsiders to whom they owed nothing. Filipino people were foreigners in the domestic space. Meanwhile, when it came to the Philippine territory, the United States managed to maintain control over the foreign archipelago as if it were domestic. As such, the deep structures of white hegemony persisted.

SEVEN   EMPIRE AS AID, 1945–1947

On July 4, 1946, the United States relinquished sovereignty over the Philippines. To proclaim Philippine independence and inaugurate the new republic, Philippine and U.S. politicians gathered in Luneta Park, Manila. General Douglas MacArthur, High Commissioner Paul McNutt, Senator Millard Tydings (D-MD), and Representative C. Jasper Bell (D-MO) were among those present. McNutt read the proclamation of independence of the Philippine Republic and Manuel Roxas was sworn in as president. Although he was not present for the ceremony, U.S. President Harry Truman sent a message broadcast in the Philippines. He noted that while the new Philippine Republic would face challenges of independence, the United States would "continue to assist the Philippines in every way possible." While "a formal compact is being dissolved," he added, "the compact of faith and understanding between two people can never be dissolved." The United States and the Philippines would "be closely bound together for many years to come," as they had been for the past forty-eight years. Truman concluded his address by underscoring the significance of U.S.–Philippine cooperation for global politics, stating: "The United States, and its partner of the Pacific, the Philippine Republic, have already charted a pattern of relationships for all the world to study. Together in the future, our two countries must prove the soundness and the wisdom of this

FIGURE 7.1. Lowering the U.S. Flag and Raising the Philippine Flag. Luneta Park, Manila, Philippines. Source: Presidential Museum and Library of the Philippines, Manila, Philippines.

great experiment in Pacific democracy."[1] U.S. politicians heralded this day as an achievement for the Philippines, ushering in a new age of democracy in Asia. The Philippines would be the model.

Despite celebrating U.S.–Philippine relations as a partnership of equals rather than the extension of colonial bonds, Truman's remarks also reflect the durability of U.S. imperial rule. Truman portrayed Philippine independence not as a break with the past but as part of a continuous history. Over the course of almost fifty years of formal rule, U.S. state actors forged the terms of Philippine independence. They institutionalized ambiguity and bifurcated the foreign and domestic aspects of rule. At the same time, the changes wrought by war-making during World War II catalyzed state transformation. Just as in 1898, U.S. state actors debated the threats to white hegemony. They translated their ideas of human difference into policies that supported the transition to a new form of empire.

From the day the war ended on September 2, 1945, to the set date of Philippine independence on July 4, 1946, conversations about the relationship of the Philippine territory to the United States accelerated. In this time of rehabilitation, U.S. and Philippine state actors finalized agreements for trade, demobilization, war recovery aid, and military assistance. Drawing on its own existing racial-imperial grammar, the United States continued to exert economic and military power over the Philippine territory.[2] As Louis Pérez wrote of the Platt Amendment for Cuba (1901), the deals struck on the eve of Philippine independence similarly "deprived the republic of the essential properties of sovereignty while preserving the appearance of independence, permitting self-government but precluding self determination."[3] Julian Go remarked that "these provisions are notable because they enabled the United States to use the Philippines as it always had when it exercised direct colonial rule—namely for capital accumulation and as a nodal point in its network of national security."[4] Importantly, the United States negotiated these deals for informal empire when the Philippines was still a colony. As such, they do not represent agreements between sovereign nations but between the metropole and its colony.

While U.S. state actors maintained the deep grammar of unequal relations, they also responded to exigencies wrought through a global war. They believed that—against accusations of racism, threats of future race war, and communist uprisings—they needed to make Philippine independence seem like a new dawn. Now, to manage critiques of the United States' racial empire, U.S. state actors spoke of the imperial project as aid. As they rehabilitated and "decolonized," U.S. state actors relied on increasingly polite portrayals of Filipinos. No longer were they little brown brothers but family and friends that had come of age. U.S. state actors spoke of Filipinos as deserving. The United States owed a debt to the Philippines.

Colonial logics of dependence and obligation were both durable and flexible. The language of obligation had once been used to justify a civilizing mission and tutelage, but now U.S. state actors reframed their obligation to justify the maintenance of U.S. territorial sovereignty amidst formal plans for decolonization. After World War II, foreign aid in exchange for loyalty only applied to the Philippine territory and not to the veterans who served during World War II. Thus, U.S. state actors hid imperial relations under the guise of aid, which became a key tool of U.S. informal empire after decolonization. The "new" model of decolonization and aid, state actors argued, would provide benefits not only to Filipinos but also to the United States and the world.

This chapter discusses how administrators in the executive branch reasserted their control of colonial and foreign affairs. After providing background on the major deals and arrangements that U.S. and Philippine state actors secured, I detail how key U.S. state actors believed their approach to addressing the new Philippine problem would manage concerns about the United States' geopolitical position. Although they framed it as a break with the past, U.S. state actors from diverse political backgrounds relied on old imperial practices and logics. Members of the military, Congress, and the executive branch disguised imperial relations under the façade of aid. After showing that U.S. state actors changed the terms in which they spoke about Filipinos and the relationship of the U.S. to the territory, I discuss how they hoped post-war plans could counter global anti-U.S. sentiment. Although obscured, the United States' racial-imperial grammar continued to structure informal empire.

A NEW PHILIPPINE PROBLEM

At the end of World War II, fearing the impacts of Japanese propaganda, anti-colonial resistance, and the rising influence of communism, the United States again faced a Philippine problem: what would be the relationship of the territory to the United States? In addressing this question, the Department of the Interior, long responsible for U.S. settler colonial expansion and now also responsible for insular affairs, relied on practiced tools of racial-imperial rule.[5] Under Secretary Harold Ickes, the Interior Department—like the War Department under Elihu Root in the early 1900s— proposed plans for yet another imperial transition in the wake of war. He centralized control of information. As in the early days of U.S. overseas empire, the U.S. colonial office drafted and made recommendations for post-war economic plans in the Philippines. The Interior Department continued to vest power over foreign affairs in the U.S. executive branch. Whereas Root laid the foundations of a new overseas formal empire, Ickes built on this structure to transition to informal empire as the United States decolonized.

In characterizing the problem of Philippine independence, Ickes drew attention to domestic and international political conflict, how the United States created a dependency in the Philippines, and disorganization in the U.S. federal government. Addressing these problems would be crucial to maintaining stability in the islands and the larger region. In May 1945 Ickes wrote Truman that the situation in the Philippines "may be leading up to a condition of chaos which will prove embarrassing to the Administration in the near future, both domestically and internationally." Ickes emphasized that managing the Philippines was important to the United States' reputation. He attributed the problems of transitioning to forthcoming independence to seven factors: (1) post-war political struggles between the guerrillas and collaborators; (2) the likely election of Manuel Roxas, at the time an accused Japanese collaborator;[6] (3) the failure of the U.S. government to establish rehabilitation or trade programs for the Philippines; (4) lack of public relief programs; (5) destruction of the trade infrastructure; (6) limited financial reserves of the Philippine Commonwealth; and (7) lack of U.S. federal coordination. Ickes concluded, "Independence with chaos will blacken the reputation of the United States; it may permanently alienate the Filipinos; and it will cause ferment throughout the Far East."[7] Nevertheless, Ickes continued to support Philippine independence. Postponing independence was not a viable option, as it would undermine the United States' reputation as a leader in democracy, and the possibility of statehood raised demographic fears. For example, while not explicitly invoking racial language, Ickes noted that "the Philippines have a population of about 18 million, approximately the population of New York and New Jersey combined, and these two states have 59 members in the House of Representatives."[8] In short, although post-war conditions, a lack of money for government programs, and decentralized U.S. control could complicate conditions in the Philippines as the U.S. planned to decolonize, independence remained the preferred path forward.

Of particular concern to Ickes and other colonial officials were the political conflicts among suspected communists, Falangists (those who supported Francoist Spain), and Japanese collaborators in the Philippines. To maintain the United States' reputation and political stability in the region amid these threats, colonial officials argued for continued U.S. support of the Philippines even as it became independent. Although Ickes was preoccupied with Japanese collaborators,[9] his concern also reflected his desire to maintain control over the transition to independence. Like Ickes, High Commissioner McNutt warned that the political situation in the Philippines was "critical." Focusing on the threat of communism, he explained that the Filipino people were "ravaged and demoralized by the crudest and most destructive of wars, politically split between loyalists and enemy collaborators, with several sizeable well-armed dissident groups still at large (Mohamedan elements, certain bands of ex guerrillas, the Agrarians usually known as the Hukbalajaps [sic])." Years of war had deepened inequality and political divides, and a democratic socialist or popular front movement was building among Filipino peasants. Therefore, he claimed, "it does not at this moment seem humanly possible for the Filipino people . . .to cope with the coincidence of political independence, sharp downward revision of economic standards, budgetary bankruptcy, and rehabilitation."[10] If the United States wanted to control potential communist uprisings and maintain its own influence in the Philippines, then, McNutt argued, the United States must support Filipinos in rebuilding the archipelago post-war and to prepare for independence.

Not only were U.S. officials concerned about communism but purported collaboration and support from Falangists threatened U.S. interests. Memos among Interior leadership identify cooperation among Falangists such as Andres Soriano, who served as an advisor to MacArthur, Roxas, and Japanese collaborators. The Interior noted that MacArthur and these Filipinos overlooked the efforts of the Hukbalahap who fought against the Japanese. And although the Interior worried about communist influence, they also worried about how MacArthur, Falangists, and Nationalists in the Philippines handled collaboration, possibly fueling Filipino peasant movements' complaints.[11]

U.S. colonial officials hoped to resolve these political challenges in the short time frame leading up to Philippine independence. Rather than entertain other possibilities such as postponing independence or making the Philippines the forty-ninth state, the U.S. executive branch again turned to a strategy of colonial rule. By centralizing power and information control under the executive's purview, Ickes managed yet another political conflict. He explained that "military operations; strict Army censorship; the resistance of General MacArthur to effective action by the civilian agencies; and the lack of any authorized United States official of general responsibility, namely, a High Commissioner" limited the executive branch's information about the Philippines. As a result, the U.S. government could not easily establish a rehabilitation or trade program. War shaped these conditions, but they were all problems exacerbated by military rule and the lack of centralized leadership attentive to civilian affairs. Ickes identified a lack of coordination among four U.S. civil agencies, including the Alien Property Custodian, the Treasury Department, the War Damage Corporation, and the Foreign Economic Administration. He was especially concerned by the United States' reliance on military authorities, namely MacArthur. Believing no one could appropriately coordinate Philippine civilian affairs, Ickes turned to an existing colonial practice: he recommended that the president appoint a new high commissioner to restore stability. He warned that without this measure, the road to Philippine independence would be even more cumbersome. Ickes noted that executive control should not be understood as "an infringement of Philippine autonomy." Rather, the high commissioner would "bring about a transfer of complete autonomy to the Philippines." Additionally, he recommended another colonial practice: establish a new survey commission under the authority of the U.S. president.[12]

In proposing these solutions for the transition to independence, Ickes even acknowledged them as reliable colonial practices. Relating the situation to the early years of U.S. rule in the Philippines, Ickes noted that "President McKinley sent a similar mission to the Philippines during the chaotic period following the war with Spain. The statesmenlike report of this mission laid the foundation for decades of progress. Again, in 1921, the Wood Forbes Mission cleared the atmosphere following a difficult period." To recover from the chaos of war and usher in Philippine independence, Ickes argued that the United States should reinstate centralized control of information through the high commissioner and under the colonial office of the Interior Department. In July 1945, President Truman issued an executive order establishing the Philippine Survey Commission, which would report to the secretary of the interior.

SOLVING THE PHILIPPINE PROBLEM

In addition to centralizing control, the U.S. executive branch—led by the Interior and the Office of the Territories—promoted three geostrategic aims that would secure the place of the Philippine territory in the U.S. empire. First, they wanted to maintain favorable trade and investment relations in Asia. The Philippines, as the established outpost of the United States in Asia, would continue to be central to this program. Second, U.S. state actors wanted to maintain regional political influence through economic support. While the United States defeated Japan, U.S. state actors worried about the rise of communism in Asia and the threat it posed to U.S. capitalist development. Against communism, U.S. state actors promoted U.S. capitalism under the pretense of democracy. Anti-communist efforts were part of how the United States claimed its exceptionalism in the post-war period.[13] Third, to maintain U.S. influence in the region, state actors believed that retaining United States military outposts in the Philippines would be crucial to a broader military strategy in Asia. In short, U.S. state actors, led by the Department of the Interior and the executive branch, planned for the continuation of U.S. control not only of the islands but also to spread the U.S. political and economic system across the region. Ickes warned that if the United States did not pursue these goals, they might face economic collapse of the Philippines and fuel more anti-U.S. propaganda Asia.

Although U.S. state actors—including the U.S. president, former colonial officials, members of the Department of the Interior, and legislators—had reached consensus about maintaining imperial relations with the Philippines, some state actors wondered if pursuing these goals would damage the United States' global reputation. The State Department warned that the United States should refrain from outwardly influencing Philippine trade, investment, military, and domestic policy. Assistant Secretary of State Dean Acheson wrote that these deals "should not be entered into until the Philippines are an independent nation." Otherwise, it would seem as if the United States pushed agreements on its colony. Acheson suggested delaying the timing of U.S.–Philippine deals. He wrote that acts and deals for trade "should be freely negotiated between two independent governments on a mutually satisfactory basis." Acheson underscored that the Philippines "are still under our Flag." Reaching deals with the Philippines while it was a colony would "inevitably create a most unfavorable world impression of United States [*sic*] intentions."[14] Writing on the question of military bases, the director of Far Eastern Affairs of the State Department John Carter Vincent also believed that the United States "should not force the Philippines to grant this Government such extensive jurisdiction in time of peace."[15] He thought a military agreement would be "regarded not merely by the Filipino people but by other friendly Far Eastern peoples as a revival of extraterritoriality." This, however, was not so much a revival of extraterritoriality as the continuation of U.S. rule. He continued "that this country's good will [*sic*] among Far Eastern peoples would suffer without commensurate advantage to this country."[16] Notably, although the State Department registered its concern about how the United States negotiated these deals, they did not object in principle to the approach to foreign affairs. Rather, their warnings highlight that concerns about global reputation mattered as state actors managed U.S. foreign relations.

Although the State Department worried about the potential blemish to the United States' reputation, most U.S. state actors—Republican and Democrat alike—believed these strategic goals would improve the United States' reputation in the world. Like in 1898, the close of World War II and preparations for Philippine independence raised questions about the relationship of the Philippines to the United States and what it meant for the United States on the world stage. Whereas in 1898 imperialists had to convince their nativist and isolationist counterparts of overseas intervention and rule, in 1946, U.S. state actors had largely reached a consensus over what to do in the Philippines. World War II also helped settle these conflicts. Japan's attack on the Philippines affirmed the geostrategic and military importance of the islands. Isolationists no longer claimed that a territory far off in the Pacific did not matter. By 1946, only the State Department registered concerns that these deals should not be reached while the Philippines was still a colony.

Executive administrators and legislators pursued the Philippine Trade Act, the Philippine Rehabilitation Act, the Military Assistance Act, and the Military Bases Agreement. Through these arrangements, administrators influenced legislators, pushing an imperial model for post-war, interstate relations between a former colony and the United States. The Philippine Trade Act and the Rehabilitation Act were aimed at strengthening the Philippine economy and combatting the spread of communism. These two pieces of legislation were crucial to how the United States transitioned from formal empire to ostensibly race-neutral foreign affairs in the Philippines. Whereas the legislative rider to the 1946 Rescission Act that reclassified Filipino veterans (see Chapter 6) only took up four pages in the transcripts from Congressional Records and Hearings, debates over the Philippine Trade and Rehabilitation Acts alone span over 1100 pages over the course of eight months. Members of Congress considered trade and aid to be of paramount importance for foreign relations. The Military Assistance Act, meanwhile, supported military and geostrategic priorities in Asia. While there are less than 100 pages of Congressional debate and hearing over the Military Assistance Act, the Joint Chiefs of Staff (JCS), with the Departments of the Interior, War, Navy, and State, discussed and negotiated the Military Bases Agreement for years. The agreement became part of the U.S. military strategy in Asia and proved to be a model for future post–World War II and postcolonial interventions.

Below, I provide detail about the debates and terms of the four agreements. Politicians from both sides of the aisle and from the legislative and executive branches supported the continuation of U.S. colonial policies in the

TABLE 7.1.   U.S.–Philippine Arrangements at the End of World War II

ACT OF U.S. CONGRESS	MAJOR PROVISIONS	MATERIAL JUSTIFICATIONS
1946 Philippine Trade Act	Free trade (for a period of eight years, followed by a twenty-five-year phase out period in which preferences would be reduced by 4 percent/year) and equal rights for U.S. citizens and corporations in natural resource investment and development	Trade Military Security Democracy in Asia
1946 Philippine Rehabilitation Act	Payment of war damages and restoration of Philippine industry and infrastructure	Economic Support Democracy in Asia
1946 Republic of the Philippines Military Assistance Act	Provides military assistance to the Philippines for the purposes of maintaining national security and to help build defensive military operations	Military Security
1947 Military Bases Agreement	Ninety-nine-year lease on over 150,000 acres of the Philippine territory for U.S. military bases	Military Security

Philippines. With the *Filipino* question largely resolved by keeping most Filipinos out of the metropole, U.S. state actors had fewer quibbles with U.S. influence and control of the archipelago. Even as conflict over Philippine policy had tempered, the U.S. executive branch continued to dominate the process of colonial and foreign policymaking.

Stabilizing the Post-War Economy: The Philippine Trade Act
The Philippine Trade Act, which passed two months before the set date of Philippine independence on April 30, 1946, encouraged the continuation of trade between the United States and the Philippines as well as U.S. capital investment in the archipelago. Although the 1934 Philippine Independence Act discussed in Part II set the Philippines on a path toward independence and planned to end reciprocal free trade between colony and metropole, after World War II, the United States extended this "special" relationship. In debates about independence and the 1946 Philippine Trade Act, state actors focused on tariffs and quotas for Philippine sugar imports to the United States.

As a U.S. colony, the economic arrangements for the Philippines under the Trade Act had historical antecedents in decades of U.S. colonial rule. The act provided for free entry of Philippine articles to the United States and U.S. articles to the Philippines until July 3, 1954, with twenty years of declining preferences. Regarding sugar, the act also maintained an absolute quota of 850,000 long tons of sugar, of which 50,000 could be refined or direct consumption sugar until January 1, 1974. After this period, the sugar quota would be reduced by half until July 3, 1974. As U.S. state actors claimed that free trade and sugar quotas would stabilize the Philippine economy and secure U.S. geopolitical interests in the region, they also tied free trade to a clause that gave U.S. citizens the right to develop and own natural resources and industry in the Philippines. This was known as "parity."[17]

Although it passed by voice vote and without opposition,[18] the Trade Act was the most publicly debated piece of post-war legislation about the Philippines. The debate took so long not because U.S. state actors objected to the infringement on Philippine sovereignty but because trade legislation was a compromise of different U.S. interests. Legislators representing U.S. business interests hoped to eliminate competition with Philippine products. Years before Congress considered the Trade Act, U.S. colonial bureaucrats hoped to convert land for sugar production and build domestic agriculture, manufacturing, and industries. U.S. industry and investors in the Philippines also wanted to protect their interests in the colony. Within the U.S. government, the Interior and the BIA believed that free trade would help secure stability in the Philippines. They claimed that ending trade preferences would destroy the Philippine economy. After all, even before 1898, the United States had long been the largest buyer of Philippine goods. And over the years of formal U.S. rule, the United States increased its consumption of Philippine products, including sugar, abaca, coconut oil, copra, tobacco, lumber, and pineapple. Thus, even as free trade would keep the Philippines dependent on the United States, U.S. colonial bureaucrats could also argue that it would in fact help stabilize the post-war Philippine economy.[19]

Not all U.S. state actors agreed with the Interior's plans for trade, however. In March 1945, the U.S. State Department put forward a plan to end quotas. Authored by Assistant Secretary of State William L. Clayton, Jr., the State Department's policy advocated for ending quotas and preferences and bringing U.S.–Philippine trade relations in line with the rest of the United States' multilateralist trade policy. The major difference with the Interior's plan was the faster timeline of phasing out preferences and the rejection of quotas. The Treasury Department supported the plan, suggesting that encouraging ongoing reliance on the export of sugar to the U.S. market was bad for the Philippine economy.[20] In the Philippines, some Filipino elites like Joaquín Miguel Elizalde supported this plan, though his power had waned.

In response to the State Department, the Interior Department argued that special concessions for the Philippines did not contradict the State Department's global plans. After all, E. D. Hester noted, the Philippines was also giving the U.S. military bases, free trade, and investment rights. The Interior also objected to the State Department's plan by arguing that the Philippine economy would suffer, and this could jeopardize a future ally in the Pacific. As a general plan for decolonization, the Interior argued that ending quotas and preferences could damage colonial economies and might lead colonized nations to ally with other powers, such as Russia. The War and Navy Departments agreed that geopolitical and military strategy were at stake.[21] So too did Manuel Roxas support the Interior Department's plan for Philippine rehabilitation.

When the United States recaptured the Philippines, the Department of the Interior, not the State Department, designed the post-war trade agreements.

At the recommendation of Ickes, Paul McNutt, former high commissioner to the Philippines and current chair of the War Manpower Commission, traveled to the Philippines to assess the political and economic situation on the islands. With the United States again exercising sovereignty over the islands, the powers of the high commissioner were restored, and McNutt, acting under the executive branch and the Interior, had wide discretion. McNutt pushed the Interior's policies for U.S. capital investment. Together, McNutt, Hester, and Richard Ely drafted the trade bill for Representative Bell, who introduced it in the House. Filipino elites also supported that Trade Act, hoping that it would return the Philippines to its pre-war conditions.[22]

Although, by the time it passed, the 1946 Trade Act was relatively non-controversial in the United States, the Philippine Congress had to amend its Constitution to give U.S. citizens parity, or equal rights, to Filipinos in natural resource ownership and development. If the Philippines did not agree, then the U.S. president could suspend or end the trade agreement. U.S. Congress also tied this deal to a package for rebuilding the war-damaged Philippine economy, discussed below. To pass the bill with the parity agreement, U.S. politicians had to amend the Philippine Constitution.[23] They worked with Philippine leadership to obscure concerns that the United States coerced the Philippines. A State Department memo highlighted how President Roxas and High Commissioner McNutt endeavored to pass the parity agreement before the Philippines became independent. If they waited until after Philippine independence, then the Philippine Supreme Court "might construe the executive agreement as a treaty, since there was nothing in Philippine law or the Constitution about trade agreements."[24] Amending the constitution would be no easy task, however. Roxas would need a three-fourths majority, and he "was doubtful whether he could carry" this vote. Nevertheless, under Roxas, the Philippine Congress successfully passed the amendments to the Philippine Constitution. He succeeded by convincing his party to bar nine other representatives from the Philippine Congress. Roxas's party claimed that "there had been fraud and terror in Central Luzon [the region where these representatives were from]."[25] These nine, who Roxas cast as possible communist sympathizers, would have voted against the amendments. Without their presence, the amendments for parity passed.

The State Department continued to oppose the Interior's proposed Trade Act, arguing that the parity clause was inconsistent with current U.S. foreign policy. Secretary of State James F. Byrnes warned President Truman that the provision of the Trade Act "requiring the Philippines to grant Americans in the Philippines broad special favors and, consequently, to discriminate against all other countries, are inconsistent with our promise to grant the Philippines genuine independence and may be expected to have unfortunate repercussions on our international relations, especially in the Far East." Byrnes went on to note that not only were Philippine officials opposed, but so too had the Soviet press "cited them as an example of 'the rising tide of reactionary forces' in the Anglo-Saxon countries." Byrnes argued it was hypocritical for the United States to demand this privileged position in the Philippine economy when the United States protested policies that discriminated against the United States in other countries.[26] Assistant Secretary of State Acheson wrote Truman, noting that "a considerable body of domestic and foreign criticism has already been directed at certain provisions of the Philippine Trade Act which call for privileged status for United States business interests in the Philippines." He continued, noting critiques of "the methods used for ensuring that the Filipinos enter into the Executive Agreement on Trade Relations, for example, withholding payments over $500 for rehabilitation until they do so." Acheson argued that such global critiques of the United States would "be very costly to United States prestige and will do much to impair the laudable record of fair dealing hitherto maintained by the United States in its Philippine relations."[27] Against the protests of nine Filipino legislators and the U.S. State Department, U.S. state actors in the Interior and their legislator allies passed the Trade Act, which Truman signed. In doing so, the United States extended metropole-colony trade relations and deviated from standard international trade relations.

Securing U.S.-led Development: The Philippine Rehabilitation Act

In addition to circumscribing Philippine sovereignty through the parity agreement, the U.S. Congress tied to the Trade Act to a package for rebuilding the war-damaged Philippine economy: the Rehabilitation Act. Even before the end of the war, U.S. state actors noted the importance of assisting the Philippines on the road to economic security and independence. President Truman, for example, stated, "The Filipino people, whose heroic and loyal stand in this war has won the affection and admiration of the American people, will be fully assisted by the United States in the great problem of rehabilitation and reconstruction which lies ahead."[28] Providing aid to rebuild the Philippine economy was a key part of the U.S. strategy to secure influence in the region.

The Rehabilitation Act, which passed with no opposition,[29] provided terms for the compensation of war damage, the disposal of U.S. surplus property to help with repairs, the restoration and improvement of public property and public services, training of Filipino workers, and the oversight of these projects by the U.S. high commissioner.[30] The act also encouraged economic development, but at a cost. Under section 601 of the act, it said that "no payments under title I of the Act in excess of $500 shall be made until an executive agreement shall have been entered into between the President of the United States and the President of the Philippines, and such agreement shall have become effective according to its terms, providing for trade relations between the United States and the Philippines."[31] In other words, the U.S. Congress would not allow any substantial war payments until the Philippine government approved the aforementioned Trade Act with the parity agreement. The U.S. Congress would only rebuild the Philippine economy if the United States received economic rights of investment and free trade in return.

As during the colonial period, the high commissioner—as the U.S. executive branch incarnate in the Philippines—would oversee the rebuilding of the Philippine economy. Even after Philippine independence, the United States managed Philippine finances. The Trade Act required the independent Philippines to consult with the United States about how to finance Philippine rehabilitation efforts. In September 1946, Philippine President Roxas inquired if, according to Section 342 of the Philippine Trade Act, the government could withdraw from the Treasury reserves allocated for Philippine rehabilitation without requiring the approval of the U.S. president. Roxas consulted with McNutt (who had seamlessly transitioned from high commissioner to U.S. ambassador to the Philippines, in yet another example of imperial continuity) about how the Philippines could expedite economic rehabilitation. McNutt suggested Roxas finance the bank "through proceeds sale surplus and currency conversion program." This way, McNutt hoped, "sufficient capital could be obtained from these sources to finance bank until Export Import Bank and International Bank prepared to consider rehabilitation loan to Philippine Govt."[32] As in the early days of U.S. empire in the archipelago, U.S. state actors managed Philippine finances and development, though now they concealed imperial continuity behind the pretense of aid.

In the Philippine Trade Act and the Philippine Rehabilitation Act, members of the U.S. Congress demonstrated they were more concerned with U.S. geopolitical and material control over the Philippine territory than debts owed to soon-to-be former colonial subjects. For example, the U.S. Senate allocated $400 million for the Philippine Rehabilitation Act—a notably higher sum than the $20 million estimated cost for providing benefits to Filipino veterans discussed in Chapter 6—$5 million of which was for restoration of U.S. property and $120 million for public services, including roads, port facilities, and public health.[33] And for the most part, Congress saw this as money well spent. Although Congress revoked Filipino veterans' status, the United States did, in fact, have the resources to keep their promise. The priority, however, was using this money to maintain territorial control and influence in the archipelago. Senator Carl Hayden (D-AZ) even commented that the Department of the Interior should not pursue money for Filipino veterans' benefits because "it might have an unfavorable reaction on the trade and war damage bill."[34] In the face of forthcoming independence and the end of the war, U.S. politicians wanted to maintain favorable trade and investment relations in Asia. They saw the Philippine territory, not people, as central to this program.

Strengthening U.S. Geostrategy: The Military Assistance and Bases
In addition to deals for trade and rehabilitation, U.S. military leaders and members of the executive branch secured informal empire and circumscribed Philippine sovereignty through military assistance to the Philippines. Rather than deals between sovereign nation states, the 1946 Military Assistance Act and the 1947 Military Bases Agreement, like the Trade Act, parity clause, and the Rehabilitation Act, were deals between an imperial power and its colony. The Military Assistance Act provided for instruction and training of military and naval personnel of the Philippines, maintenance and repair of equipment, and the transfer of arms and ammunition. In the Military Bases Agreement, the Philippine government granted the United States bases on a ninety-nine-year lease. Discussions of U.S. military assistance and bases in the islands have roots in the years of formal imperial rule, dating back to debates over the 1930s Philippine independence legislation. Although negotiations over U.S. military influence in the Philippines proceeded in fits and starts, the United States and the Philippines reached agreements that extended U.S. sovereignty over the Philippines.

Prior to World War II, imperialists and nativist-isolationists disagreed about the military importance of the Philippines. As Chapter 5 discussed, however, Japan's attacks on Hawai'i and the Philippines shifted priorities. In 1942, the JCS was already considering sites for bases that could "be used by an 'international police force' that would preserve the peace after the defeat of the Axis."[35] Nevertheless, the JCS did not settle the issue of bases in 1942. Instead, they deemed that, while the 1934 legislation allowed for the U.S. president to maintain bases in the Philippines, this matter should be settled after the Philippines was "liberated." For only after liberation, the JCS claimed, could the Philippines be brought back to a civil government and prepare for independence. With relative stability, the U.S. Army and Navy could reexamine which bases were of strategic importance.[36]

Wartime activities and anxieties about U.S. military strategy, however, hastened concerns about U.S. strategy in Asia. In 1943, Japan declared they would grant immediate independence to the Philippines. Concerns about Japanese promises of independence and the rising importance of the Philippines as a strategic site for the United States in the Pacific accelerated plans to settle the bases issue.[37] In the JCS meeting on December 21, 1943, Admiral William D. Leahy emphasized that "bases in the Philippines might be essential to any action that we might have to take against Japan before the defense of the Islands would again be necessary."[38] Although support for settling the matter increased, arrangements proceeded slowly, as the executive branch coordinated with the different branches of U.S. government and the Philippine Commonwealth.

The debates and agreements highlighted the U.S. executive branch's discretionary power and the symbolic sovereignty of the Philippines. For example, in 1944, the U.S. Congress passed a resolution concerning the eventual independence of the Philippines.[39] In addition to affirming the United States' commitment to "drive the treacherous, invading Japanese from the Philippine Islands, restore as quickly as possible the orderly and free democratic processes of the government of the Filipino people," the resolution allowed the U.S. president to acquire military bases in addition to those specified by the 1934 Tydings–McDuffie Act, as was deemed necessary "for the mutual protection of the Philippine Islands and of the United States." This was a crucial step toward securing U.S. military influence in the region, and the resolution vested discretionary authority in the president of the United States to withhold or acquire and retain such bases. Once again, the executive branch affirmed its power to manage foreign affairs.

On May 14, 1945, President Truman and President Osmeña signed a preliminary agreement on U.S. military and naval bases in the Philippines that tied the fates of the United States and the Philippines and guaranteed preferences for the United States in the islands.[40] The agreement dictated that U.S. and Philippine military plans "will be closely integrated in order to ensure the full and mutual protection of the U.S. and the Philippines" and that "no nation other than the U.S. or the Philippines is to be permitted to establish or make use of any bases in the Philippines without the prior agreement of both the U.S. and Philippine Governments."[41] The United States would keep special rights in the Philippine territory after independence. It was then left to the navy and the army to determine which sites they wanted to retain.

The War and Navy Departments believed bases to be "essential . . .even in time of peace." They also claimed "that the exercise of such jurisdiction is necessary to [the U.S.] military program and position in the Islands."[42] Admiral Forrest P. Sherman argued bases were "essential to the security of the United States, its possessions, the Western Hemisphere, and the Philippines."[43] The JCS considered Philippine bases as "spring boards from which the United States armed forces may be projected."[44] In their report, the JCS, noted that bases supported the U.S. military as it worked "to uphold [U.S.] national policies and interests in the Far East."[45] McNutt also supported a plan for bases, saying that they would aid "supply, repair, and staging activities for all our armed forces in the Far East. . . .Committed as we are to a long-time occupation of Japan, to a strong policy in Asia, the Philippines are designed to play a major role in our diplomacy in the Orient."[46]

Geostrategic concerns were not only on the minds of the military and colonial officials. In 1946, U.S. Congress passed an act to provide military assistance to the Philippines, another critical step toward maintaining U.S. executive and military influence over the Philippines after independence.[47] Representative Sol Bloom (D-NY) introduced the Republic of the Philippines Military Assistance Act. The aims of the act were to maintain national security and to lay the foundation for future military cooperation. Secretary of State James Byrnes voiced his support for military assistance, stating, "I firmly believe that the national interest, our duty to the people of the Philippines, and considerations of good conscience require that the United States continue to provide military assistance to the Republic of the Philippines to permit that nation in post-independence status to organize and maintain a military force for national security and defense."[48] The act allowed the U.S. president to use his discretion to provide for instruction and training of military and naval personnel of the Philippines, maintenance and repair of equipment, and transferring arms and ammunition. In exchange, the Philippines gave the U.S. president oversight over transfers and use of the property. While this power was vested in the president, he delegated authority to carry out this law to executive administrators: the secretaries of state, war, and navy. War and Navy established a Joint U.S. Military Advisory Group (JUSMAG). This organization was the first of its kind, and would not only manage military aid, but also advise the Philippine government.[49] The Military Assistance Act, then, is another example of executive innovation in its control over foreign affairs.

Finally, after much negotiation, in 1947, the United States and the new Philippine Republic signed the Military Bases Agreement (MBA). While this was signed after independence, the aforementioned preparations happened during the colonial period. In part, it took a long time to reach a bases agreement because President Roxas could not secure support from the Philippine government. Roxas blamed this on "communistic" elements of his government.[50] During negotiations, McNutt hoped that the U.S. government could assuage the Philippine public that the United States was "devoted to peace" and "will not impose its will upon another nation" or "ask concessions from a weaker power against the will of the people and the government of that power." He suggested the United States make a "solemn compact for the mutual defense of the Philippines," which could help Roxas manage those in "his own administration who are privately sabotaging his foreign policy."[51]

In light of prolonged negotiations that threatened global perceptions of the United States, even the U.S. military establishment reconsidered the importance of the Philippines for U.S. geopolitical strategy. The State Department, in consultation with the Departments of War and Navy, counseled against McNutt's proposed speech. In particular, they objected to suggestions that there was a solemn compact between the United States and the Philippines, since the bases agreement was not yet reached. Secretary of War Patterson threatened that if a deal could not soon be reached, he would reevaluate the United States' strategic need for bases in the Philippines.[52] Secretary Patterson also noted that Army Chief of Staff General Dwight D. Eisenhower believed that "future good relations of the two nations" was more important than army bases.[53] In response, Roxas continued to assure McNutt that the Philippines wanted the bases and did not want the U.S. military to withdraw.[54]

Despite the hiccups, the newly founded Philippine Republic and the United States reached a consensus and extended years of colonial relations into a new era. According to the terms of the MBA, the Philippines could be treated as an extension of the United States in Asia. The Philippine government also agreed to allow U.S. military bases in the Philippines on a ninety-nine-year lease.[55] In addition to granting land to the United States, the MBA maintained aspects of U.S. sovereignty abroad, most notably in the jurisdiction of U.S. courts. In effect, the MBA granted sovereignty to the United States and limited Philippine control. According to the agreement, the United States had both legal and territorial authority to construct bases, exercise jurisdiction over civil and criminal offences, and extract natural resources.[56] The United States gained hundreds of thousands of acres of military bases. In a striking limitation to Philippine sovereignty, the Philippine government could not "grant, without prior consent of the United States, any bases or any rights, power, or authority whatsoever, in or relating to bases" to a polity other than the United States.[57] The Philippines—at least the acres reserved for bases—still belonged to the United States, and they would help secure U.S. influence in the region. While the MBA was not the first of its kind, it was a watershed moment for the U.S. empire, as it gained major military bases in Asia to serve as launching points in future wars.[58]

DISGUISING EMPIRE IN POLITE TERMS

To secure imperial trade, rehabilitation, and military assistance agreements in an era of decolonization, state actors disguised U.S.–Philippine relations in terms that were not explicitly hierarchical. They invoked colonial language of Filipino dependency and loyalty to cast U.S. imperial interest as benevolent support in politically and economically uncertain times. Whereas nativist-isolationist state actors cited Filipino dependency as rationale for exclusion (Chapter 4) and did not remunerate Filipinos for their loyalty (Chapter 6), when it came to colonial policy in the archipelago, U.S. state actors argued that the United States owed a great debt to Filipinos for their loyalty and dependency. In the form of U.S.-led rehabilitation and free trade, the United States would support the emerging nation. Even as they reframed empire as aid, U.S. state actors and Filipino elite did not abandon earlier logics of polite racism. They spoke of the Philippines as having come of age during decades of U.S. rule. The tutelary project worked. Filipinos proved their maturity to their Anglo-Saxon father figures. As they maintained U.S. extraterritorial sovereignty, U.S. state actors relied on justifications that both stemmed from and veiled logics of colonial and racial difference.

Filipinos as Dependent and Loyal

U.S. politicians argued that the Philippines, although it was soon-to-be independent, was still in need of ongoing support. Although claims of inherent dependency served as justification for reclassifying and excluding Filipinos in the 1930s, now, U.S. state actors recognized that they made Filipinos dependent. Over nearly fifty years, the United States had developed the Philippine economy to serve U.S. interests. In 1946, McNutt wrote Richard R. Ely, executive assistant to the high commissioner, citing concerns about Philippine dependence as his rationale for supporting the Philippine Trade Act. He noted that because the United States had free trade and preferential trade with the Philippines between 1909 and 1941, the territory was not prepared for political independence. McNutt continued, stating "it should be obvious that after over 30 years of forced development into almost complete economic dependence a sudden reversal of economy is impossible without courting disaster. The mistake was ours and we have an obligation to adopt remedial measures which will not destroy Philippine economy."[59] Similarly, the Assistant Secretary of State and former High Commissioner to the Philippines Francis B. Sayre wrote in *The Atlantic*: "Because the present economic dependence of the Filipinos upon the United States is largely of our own making, and because it is to our own interest to build for future stability in the Pacific, the Filipino people must be given their independence under such conditions as will assure them sound economic foundations for their future. The American people will not be content with anything less."[60] Free trade, which McNutt and Sayre acknowledged as having made the Philippines dependent, was also held up as the solution.

It was not only colonial administrators, but also legislators too referenced ideas of Philippine dependency to justify informal empire. Representative A. Willis Robertson (D-VA), for example, supported the trade program as an effort to "restore the Philippine Islands," but also as an undertaking "not with foreigners, but those who for many years have been our wards."[61] Senator David Walsh (D-MA) from the Committee on Finance wrote that "the United States is deeply concerned in the welfare of the Islands."[62] State actors no longer spoke of Filipinos' status as wards and dependents in biological or essentialist terms. Instead, when it came to free trade and natural resource development, U.S. state actors argued that the United States cultivated dependency. As such, they argued Filipinos needed U.S. aid. Notably, these arguments were only used to justify U.S. control over the islands and not to reward rights or benefits to Filipino people.

Just as invocations of dependency were malleable, so too were loyalty-based arguments. Although legislators only symbolically invoked Filipino loyalty and did not uphold the United States' obligation to Filipino veterans, U.S. state actors cited Filipino loyalty as grounds to maintain U.S. influence over the Philippine territory. For example, Representative Karl Stefan (R-NE) stated, "Gentlemen, I ask your support for the Philippine Trade Act of 1946—the first forward step on the road to true liberty for a brave and an honorable people."[63] Representative Emily T. Douglas (D-IL, at large), referring to U.S. trade policy toward the Philippines, noted that while "many Europeans in the Orient and some Americans at home" scrutinized U.S. policy and "called us soft for acting in such an idealistic fashion," U.S. imperial policies "were not only right, but they also proved their worth in the years of crisis." She noted that "the Filipinos fought with us as true comrades in arms," and that "by so doing, they paid off any debt they may have owed us and place us instead greatly in their debt." In exchange, the United States ought to abide by "generosity of treatment" and recall Filipino loyalty as they decided on future policies toward the Philippines.[64] The ostensibly race-neutral language of loyalty may not have helped Filipino people maintain their rights, but U.S. state actors used it to justify informal empire.

Colonial Extraction as U.S. Debt

U.S. and Philippine state actors argued that because of Philippine dependency and loyalty, the United States had a debt to the emerging nation. Although the method of payment extended U.S. colonial policy, state actors disguised free trade and U.S. capital investment in the islands as aid to struggling Filipinos. Representative John D. Dingell, Sr. (D-MI), chairman of the Ways and Means

Subcommittee that revised the Bell Trade Act, drew attention to devastation from war.[65] Dingell argued that after the "tragic tidal wave of war," the Philippines "are destitute and devastated." "The people are confused and desperate," and "for 4 years the people of the Philippines fought our war, the war of the United States against Japan, against the Axis." Dingell argued that in the ten months since the war's end, the United States had "done very little to recognize this valorous service of a great and heroic people," who had not only sacrificed their lives in war, but also "the fruits of their land" and "their national economy." To not support free trade was cowardly. For example, Dingell argued against proposals to cut the Philippine quota from 1,000,000 short tons (the quota before the war) to 102,000 short tons. He said that this was a "niggardly action, which tells the world that we are weighing in the balance of 102,000 short tons of sugar quota against the unlimited heroism and sacrifices of a great people in the cause of democracy. What a cheap way of paying off our obligation. What a miserly way of reckoning our debt to a heroic people."[66]

The sponsor of the Trade Act, Representative Bell, also spoke of U.S. duty to the Philippines when arguing for the Rehabilitation Act. While he acknowledged the material benefits of the bill to the United States, Bell also emphasized that the United States owed Filipinos for their loyalty. Using the same language as Truman's statement accompanying the Rescission Act (that the U.S. had a "moral obligation . . .to look after the welfare of the Philippine Army veterans"), Bell stated that the United States had "a moral obligation" to the Philippines, "a gallant little country whose people fought with unfailing loyalty and courage in the recent conflict."[67] Unlike in pre-war debates over trade and sugar, state actors like Dingell and Bell framed colonial policy as a U.S. debt and obligation to suffering Filipinos rather than as only for the material benefit of the United States.

Of course, as state actors concealed colonial relations, they also believed trade and U.S.-led rehabilitation would serve the United States. Bell, for example, argued that "if we do not pass this bill we will be depriving this country of vast amounts of trade" and that voting down the Rehabilitation Act would "dry up a golden stream of commerce that will bring wealth and welfare to both countries."[68] It was both in the U.S. material interests and U.S. duty, then, to aid the Philippines. As he argued in favor of maintaining the pre-war sugar quota, Dingell claimed that the Trade Act not only "rehabilitated the economy of the Philippine Islands," but also could "restore the dignity of man and thus to [*sic*] bring about the maximum possible and the earliest possible restoration of a two-way trade." This would "induce capital," specifically U.S. capital, "which has been heavily entrenched in this Pacific paradise, to resume its active and productive role in rebuilding of the sugar mills, the mine tipples, the mills, and industry in general, in order to bring about prosperity among the Filipino people." If the United States did not support the Philippine economy, then, Dingell claimed, they "will have failed in all our efforts in the Philippines and the Far East."[69] Free trade was part of the United States' obligation to loyal Filipinos, and if the United States did not deliver, it risked not only losing capital but also compromising its reputation and position in Asia.

Filipinos Coming of Age

Even as U.S. state actors cited loyalty and reframed dependency and U.S. colonial extraction in ways that evaded explicit racial logics, they still clung to polite racist logics of tutelage. In a draft called "The Philippines Come of Age," Secretary of the Interior Ickes referred to the Philippines as soon reaching its "political maturity." He cautioned that independence did not mean that "the United States would be relieved of the duty of solving or paying attention to the Islands or their problems." He continued, "As a matter of fact, this is the attitude with which many in the United States have approached the problem of the Philippines. It is an attitude reminiscent of the righteous parent who brings up his child the best way that he knows how, and, when that child reaches his maturity, the parent leads him forth into the world and says, 'you are on your own now.'" Ickes argued that "in more than one respect this has been the attitude of the United States," which he qualified was "not to say that the United States has not been a good parent." He noted, for example, that "we have provided the Philippines with a better education than most colonies. We have seen to it that the Filipino people were healthy and we have provided the Islands with a large allowance in terms of trade preferences and governmental expenditures." The United States raised its child well. "The gallantry and bravery of those Filipinos who fought side by side with the Americans on Bataan and Corregidor, the utter failure of the Japanese to win the Filipinos over to the Greater Asia Sphere of Co-Prosperity, and a thousand acts of heroism in defense of the United States" made clear the United States' success "as more than a good parent."[70]

Drawing on the familial tutelage metaphor, Ickes argued that the United States needed to protect a smaller, emerging nation, like the Philippines.

A good parent did not leave their child to fend for themselves, even as they came of age. Thus, although the United States devotedly completed its mission to raise the Philippines to maturity, Ickes emphasized "that there is a difference between training a boy to take his place in a community of his people and training a country to take its place in a community of nations." To avoid a situation in which the Philippines could be "stepped on" or "crushed and gobbled up by the stronger countries,"[71] Ickes argued for that the Philippine Trade Act would help address economic problems in the Philippines. In the House, Robertson also referenced the years of relationship as years of tutelage, noting that U.S.–Philippine relations were important for future U.S. geopolitical interests: "Throughout the Orient our ideals are being challenged by communism. The challenge of an idea cannot be successfully met by force. . . . We have taught the Filipino people our principles of democracy. In the survival of those teachings we have a crucial stake. If they are to survive in the Philippines, they must have economic as well as political independence."[72] Thus, Robertson argued that because the Philippines was taught by the United States, the United States must continue to support the Philippines through free trade.

During preparations for independence, Filipino elites also invoked the language of tutelage. As previously discussed, Roxas fought for a twenty-eight-year relationship in which U.S. investors would receive equal natural resource investment rights as Filipino investors. To show his support for the parity agreement and defend against accusations that he was compromising Philippine sovereignty, he argued that parity was not "an abridgment of sovereignty" but "an exercise of sovereignty by the Filipino people."[73] Roxas claimed that the United States "realizes just as a good man should realize when he raises a child to age and maturity that he has some obligations to that child and that he does not discharge that obligation by turning him out of doors into the cold without any assurance of a livelihood for him."[74] He cast the Philippines as a dependent of the United States even as he prepared for independence. At the same time, for such Filipino elites, given the constraints and systems of colonial rule, referring to their emerging nation as a child was not merely a belittling gesture. Rather, these political leaders appealed to the United States for recognition of their growth. They were no longer savages, as was thought to be the case when the United States first colonized the archipelago. Now, Filipinos were well-trained children of the United States, ready to take on more responsibility. And they were still teachable and thus attractive participants in ongoing reciprocal economic and military relations. For Filipino elites, being a child of the United States, then, was not oppositional to independence, and in fact could provide material benefits.

As U.S. state actors drew on the decades-long relationship with the Philippines to justify empire as aid, they spoke in less explicitly hierarchical familial terms. Instead, they recast U.S.–Philippine relations as based on friendship and fraternity. For example, on October 3, 1945, President Truman issued a statement on Philippine rehabilitation, noting that "this program will, of course, reflect the traditional friendship of the people of the United States and of the Philippines, and it will take account of the heroic and loyal conduct of the Filipinos during the war."[75] Similarly, speaking in favor of the Trade Act, Representative Stefan (R-NE) called upon "our bond of friendship with the Filipino people," which, he argued, "does not alone extend deep into our common yesterdays, but through today and into our common tomorrow." He continued, "We need this brotherhood in peace as we have needed it in war. We need it for the sake of the Filipinos. We need it for our own sake."[76] Stefan not only portrayed U.S. rehabilitation of the Philippines as rooted in decades of friendship but also as in the United States' self-interest. As he and Truman redefined empire as aid, they also disguised the colonial relationship as friendship.

A NEW MODEL OF DEMOCRACY AS COUNTERPROPAGANDA

As administrators and legislators both drew on and disguised the existing racial-imperial grammar, they hoped that deals for trade, rehabilitation, and military assistance could improve the United States' global reputation. They presented the United States' informal empire as a new model for democracy. Not only were Filipinos owed something for their loyalty, but in the context of the Cold War, U.S. state actors argued that economic, political, and military influence—key features of the U.S. racial-imperial grammar in the Philippines—were evidence of the United States' democratic and anti-imperialist aims. Filipinos became allies against threats to U.S. hegemony.

Colonial administrators upheld how U.S. influence in the Philippines was crucial to the U.S. war effort and suggested that it would serve as a model for the world. Four months before Philippine independence, Ickes stated, "We have made our policy in the Philippines the basis of our propaganda in the Far East. We have boasted about the imminent independence of the islands as a contrast to Japanese policy and have held it up as an example to the Asiatic people of what they may expect from us after the war."[77] For Ickes, securing the post-independence relationship between the United States and the Philippines was crucial "to assure the entrenchment of American republicanism, American democracy, economic opportunity, and social advancement in the Philippines." High Commissioner of the Philippines Paul McNutt argued: "We have boasted long of our enlightened policy in the Philippines and we have assumed that the example of their independence will serve to destroy European imperialism in Asia."[78] McNutt also called the Philippines "a branch bank of democracy, an outpost of western idealism" that would be pivotal in "the preservation of peace in the world," "set[ting] a new pattern of thinking . . .and of acting throughout the world."[79] By his estimation, the act would increase not only Philippine but widespread Asian fealty to the United States. He wrote, "On July 4, when our flag comes down in the Philippines, it will fly actually higher in the hearts and minds of the people of the Philippine and of the entire Far East than ever before in history."[80] In a world increasingly critical of racism and empire, U.S. state actors cast the end of U.S. rule in the Philippines as an opportunity to prove America's good spirit and magnanimity to the world.

Just as U.S. policy toward the Philippines would manage reputational questions, so too did U.S. state actors argue that post-war deals with the Philippines would create allies. Defending his proposal to stabilize the Philippines, Ickes argued it would create "a civil environment which will be hospitable to the conduct of military operations and the creation of a close and strong ally in that quarter of the globe."[81] Ickes and other U.S. state actors justified these neocolonial arrangements as crucial to maintaining U.S. hegemony in a post–World War II Asia. Like their imperialist forebears who distinguished U.S. rule from Spain's, McNutt and Ickes argued that U.S. policy in the Philippines was an exceptional model for the world. Even if the United States had been an empire, it was an empire unlike others. After all, they argued, the United States was preparing to transfer sovereignty to the Philippines.

During and after World War II, Democrats and former nativist-isolationists joined their imperialist counterparts in their concern for U.S. hegemony abroad. They too believed that the United States' approach to the Philippines could help improve the former's global reputation. Senator Millard Tydings (D-MD) claimed that "in the Far East our whole prestige and the future opinion of the people of Far East of the United States will depend, as it has in the past so successfully on our treatment of the Philippine Islands." He continued, saying he felt "very strongly that throughout the Far East we shall receive from our contribution, because of our accomplishment in finishing the great job we have done in the Philippine Islands, a credit which will amount to far more than any money."[82] For Senator Tydings, the success of the U.S. model in the Philippines would be taken as proof by other Asian countries of U.S. goodwill. Representative C. Jasper Bell (D-MO) reflected similar concerns about the United States' global reputation, stating: "the teeming millions of China want to know that; the people of Burma want to know that; the little countries of Europe want to know how the United States treats the people of the Philippines." He argued that "they want to know whether our boasted words of brotherhood for all men and of fairness in international dealings, the good-neighbor policy, are sincere, and whether we mean those things or whether we do not."[83] Representative J. Leroy Johnson (R-CA) echoed these sentiments, saying, "Millions of people in that part of the world are looking hopefully toward the day when they may, like the Philippines, become free and independent. No one knows how far-reaching or important our conduct may be today."[84] Legislators from states that had long fought for nativist exclusion and Philippine independence argued that this was a moment to prove the United States' anti-imperial commitments to the world. They joined their imperialist and Republican counterparts in arguing that U.S. policy toward the Philippines was a program for democracy.

CONCLUSION

In light of post-war instability, attacks on their geopolitical position, and communist and collaborationist threats, the United States executive branch worried about what the end of formal rule of the Philippines would mean for their hegemony. Like their imperialist counterparts of the early 1900s, to solve their problems, they secured executive control with input from the military. They built a program for post-war and post-independence stability on three pillars: free trade, U.S. development and investment, and military assistance. The first two were explicitly tied together: free trade in exchange for U.S. natural resource rights. The latter, military assistance, came as financial aid, equipment, and bases. U.S. state actors no longer needed formal empire; they could achieve goals of U.S. economic, military, political, and territorial control abroad through agreements with ostensibly sovereign states. This new model may appear less coercive than the early years of U.S. empire in the archipelago. U.S. state actors, led by the Department of the Interior, however, built U.S. foreign relations on the practices and logics of colonial administration. The formal terms changed, but the deep grammar of racial-imperial rule persisted.

Even before it gained independence from the United States, the Philippine Republic ceded sovereignty to the United States. Free trade, rehabilitation, and military agreements, secured while the Philippines was still a colony, entrenched the unequal relations between former ruler and subject state and affirmed the power of the executive branch to manage overseas affairs. Shalom writes, "As formal sovereignty changed hands in the Philippines, U.S. strategic and economic interests remained intact."[85] In the name of "decolonization" and "democracy," the U.S. executive branch together with Congress gutted Philippine sovereignty even before independence. As the United States decolonized, state actors continued to treat the Philippines as if it belonged to the United States. The transition to Philippine independence circumscribed Philippine sovereignty and maintained U.S. influence over the Philippine territory and its politics.

Prior to World War II, U.S. state actors equivocated over including the Philippines in the United States. Nativist state actors warned against incorporating and bestowing rights to savage and dependent people. World War II, however, demonstrated the importance of securing U.S. interests around the globe and the Philippines' strategic role. U.S. state actors reached consensus that the territory and resources of the Philippines were important and should remain (at least partially) under U.S. control even if the Philippines became nominally independent. In the newfound consensus, U.S. state actors not only spoke of the material and reputational benefits of maintaining control in the islands, but they also agreed that the United States' global position was at stake. State actors argued for continued Western control over the archipelago and invoked polite racist language as they described the Philippines.

It was not only imperialists or interventionists, however, that made these arguments. Both Republican and Democrat state actors spoke of the

Philippines and Filipinos as dependent on and loyal to the United States. Whereas nativists once argued that Filipinos were dependent and should therefore be excluded from the U.S. metropole, now politicians claimed that the United States had created the conditions of dependence. And because Filipinos were dependent, the United States owed a debt to the Philippines in the form of trade, rehabilitation, and military agreements. In other words, U.S. state actors framed the extension of U.S. imperial control in the archipelago as benevolent aid for a dutiful ward that had now come of age. Support, however, was only available to the territory and not the loyal people of the Philippines. The logic whereby the Philippines was both a ward and an independent country dated back to and was rooted in colonial definitions of the Philippine territory as "foreign in a domestic sense" and "belonging to, but not part of the United States."[86]

These two chapters addressed how U.S. state actors disguised explicit racial-imperial rule as ostensibly race-neutral foreign affairs. On the one hand, they abrogated rights promised to Filipino people. On the other, they concealed the hierarchical relations of empire under the guise of aid. As in Part II, U.S. state actors took advantage of the flexible colonial relationship established in the *Insular Cases*. They continued to hide traces of empire at home and erase explicitly vulgar racial logics of rule abroad. They claimed they had no obligation to colonial subjects while, at the same time, continuing to lay claim to the Philippine territory and resources. By effacing promises made to Filipino people and citing forthcoming independence, U.S. state actors argued Filipinos had no rights in the metropole. Likewise, with forthcoming independence, economic and military assistance could be framed as generous foreign aid. The archipelago deserved support, but people who sacrificed their lives did not. It was only in the context of acts that would strengthen the United States' economic position and political influence in the Philippines and Asia—rather than acts about the social welfare benefits and citizenship owed to actual, individual Filipinos—that U.S. state actors invoked the dependence and welfare of Filipinos as a rationale for helping them.

CONCLUSION

THE EMPIRE'S NEW CLOTHES

To some observers, the end of World War II ushered in the end of empire and racial rule. In 1946, the United States recognized Philippine independence, and other imperial powers in Asia soon followed suit. Great Britain recognized the independence of Burma, India, and Pakistan in 1947 and Sri Lanka in 1948. The Dutch did the same for Indonesia in 1949. Not only did empires relinquish sovereign claims abroad, but some metropolitan legislatures also lifted racial exclusions to migration and naturalization. In the United States, Chinese individuals gained the right to naturalize in 1943 and Asian Indians and Filipinos in 1946. In 1946, France rebranded its empire as the French Union, a federation of France and its colonies. Colonized people now possessed the "qualities" of citizenship, which eliminated, at least in law, unequal socioeconomic treatment of colonial subjects.[1] In 1948, Great Britain passed new nationality legislation expanding the rights—including for migration—of people in their dominions.[2]

In this period, former empires contended with their histories of hierarchical rule. It may seem that imperial state actors developed an increasingly progressive orientation toward race and empire after World War II. After all, from France and Britain to the United States, metropolitan state actors passed new legislation, made promises of unity under a federation, and flirted with possibilities of self-government. In the United States, how politicians discussed Filipinos and imperial rule over the Philippines changed. Explicitly and vulgarly racist arguments for excluding Filipinos from the metropole and for ruling over Filipinos all but died away. The era of formal empire ended.

Yet, this was not a new dawn. Examination of supposed decolonization lays bare imperial continuity. While peddling the fiction that they had changed, white empires continued violent suppression and unequal treatment of colonial subjects.[3] France retook its colony of Indochina from Japan during World War II Despite repeated declarations of independence by Vietnam and Cambodia, the French empire did not recognize these countries' sovereignty until 1954. The British, though they had promised their colonies a path to self-government, attempted to crush the Malaysian Communist Party and guerrillas in Burma who had fought against the Japanese Occupation.[4] Before recognizing Indonesian independence, the Dutch violently responded to Indonesia's 1945 declaration of independence.[5] Just two years before the United States recognized Philippine independence, they reimposed colonial rule in their project of "liberation" from the Japanese. As the war ended, the United States suppressed and denied military benefits, going back on promises of equality made to veterans who served in the war.

Concerned about anti-colonial nationalist agitation, imperial state actors sought ways to reassert their dominance over the colonies Japan had occupied during the war. In April 1946, less than three months before Philippine independence, Senator Robert A. Taft (R-OH), son of former President and head of the Philippine Commission William Howard Taft, declared his support for continuing the imperial relationship that his father had a crucial role in shaping. Speaking in favor of the 1946 Trade Act, he stated, "We are responsible for having built up the economy of the Philippines based on particular tariffs applicable to Philippine industries. . . .I think we should recognize permanently a special relationship with the Philippines and not pretend that 20 years from now it is going to be any different from what it is today, after they become free in July." Taft compared forthcoming Philippine independence to the United States' relationship with Cuba and Britain's special relationships with its former colonies. He also cited military bases as evidence of the permanent relationship between the United States and the Philippines. The bases would keep the Philippines tied to the United States politically and serve as "an American outpost." And the United States would continue to act as a "big brother" to the Philippines.[6] As Taft's statement underscores, from the early days of U.S. rule over the Philippines, the United States secured trade deals, developed the economy for U.S. interests, relied on military labor, and invested in the territory as a strategic outpost. Even as the era of formal empire ended, U.S. state actors advocated for imperial continuity.

U.S. state actors also faced new conditions wrought through World War II. As they responded to calls for racial equity, threats of anti-colonial nationalist uprisings, and communism, however, the United States led their European counterparts in reinscribing a white hegemonic rule. While the explicit language of their racial-imperial grammar disappeared from justifications for U.S.–Philippine relations, notions of subordination and loyalty to Western ideals remained. U.S. federal state actors changed how they talked about overseas influence. Formerly isolationist and imperialist federal state actors united in their vision of U.S. hegemony. They justified this plan in polite and racially inevident terms, refashioning racial-imperial rule as political divisions that obscured and reinscribed global racial hierarchies. U.S. state actors showed that empire could endure.

STATE FORMATION THROUGH WAR-MAKING AND CONFLICTS OVER WHITE HEGEMONY

To explain both the transformations and persistence of empire, this book charted how, in making war, U.S. federal state actors confronted their fears about threats to U.S. white hegemony. As they answered questions about who "we" are opposed to "them," members of the U.S. Congress, the executive branch, and the U.S. Supreme Court grappled with the relationship of the United States to the Philippines and its people. Analogies were especially useful: who are "we" like; and, by contrast, who are "they" like? U.S. state actors differentiated Filipinos from their ideal Anglo-Saxon white population in the United States.

At the beginning of the story, in 1898, the United States went to war against Spain and for four more years continued to fight the Philippines in their own war of independence. As the United States claimed sovereignty over new, nonwhite people, nativist-isolationists and imperialists agreed that the United States should remain a white nation. They disagreed, however, over

TABLE C.1. Characterizations of Filipinos' Racial Status
Relative to U.S. and Other Nonwhite, Outsider Populations

EVENTS	YEARS AND CORRESPONDING BOOK PART	WHITE HEGEMONY AT HOME	WHITE HEGEMONY ABROAD
Spanish–American War	1898–1913 (Part I)	Filipinos are biologically inferior racial outsiders like domestic nonwhites.	Filipinos are uncivilized children capable of learning under U.S. tutelage.
Election of Democrats, World War I, the Great Depression, and pre-World War II	1913–1941 (Part II)	Filipinos are racial outsiders like domestic nonwhites. Specifically, they are Asian aliens.	Filipinos are loyal subjects and wards.
World War II	1941–1945 (Part II)	Filipinos are allies against Japanese but are still outsiders.	Filipinos are loyal allies.
End of World War II and Philippine independence	1945–1946 (Part III)	Filipinos are allies against communism and for U.S. democracy in the East (loyal) but are outsiders to the United States.	

the best way to maintain white hegemony. There were two camps. Nativist-isolationists, who would rather halt territorial expansion than risk browning the nation, relied on vulgarly racist claims that underscored the inherent biological difference between Filipinos and U.S. whites. Taking the Philippines risked the inclusion of nearly seven million Filipinos as potential U.S. citizens. These state actors, primarily Southern and West Coast legislators, compared Filipinos to unwanted nonwhite populations in the U.S. metropole. Imperialists, however, saw the possibilities for global white hegemony. They believed they could expand U.S. sovereignty to new territories without abiding by the promise of equal citizenship. Speaking in politely racist terms, they characterized Filipinos as little brown brothers capable of learning the art of self-government under U.S. tutelage. Imperialists made claims of cultural difference between Filipinos and U.S. whites. Initially motivated by their commitment to either domestic or global white hegemony, U.S. state actors came to different conclusions about the relationship of the United States, its colony, and the world.

Unable to reconcile commitments to racial exclusion from the metropole and imperial expansion abroad, in the *Insular Cases* of the early 1900s, the U.S. Supreme Court translated explicitly racial concerns into new legal and institutional forms. By institutionalizing ambiguity as the foundation of U.S. overseas colonialism, the Supreme Court cemented conflicts over white hegemony into legal and administrative structures. With a legislative branch hostile to overseas empire, the executive branch, led by the War Department, stepped in to build an institutionally autonomous and powerful foreign affairs state.

A flexible legal structure for managing colonial people and territory allowed for both legislative and executive discretionary treatment of Filipinos and the Philippines. From the early 1900s through 1941, nativist-isolationists and imperialists bifurcated domestic and foreign aspects of imperial rule as they autonomously managed each. The nativist-isolationist faction wielded power within the legislative branch, and they aimed to preserve the white racial order at home. They continued to see Filipinos in light of domestic racial problems, primarily in reference to earlier waves of Asian migrants. They cast Filipinos as biologically inferior and undesirable dependent wards. And while predominating "scientific" ideas of race at the time classified Filipinos as distinct from Asians, isolationists lumped Filipinos into this category as a basis for claiming they were unassimilable aliens. Characterizing Filipinos as Asian outsiders supported isolationists' claims that Filipinos could not be considered part of the United States. They passed legislation to limit Filipino migration, settlement, and naturalization. As they cast Filipinos as Asian outsiders and excluded them from the demographic definition of the polity, nativist-isolationist legislators hid the fact of empire at home.

Imperialists, meanwhile, were dedicated to expanding white hegemony abroad. They saw the Philippines as an important stepping-stone to Asia and an outpost of U.S. influence abroad. Through their control of the executive branch, they laid down a program of tutelage in the Philippines, training Filipinos in the art of civilized government and "modern" industrial development. U.S. imperialists also invested in Philippine agricultural industries and natural resource development. They argued that the Philippine economy (and Filipinos) needed support in developing toward a civilized nation. To accomplish this, U.S. imperialist state actors claimed oversight of the Philippine colonial government. They tied Philippine industries to the United States' economy through trade arrangements. Because imperialists saw the Philippines as geostrategically important to the United States, they installed military bases and trained the Filipino military. When it came to U.S. economic and military interests, imperialist state actors included the Philippine territory in geographic definitions of the polity.

The bifurcation of the domestic and foreign aspects of racial-imperial rule was in place when World War II arrived on U.S. shores in 1941. When the Japanese attacked Hawai'i and the Philippines, formerly nativist-isolationist state actors joined their imperialist counterparts in seeing Japan as the most pressing racial threat. At the same time, formerly imperialist state actors had established a system of U.S. influence abroad that was no longer explicitly racial but built on trade, aid, and military agreements. In light of concerns of another global war, those preoccupied with the spread of white hegemony abroad avoided explicit mention of race and spoke of the Philippines as a strategic site and Filipinos as loyal U.S. nationals. The utility of the islands and the deracialized characterization of Filipinos as loyal brothers in arms gained traction. The United States even promised expedited naturalization and social welfare benefits to Filipinos who served for the United States in World War II. Filipinos proved their loyalty in war as the United States turned to a new racialized enemy in Asia, the Japanese. Faced with a war against Japan, U.S. federal state actors hid race from the foreign aspects of U.S. imperial rule of the Philippines.

After World War II, no longer did U.S. state actors speak of Filipinos in vulgarly or even explicitly racist terms. Instead, they disguised U.S.–Philippine relations in nonhierarchical terms. They characterized Filipinos as loyal former wards who had come of age under U.S. tutelage. Faced with rising concerns about communism and colonial uprisings, formerly isolationist politicians joined their imperialist counterparts in constructing Filipinos in politely racist ways, as "good Asians" and allies in democracy. As the promised date of Philippine independence arrived, U.S. state actors argued that the Philippines was proof of the United States' anti-imperial aims. Not only that, but the archipelago served as the United States' exemplar of democratic tutelage. Filipinos' democratic training under the United

States, their loyal wartime service, and their new status as U.S. allies, however, did not mean they would be included in demographic definitions of the United States. Although the United States promised Filipino veterans citizenship and rights in exchange for their service, Congress rescinded these promises after the war. U.S. state actors now ignored their colonial obligation to Filipinos.

By portraying U.S. Filipinos as loyal, however, U.S. state actors veiled ongoing U.S. imperial influence in the islands. After World War II and Philippine independence, U.S. state actors argued that in exchange for Filipino loyalty, the United States should aid the emerging Philippine Republic. The U.S. executive branch and the U.S. Congress extended colonial trade arrangements, provided Philippine natural resource rights to U.S. citizens, and maintained military bases in the archipelago. In the name of development, aid, and political stability, the U.S. executive branch continued to intervene in both Philippine and global politics. Filipinos' colonial loyalty and coming of age under the United States did not gain them equal rights but provided cover for continuing U.S. racial-imperial rule in the Philippines. By the end of World War II and in the transition to Philippine independence, U.S. federal state actors removed explicit mention of racial difference from discourse about U.S. imperial influence abroad. By making war and debating the relationships among the United States, the Philippines, and the world, U.S. state actors transformed how they managed the world outside their nation's metropolitan borders.

ENDURING EMPIRE AFTER 1946 AND BEYOND THE PHILIPPINES

War-making and debates over white hegemony shaped U.S. racial-imperial rule in the Philippines. At the same time, the transformations to the United States' grammar of rule extend beyond 1946 and beyond the Philippines. The United States still maintains ambiguous sovereign relations with the territories of Puerto Rico, Guåhan, American Sāmoa, the U.S. Virgin Islands, the Commonwealth of the Northern Mariana Islands, and its former trust territories of the Federated States of Micronesia, the Republic of the Marshall Islands, and the Republic of Palau. Years of formal rule in the Pacific and infrastructural development in World War II also laid a path toward new strategies of informal empire.[7] While it is beyond the scope of this book to explore how U.S.

empire endures after 1946 and beyond the Philippines, future work can ask how the language of race, economics, and political influence has co-evolved and changed. Have politicians continued to avoid explicit and vulgar claims of biological inferiority when speaking about people under the influence of the United States? If the vocabulary has changed, does the underlying system of hierarchical relations—concretized in law and administrative structure—remain? Grounded in the insights from the case of U.S. rule over the Philippines, I briefly draw attention to how the United States—through executive control, economic arrangements, political repression, and militarization—has both made racial-imperial rule endure and refashioned it in other terms.[8]

For decades, the executive branch rehearsed their program of free trade, agricultural and technological "modernization," and economic development in the Philippines. Years of formal imperial rule laid an important foundation for how the United States would shape global economic arrangements not in the name of empire but development.[9] Like in the colonial period, the U.S. executive branch—including the Departments of Interior, State, and War—controlled post-war Philippine policy, often with little input from the U.S. Congress.[10] Meanwhile, the systems of executive-led imperial influence that the United States developed over fifty years in the Philippines also shaped U.S. intervention beyond the territory. Alongside preparations for Philippine independence and post-war policy, the United States created a mandate over Japan and its former colonies, including Korea. The U.S. executive branch created the Point Four Program to incentivize corporate investment and development in the world more broadly. Through the program, which offered technical assistance and capital to "underdeveloped" countries in Asia, Africa, and Latin America, the Interior—a department that had historically managed colonial affairs—expanded its global influence.

Ideas of racial difference continued to shape U.S. foreign policy and the administration of aid. Believing that Europe was more civilized and deserving, U.S. state actors not only provided more aid but also structured their agreements with Europeans in more equal terms. The United States created the Marshall Plan (for economic assistance to Western Europe) and multilateral alliances—like the General Agreement on Tariffs and Trade (GATT) and the North Atlantic Treaty Organization (NATO). In these arrangements, U.S. state actors conceived of Europeans as partners in rehabilitation and governance. Such programs did not exist for the rest of the world, however.

While the United States built alliances with and among European countries, U.S. officials argued that Asians were too different from people of the United States. U.S. state actors justified hierarchical and bilateral U.S.-led post-war development in Japan, Korea, Taiwan, and Vietnam by referencing fears about pan-Asian alliances and communism as well as ideas of Asian alienage and inferiority.[11] The United States also provided significantly less aid for non-European countries. In 1948, the Marshall Plan designated $13.3 billion dollars to bolster post-war European economies. For the rest of the world, President Harry Truman framed the Point Four Program, like the Philippine Trade and Rehabilitation Acts, as providing "necessary" aid. In contrast to the Marshall Plan, the Point Four Program allocated only $34.5 million. A precursor to the United States Agency for International Development (USAID), the Point Four Program also extended practices of U.S. informal empire in Latin America through the Institute for Inter-American Affairs (IIAA).[12]

Just as the ideas of racial difference structured informal empire under the mantle of aid, in the post–World War II era, U.S. state actors transformed overt war into counterinsurgency.[13] Racial divisions became political ones: Black, brown, and yellow formerly colonized people posed anti-colonial, nationalist, communist, and terrorist threats to U.S. global hegemony. U.S. officials continued to treat the Philippines as a laboratory for perfecting imperial influence and U.S. hegemony.[14] In the 1950s, U.S. state actors declared that Philippine anti-communist efforts were the "the first victory over Asian communism."[15] General Edward Lansdale, who supervised intelligence operations against the Huks, exported his practices and institutions to Vietnam. CIA director Allen Dulles invited Lansdale to form a private paramilitary organization not only for Asian but also for Latin American anti-communist interventions.[16] As U.S. state actors engaged in political repression and counterinsurgency, they avoided explicit mention of race or exercising formal imperial sovereignty. Since 1946, to manage threats against suspected communists and terrorists in Afghanistan, USAID carried on the work of empire under the banner of aid, development, and democracy.[17] Aid—accompanied by "anti-terrorist" surveillance, regulation, and policing, all of which call back to the colonial era—continues to be part of a flexible system of imperial management that allows the United States to exert its influence outside its sovereign borders.[18] Under the veil of supporting allied governments and managing communist and terrorist threats, the United States has maintained its global hegemony.

U.S. occupations and wars against purported anti-colonial nationalists, communists, and terrorists were made possible by another pillar of U.S. empire: militarization. Even as the United States disavowed formal and explicit racial-imperial rule, bases—as sites of formal sovereign control—remained. Within the Philippines, on the Subic Bay Naval and Clark Air Bases, the United States continued to exert legal and administrative oversight after formal decolonization. From 1946 to 1991, the U.S. Navy could collect tax, distribute utilities and business licenses, search without a warrant, and conduct deportations.[19] By continuing to treat the Philippines as an extension of the United States' territory, U.S. state actors maintained territorial sovereignty over the archipelago and expanded U.S. geopolitical influence in Asia and the world. Although the Philippine government did not renew the Military Bases Agreement (which expired in 1991), in 1999, the United States and the Philippines signed a new agreement extending U.S. military influence. The Visiting Forces Agreement (VFA) allows the U.S. military access to Philippine airports and ports and to conduct military training and exercises in the archipelago. The old bases continue to serve as logistical hubs for the U.S. military.[20]

The Philippine Military Assistance Act of 1946 and the Military Bases Agreement of 1947 not only laid the groundwork for ongoing U.S. military influence in the archipelago, they also served as precursors to the U.S. National Security Council's strategy in the Cold War.[21] Beyond the Philippines, the United States increased military spending and secured what scholars have called its "bases of empire,"[22] "settler garrison,"[23] and "pointillist empire."[24] From Guantánamo to its installations in Iraq, the United States military maintains partial or semi-sovereign arrangements.[25] The United States still has bases in Guåhan and Puerto Rico, and its former mandate country Japan. The most well-known example of this is Okinawa.[26] The United States also limits foreign nations' sovereignty through Status of Forces Agreements (SOFAs), which—like the Military Bases Agreement of 1947—define the legal status of the U.S. military in foreign countries and the extent to which the foreign government's laws apply to U.S. soldiers. While the United States shares more jurisdiction with predominantly white host countries, it is more likely to withhold or limit shared governance from nonwhite states.[27] U.S. empire is still grounded in racialized territorial and legal control, albeit not in the wholesale claim to another polity.

Through militarization, political repression, and executive branch control over economic arrangements and aid, the United States maintains extraterritorial and hierarchical influence over not only the Philippines but the larger world. As U.S. state actors made war, they also made a durable and flexible form of hierarchical rule. Although the world looks different from when the United States first colonized the Philippines in 1898, ideas of racial difference continue to shape U.S. foreign policy. When formal empire ended in the Philippines, by portraying imperial influence as development, aid, and support for democracy, U.S. state actors found new ways to shape the lives of nonwhite people abroad. And they have since spread and developed these practices around the world.

IMPLICATIONS FOR STUDYING STATE TRANSFORMATION

This book began by asking how a system of rule could evolve without disrupting the foundational structure of inequality. Racial-imperial grammars of rule evolve over time and in response to war, but, as this study shows, logics of human difference and the commitment to white hegemony endure. By taking a historical and institutional approach, this book offers three insights for the study of racial and imperial state transformation more broadly. First, state actors cement ideas of human difference in laws, policies, and institutional structures that are not explicitly racial or imperial. Second, war-making catalyzes conflict over strategic aims. Unable to resolve disagreements, state actors institutionalize flexible and ambiguous laws. Third, and finally, while ambiguity enables a range of foreign and domestic policies, commitment to narrow ideas of the nation constrains possibilities for structural change. By examining how state actors disguise hierarchical rule, how they institutionalize ambiguity, and how enduring national ideologies limit the path of state formation, studies of state transformation can explain both continuity and change.

Studying state activity that is not, on its surface, about race or empire reveals the many sites in which state actors secure unequal rule. To study how power operates, we must look for where power seeks power. Different groups embed their interests in parts of the state that are relevant to them. In the case of U.S. rule over the Philippines, imperialists in the executive branch shaped policy about trade and development abroad. Isolationists in Congress took control over naturalization and migration at home. Studying each of these groups on their own conceals the reach of empire and the racial motivations that undergird ostensibly race-neutral policy. Most scholars of race would agree that just because something is not racist on its surface does not mean that it is not racist in intent or effect. Studying the historical development of policy, precedents, and how justifications change over time can shed light on how race informs politics without its explicit mention. For instance, foreign policy—as in trade agreements and economic and military aid—does more than secure geopolitical or material interests. It also advances white hegemony. Acts about migration and naturalization not only manage the racial demography of the purported nation, but they also define the state's relationship to subjugated territories and inhabitants of these places. Through laws about movement and citizenship, metropolitan state actors define what they owe to colonial subjects. Analyzing laws that do not explicitly address race or empire unveils how state actors construct enduring systems of inequality.

Just as we need to reveal the range of laws that support white hegemonic rule at home and abroad, we must also pay attention to variation in state actors' positions. Moments of disagreement illuminate how state actors debate, reconfigure, and often conceal said rule. War-making—preparing for, fighting in, and recovering from war—is an especially productive site of state formation. State actors consider how to define the nation in geographic and demographic terms, what they owe to their people, and how to secure their victories. When state actors disagree and evaluate the most pressing threat to their hegemony in divergent ways, ambiguity allows them to operate in isolation from one another. This may look like incoherent rule. Discretionary law-making and polysemous classification, however, are the downstream effects of legal compromises intended to satisfy two or more intractable sides. By bifurcating rule, state actors from different camps can operate with relative institutional autonomy from one another. Such independence allows them to try on a range of strategies for maintaining and spreading their influence. By decoupling domestic and foreign aspects of rule, state actors can carry out imperial relations under a new banner: foreign affairs. They can manage colonial subjects in the metropole as aliens. By institutionalizing ambiguity, bifurcating rule, and disguising empire, state actors manage conflicts and conceal the persistence of hierarchical and unequal rule.

Although ambiguity enables a range of practices, the enduring commitment to narrow definitions of the nation constrains meaningful structural transformation. Studies of state formation, then, must also be attentive to how the commitment to national ideologies and projects of hegemony structure law, policy, and institutions. After the Court institutionalized ambiguity in *Downes v. Bidwell*, state actors reevaluated and restructured their relationship to the Philippines, all while maintaining the U.S. racial-imperial grammar. The 1902 Organic Act, the 1916 Jones Act, the 1934 Tydings–McDuffie Act, and the 1946 Trade, Rehabilitation, and Military Assistance Acts created new possibilities for political arrangements, racial characterizations, and interstate arrangements. Rather than providing alternatives to imperial sovereignty, however, state actors reaffirmed their commitment to white hegemony. The independence promised and then granted to the Philippines maintained unequal relations in trade and cemented racial exclusion. None of the acts provided aid without substantial benefit to the United States, nor did they offer repair or restitution. While each of these acts appear to be progressive steps toward "decolonialization," they did not restructure power relations or redistribute resources. Empire endured through the persistence of narrow and racist notions of the ideal "nation," the institutionalization of ambiguity, and the implementation of hierarchical governance in policy that is ostensibly not about race or empire. The terms of rule may change, but the deep grammar remains in place.

Perhaps this seems like a dismal place to end this book. I have argued that even when they have different interests, powerful people institutionalize domestic and global inequalities. Anti-racist and anti-colonial strategies have not emerged from the political debates of federal state actors. Both isolation in the form of "America first" polices and intervention in the form of foreign aid and diplomacy are positions rooted in a commitment to white hegemonic rule. We must then disrupt this two-sided debate with an alternative approach to thinking about human difference and sovereignty. While this book is not about the Filipinos and their allies who endured empire and envisioned anti-colonial possibilities,[28] I hope close attention to how state actors secure empire can provide insights for studying and dismantling racial-imperial rule. By paying attention to how state actors debate rule and institutionalize ambiguity, we can analyze the political consequences that follow, isolate structural weaknesses, and discover paths not taken. The alternative visions of Filipino intellectuals, migrant workers, guerilla fighters, communist peasants, and even political elites provide some examples of other ways to conceive of the relationship among an empire state, racialized people, and the wider world. In our scholarship and struggles to challenge racial-imperial formations, then, we must not only identify the problems with paths taken as I have here but also look beyond the state to build a better and more just world.

NOTES

Introduction

1. This committee, formed on December 8, 1899, was tasked with understanding the conditions in former Spanish territories including the Philippines, Puerto Rico, and Cuba.

2. *Downes v. Bidwell*, 182 U.S. 244 (1901).

3. U.S. Congress, House, The Committee on Insular Affairs, Statement of Hon. William H. Taft, President of the Board of Commissioners to the Philippine Islands, 57th Congress, 1st and 2nd Sessions, February 21, 1902, 198.

4. U.S. Congress, House, The Committee on Insular Affairs, Statement of Hon. Felipe Buencamino, through Mr. Frank L. Joannini, Interpreter, 57th Congress; 1st and 2nd Sessions, May 31, 1902, 236; 271.

5. *An Act Temporarily to provide for the administration of the affairs of civil government in the Philippine Islands, and for other purposes,* Public Law 57-235 (1902).

6. Richard L. Watson Jr., "Furnifold Simmons and the Politics of White Supremacy," in *Race, Class and Politics in Southern History: Essays in Honor of Robert F. Durden,* ed. Jeffrey J. Crow et al. (Louisiana State University Press, 1989), 126–72.

7. Senator Simmons, speaking on S. 2295, "Civil Government for the Philippine Islands," on April 28, 1902, in 57th Congress, 1st Session, *Congressional Record* 35, pt. 5: 4759.

8. I refer to U.S. politicians, bureaucrats, and justices in the federal (or national) government of the United States as federal state actors or sometimes simply state actors. This book is primarily concerned with the ideologies and activities of those in the federal government, not state governments like North Carolina or Wisconsin.

9. David Theo Goldberg, *The Racial State* (Blackwell Publishers, 2002); Mahmood Mamdani, *Citizen and Subject: Contemporary Africa and the Legacy of Late Colonialism* (Princeton University Press, 1996); Andreas Wimmer, *Nationalist Exclusion and Ethnic Conflict: Shadows of Modernity* (Cambridge University Press, 2002).

10. *Cherokee Nation v. Georgia*, 30 U.S. 1 (1831).

11. Julia Adams, "Principals and Agents, Colonialists and Company Men: The Decay of Colonial Control in the Dutch East Indies," *American Sociological Review* 61, no. 1 (1996): 12–28; Karen Barkey, *Empire of Difference: The Ottomans in Comparative Perspective* (Cambridge University Press, 2008); Lauren Benton, *A Search for Sovereignty: Law and Geography in European Empires, 1400–1900* (Cambridge University Press, 2010); Christina Duffy Burnett and Burke Marshall, eds., *Foreign in a Domestic Sense: Puerto Rico, American Expansion, and the Constitution* (Duke University Press, 2001); Achille Mbembe, *On the Postcolony* (University of California Press, 2001); Sally Engle Merry, *Colonizing Hawai'i: The Cultural Power of Law* (Princeton University Press, 2000); Ann Laura Stoler and Frederick Cooper, "Between Metropole and Colony: Rethinking a Research Agenda," in *Tensions of Empire: Colonial Cultures in a Bourgeois World*, ed. Ann Laura Stoler and Frederick Cooper (University of California Press, 1997), 1–56; Nicholas Hoover Wilson, *Modernity's Corruption: Empire and Morality in the Making of British India* (Columbia University Press, 2023).

12. On imperial durability, see: Ann Laura Stoler, *Duress: Imperial Durabilities in Our Times* (Duke University Press, 2016). On durable inequality, see: Charles Tilly, *Durable Inequality* (University of California Press, 1998).

13. While critical discourse studies have explored the relationships of discourse, power, and racism, I use grammar as a metaphor for understanding how a system can both endure and change. See: Teun A. Van Dijk, *Elite Discourse and Racism* (SAGE, 1993); Teun A. van Dijk, *Discourse as Structure and Process* (SAGE, 1997); Theo Van Leeuwen, *Discourse and Practice: New Tools for Critical Discourse Analysis* (Oxford University Press, 2008); Gloria Wekker, *White Innocence: Paradoxes of Colonialism and Race* (Duke University Press, 2016); Ruth Wodak and Martin Reisigl, "Discourse and Racism," in *The Handbook of Discourse Analysis*, ed. Deborah Tannen et al. (John Wiley & Sons, Ltd., 2015), 576–96.

14. When speaking of an imperial and racial grammar, scholars have referred to the layers of meaning, codes, cultural fictions, architectures and rules of discourse, and a system by which we name and value. Both racial and imperial grammars are practiced and embodied. See: Eduardo Bonilla-Silva, "The Invisible Weight of Whiteness: The Racial Grammar of Everyday Life in Contemporary America," *Ethnic and Racial Studies* 35, no. 2 (February 1, 2012): 173–94; Erica R. Edwards, *The Other Side of Terror: Black Women and the Culture of US Empire* (NYU Press, 2021); Caroline Knowles, *Race and Social Analysis* (SAGE, 2003); Dylan Rodríguez, *Suspended Apocalypse: White Supremacy, Genocide, and the Filipino Condition* (University of Minnesota Press, 2010); Ann Laura Stoler and Frederick Cooper, "Between Metropole and Colony: Rethinking a Research Agenda," in *Tensions of Empire: Colonial Cultures in a Bourgeois World*, ed. Ann Laura Stoler and Frederick Cooper (University

of California Press, 1997), 1–56; Hortense Spillers, "Mama's Baby, Papa's Maybe: An American Grammar Book," *Diacritics* 17, no. 2 (1987): 64–81; Patrick Wolfe, "Settler Colonialism and the Elimination of the Native," *Journal of Genocide Research* 8, no. 4 (2006): 387–409.

15. Consider: (1) "they" as a singular pronoun; (2) "for whom is the gift?" versus "who is the gift for?"; (3) "if I were a carpenter" versus "if I was a carpenter."

16. Rick Baldoz, *The Third Asiatic Invasion: Migration and Empire in Filipino America, 1898–1946* (NYU Press, 2011); Hana E. Brown, "Who Is an Indian Child? Institutional Context, Tribal Sovereignty, and Race-Making in Fragmented States," *American Sociological Review* 85, no. 5 (October 1, 2020): 776–805; David Scott Fitz-Gerald and David Cook-Martín, *Culling the Masses* (Harvard University Press, 2014); Cybelle Fox, *Three Worlds of Relief: Race, Immigration, and the American Welfare State from the Progressive Era to the New Deal* (Princeton University Press, 2012); Gary Gerstle, *American Crucible: Race and Nation in the Twentieth Century* (Princeton University Press, 2002); Evelyn Nakano Glenn, "Settler Colonialism as Structure: A Framework for Comparative Studies of US Race and Gender Formation," *Sociology of Race and Ethnicity* 1, no. 1 (2015): 52–72; Ian Haney-López, *White by Law: The Legal Construction of Race* (NYU Press, 1996); Mara Loveman, *National Colors: Racial Classification and the State in Latin America* (New York: Oxford University Press, 2014); Marisela Martinez-Cola, "Visibly Invisible: TribalCrit and Native American Segregated Schooling," *Sociology of Race and Ethnicity* 6, no. 4 (October 1, 2020): 468–82; G. Cristina Mora, *Making Hispanics: How Activists, Bureaucrats, and Media Constructed a New American* (University of Chicago Press, 2014); Mae M. Ngai, *Impossible Subjects: Illegal Aliens and the Making of Modern America* (Princeton University Press, 2004); Aziz Rana, *The Two Faces of American Freedom* (Harvard University Press, 2010); George Steinmetz, *The Devil's Handwriting: Precoloniality and the German Colonial State in Qingdao, Samoa, and Southwest Africa* (University of Chicago Press, 2007).

17. Both "imperial formation" and "racial formation" borrow from the term "social formation," which refers to the "concrete complex comprising economic practice, political practice, and ideological practice at a certain place and stage of development." Louis Althusser et al., *Reading Capital: The Complete Edition* (Verso Books, 2016), 313. See also: Michael Omi and Howard Winant, *Racial Formation in the United States* (Routledge, 1994), 55; Ann Laura Stoler and Carole McGranahan, "Introduction: Refiguring Imperial Terrains," in *Imperial Formations*, ed. Ann Laura Stoler et al. (SAR Press, 2007), 8.

18. Because my discussion of Filipinos centers on the perspectives U.S. state actors had about them, this book attends to how the United States constructed its own national boundaries in relation to a Philippine nation that was likewise under construction. The reader should not assume the coherence of the Philippine nation; indeed, Chapter 2 demonstrates how ideas about who constituted the group of "Filipinos" were in flux. See: Patricio N. Abinales, *Making Mindanao: Cotabato and Davao in the Formation of the Philippine Nation-State* (Ateneo University Press, 2000); Patricio N. Abinales, "American Rule and the Formation of Filipino 'Colonial Nationalism,'"

Japanese Journal of Southeast Asian Studies 39, no. 4 (2002): 604–21; Oliver Charbonneau, *Civilizational Imperatives: Americans, Moros, and the Colonial World* (Cornell University Press, 2020); Adrian De Leon, *Bundok: A Hinterland History of Filipino America* (University of North Carolina Press, 2023); Moon-Kie Jung, *Reworking Race: The Making of Hawaii's Interracial Labor Movement* (Columbia University Press, 2006).

19. Henry William Brands, *Bound to Empire: The United States and the Philippines* (Oxford University Press, 1992); Michael Cullinane, "Playing the Game: The Rise of Sergio Osmeña 1898–1907," in *Philippine Colonial Democracy*, ed. Ruby R. Paredes (Ateneo de Manila University Press, 1988), 70–113; Michael Cullinane, *Ilustrado Politics: Filipino Elite Responses to American Rule, 1898–1908* (Ateneo de Manila University Press, 1989); Augusto Fauni Espiritu, *Five Faces of Exile: The Nation and Filipino American Intellectuals* (Stanford University Press, 2005); Paul A. Kramer, *The Blood of Government: Race, Empire, the United States, and the Philippines* (University of North Carolina Press, 2006); Alfred W. McCoy, "Quezon's Commonwealth: The Emergence of Philippine Authoritarianism," in *Philippine Colonial Democracy*, ed. Ruby R. Paredes (Ateneo de Manila University Press, 1988), 114–60; Alfred W. McCoy, "Sugar Barons: Formation of a Native Planter Class in the Colonial Philippines," in *Plantations, Proletarians and Peasants in Colonial Asia*, ed. Henry Bernstein, Tom Brass, and E. Valentine Daniel (Routledge, 1993); Ruby R. Paredes, ed., *Philippine Colonial Democracy* (Ateneo de Manila University Press, 1988).

20. Leia Castañeda Anastacio, *The Foundations of the Modern Philippine State: Imperial Rule and the American Constitutional Tradition in the Philippine Islands, 1898–1935* (Cambridge University Press, 2016); Julian Go, *American Empire and the Politics of Meaning: Elite Political Cultures in the Philippines and Puerto Rico During U.S. Colonialism* (Duke University Press, 2008).

21. For discussion of a research agenda that brings the metropole and colony and the foreign and domestic into the same analytic frame, see: Tony Ballantyne and Antoinette Burton, *Empires and the Reach of the Global: 1870–1945* (Harvard University Press, 2012); Amy Kaplan, *The Anarchy of Empire in the Making of US Culture* (Harvard University Press, 2005); Paul A. Kramer, *The Blood of Government: Race, Empire, the United States, and the Philippines* (University of North Carolina Press, 2006); Ann Laura Stoler and Frederick Cooper, "Between Metropole and Colony: Rethinking a Research Agenda," in *Tensions of Empire: Colonial Cultures in a Bourgeois World*, ed. Ann Laura Stoler and Frederick Cooper (University of California Press, 1997), 1–56.

22. Because the Spanish–American War began not as a war between the United States and Spain but with the Cuban and then the Filipino struggle for independence from Spain, Louis Pérez refers to the war as the War of 1898. Although the struggle of colonized people was the impetus for the war, because I focus on the conflict once the United States entered the war, I mostly refer to the war as the Spanish–American War. See: Louis A Pérez, *The War of 1898: The United States and Cuba in History and Historiography* (University of North Carolina Press, 1998).

23. Mary Dudziak, "Making Law, Making War, Making America," in *The Cambridge History of Law in America: Volume 3: The Twentieth Century and After (1920–)*, ed. Christopher Tomlins and Michael Grossberg (Cambridge University Press, 2008),

680–717; Paul Frymer, *Building an American Empire: The Era of Territorial and Political Expansion* (Princeton University Press, 2017); Michael Mann, *States, War, and Capitalism: Studies in Political Sociology* (Basil Blackwell, 1988); Charles Tilly, *Coercion, Capital, and European States, AD 990–1990* (Oxford Blackwell, 1992). But see: Miguel Angel Centeno, *Blood and Debt: War and the Nation-State in Latin America* (Penn State Press, 2002).

24. On institutional braiding, see Ira Katznelson, "Flexible Capacity: The Military and Early American Statebuilding," in *Shaped by War and Trade: International Influences on American Political Development*, ed. Ira Katznelson and Martin Shefter (Princeton University Press, 2002).

25. Daniel Immerwahr, *How to Hide an Empire: A History of the Greater United States* (Farrar, Straus and Giroux, 2019); Ira Katznelson, *When Affirmative Action Was White: An Untold History of Racial Inequality in Twentieth-Century America* (W. W. Norton, 2005); Daniel Kryder, *Divided Arsenal: Race and the American State During World War II* (Cambridge University Press, 2001); Catherine Lutz and Cynthia Enloe, *The Bases of Empire: The Global Struggle Against US Military Posts* (NYU Press, 2009); Suzanne Mettler, *Soldiers to Citizens: The GI Bill and the Making of the Greatest Generation* (Oxford University Press, 2005); James T. Sparrow, *Warfare State: World War II Americans and the Age of Big Government* (Oxford University Press, USA, 2011).

26. W.E.B. Du Bois, "The Souls of White Folk," in *Darkwater: Voices from within the Veil* (Humanity Books, 1920), 46.

27. J. A. Hobson, *Imperialism: A Study* (Liberty Fund, 2004); Vladimir Lenin, *Imperialism: The Highest Stage of Capitalism* (Resistance Books, 1999); George Padmore, *Africa and World Peace* (Routledge, 1972).

28. Michel Foucault, *"Society Must Be Defended": Lectures at the Collège de France, 1975–1976*, vol. 1 (Picador, 1997).

29. Ned Blackhawk, *Violence over the Land: Indians and Empires in the Early American West* (Harvard University Press, 2006), 5.

30. Mary L. Dudziak, *War Time: An Idea, Its History, Its Consequences* (Oxford University Press, 2012); Nikhil Pal Singh, *Race and America's Long War* (University of California Press, 2017).

31. Political scientists note that perceptions of state power change as a result of war. See for example: Robert Jervis et al., *Psychology and Deterrence* (Johns Hopkins University Press, 1985); Fareed Zakaria, *From Wealth to Power: The Unusual Origins of America's World Role* (Princeton University Press, 1999).

32. Pierre Bourdieu, "Rethinking the State: Genesis and Structure of the Bureaucratic Field," in *State/Culture*, ed. George Steinmetz (Cornell University Press, 1999), 53–75; Philip S. Gorski, *The Disciplinary Revolution: Calvinism and the Rise of the State in Early Modern Europe* (University of Chicago Press, 2003); Mara Loveman, "The Modern State and the Primitive Accumulation of Symbolic Power," *American Journal of Sociology* 110, no. 6 (2005): 1651–83; Jonathan Wyrtzen, *Worldmaking in the Long Great War: How Local and Colonial Struggles Shaped the Modern Middle East* (Columbia University Press, 2022).

33. Nikhil Singh, "Racial Formation in an Age of Permanent War," in *Racial Formation in the Twenty-First Century*, ed. Daniel Martinez HoSang et al. (University of California Press, 2012), 292.

34. For discussion of racial threat, see: Lawrence D. Bobo, "Prejudice as Group Position: Microfoundations of a Sociological Approach to Racism and Race Relations," *Journal of Social Issues* 55, no. 3 (1999): 445–72.

35. Kramer, *The Blood of Government*, 28–29; 30.

36. Frymer, *Building an American Empire*; Walter Johnson, *River of Dark Dreams* (Harvard University Press, 2013); Heather Cox Richardson, *West from Appomattox: The Reconstruction of America after the Civil War* (Yale University Press, 2007); Richard White, *The Republic for Which It Stands: The United States During Reconstruction and the Gilded Age, 1865–1896* (Oxford University Press, 2017).

37. Blackhawk, *Violence over the Land*, 5.

38. Frymer, *Building an American Empire*.

39. Aziz Rana, *The Two Faces of American Freedom* (Harvard University Press, 2010); Frymer, *Building an American Empire*.

40. Ethan Davis, "An Administrative Trail of Tears: Indian Removal," *American Journal of Legal History* 50, no. 1 (January 1, 2010): 49–100; Stephen J. Rockwell, *Indian Affairs and the Administrative State in the Nineteenth Century* (Cambridge University Press, 2010).

41. Brian DeLay, *War of a Thousand Deserts: Indian Raids and the U.S.-Mexican War* (Yale University Press, 2008).

42. Roxanne Dunbar-Ortiz, *An Indigenous Peoples' History of the United States* (Beacon Press, 2014); Frymer, *Building an American Empire*.

43. Blackhawk, *Violence over the Land*; Robert M. Utley, *The Indian Frontier 1846–1890* (University of New Mexico Press, 2003).

44. Richard Griswold del Castillo, *The Treaty of Guadalupe Hidalgo: A Legacy of Conflict* (University of Oklahoma Press, 1992).

45. Johnson, *River of Dark Dreams*, 307–8; Frymer, *Building an American Empire*, 132; 140–41.

46. Gerald Horne, *Race to Revolution: The U.S. and Cuba During Slavery and Jim Crow* (NYU Press, 2014); Johnson, *River of Dark Dreams*; Robert E. May, *The Southern Dream of a Caribbean Empire, 1854–1861* (University Press of Florida, 1973).

47. Frymer, *Building an American Empire*; Johnson, *River of Dark Dreams*; Matthew Karp, *This Vast Southern Empire: Slaveholders at the Helm of American Foreign Policy* (Harvard University Press, 2016); Pérez, *The War of 1898*.

48. In his opinion for the court, Justice Taney also differentiated the treatment of people of African descent from Native Americas, arguing that the former were never free people.

49. Moon-Kie Jung, *Beneath the Surface of White Supremacy: Denaturalizing U.S. Racisms Past and Present* (Stanford University Press, 2015).

50. Richardson, *West from Appomattox*, 3.

51. Sam Erman, *Almost Citizens: Puerto Rico, the U.S. Constitution, and Empire* (Cambridge University Press, 2018).

52. W.E.B. Du Bois, *Black Reconstruction in America, 1860–1880* (The Free Press, 1935).

53. Du Bois, *Black Reconstruction in America*; Eric Foner, *Reconstruction: America's Unfinished Revolution, 1863–1877* (Harper Collins, 2011).

54. Du Bois, *Black Reconstruction in America*; Foner, *Reconstruction*; Evelyn Nakano Glenn, *Unequal Freedom: How Race and Gender Shaped American Freedom and Labor* (Harvard University Press, 2002); Richard M. Valelly, *The Two Reconstructions: The Struggle for Black Enfranchisement* (University of Chicago Press, 2009).

55. Ian Millhiser, *Injustices: The Supreme Court's History of Comforting the Comfortable and Afflicting the Afflicted* (Nation Books, 2015). See especially *Slaughterhouse Cases* (1872) and the *Civil Rights Cases* (1883).

56. Fox, *Three Worlds of Relief*; Glenn, *Unequal Freedom*; Goldberg, *The Racial State*; Rogers M. Smith, Civic Ideals: Conflicting Visions of Citizenship in US History (Yale University Press, 1997).

57. For a discussion on the scholarly history of the term "settler colonialism," see Maile Renee Arvin, *Possessing Polynesians: The Science of Settler Colonial Whiteness in Hawai'i and Oceania* (Duke University Press, 2019); Frederick E. Hoxie, "Retrieving the Red Continent: Settler Colonialism and the History of American Indians in the US," *Ethnic and Racial Studies* 31, no. 6 (September 1, 2008): 1153–67; Patrick Wolfe, "Settler Colonialism and the Elimination of the Native."

58. Stephen Cornell, *The Return of the Native: American Indian Political Resurgence* (Oxford University Press, 1988); Vine Deloria, *Custer Died for Your Sins: An Indian Manifesto* (University of Oklahoma Press, 1969); Dunbar-Ortiz, *An Indigenous Peoples' History of the United States*; Reginald Horsman, *Race and Manifest Destiny* (Harvard University Press, 1981).

59. Although Congress did not legislate wholesale citizenship for American Indians until 1924, it is worth noting that the granting of citizenship to American Indians is not a simple victory for a multicultural empire state but rather a denial of American Indian nations and sovereignty.

60. Dunbar-Ortiz, *An Indigenous Peoples' History of the United States*; Heather Cox Richardson, *Wounded Knee: Party Politics and the Road to an American Massacre* (Basic Books, 2010); Robert Marshall Utley, *The Last Days of the Sioux Nation: Second Edition* (Yale University Press, 2004).

61. For discussion of the importance of the Reconstruction era in reshaping the concept of citizenship and the practices of white supremacy see: Erman, *Almost Citizens*; Matthew Frye Jacobson, *Barbarian Virtues: The United States Encounters Foreign Peoples at Home and Abroad, 1876–1917* (Macmillan, 2001).

62. Benedict Anderson, *Imagined Communities: Reflections on the Origin and Spread of Nationalism* (Verso Books, 1983), on "imagined communities."

63. Fredrik Barth, *Ethnic Groups and Boundaries: The Social Organization of Culture Difference* (Waveland Press, 1969); Stuart Hall, "Race, the Floating Signifier," in *Selected Writings on Race and Difference*, ed. Paul Gilroy and Ruth Wilson Gilmore (Duke University Press, 2021), 359–73; Richard Jenkins, "Rethinking

Ethnicity: Identity, Categorization and Power," *Ethnic and Racial Studies* 17, no. 2 (1994): 197–223; Andreas Wimmer, "The Making and Unmaking of Ethnic Boundaries: A Multilevel Process Theory," *American Journal of Sociology* 113, no. 4 (2008): 970–1022.

64. Max Weber, *Economy and Society* (1922; University of California Press, 1968), 43–6.

65. For work on how different European migrants became "white" in the United States, see: James Baldwin, "On Being White and Other Lies," *Essence*, 1984; Thomas A. Guglielmo, *White on Arrival: Italians, Race, Color, and Power in Chicago, 1890–1945* (Oxford University Press, 2004); Noel Ignatiev, *How the Irish Became White* (Routledge, 1995); Matthew Frye Jacobson, *Whiteness of a Different Color* (Harvard University Press, 1999); David R. Roediger, *The Wages of Whiteness: Race and the Making of the American Working Class* (Verso Books, 1991).

66. Horsman, *Race and Manifest Destiny.*

67. Many Filipinos would also argue that they have less in common with Asians. In fact, many Asians and Latinx/es, while sometimes banding together to assert a shared panethnic identity, see themselves as quite distinct and prefer to refer to themselves by their country of origin. See Yen Espiritu, *Asian American Panethnicity: Bridging Institutions and Identities* (Temple University Press, 1992); Mora, *Making Hispanics*; Anthony Christian Ocampo, *The Latinos of Asia: How Filipino Americans Break the Rules of Race* (Stanford University Press, 2016); Dina G. Okamoto, *Redefining Race: Asian American Panethnicity and Shifting Ethnic Boundaries* (Russell Sage Foundation, 2014).

68. Whereas white or Black or African American are each a single box on the Census form, by aggregating the counts for Chinese, Japanese, Filipino, Korean, Asian Indian, Vietnamese, and Other Asian, the Census reports data on the "Asian" population.

69. See also Rodríguez, *Suspended Apocalypse.*

70. Scholars have debated the definitions of these terms, arguing that we should or shouldn't differentiate between race and ethnicity. The former think of race as referencing biological difference and ethnicity as cultural; race as imposed and ethnicity as asserted; race as invariably an assertion of power, while this may not be true for ethnicity; and that race connotes hierarchical thinking. See, for example, Stephen Cornell and Douglas Hartmann, *Ethnicity and Race: Making Identities in a Changing World* (SAGE Publications, 1998). Others are more flexible in their definitions, reflecting a spatially and temporally situated approach to thinking about race and ethnicity.

71. D. Ferreira da Silva, "Facts of Blackness: Brazil Is Not (Quite) the United States . . .and Racial Politics in Brazil?," *Social Identities* 4, no. 2 (1998): 201–34; Mara Loveman, "Making 'Race' and Nation in the United States, South Africa, and Brazil: Taking Making Seriously," *Theory and Society* 28, no. 6 (1999): 903–27; Mara Loveman, *National Colors: Racial Classification and the State in Latin America* (New York: Oxford University Press, 2014); Tianna S. Paschel, *Becoming Black Political Subjects:*

Movements and Ethno-racial Rights in Colombia and Brazil (Princeton University Press, 2016); Peter Wade, *Race and Ethnicity in Latin America* (Pluto Press, 1997).

72. Omi and Winant, *Racial Formation in the United States*. On the Philippines, see: Julian Go, "'Racism' and Colonialism: Meanings of Difference and Ruling Practices in America's Pacific Empire," *Qualitative Sociology* 27, no. 1 (2004): 35–58; Lanny Thompson, *Imperial Archipelago: Representation and Rule in the Insular Territories under U.S. Dominion after 1898* (University of Hawai'i Press, 2010).

73. Cornell, *The Return of the Native*; Omi and Winant, *Racial Formation in the United States*; Wade, *Race and Ethnicity in Latin America*.

74. For a similar diagnosis of the tensions of studying how race is socially constructed while also relying on racial categories, see: Ada Ferrer, *Insurgent Cuba: Race, Nation, and Revolution, 1868–1898* (University of North Carolina Press, 1999).

75. Arjun Appadurai, "Number in the Colonial Imagination," in *Orientalism and the Postcolonial Predicament: Perspectives on South Asia* (University of Pennsylvania Press, 1993), 314–39; David Theo Goldberg, "Taking Stock: Counting by Race," in *Racial Subjects: Writing on Race in America* (Routledge, 1997), 27–58; Ian Hacking, "Making Up People," in *Reconstructing Individualism: Autonomy, Individuality, and the Self in Western Thought*, ed. Thomas C. Heller et al. (Stanford University Press, 1986), 222–36; Moon-Kie Jung and Tomás Almaguer, "The State and the Production of Racial Categories," in *Race and Ethnicity: Across Time, Space, and Discipline*, ed. Rodney D. Coates (Leiden, Netherlands: Brill, 2004), 55–72.

76. For discussion of "vulgar racism," see: Frantz Fanon, "Racism and Culture," in *Toward the African Revolution*, trans. Haakon Chevalier (Grove Press, 1967), 32, 35; Takashi Fujitani, *Race for Empire: Koreans as Japanese and Japanese as Americans during World War II* (University of California Press, 2011), 7–9, 24–5. See also: Rick Baldoz, "The Racial Vectors of Empire: Classification and Competing Master Narratives in the Colonial Philippines," *Du Bois Review: Social Science Research on Race* 5, no. 1 (April 2008): 69–94; Sunmin Kim, *The Unruly Facts of Race: The Politics of Knowledge Production in the Early 20th Century Immigration Debate* (University of Chicago Press, 2025). Baldoz uses the term "aversive racism" to describe the position of anti-imperialists. What I refer to as "vulgar racism" is what Kim calls racial essentialism, based in categorical difference.

77. Stephen R. Mallory II speaking to the Senate on "Acquisition of Territory," on January 26, 1899, 55th Congress, 3rd Session, *Congressional Record* 32, pt. 1: 1067–69.

78. For discussion of "polite racism," see Fujitani, *Race for Empire*, 22–25. See also Fanon, "Racism and Culture," on cultural racism; Baldoz, "The Racial Vectors of Empire"; and Kim, *The Unruly Facts of Race*. Baldoz refers to imperialists' racial arguments about tutelage as paternalistic racism. Referring to the idea that inferior Europeans can overcome racial difference, Kim writes of racial liberalism.

79. U.S. Congress, House, The Committee on Insular Affairs, Statement of Hon. William H. Taft, President of the Board of Commissioners to the Philippine Islands, 57th Congress, 1st and 2nd Sessions, February 21, 1902, 120–21.

80. Moon-Kie Jung and Yaejoon Kwon, "Theorizing the US Racial State: Sociology Since Racial Formation," *Sociology Compass* 7, no. 11 (2013): 927–40; Jung, *Beneath*

the Surface of White Supremacy; katrina quisumbing king, "Recentering U.S. Empire: A Structural Perspective on the Color Line," *Sociology of Race and Ethnicity* 5, no. 1 (2019): 11–25.

81. Richard Alba, *Blurring the Color Line* (Harvard University Press, 2009); Richard Alba and Victor Nee, *Remaking the American Mainstream: Assimilation and Contemporary Immigration* (Harvard University Press, 2009); Richard Alba and Nancy Foner, *Strangers No More: Immigration and the Challenges of Integration in North America and Western Europe* (Princeton University Press, 2015); Alejandro Portes and Min Zhou, "The New Second Generation: Segmented Assimilation and Its Variants," *The Annals of the American Academy of Political and Social Science* 530, no. 1 (1993): 74–96; Mary C. Waters, *Black Identities: West Indian Immigrant Dreams and American Realities* (Harvard University Press, 2009).

82. Leisy J. Abrego, *Sacrificing Families: Navigating Laws, Labor, and Love Across Borders* (Stanford University Press, 2014); Yen Le Espiritu, *Home Bound: Filipino American Lives Across Cultures, Communities, and Countries* (University of California Press, 2003); Yen Le Espiritu, *Body Counts: The Vietnam War and Militarized Refugees* (University of California Press, 2014); Cecilia Menjívar, "Liminal Legality: Salvadoran and Guatemalan Immigrants' Lives in the United States," *American Journal of Sociology* 111, no. 4 (January 1, 2006): 999–1037.

83. Ngai, *Impossible Subjects*.

84. FitzGerald and Cook-Martín, *Culling the Masses*; Madeline Y. Hsu, *The Good Immigrants: How the Yellow Peril Became the Model Minority* (Princeton University Press, 2017); Paul A. Kramer, "Power and Connection: Imperial Histories of the United States in the World," *American Historical Review* 116, no. 5 (December 2011): 1348–92; Paul A. Kramer, "Imperial Openings: Civilization, Exemption, and the Geopolitics of Mobility in the History of Chinese Exclusion, 1868–1910," *The Journal of the Gilded Age and Progressive Era* 14, no. 3 (2015): 317–47.

85. Dating the end of the Philippine–American War varies. See Patricio N. Abinales and Donna J. Amoroso, *State and Society in the Philippines* (Rowman & Littlefield Publishers, 2005).

86. See Simeon Man, *Soldiering Through Empire: Race and the Making of the Decolonizing Pacific* (University of California Press, 2018). For example, he writes, "the bipolar divide between communism and liberal democracy that structured U.S. global politics after 1945 indeed produced new categories of difference that at first glance do not appear to be rooted in race" (3). According to Man, this transformation relied on Asians being cast as either "good" or "bad." This book is an attempt to show how new categories in practices were rooted in race by tracing policy, law, and transformations to state structure.

Chapter 1

1. Michael Patrick Cullinane, "Imperial 'Character': How Race and Civilization Shaped Theodore Roosevelt's Imperialism," in *America's Transatlantic Turn: Theodore Roosevelt and the "Discovery" of Europe*, ed. Hans Krabbendam and John M. Thompson (Palgrave Macmillan, 2012), 31–47; Kristin L. Hoganson, *Fighting for*

American Manhood: How Gender Politics Provoked the Spanish-American and Philippine-American Wars (Yale University Press, 1998).

2. Thomas G. Dyer, *Theodore Roosevelt and the Idea of Race* (LSU Press, 1992).

3. Theodore Roosevelt, *The Strenuous Life* (G. P. Putnam's, 1901), 19.

4. Theodore Roosevelt, "The Issues of 1900," in *Campaigns and Controversies* (Scribner, 1926), 370.

5. Adam D. Burns, "Adapting to Empire: William H. Taft, Theodore Roosevelt, and the Philippines, 1900–08," *Comparative American Studies An International Journal* 11, no. 4 (2013): 418–33.

6. Theodore Roosevelt, *The Letters of Theodore Roosevelt*, ed. Elting E Morison, vol. 7 (Harvard University Press, 1951), 761–62.

7. Ann Laura Stoler et al., eds., *Imperial Formations* (SAR Press, 2007), xii.

8. Kwame Nkrumah, *Neo-Colonialism: The Last Stage of Imperialism*, 1965.

9. Michael Mann, "American Empires: Past and Present," *Canadian Review of Sociology/Revue Canadienne de Sociologie* 45, no. 1 (2008): 7–50.

10. Julian Go, *Patterns of Empire: The British and American Empires, 1688 to the Present* (Cambridge University Press, 2011), 11.

11. Stoler et al., *Imperial Formations*; Go, *Patterns of Empire*, 11.

12. For discussion on U.S. exceptionalism, see Go, *Patterns of Empire*, especially Chapters 2 and 3, as they relate to debunking claims about the United States' liberal democratic form of empire in the Philippines.

13. David Kenneth Fieldhouse, *The Colonial Empires: A Comparative Survey from the Eighteenth Century* (McMillan Press Limited, 1982); Stanley Karnow, *In Our Image: America's Empire in the Philippines* (Ballantine Books, 1989); Tony Smith, *America's Mission: The United States and the Worldwide Struggle for Democracy* (Princeton University Press, 1994).

14. Bruce Cumings, "Is America an Imperial Power?," *Current History* 102, no. 667 (2003): 355–60; Victor Davis Hanson, "What Empire?," in *The Imperial Tense: Prospects and Problems of American Empire*, ed. Andrew J. Bacevich (Ivan R. Dee, 2003), 146–55; A. G. Hopkins, *American Empire: A Global History* (Princeton University Press, 2018). Critiques of this perspective are plentiful, in addition to Go, *Patterns of Empire*: Daniel Immerwahr, *How to Hide an Empire: A History of the Greater United States* (Farrar, Straus and Giroux, 2019); Amy Kaplan, "'Left Alone with America': The Absence of Empire in the Study of American Culture," in *Cultures of United States Imperialism*, ed. Amy Kaplan and Donald E. Pease (Duke University Press, 1993): 11; William Appleman Williams, "The Frontier Thesis and American Foreign Policy," *Pacific Historical Review* 24, no. 4 (1955): 379–95.

15. Mann, "American Empires."

16. Niall Ferguson, *Colossus: The Price of America's Empire* (Penguin Press, 2004); G. John Ikenberry, "America's Imperial Ambition," *Foreign Affairs*, September 1, 2002, 44–60.

17. Earl C. Ravenal, "What's Empire Got to Do with It? The Derivation of America's Foreign Policy," *Critical Review* 21, no. 1 (January 1, 2009): 21–75; Jeremi Suri, "The Limits of American Empire: Democracy and Militarism in the Twentieth and

Twenty-First Centuries," in *Colonial Crucible: Empire in the Making of the Modern American State*, ed. Alfred W. McCoy and Francisco A. Scarano (University of Wisconsin Press, 2009), 523–31.

18. Prasenjit Duara, "The Imperialism of 'Free Nations': Japan, Manchukuo and the History of the Present," in *Imperial Formations*, ed. Ann Laura Stoler et al. (SAR Press, 2007), 211–39; Michael Mann, *Incoherent Empire* (Verso, 2005); William Appleman Williams, *The Tragedy of American Diplomacy*, 2nd rev. and enl. ed. (Dell Pub. Co., 1972); William Appleman Williams, *Empire as a Way of Life: An Essay on the Causes and Character of America's Present Predicament, Along with a Few Thoughts About an Alternative* (Oxford University Press, 1980). For discussion of "imperialism of free trade," defined by Robinson and Gallagher, see: Ronald Robinson and John Gallagher, "The Imperialism of Free Trade," *Economic History Review* 6, no. 1 (1953): 1–15.

19. For discussion of how critical revisionist accounts of U.S. empire reinscribe U.S. exceptionality, see: Go, *Patterns of Empire*.

20. For discussion of the blurry distinction between formal and informal empire, see: Paul A. Kramer, "Power and Connection: Imperial Histories of the United States in the World," *American Historical Review* 116, no. 5 (December 2011): 1348–92.

21. David Keanu Sai, "The American Occupation of the Hawaiian Kingdom: Beginning the Transition from Occupied to Restored State" (PhD diss., University of Hawai'i at Manoa, 2008).

22. Wesley Attewell, *The Quiet Violence of Empire: How USAID Waged Counterinsurgency in Afghanistan* (University of Minnesota Press, 2023); Sasha Davis, *The Empires' Edge: Militarization, Resistance, and Transcending Hegemony in the Pacific* (University of Georgia Press, 2015); Juliet Nebolon, *Settler Militarism: World War II in Hawai'i and the Making of US Empire* (Duke University Press, 2024); Setsu Shigematsu and Keith L. Camacho, *Militarized Currents: Toward a Decolonized Future in Asia and the Pacific* (University of Minnesota Press, 2010).

23. Go, *Patterns of Empire*; Hopkins, *American Empire*; Paul Kennedy, *The Rise and Fall of the Great Powers: Economic Change and Military Conflict from 1500 to 2000* (Knopf Doubleday Publishing Group, 1987); Atul Kohli, *Imperialism and the Developing World: How Britain and the United States Shaped the Global Periphery* (Oxford University Press, 2020); Fareed Zakaria, *From Wealth to Power: The Unusual Origins of America's World Role* (Princeton University Press, 1999).

24. Brian DeLay, *War of a Thousand Deserts: Indian Raids and the US-Mexican War* (Yale University Press, 2008); Greg Grandin, *Empire's Workshop: Latin America, the United States, and the Rise of the New Imperialism* (Henry Holt and Company, 2006); Louis A. Pérez, *The War of 1898: The United States and Cuba in History and Historiography* (University of North Carolina Press, 1998).

25. Go, *Patterns of Empire*, 221.

26. Matthew Frye Jacobson, *Barbarian Virtues: The United States Encounters Foreign Peoples at Home and Abroad, 1876–1917* (Macmillan, 2001); Eric T. L. Love, *Race Over Empire: Racism and US Imperialism, 1865–1900* (University of North Carolina Press, 2004); Colin D. Moore, *American Imperialism and the State, 1893–1921* (Cambridge University Press, 2017).

27. Antony Anghie, *Imperialism, Sovereignty and the Making of International Law* (Cambridge University Press, 2007); Zoltán I. Búzás, "The Color of Threat: Race, Threat Perception, and the Demise of the Anglo-Japanese Alliance (1902–1923)," *Security Studies* 22, no. 4 (October 1, 2013): 573–606; Bianca Freeman et al., "Race in International Relations: Beyond the 'Norm Against Noticing,'" *Annual Review of Political Science* 25 (May 12, 2022): 175–96.

28. Oliver Cromwell Cox, *Caste, Class, & Race* (Doubleday, 1948); W.E.B. Du Bois, *Black Reconstruction in America, 1860–1880* (The Free Press, 1935); Cyril Lionel Robert James, *The Black Jacobins: Toussaint L'Ouverture and the San Domingo Revolution* (Penguin UK, 1989); Cedric J. Robinson, *Black Marxism: The Making of the Black Radical Tradition* (UNC Press Books, 1983); Walter Rodney, *How Europe Underdeveloped Africa* (Verso Books, 1972).

29. Muriam Haleh Davis, *Markets of Civilization: Islam and Racial Capitalism in Algeria* (Duke University Press, 2022).

30. George Steinmetz, *The Devil's Handwriting: Precoloniality and the German Colonial State in Qingdao, Samoa, and Southwest Africa* (University of Chicago Press, 2007), 490–505.

31. Derrick Bell, *Faces at the Bottom of the Well: The Permanence of Racism* (Basic Books, 1992); Ian Haney-López, *Dog Whistle Politics: How Coded Racial Appeals Have Reinvented Racism and Wrecked the Middle Class* (Oxford University Press, 2014).

32. Eduardo Bonilla-Silva, "Rethinking Racism: Toward a Structural Interpretation," *American Sociological Review* 62, no. 3 (June 1997): 465–80; Michael Omi and Howard Winant, *Racial Formation in the United States* (Routledge, 1994), 79. Omi and Winant also define the racial order as "the social meaning and political role played by race" (88).

33. Omi and Winant, *Racial Formation in the United States*. See also: Gary Gerstle, *American Crucible: Race and Nation in the Twentieth Century* (Princeton University Press, 2002); Desmond S. King and Rogers M. Smith, "Racial Orders in American Political Development," *American Political Science Review* 99, no. 1 (February 2005): 75–92; Rogers M. Smith, *Civic Ideals: Conflicting Visions of Citizenship in US History* (Yale University Press, 1997). In each of these accounts, equality, democracy, and civic inclusion are counterposed to a racial exclusionary, white supremacist creed.

34. Lawrence Bobo et al., "Laissez-Faire Racism: The Crystallization of a Kinder, Gentler, Antiblack Ideology," in *Racial Attitudes in the 1990s: Continuity and Change*, ed. Steven A. Tuch and Jack K. Martin (Praeger, 1997), 15–42; Eduardo Bonilla-Silva, *Racism Without Racists: Color-Blind Racism and the Persistence of Racial Inequality in the United States* (Rowman & Littlefield Publishers, 2006); Michael Kingsley Brown et al., *Whitewashing Race: The Myth of a Color-Blind Society* (University of California Press, 2023); Leslie G. Carr, *"Colorblind" Racism* (Sage, 1997); Tyrone A. Forman, "Color-Blind Racism and Racial Indifference: The Role of Racial Apathy in Facilitating Enduring Inequalities," in *The Changing Terrain of Race and Ethnicity*, ed. Maria Krysan and Amanda E. Lewis (Russell Sage, 2004), 43–66; Charles A. Gallagher, "Color-Blind Privilege: The Social and Political Functions of Erasing the Color Line in Post Race America," *Race, Gender & Class* 10, no. 4 (2003), 22–37;

Matthew W. Hughey et al., "Paving the Way for Future Race Research: Exploring the Racial Mechanisms within a Color-Blind, Racialized Social System," *American Behavioral Scientist* 59, no. 11 (2015): 1347–57; Robert C. Smith, *Racism in the Post-Civil Rights Era: Now You See It, Now You Don't* (State University of New York Press, 1996).

35. Etienne Balibar and Immanuel Maurice Wallerstein, *Race, Nation, Class: Ambiguous Identities* (Verso, 1991); Martin Barker, *The New Racism: Conservatives and the Ideology of the Tribe* (Junction Books, 1981).

36. Claire Jean Kim, "The Racial Triangulation of Asian Americans," *Politics & Society* 27, no. 1 (1999): 105–38.

37. For exceptions, see: Haney-López, *Dog Whistle Politics*; Naomi Murakawa, *The First Civil Right: How Liberals Built Prison America* (Oxford University Press, 2014). To explain the rise of colorblind racism and how the terms of racism change, Haney-López shows that changes in party strategy since the 1960s shaped the use of racially coded language in politics. In her historical analysis of racism and mass incarceration in the United States, Murakawa identifies seeds of the transition to colorblind racism in the 1940s. She shows that it was not only post–Civil Rights conservative backlash but earlier liberal acknowledgment of racism and ideas of race neutrality that expanded the scope of the federal state and formed the carceral state.

38. Omi and Winant, *Racial Formation in the United States*, 66. For an account of continuity and persistence of U.S. racist institutions and Black Americans, see: Loïc Wacquant, "Deadly Symbiosis: When Ghetto and Prison Meet and Mesh," *Punishment & Society* 3, no. 1 (January 1, 2001): 95–133.

39. Takashi Fujitani, *Race for Empire: Koreans as Japanese and Japanese as Americans during World War II* (University of California Press, 2011); Daniel Martinez HoSang et al., eds., *Racial Formation in the Twenty-First Century* (University of California Press, 2012); Nikhil Pal Singh, *Black Is a Country: Race and the Unfinished Struggle for Democracy* (Harvard University Press, 2004).

40. Murakawa, *The First Civil Right*, 11.

41. W.E.B. Du Bois, "The Souls of White Folk," in *Darkwater: Voices from within the Veil* (Humanity Books, 1920), 55–74; W.E.B. Du Bois, "Prospect of a World Without Race Conflict," *American Journal of Sociology* 49, no. 5 (1944): 450–56; Marilyn Lake and Henry Reynolds, *Drawing the Global Colour Line: White Men's Countries and the Question of Racial Equality* (Melbourne University Publishing, 2008).

42. Benedict Anderson, *Imagined Communities: Reflections on the Origin and Spread of Nationalism* (Verso Books, 1983); Immerwahr, *How to Hide an Empire*.

43. Rick Baldoz, "The Racial Vectors of Empire: Classification and Competing Master Narratives in the Colonial Philippines," *Du Bois Review: Social Science Research on Race* 5, no. 1 (April 2008): 69–94.

44. Moon-Kie Jung, *Beneath the Surface of White Supremacy: Denaturalizing U.S. Racisms Past and Present* (Stanford University Press, 2015), 38.

45. David Scott FitzGerald and David Cook-Martín, *Culling the Masses* (Harvard University Press, 2014); Moon-Kie Jung, *Reworking Race: The Making of Hawaii's*

Interracial Labor Movement (Columbia University Press, 2006); Mara Loveman, *National Colors: Racial Classification and the State in Latin America* (Oxford University Press, 2014).

46. Fujitani, *Race for Empire*. See also: Jodi Melamed, *Represent and Destroy: Rationalizing Violence in the New Racial Capitalism* (University of Minnesota Press, 2011).

47. Jacobson, *Barbarian Virtues*.

48. Kim, *The Unruly Facts of Race*.

49. Madeline Y. Hsu, *The Good Immigrants: How the Yellow Peril Became the Model Minority* (Princeton University Press, 2017); Erika Lee, *At America's Gates: Chinese Immigration During the Exclusion Era, 1882–1943* (University of North Carolina Press, 2003); Erika Lee, *The Making of Asian America: A History* (Simon and Schuster, 2015); Simeon Man, *Soldiering Through Empire: Race and the Making of the Decolonizing Pacific* (University of California Press, 2018); Ellen D. Wu, *The Color of Success: Asian Americans and the Origins of the Model Minority* (Princeton University Press, 2013).

50. Frantz Fanon, "Racism and Culture," in *Toward the African Revolution*, trans. Haakon Chevalier (New York: Grove Press, 1967), 35–7; Fujitani *Race for Empire*.

51. Michel Foucault, *"Society Must Be Defended": Lectures at the Collège de France, 1975–1976*, vol. 1 (Picador, 1997).

52. Ann Stoler, "Sexual Affronts and Racial Frontiers: European Identities and the Cultural Politics of Exclusion in Colonial Southeast Asia," *Comparative Studies in Society and History* 34, no. 3 (1992): 514–51; Ann Laura Stoler, *Carnal Knowledge and Imperial Power: Race and the Intimate in Colonial Rule* (University of California Press, 2010).

53. Julian Go, "'Racism' and Colonialism: Meanings of Difference and Ruling Practices in America's Pacific Empire," *Qualitative Sociology* 27, no. 1 (2004): 35–58; Daniel P. S. Goh, "States of Ethnography: Colonialism, Resistance, and Cultural Transcription in Malaya and the Philippines, 1890s–1930s," *Comparative Studies in Society and History* 49, no. 1 (2007): 109–42; Sally Engle Merry, *Colonizing Hawai'i: The Cultural Power of Law* (Princeton University Press, 2000); Elizabeth A. Povinelli, *The Cunning of Recognition: Indigenous Alterities and the Making of Australian Multiculturalism* (Duke University Press, 2002); Steinmetz, *The Devil's Handwriting.*

54. Stuart Hall, "The West and the Rest: Discourse and Power [1992]," in *Essential Essays*, vol. 2, ed. David Morley (Duke University Press, 2019), 141–84; Lisa Lowe, *The Intimacies of Four Continents* (Duke University Press, 2015); Aníbal Quijano and Immanuel Wallerstein, "Americanity as a Concept, or the Americas in the Modern World-System," *International Social Science Journal* 44, no. 4 (1992): 549–57; Cedric J. Robinson, *Black Marxism: The Making of the Black Radical Tradition* (UNC Press Books, 1983).

55. Yael Berda, *Colonial Bureaucracy and Contemporary Citizenship* (Cambridge University Press, 2022).

56. Lauren Benton, *Law and Colonial Cultures: Legal Regimes in World History, 1400–1900* (Cambridge University Press, 2002); Ilana Feldman, *Governing Gaza: Bureaucracy, Authority, and the Work of Rule, 1917–1967* (Duke University Press, 2008);

Diana S. Kim, *Empires of Vice: The Rise of Opium Prohibition Across Southeast Asia* (Princeton University Press, 2020).

57. Go, *American Empire and the Politics of Meaning*; Reynaldo Clemeña Ileto, *Pasyon and Revolution: Popular Movements in the Philippines, 1840–1910* (Ateneo de Manila University Press, 1997); Vicente L. Rafael, *Contracting Colonialism: Translation and Christian Conversion in Tagalog Society Under Early Spanish Rule* (Duke University Press, 1992); Jonathan Wyrtzen, *Making Morocco: Colonial Intervention and the Politics of Identity* (Cornell University Press, 2016).

58. Ada Ferrer, *Insurgent Cuba: Race, Nation, and Revolution, 1868–1898* (University of North Carolina Press, 1999); Go, *American Empire and the Politics of Meaning*; Lanny Thompson, *Imperial Archipelago: Representation and Rule in the Insular Territories under U.S. Dominion after 1898* (University of Hawai'i Press, 2010).

59. Laura Briggs, *Reproducing Empire: Race, Sex, Science, and US Imperialism in Puerto Rico* (University of California Press, 2002); Eileen Findlay, *Imposing Decency: The Politics of Sexuality and Race in Puerto Rico, 1870–1920* (Duke University Press, 1999); Victor Román Mendoza, *Metroimperial Intimacies: Fantasy, Racial-Sexual Governance, and the Philippines in U.S. Imperialism, 1899–1913* (Duke University Press, 2015); Stoler, *Carnal Knowledge and Imperial Power*.

60. John D'Emilio and Estelle B. Freedman, *Intimate Matters: A History of Sexuality in America* (University of Chicago Press, 1997); Philippa Levine, *Prostitution, Race, and Politics: Policing Venereal Disease in the British Empire* (Psychology Press, 2003); Gary B. Nash, "The Hidden History of Mestizo America," *The Journal of American History* 82, no. 3 (1995): 941–64; Vicente Rafael, "Colonial Domesticity: Engendering Race at the Edge of Empire, 1899–1912," in *White Love and Other Events in Filipino History* (Duke University Press, 2000), 52–75; Emmanuelle Saada, *Empire's Children: Race, Filiation, and Citizenship in the French Colonies* (University of Chicago Press, 2011); Ann Laura Stoler, "Tense and Tender Ties: The Politics of Comparison in North American History and (Post) Colonial Studies," *Journal of American History* 88, no. 3 (2001): 829–65; Ann Laura Stoler, ed., *Haunted by Empire: Geographies of Intimacy in North American History* (Duke University Press, 2006); Laura Wexler, *Tender Violence: Domestic Visions in an Age of U.S. Imperialism*, Cultural Studies of the United States (University of North Carolina Press, 2000).

61. Stoler, "Tense and Tender Ties," 831.

62. Lowe, *The Intimacies of Four Continents*.

63. Allan E. S. Lumba, *Monetary Authorities: Capitalism and Decolonization in the American Colonial Philippines* (Duke University Press, 2022).

64. Briggs, *Reproducing Empire*; Findlay, *Imposing Decency*. See Chapters 4 and 6.

65. Hannah Arendt, *The Origins of Totalitarianism* (Harcourt, Brace and Company, 1973); Aimé Césaire, *Discourse on Colonialism* (1955; Monthly Review Press, 1972); Foucault, *"Society Must Be Defended"*; Julian Go, *Policing Empires: Militarization, Race, and the Imperial Boomerang in Britain and the US* (Oxford University Press, 2023); Zine Magubane, *Bringing the Empire Home: Race, Class, and Gender in Britain and Colonial South Africa* (University of Chicago Press, 2004).

66. Du Bois, "The Souls of White Folk."

67. Alfred W. McCoy and Francisco A. Scarano, eds., *Colonial Crucible: Empire in the Making of the Modern American State* (University of Wisconsin Press, 2009).

68. Julian Go, "Reverberations of Empire: How the Colonial Past Shapes the Present," *Social Science History* 48, no. 1 (February 2024): 1–18; Ann Laura Stoler, *Duress: Imperial Durabilities in Our Times* (Duke University Press, 2016), 26.

69. Mbembe, *On the Postcolony*.

70. Arjun Appadurai, "Number in the Colonial Imagination," in *Orientalism and the Postcolonial Predicament: Perspectives on South Asia* (University of Pennsylvania Press, 1993), 314–39; Yael Berda, *Colonial Bureaucracy and Contemporary Citizenship* (Cambridge University Press, 2022); Yannick Coenders, "Colonial Recursion: State Categories of Race and the Emergence of the 'Non-Western Allochthone,'" *American Journal of Cultural Sociology* 12 (May 8, 2024); Ricarda: 698–729; Hammer, "Decolonizing the Civil Sphere: The Politics of Difference, Imperial Erasures, and Theorizing from History," *Sociological Theory* 38, no. 2 (June 1, 2020): 101–21; Wyrtzen, *Making Morocco*.

71. Anghie, *Imperialism, Sovereignty and the Making of International Law*; Getachew, *Worldmaking after Empire*; Stuart Hall, "The West and the Rest: Discourse and Power," in *Race & Racialization, Second Edition: Essential Readings*, ed. Tania Das Gupta et al. (Canadian Scholars, 2018), 85–95; Alexandre I. R. White, *Epidemic Orientalism: Race, Capital, and the Governance of Infectious Disease* (Stanford University Press, 2023).

72. Martin F. Manalansan and Augusto Espiritu, *Filipino Studies: Palimpsests of Nation and Diaspora* (NYU Press, 2016); Angel Adams Parham, *American Routes: Racial Palimpsests and the Transformation of Race* (Oxford University Press, 2017).

73. Julia Adams, "Principals and Agents, Colonialists and Company Men: The Decay of Colonial Control in the Dutch East Indies," *American Sociological Review* 61, no. 1 (1996): 12–28; Karen Barkey, *Empire of Difference: The Ottomans in Comparative Perspective* (Cambridge University Press, 2008); Frederick Cooper and Ann Laura Stoler, *Tensions of Empire: Colonial Cultures in a Bourgeois World* (University of California Press, 1997); Malick W. Ghachem, *The Old Regime and the Haitian Revolution* (Cambridge University Press, 2012); Julian Go, *American Empire and the Politics of Meaning: Elite Political Cultures in the Philippines and Puerto Rico During U.S. Colonialism* (Duke University Press, 2008); Kim, *Empires of Vice*; Uday S. Mehta, "Liberal Strategies of Exclusion," in *Tensions of Empire: Colonial Cultures in a Bourgeois World*, ed. Frederick Cooper and Ann Laura Stoler (University of California Press, 1997), 59–86; Rasmus Sielemann, "Governing the Risks of Slavery: State-Practice, Slave Law, and the Problem of Public Order in 18th Century Danish West Indies," *Rethinking the Colonial State, Political Power and Social Theory* 33 (January 1, 2017): 81–108.

74. Baldoz, *The Third Asiatic Invasion*; Christina Duffy Burnett and Burke Marshall, eds., *Foreign in a Domestic Sense: Puerto Rico, American Expansion, and the Constitution* (Duke University Press, 2001); Sam Erman, *Almost Citizens: Puerto Rico, the U.S. Constitution, and Empire* (Cambridge University Press, 2018); Veta R. Schlimgen, *Neither Citizens nor Aliens: Filipino "American Nationals" in the US Empire, 1900–1946* (University of Oregon Press, 2010); Bartholomew H. Sparrow, *The*

Insular Cases and the Emergence of American Empire (University Press of Kansas, 2006).

75. This approach is compatible with those that draw on field theory to map variations and change in the colonial state. See: Steinmetz, *The Devil's Handwriting*; Wyrtzen, *Making Morocco*.

76. See also: Baldoz, "The Racial Vectors of Empire."

77. Paul A. Kramer, *The Blood of Government: Race, Empire, the United States, and the Philippines* (University of North Carolina Press, 2006), 116.

78. Although considered an epithet at the time, the term Mugwumps refers to politicians who split from the Republican party. Most of them switched parties in 1884 to support the Democratic candidate, Grover Cleveland. As a group, they opposed corruption and patronage in the Republican party.

79. Robert L. Beisner, *Twelve Against Empire: The Anti-Imperialists, 1898–1900* (McGraw-Hill, 1968); M. Cullinane, *Liberty and American Anti-Imperialism: 1898–1909* (Springer, 2012); Kramer, *The Blood of Government*, 116–21; Love, *Race Over Empire*; Erin L. Murphy, *No Middle Ground: Anti-Imperialists and Ethical Witnessing during the Philippine-American War* (Rowman & Littlefield, 2019). See also: Jacobson, *Barbarian Virtues*, where Jacobson writes that those against empire "were so varied as to preclude any viable political coalition" (228).

80. Baldoz, *The Third Asiatic Invasion*.

81. For more on how the United States is not an isolationist country and how U.S. intervention in Latin America shaped U.S. national identity, see: Brian Loveman, *No Higher Law: American Foreign Policy and the Western Hemisphere Since 1776* (University of North Carolina Press, 2010).

82. Hoganson, *Fighting for American Manhood*; Heather Cox Richardson, *West from Appomattox: The Reconstruction of America after the Civil War* (Yale University Press, 2007).

83. Hoganson, *Fighting for American Manhood*, 112–23.

84. Mark Elliott, "'Our God-Given Mission': Reconstruction and the Humanitarian Nationalism of the 1890s," in *Reconstruction and Empire: The Legacies of Abolition and Union Victory for an Imperial Age*, ed. David Prior (Fordham University Press, 2022), 161–90; Susan K. Harris, *God's Arbiters: Americans and the Philippines, 1898–1902* (New York: Oxford University Press, 2011); Julia Irwin, *Making the World Safe: The American Red Cross and a Nation's Humanitarian Awakening* (Oxford University Press USA, 2013); Ian Tyrrell, *Reforming the World: The Creation of America's Moral Empire* (Princeton University Press, 2010).

85. Pérez, *The War of 1898*, 41.

86. Rudyard Kipling, "White Man's Burden," *McClure's Magazine*, February 1899.

87. For further discussion of coexisting ideas of biological and cultural difference today in the United States and Italy, see: Ann Morning and Marcello Maneri, *An Ugly Word: Rethinking Race in Italy and the United States* (Russell Sage Foundation, 2022).

88. Fujitani, *Race for Empire*, 2011.

89. Christopher T. Fan, "Melancholy Transcendence: Ted Chiang and Asian American Postracial Form," *Post45*, November 5, 2014.

90. Paul J. DiMaggio and Walter W. Powell, "Introduction," in *The New Institutionalism in Organizational Analysis*, ed. Walter W. Powell and Paul J. DiMaggio (University of Chicago Press, 1991), 1–40; Mark C. Suchman and Lauren B. Edelman, "Legal Rational Myths: The New Institutionalism and the Law and Society Tradition," *Law & Social Inquiry* 21, no. 4 (1996): 903–41.

91. James Mahoney, "Path Dependence in Historical Sociology," *Theory and Society* 29, no. 4 (2000): 507–48; James Mahoney and Kathleen Thelen, "A Theory of Gradual Institutional Change," in *Explaining Institutional Change: Ambiguity, Agency, and Power*, ed. James Mahoney and Kathleen Thelen (Cambridge University Press, 2010), 1–37; James Mahoney and Kathleen Thelen, *Advances in Comparative-Historical Analysis* (Cambridge University Press, 2015); Bruno Palier, "Ambiguous Agreement, Cumulative Change: French Social Policy in the 1990s," in *Beyond Continuity: Institutional Change in Advanced Political Economies*, ed. Wolfgang Streeck and Kathleen Thelen (Oxford University Press, 2005), 127–44; Eric Schickler, *Disjointed Pluralism: Institutional Innovation and the Development of the U.S. Congress* (Princeton University Press, 2001).

92. Leia Castañeda Anastacio, *The Foundations of the Modern Philippine State: Imperial Rule and the American Constitutional Tradition in the Philippine Islands, 1898–1935* (Cambridge University Press, 2016), 5. See also: Go, *American Empire and the Politics of Meaning*, 2008; Ruby R. Paredes, ed., *Philippine Colonial Democracy* (Ateneo de Manila University Press, 1988).

93. John Dower, *War without Mercy: Race and Power in the Pacific War* (Knopf Doubleday Publishing Group, 2012).

Part 1

1. Dating the end of the Philippine–American War (or, as it is known to many in the United States, the Philippine Insurrection) varies. On July 4, 1902, President Roosevelt declared an end to the war. Guerrilla resistance continued until 1906.

2. Paul A. Kramer, *The Blood of Government: Race, Empire, the United States, and the Philippines* (University of North Carolina Press, 2006); Lanny Thompson, *Imperial Archipelago: Representation and Rule in the Insular Territories under U.S. Dominion after 1898* (University of Hawai'i Press, 2010).

3. Louis Hartz, *The Liberal Tradition in America: An Interpretation of American Political Thought Since the Revolution* (Houghton Mifflin Harcourt, 1955); Samuel P. Huntington, *American Politics: The Promise of Disharmony* (Harvard University Press, 1981); Gunnar Myrdal, *An American Dilemma: The Negro Problem and Modern Democracy* (Routledge, 1944).

4. Gary Gerstle, *American Crucible: Race and Nation in the Twentieth Century* (Princeton University Press, 2002); Rogers M. Smith, *Civic Ideals: Conflicting Visions of Citizenship in US History* (Yale University Press, 1997).

5. Evelyn Nakano Glenn, "Settler Colonialism as Structure: A Framework for Comparative Studies of US Race and Gender Formation," *Sociology of Race and Ethnicity* 1, no. 1 (2015): 52–72; Moon-Kie Jung, *Beneath the Surface of White Supremacy: Denaturalizing U.S. Racisms Past and Present* (Stanford University Press, 2015).

6. Aziz Rana, *The Two Faces of American Freedom* (Harvard University Press, 2010); Paul Frymer, *Building an American Empire: The Era of Territorial and Political Expansion* (Princeton University Press, 2017).

7. Mae M. Ngai, *Impossible Subjects: Illegal Aliens and the Making of Modern America* (Princeton University Press, 2004); Roger Daniels, *Guarding the Golden Door: American Immigration Policy and Immigrants since 1882* (New York: Farrar, Straus and Giroux, 2004).

8. The Asiatic Barred Zone did not include the Philippines, as it was a U.S. colony. Neither did it include Japan, as the United States and Japan agreed the latter would limit emigration.

9. Ian Haney-López, *White by Law: The Legal Construction of Race* (NYU Press, 1996).

10. Ngai, *Impossible Subjects*.

11. Kristin L. Hoganson, *Fighting for American Manhood: How Gender Politics Provoked the Spanish-American and Philippine-American Wars* (Yale University Press, 1998); Eric T. L. Love, *Race Over Empire: Racism and US Imperialism, 1865–1900* (University of North Carolina Press, 2004).

12. Louis A. Pérez, *The War of 1898: The United States and Cuba in History and Historiography* (University of North Carolina Press, 1998); Walter Johnson, *River of Dark Dreams* (Harvard University Press, 2013).

13. According to Hoganson, gender drew jingoists together and helped justify intervention. By asserting that American manhood was at stake, jingoes could make economic, strategic, and political justifications for war. I agree with this assertion and emphasize not only manhood, but *white* manhood as a key motivating ideology for war and empire. War in Cuba, as Hoganson argues, was an opportunity to build American manhood. This remained true in the Philippines, but in keeping a far-off archipelago, imperialists relied more on ideas of racial difference.

14. William T. McKinley, *Message of the President of the United States Communicated in the Two Houses of Congress on the Relations of the United States to Spain* (Washington, D.C.: Government Printing Office, 1898), 11.

15. While first a Republican, Teller organized Silver Republicans to leave the party in 1896. He remained a Silver Republican until 1903, when he became a Democrat.

16. Heather Cox Richardson, *West from Appomattox: The Reconstruction of America after the Civil War* (Yale University Press, 2007), 319.

17. Kramer, *The Blood of Government*, 93.

18. Love, *Race Over Empire*, 159–60.

19. Bartholomew H. Sparrow, *The Insular Cases and the Emergence of American Empire* (University Press of Kansas, 2006), 65–67.

20. Love, *Race Over Empire*, 167–68.

21. Aguinaldo quoted in Leonard Y. Andaya, "Ethnicity in the Philippine Revolution," in *1898, España y el Pacífico: interpretación del pasado, realidad del presente*, ed. Miguel Luque Talaván et al. (Asociación Española de Estudios del Pacífico, 1999), 73–74.

22. Patricio N. Abinales and Donna J. Amoroso, *State and Society in the Philippines* (Rowman & Littlefield Publishers, 2005); Kramer, *The Blood of Government*, 36–77.

23. Abinales and Amoroso, *State and Society in the Philippines*.

24. U.S. Congress, House, Committee on Insular Affairs, Secretary Elihu Root on Public Lands and Franchises Committee of Insular Affairs, 57th Congress, 1st Session, Jan. 23, 1902, 53.

25. U.S. Congress, Senate, Committee on the Philippines, *Affairs in the Philippine Islands: Hearings before the Committee on the Philippines*, 57th Congress, 1st Session, February 7, 1902.

26. Ngai, *Impossible Subjects*, 98.

27. Henry Gannet, "The Philippine Islands and Their People (Reprinted from the National Geographic Magazine, March)," March 1, 1904, Presented to the Senate by Henry Cabot Lodge, 58th Congress, 2nd Session: 13–14.

28. Senator Simmons on Civil Government for the Philippine Islands, on April 28, 1902, 57th Congress, 1st Session, *Congressional Record* 35, pt. 5: 4755.

29. See Julian Go, "Introduction: Global Perspectives on the US Colonial State in the Philippines," in *The American Colonial State in the Philippines* (Duke University Press, 2003), 6.

Chapter 2

1. William Day, letter to President William McKinley, October 28, 1898, McKinley Letter Collection (1898), Roosevelt Papers, Library of Congress.

2. As noted by Democratic Senator Edward Carmack. Senator Carmack, "Civil Government for the Philippine Islands," speaking on S. 2295, on April 25, 1902, 57th Congress, 1st Session, *Congressional Record* 35, pt. 5: 4673.

3. Because the term refers to cases about the relationship of the United States to its territories, there is some debate about what counts as an "insular case." Trías Monge (1999), for example, counts cases from 1901. Rivera Ramos (2001) refers to the first nine cases, which range from 1901 to 1914, and Malavet (2004) includes cases up to 1979. See Pedro A. Malavet, *America's Colony: The Political and Cultural Conflict Between the United States and Puerto Rico* (NYU Press, 2004); Efrén Rivera Ramos, "Deconstructing Colonialism: The 'Unincorporated Territory' as a Category of Domination," in *Foreign in a Domestic Sense: Puerto Rico, American Expansion, and the Constitution*, ed. Christina Duffy Burnett and Burke Marshall (Duke University Press, 2001), 104–19; José Trías Monge, *Puerto Rico: The Trials of the Oldest Colony in the World* (Yale University Press, 1999).

4. Julian Go, "'Racism' and Colonialism: Meanings of Difference and Ruling Practices in America's Pacific Empire," *Qualitative Sociology* 27, no. 1 (2004): 35–58; Lanny Thompson, *Imperial Archipelago: Representation and Rule in the Insular Territories under U.S. Dominion after 1898* (University of Hawai'i Press, 2010).

5. Julian Go, *American Empire and the Politics of Meaning: Elite Political Cultures in the Philippines and Puerto Rico During U.S. Colonialism* (Duke University Press, 2008); George Steinmetz, *The Devil's Handwriting: Precoloniality and the German Colonial State in Qingdao, Samoa, and Southwest Africa* (University of Chicago Press, 2007).

6. Carman F. Randolph, "Constitutional Aspects of Annexation. Part First," *Harvard Law Review* 12, no. 5 (1898): 309.

7. Senator Simmons, "Civil Government for the Philippine Islands," speaking on S. 2295, April 28, 1902, 57th Congress, 1st Session, *Congressional Record* 35, pt. 5: 4759.

8. As quoted in Eric T. L. Love, *Race Over Empire: Racism and US Imperialism, 1865–1900* (University of North Carolina Press, 2004), 184.

9. U.S. Congress, Senate, Committee on the Philippines, *Affairs in the Philippine Islands: Hearings before the Committee on the Philippines*, 57th Congress, 1st Session. May 23, 1902, 2673, 2694.

10. U.S. Congress, Senate, Committee on the Philippines, *Affairs in the Philippine Islands: Hearings before the Committee on the Philippines*, 57th Congress, 1st Session, February 15, 1902, 322.

11. Randolph, "Constitutional Aspects of Annexation. Part First," 309–10. See also Simeon E. Baldwin, "The Constitutional Questions Incident to the Acquisition and Government by the United States of Island Territory," *Harvard Law Review* 12, no. 6 (1899): 407.

12. John H. Parker, "Conditions in the Philippines," October 13, 1900, Special Correspondence, Box 162, Theodore Roosevelt, Elihu P. Root Papers, Manuscript Division, Library of Congress, Washington, D.C.

13. Theodore Roosevelt, letter to Elihu P. Root, February 18, 1902, Special Correspondence, Box 162, Theodore Roosevelt, Elihu P. Root Papers, Manuscript Division, Library of Congress, Washington, D.C.

14. Some scholars have argued that U.S. state actors exported American Indian policy to the Philippines. See: Katharine Bjork, *Prairie Imperialists: The Indian Country Origins of American Empire* (University of Pennsylvania Press, 2018); Anne Paulet, *The Only Good Indian Is a Dead Indian: The Use of United States Indian Policy as a Guide for the Conquest and Occupation of the Philippines, 1898–1905* (Rutgers University, 1995); Walter L. Williams, "United States Indian Policy and the Debate over Philippine Annexation: Implications for the Origins of American Imperialism," *The Journal of American History* 66, no. 4 (1980): 810–31.

15. Christopher Capozzola, *Bound by War: How the United States and the Philippines Built America's First Pacific Century* (Basic Books, 2020), 13–15; Edward M. Coffman, "Batson of the Philippine Scouts" *Parameters* 7, no. 3 (1977): 68.

16. Paul A. Kramer, *The Blood of Government: Race, Empire, the United States, and the Philippines* (University of North Carolina Press, 2006), 113–15; Alfred McCoy, "The Colonial Origins of Philippine Military Traditions," in *The Philippine Revolution of 1896: Ordinary Lives in Extraordinary Times* (Ateneo de Manila University Press, 2001), 83–124.

17. Go, "'Racism' and Colonialism: Meanings of Difference and Ruling Practices in America's Pacific Empire"; Thompson, *Imperial Archipelago*.

18. Virginia R. Dominguez, "When the Enemy Is Unclear: US Censuses and Photographs of Cuba, Puerto Rico, and the Philippines from the Beginning of the Twentieth Century," *Comparative American Studies An International Journal* 5, no. 2 (June 2007): 173–203; Go, "'Racism' and Colonialism"; Thompson, *Imperial Archipelago*.

19. See Eduardo Bonilla-Silva, "The Essential Social Fact of Race," *American Sociological Review* 64, no. 6 (1999): 899–906.

20. Baldwin, "The Constitutional Questions Incident to the Acquisition and Government by the United States of Island Territory," 407. Baldwin is more explicit than Randolph on these points.

21. Baldwin, "The Constitutional Questions Incident," 415.

22. Baldwin, "The Constitutional Questions Incident"; Christina Duffy Burnett and Burke Marshall, eds., *Foreign in a Domestic Sense: Puerto Rico, American Expansion, and the Constitution* (Duke University Press, 2001); Randolph, "Constitutional Aspects of Annexation. Part First"; Carman F. Randolph, "The Insular Cases," *Columbia Law Review* 1, no. 7 (1901): 436–70; Bartholomew H. Sparrow, *The Insular Cases and the Emergence of American Empire* (University Press of Kansas, 2006).

23. Burnett and Marshall, *Foreign in a Domestic Sense*; Christopher Columbus Langdell, "The Status of Our New Territories," *Harvard Law Review* 12, no. 6 (1899): 365–92; Sparrow, *The Insular Cases and the Emergence of American Empire*; James Bradley Thayer, "Our New Possessions," *Harvard Law Review* 12, no. 7 (1899): 464–85; Trías Monge, *Puerto Rico: The Trials of the Oldest Colony in the World.*

24. Abbott Lawrence Lowell, "The Status of Our New Possessions: A Third View," *Harvard Law Review* 13, no. 3 (1899): 155–76.

25. Lowell, "The Status of Our New Possessions: A Third View." See also Thompson, *Imperial Archipelago*, 190.

26. Burnett and Marshall, *Foreign in a Domestic Sense*; Sparrow, *The Insular Cases and the Emergence of American Empire*; Trías Monge, *Puerto Rico: The Trials of the Oldest Colony in the World.*

27. Sam Erman, *Almost Citizens: Puerto Rico, the U.S. Constitution, and Empire* (Cambridge University Press, 2018).

28. Moon-Kie Jung, *Beneath the Surface of White Supremacy: Denaturalizing U.S. Racisms Past and Present* (Stanford University Press, 2015), 63.

29. Sparrow, *The Insular Cases and the Emergence of American Empire*, 5.

30. Sam Erman, "Meanings of Citizenship in the US Empire: Puerto Rico, Isabel Gonzalez, and the Supreme Court, 1898 to 1905," *Journal of American Ethnic History* 27, no. 4 (2008): 6.

31. April Merleaux, *Sugar and Civilization: American Empire and the Cultural Politics of Sweetness* (UNC Press Books, 2015), 30–31.

32. Merleaux, *Sugar and Civilization*, 45–46.

33. *De Lima v. Bidwell*, 182 U.S. 1 (1901).

34. *De Lima v. Bidwell*, 182 U.S. 1 (1901).

35. William M. Stewart, William Lindsay, and Augustus Bacon speaking on "Policy Regarding the Philippine Islands," on February 14, 1899, 55th Congress, 3rd Session, *Congressional Record* 32, pt. 2: 1830–47.

36. *Fourteen Diamond Rings v. United States*, 183 U.S. 176 (1901).

37. *Fourteen Diamond Rings v. United States*, 183 U.S. 176 (1901).

38. *Foraker Act*, Section 3, Public Law 56-191 (1900).

39. The implications of this case would extend to other imports, including sugar. The Sugar Trust, run by the American Sugar Refining Company, actively opposed free

trade for Puerto Rican imported sugar and therefore did not want the United States to annex the territories as states and give them free trade. Although Puerto Rican sugar production did not threaten domestic sugar, if the imports were not taxed, then Puerto Rico would be treated as a state (Sparrow, *The Insular Cases and the Emergence of American Empire*, 70–76.)

40. Only one justice wrote the Court's opinion, and four other justices concurred but did not join the opinion of the Court.

41. *Downes v. Bidwell*, 182 U.S. 244 (1901).

42. Burnett and Marshall, *Foreign in a Domestic Sense*, 13–17.

43. The plaintiff's name was actually González, but the court case is written as Gonzales.

44. The Philippine equivalent to the 1900 Foraker Act for Puerto Rico.

45. Circular No. 97, August 2, 1902, in *Circular Instructions of the Treasury Department Relating to the Tariff, Navigation, and Other Laws for the Year Ended December 31, 1902* (Washington, D.C.: Treasury Department, 1903); Transcript of Record, No. 225, *Gonzales v. Williams*, 192 U.S. 1, 3–6.

46. For discussion of Collazo as well as the struggle for Puerto Rican citizenship, see Erman, "Meanings of Citizenship in the US Empire."

47. *Downes v. Bidwell*, 182 U.S. 244 (1901).

48. *Downes v. Bidwell*, 182 U.S. 244 (1901).

49. *Downes v. Bidwell*, 182 U.S. 244 (1901).

50. U.S. Congress, Senate, Committee on the Philippines, *Affairs in the Philippine Islands: Hearings before the Committee on the Philippines*, 57th Congress, 1st Session, May 21, 1902, 2673.

51. *Act Temporarily to provide for the administration of the affairs of civil government in the Philippine Islands, and for other purposes*, Public Law 57-235 (1902). This provision, other than referring to the Philippines rather than "Porto Rico," is identical to that written in the 1900 Foraker Act (or Puerto Rican Organic Act). In the Puerto Rican Organic Act, however, it reads: "and they, together with such citizens of the United States as may reside in Porto Rico, shall constitute a body politic under the name of The People of Porto Rico, with governmental powers as hereinafter conferred, and with power to sue and be sued as such."

52. U.S. Congress, Senate, April 21, 1902, 57th Congress, 1st Session, *Congressional Record* 35, pt. 5: 4477.

53. U.S. Congress, Senate, April 21, 1902, 57th Congress, 1st Session, *Congressional Record* 35, pt. 5: 5213.

54. *Gonzales v. Williams*, 192 U.S. 1 (1904).

55. *Gonzales v. Williams*, 192 U.S. 1 (1904).

56. *Gonzales v. Williams*, 192 U.S. 1 (1904).

57. U.S. Congress, Senate, Committee on the Philippines, *Affairs in the Philippine Islands: Hearings before the Committee on the Philippines*, 57th Congress, 1st Session, February 15, 1902, 322.

58. Senator Morgan speaking on "Civil Government for the Philippines" on May 29, 1902, 57th Congress, 1st Session, *Congressional Record* 35, pt. 6: 6089; 6091.

59. Veta Schlimgen, "The Invention of 'Noncitizen American Nationality' and the Meanings of Colonial Subjecthood in the United States," *Pacific Historical Review* 89, no. 3 (July 3, 2020): 317–46.

60. Christina Duffy Burnett, "Empire and the Transformation of Citizenship," in *Colonial Crucible: Empire in the Making of the Modern American State*, ed. Alfred W. McCoy and Francisco A. Scarano (University of Wisconsin Press, 2009), 335. This language is like that described by Patricia Hill Collins (2001) in referring to how the United States has navigated the tensions between liberal individual rights and racial exclusion of Black people. She uses the experience of Black women as domestic workers who are "like one of the family" to demonstrate the subordination of rights to racial Others.

61. Erman, "Meanings of Citizenship in the US Empire," 16.

62. Justice William Day, like Coudert, proposed a new term, "liegeman," as something in between alien and citizen (Erman, "Meanings of Citizenship in the US Empire," 20).

63. U.S. Constitution, article 4, section 3, clause 2: "power to dispose of and make all needful rules and regulations respecting the territory or other property belonging to the United States."

64. *Downes v. Bidwell*, 182 U.S. 244 (1901).

65. Senator Vest speaking on "Army Appropriation Bill," on February 25, 1901, 56th Congress, 2nd Session, *Congressional Record* 34, pt. 3: 2956.

66. *Downes v. Bidwell*, 182 U.S. 244 (1901).

67. *Downes v. Bidwell*, 182 U.S. 244 (1901).

68. *Downes v. Bidwell*, 182 U.S. 244 (1901).

69. *Downes v. Bidwell*, 182 U.S. 244 (1901).

70. *Downes v. Bidwell*, 182 U.S. 244 (1901).

71. Juan R. Torruella, "One Hundred Years of Solitude: Puerto Rico's American Century," in *Foreign in a Domestic Sense: Puerto Rico, American Expansion, and the Constitution*, ed. Christina Duffy Burnett and Burke Marshall (Duke University Press, 2001), 241–50.

Chapter 3

1. William McKinley, "Benevolent Assimilation Proclamation," December 21, 1898.

2. Mark Elliott, "'Our God-Given Mission': Reconstruction and the Humanitarian Nationalism of the 1890s," in *Reconstruction and Empire: The Legacies of Abolition and Union Victory for an Imperial Age*, ed. David Prior (Fordham University Press, 2022), 176.

3. Simeon E. Baldwin, "The Constitutional Questions Incident to the Acquisition and Government by the United States of Island Territory," *Harvard Law Review* 12, no. 6 (1899): 415.

4. Colin D. Moore, *American Imperialism and the State, 1893–1921* (Cambridge University Press, 2017).

5. Moore, *American Imperialism and the State,* xiv.

6. Before Root, the assistant secretary of war, George De Rue Meiklejohn, built the precursors to the BIA. Romeo V. Cruz, *America's Colonial Desk and the Philippines, 1898–1934* (University of the Philippines Press, 1974), 23–5, 30–40.

7. U.S. Congress, Senate, *Gazetteer of the Philippine Islands,* 57th Congress, 1st Session, 1902, serial 4240, 239.

8. Cruz, *America's Colonial Desk and the Philippines,* vii. Cruz also argues that the BIA, in part because it was not an official colonial office, had latitude to take action that European colonial offices "would dare not do" (55).

9. For information on the Rube Goldberg State, see also Elisabeth S. Clemens, "Lineages of the Rube Goldberg State: Building and Blurring Public Programs, 1900–1940," in *Rethinking Political Institutions: The Art of the State,* ed. Ian Shapiro et al. (NYU Press, 2006), 380–443.

10. See, for example, 1905 Naval Appropriations Bill passed on March 3; 1909 Philippine Tariff Act and US Tariff Revision Act passed on August 5.

11. Moore argues that the "external state," meaning the part of the state concerned with imperial or foreign affairs, emerged from Congress's lack of interest in foreign affairs. Where Moore argues Congress designed the colonial state to fail, I emphasize the Courts enabled political discretion, which, faced with a lack of interest, gave rise to administrative discretion and control.

12. Castañeda Anastacio argues that over the course of U.S. rule, U.S. state actors worked to balance the two. Leia Castañeda Anastacio, *The Foundations of the Modern Philippine State: Imperial Rule and the American Constitutional Tradition in the Philippine Islands, 1898–1935* (Cambridge University Press, 2016).

13. Charles Edward Magoon, *Reports on the Law of Civil Government in Territory Subject to Military Occupation by the Military Forces of the United States: Submitted to Hon. Elihu Root, Secretary of War* (U.S. Government Printing Office, 1902), 236.

14. Magoon, *Reports on the Law of Civil Government in Territory Subject to Military Occupation by the Military Forces of the United States,* 216.

15. Magoon, *Reports on the Law of Civil Government in Territory Subject to Military Occupation by the Military Forces of the United States,* 220.

16. Magoon, *Report on the Legal Status of the Territory and Inhabitants of the Islands Acquired by the United States During the War with Spain,* 13.

17. Magoon, *Report on the Legal Status of the Territory and Inhabitants of the Islands Acquired by the United States During the War with Spain,* 38.

18. Elihu Root, "The Civil Government of the Philippines," in *The Military and Colonial Policy of the United States: Addresses and Reports by Elihu Root,* Legal Classics Library (Harvard University Press, 1916), 252–53.

19. Margot Canaday, *The Straight State: Sexuality and Citizenship in Twentieth-Century America* (Princeton University Press, 2009); Oz Frankel, *States of Inquiry: Social Investigations and Print Culture in Nineteenth-Century Britain and the United States* (Johns Hopkins University Press, 2006); Sunmin Kim, *The Unruly Facts of Race: The Politics of Knowledge Production in the Early 20th Century Immigration Debate* (University of Chicago Press, 2025).

20. Root, "The Civil Government of the Philippines," 286–87.

21. Senator Tillman, speaking on "Army Appropriation Bill," on February 25, 1901, 56th Congress, 2nd Session, *Congressional Record* 34, pt. 3: 2958.

22. Senator Tillman, speaking on "Army Appropriation Bill," on February 25, 1901, 56th Congress, 2nd Session, *Congressional Record* 34, pt. 3: 2957.

23. David V. Holtby, "Connected Lives: Albert Beveridge, Benjamin Tillman, and the Grand Army of the Republic," in *Reconstruction and Empire: The Legacies of Abolition and Union Victory for an Imperial Age*, ed. David Prior (Fordham University Press, 2022), 191–213; D. J. Polite, "The Lynching of Frazier Baker: Violence from Reconstruction to Empire," in *Reconstruction and Empire: The Legacies of Abolition and Union Victory for an Imperial Age*, ed. David Prior (Fordham University Press, 2022), 214–38.

24. "Commission to Visit Porto Rico [*sic*], the Philippines, and Cuba," March 2, 1901, 56th Congress, 2nd Session, *Congressional Record* 34, pt. 4: 3567–69.

25. Philip C. Jessup, *Elihu Root* (Dodd Mead, 1938), 359; Richard William Leopold, *Elihu Root and the Conservative Tradition* (Little, Brown, 1954), 36; Moore, *American Imperialism and the State*, 88.

26. U.S. Congress, Senate, *In relation to the suppression of insurrection in, and to the government of, the Philippine Islands, ceded by Spain to the United States by the treaty concluded at Paris on the 10th day of December, 1898*, S. 2355, 56th Congress, 1st Session, Introduced on January 11, 1900.

27. Senator Spooner, "Amendment intended to be proposed by Mr. Spooner to the bill (H.R. 14017) making appropriations for the support of the Army," on February 8, 1901, 56th Congress, 2nd Session, *Congressional Record* 34, pt. 3: 2117.

28. Senator Morgan, speaking on "Army Appropriation Bill," on February 25, 1901, 56th Congress, 2nd Session, *Congressional Record* 34, pt. 3: 2967.

29. *An Act making appropriation for the support of the Army for the fiscal year ending June thirtieth, nineteen hundred and two*, Public Law 56-803 (1901).

30. Senator Caffery, speaking on "Army Appropriation Bill," on February 25, 1901, 56th Congress, 2nd Session, *Congressional Record* 34, pt. 3: 2961–63.

31. Senator Vest, speaking on "Army Appropriation Bill," on February 25, 1901, 56th Congress, 2nd Session, *Congressional Record* 34, pt. 3: 2956.

32. Senator Bacon, speaking on "Army Appropriation Bill," on February 25, 1901, 56th Congress, 2nd Session, *Congressional Record* 34, pt. 3: 2957.

33. Senator Tillman, speaking on "Army Appropriation Bill," on February 25, 1901, 56th Congress, 2nd Session, *Congressional Record* 34, pt. 3: 2957.

34. *An Act Temporarily to provide for the administration of the affairs of civil government in the Philippine Islands, and for other purposes*, Public Law 57-235 (1902). See Moore, *American Imperialism and the State*, 95–96.

35. Root to Taft, January 21, 1901, Root Papers, Semi-Official Letters, vol. 4 (in Cruz, *America's Colonial Desk and the Philippines*, 111).

36. Nerissa Balce, *Body Parts of Empire: Visual Abjection, Filipino Images, and the American Archive* (University of Michigan Press, 2016); Rick Baldoz, "The Racial Vectors of Empire: Classification and Competing Master Narratives in the Colonial Philippines," *Du Bois Review: Social Science Research on Race* 5, no. 1 (April 2008): 69–94; Cheryl Beredo, *Import of the Archive: U.S. Colonial Rule of the Philippines and the*

Making of American Archival History (Litwin Books, 2013); Mark Rice, *Dean Worcester's Fantasy Islands: Photography, Film, and the Colonial Philippines* (University of Michigan Press, 2014).

37. See: James C. Scott, *Seeing Like a State: How Certain Schemes to Improve the Human Condition Have Failed* (Yale University Press, 1998); Charles Tilly, *Coercion, Capital, and European States, AD 990–1990* (Oxford Blackwell, 1992).

38. Schurman Commission, "The Native Peoples of the Philippines," *Report of the Philippine Commission, Volume I* (Washington, D.C.: Government Printing Office, 1900). See also Rice, *Dean Worcester's Fantasy Islands: Photography, Film, and the Colonial Philippines*; Dean C. Worcester, *The Philippine Islands and Their People* (New York, London: The Macmillan Company, 1898); Dean Conant Worcester, *The Philippines Past and Present* (Macmillan Company, 1914).

39. Schurman Commission, "The Native Peoples of the Philippines," 11.

40. Mark S. Weiner, "Teutonic Constitutionalism: The Role of Ethno-Juridical Discourse in the Spanish-American War," in *Foreign in a Domestic Sense: Puerto Rico, American Expansion, and the Constitution*, ed. Christina Duffy Burnett and Burke Marshall (Duke University Press, 2001), 48–81.

41. Sixto López, *The "Tribes" in the Philippines* (New England Anti-Imperialist League, 1900).

42. Henry Gannet, "The Philippine Islands and Their People (Reprinted from the National Geographic Magazine, March)," March 1, 1904, Presented to the Senate by Henry Cabot Lodge, 58th Congress, 2nd Session: 6.

43. For discussion of Moros as wild, see Paul A. Kramer, *The Blood of Government: Race, Empire, the United States, and the Philippines* (University of North Carolina Press, 2006), 67–71, 219–320, 341.

44. Vicente L. Rafael, *White Love: Census and Melodrama in the U.S. Colonization of the Philippines* (Duke University Press, 2000).

45. Elihu Root, "The Beginnings of Civil Government," in *The Military and Colonial Policy of the United States: Addresses and Reports by Elihu Root*, Legal Classics Library (1901; Harvard University Press, 1916), 239–40.

46. Elihu Root, "Finances of the Philippines," extracted from *The Report of the Secretary of War* in *Military and Colonial Policy of the United States, Addresses and Reports* (1903; Harvard University Press, 1916), 313.

47. Theodore Roosevelt, *The Strenuous Life* (G. P. Putnam's, 1901), 19.

48. Schurman Commission, "The Native Peoples of the Philippines," 12.

49. Carman F. Randolph, "Constitutional Aspects of Annexation. Part First," *Harvard Law Review* 12, no. 5 (1898): 304.

50. James Bradley Thayer, "Our New Possessions," *Harvard Law Review* 12, no. 7 (1899): 466.

51. Christopher Columbus Langdell, "The Status of Our New Territories," *Harvard Law Review* 12, no. 6 (1899): 371.

52. This claim also erased American Indians as people who had sovereignty over their lands, thus contradicting the first argument about political sovereignty.

53. Virginia R. Dominguez, "When the Enemy Is Unclear: US Censuses and Photographs of Cuba, Puerto Rico, and the Philippines from the Beginning of the Twentieth Century," *Comparative American Studies An International Journal* 5, no. 2 (June 2007): 173–203.

54. Julian Go, "'Racism' and Colonialism: Meanings of Difference and Ruling Practices in America's Pacific Empire," *Qualitative Sociology* 27, no. 1 (2004): 39. Go quotes Cameron Forbes (Forbes 1928, vol. I, p. 166; Forbes to Higginson, Sept. 2, 1904, FP).

55. Woodrow Wilson, "The Ideals of America," *Atlantic Monthly* 90, no. 6 (1902): 721–34.

56. Go, "'Racism' and Colonialism," 27.

57. President McKinley, to Congress, December 4, 1900, McKinley Papers; Library of Congress Series 5 (3), images 377.

58. Erin L. Murphy, "In a Few Generations: Debating Race, Colonial Development, and Independence in the US Colonial Field," *Critical Sociology* 41, no. 2 (March 1, 2015): 219–35.

59. Weiner, "Teutonic Constitutionalism," refers to this as Teutonic ethno-juridical discourse. See also Albert Jeremiah Beveridge, "Our Philippine Policy," in *The Meaning of the Times: And Other Speeches* (1908; Bobbs-Merrill Company, 1968), 106–7.

60. Eric T. L. Love, *Race Over Empire: Racism and US Imperialism, 1865–1900* (University of North Carolina Press, 2004).

61. U.S. Congress, House, Committee on Insular Affairs, Statement of Hon. William H. Taft, President of the Board of Commissioners to the Philippine Islands, 57th Congress, 1st and 2nd Sessions, February 21, 1902, 120–21.

62. Both Go, "'Racism' and Colonialism," and Thompson, *Imperial Archipelago*, refer to this perspective as Lamarckian. Thompson notes that sociologists Albion Small, Franklin Giddings, and William I. Thomas (of the early Chicago school) were Lamarckian evolutionists in this vein (Thompson, 90).

63. Luke E. Wright, letter to Colonel Clarence R. Edwards. February 20, 1902, Special Correspondence, Box 161, Henry Cabot Lodge, Elihu P. Root Papers, Manuscript Division, Library of Congress, Washington, D.C.

64. Taft Commission, *Reports of the Taft Philippine Commission* (Washington, D.C.: Government Printing Office, 1901), 19.

65. President McKinley, Message to Congress, c. 1900, McKinley Papers; LoC Series 5 (3) images 715-723.

66. Glenn Anthony May, *Social Engineering in the Philippines: The Aims, Execution, and Impact of American Colonial Policy, 1900–1913* (Greenwood Press, 1980).

67. In the United States, organic acts create territorial governments and lay down the terms of how the territory will be governed or administered.

68. Theodore Roosevelt, *The Strenuous Life*, vol. 20 (Scribner, 1903), 6.

69. *Philippine Government Act,* Section 3, Public Law 57-235-1 (1902).

70. Patricio N. Abinales and Donna J. Amoroso, *State and Society in the Philippines* (Rowman & Littlefield Publishers, 2005); Kramer, *The Blood of Government.*

71. U.S. Congress, House, Committee on Insular Affairs, *Statement of Conditions in the Philippine Islands: Hearings before the Committee on Insular Affairs*, 57th Congress, 1st Session, March 5, 1902, 140.

72. Patricio N. Abinales, *Making Mindanao: Cotabato and Davao in the Formation of the Philippine Nation-State* (Ateneo de Manila University Press, 2000); Kramer, *The Blood of Government*.

73. As quoted in May, *Social Engineering in the Philippines*, 80.

74. Root, "The Civil Government of the Philippines," 272.

75. Act 74 of the Philippine Commission (1901).

76. J. Matthew Knake, "Education Means Liberty: Filipino Students, *Pensionados*, and U.S. Colonial Education," *Western Illinois Historical Review* 6, no. 1 (2014); Barbara M. Posadas and Roland L. Guyotte, "Aspiration and Reality: Occupational and Educational Choice among Filipino Migrants to Chicago, 1900–1935," *Illinois Historical Journal* 85, no. 2 (1992): 89–104.

77. Taft Commission, *Reports of the Taft Philippine Commission* (Washington, D.C.: Government Printing Office, 1901), 32.

78. May, *Social Engineering in the Philippines*, 97–98.

79. U.S. Congress, Senate, Committee on the Philippines, *Affairs in the Philippine Islands, Hearings before the Committee on the Philippines*, 57th Congress, 1st Session. March 12, 1902, 694.

80. U.S. War Department, *Special Report of William H. Taft, Secretary of War, to the President on the Philippines* (Washington, D.C.: Government Printing Office, 1909), 27.

81. *An Act Providing for the Education of Filipino Students in the United Sates and Appropriating for such purpose the sum of seventy-two thousand dollars, in money of the United States*, Philippine Commission Act No. 854 (1903). August 26, 1903. See also Knake, "Education Means Liberty: Filipino Students, Pensionados and U.S. Colonial Education"; Murphy, "In a Few Generations"; Posadas and Guyotte, "Aspiration and Reality," 89–104; Sarah Steinbock-Pratt, *Educating the Empire: American Teachers and Contested Colonization in the Philippines* (Cambridge University Press, 2019); Noel V. Teodoro, "Pensionados and Workers: The Filipinos in the United States, 1903–1956," *Asian and Pacific Migration Journal* 8, no. 1–2 (March 1, 1999): 157–78.

82. Steinbock-Pratt, *Educating the Empire*, 203.

83. Christopher Capozzola, *Bound by War: How the United States and the Philippines Built America's First Pacific Century* (Basic Books, 2020), 13–15; Edward M. Coffman, "Batson of the Philippine Scouts" (Amy War College Carlisle Barracks PA, 1977).

84. *Military Establishment Efficiency Act*, Public Law 56-192 (1901).

85. Kramer, *The Blood of Government*, 113–15; Alfred McCoy, "The Colonial Origins of Philippine Military Traditions," in *The Philippine Revolution of 1896: Ordinary Lives in Extraordinary Times* (Ateneo de Manila University Press, 2001), 83–124.

86. Cynthia Marasigan, "Race, Performance, and Colonial Governance: The Philippine Constabulary Band Plays the St. Louis World's Fair," *Journal of Asian American Studies* 22, no. 3 (October 31, 2019): 349–85; Barbara M. Posadas, *The Filipino Americans* (Bloomsbury Publishing USA, 1999), 17; Mary Talusan, "Music, Race, and

Imperialism: The Philippine Constabulary Band at the 1904 St. Louis World's Fair," *Philippine Studies* 52, no. 4 (2004): 499–526.

87. May, *Social Engineering in the Philippines*. May notes that U.S. imperialist proposals were not novel but followed the history of expansion and development in the U.S. metropole.

88. *An Act establishing a department of public instruction in the Philippine Islands*, Philippine Commission Act No. 74 (1901).

89. May, *Social Engineering in the Philippines*, 91–92.

90. Fred W. Atkinson, *The Present Educational Movement in the Philippine Islands* (Washington, D.C.: Government Printing Office, 1902); Bernard Moses Papers, Bancroft Library, scrapbook 5. As quoted in May, *Social Engineering in the Philippines*, 93.

91. May, *Social Engineering in the Philippines*, 92.

92. Luke E. Wright, to Cameron and McLaughlin, January 3, 1902. As quoted by William H. Taft in U.S. Congress, House, Committee on Insular Affairs, *Statement of the Conditions in the Philippine Islands: Hearings before the Committee on Insular Affairs*, 57th Congress, 1st Session, March 3, 1902, 100.

93. William H. Taft, to Henry Cabot Lodge, October 1, 1900, Taft Papers, Series 3, Box 63.

94. May, *Social Engineering in the Philippines*; Ruby R. Paredes, ed., *Philippine Colonial Democracy* (Ateneo de Manila University Press, 1988).

95. *An Act to revise and amend the tariff laws of the Philippine Archipelago*, Philippine Commission Act No. 230 (1901).

96. Taft Commission, *Reports of the Taft Philippine Commission* (Washington, D.C.: Government Printing Office, 1901), 59.

97. Senator Foster, May 25, 1909, 61st Congress, 1st Session, *Congressional Record* 55, pt. 3: 2373

98. *An Act temporarily to provide revenue for the Philippine Islands, and for other purposes*, Public Law 57-28 (1902).

99. May, *Social Engineering in the Philippines*.

100. Entry on Saturday May 21, 1910, Journal of W. Cameron Forbes, Volume III, April 17, 1908–March 4, 1910, W. Cameron Forbes papers, Library of Congress, Washington, D.C.: 101.

101. *1904 Democratic Party Platform*, July 6, 1904, https://www.presidency.ucsb .edu/documents/1904-democratic-party-platform.

102. *1908 Democratic Party Platform*, July 7, 1908, https://www.presidency.ucsb .edu/documents/1908-democratic-party-platform.

103. *1912 Democratic Party Platform*, June 25, 1912, https://www.presidency.ucsb .edu/documents/1912-democratic-party-platform.

104. Samuel Flagg Bemis, "American Foreign Policy and the Blessings of Liberty," *The American Historical Review* 67, no. 2 (1962): 291–305; Brian Loveman, *No Higher Law: American Foreign Policy and the Western Hemisphere Since 1776* (University of North Carolina Press, 2010), 194.

105. Gerald E. Wheeler, "Republican Philippine Policy, 1921–1933," *Pacific Historical Review* 28, no. 4 (1959): 377–90.

106. Quoted in Grayson L. Kirk, *Philippine Independence: Motives, Problems, and Prospects* (Da Capo Press, 1936), 44. See also: Harley Notter, *The Origins of the Foreign Policy of Woodrow Wilson* (Johns Hopkins University Press, 1937).

107. Roy Watson Curry, "Woodrow Wilson and Philippine Policy," *The Mississippi Valley Historical Review* 41, no. 3 (1954): 435–52. Curry notes that "various influential groups insisted" that W. Cameron Forbes, a Republican, be replaced.

108. As quoted in Curry, "Woodrow Wilson and Philippine Policy," 440.

109. Curry, "Woodrow Wilson and Philippine Policy."

110. *Philippine Autonomy Act* (Jones Law), Public Law 64-260 (1916).

111. For more on Quezon's position on Philippine independence, see: Curry, "Woodrow Wilson and Philippine Policy"; Alfred W. McCoy, "Quezon's Commonwealth: The Emergence of Philippine Authoritarianism," in *Philippine Colonial Democracy*, ed. Ruby R. Paredes (Ateneo de Manila University Press, 1988), 114–60; Richard Bruce Meixsel, "Manuel L. Quezon, Douglas MacArthur, and the Significance of the Military Mission to the Philippine Commonwealth," *Pacific Historical Review* 70, no. 2 (2001): 255–92.

112. W. Cameron Forbes, letter to Hon. Theodore Roosevelt, May 19, 1916, Forbes Series II, Vol I: 338–39.

113. Senator Clarke, January 11, 1916, 64th Congress, 1st Session, *Congressional Record* 53, pt. 1: 846. See also Curry, "Woodrow Wilson and Philippine Policy."

114. It won out over another version of the bill, which would have given a republic in 1920, because Congressional representatives thought that the Philippines needed more "training in self-government" (John A. Beadles, "The Debate in the United States Concerning Philippine Independence; 1912–1916," *Philippine Studies* 16, no. 3 (1968): 441.

115. With the exception of non-Christian tribes, who the U.S. and Filipino elite continued to view as unassimilable.

116. *Philippine Autonomy Act* (Jones Law), Public Law 64-260 (1916).

117. President Wilson, December 7, 1920, 66th Congress, 3rd Session, *Congressional Record* 60, pt. 1: 26.

Part 2

1. Daniel Immerwahr, *How to Hide an Empire: A History of the Greater United States* (Farrar, Straus and Giroux, 2019).

2. Ann Laura Stoler, *Duress: Imperial Durabilities in Our Times* (Duke University Press, 2016), 10.

3. For a discussion of World War I and European colonialism, see: W.E.B. Du Bois, "The Souls of White Folk," in *Darkwater: Voices from within the Veil* (Harcourt, Brace and Howe, 1920), 29–52; W.E.B. Du Bois, *Dusk of Dawn: An Essay Toward an Autobiography of a Race Concept* (Transaction Publishers, 1940).

4. Francis Burton Harrison, *The Corner-Stone of Philippine Independence* (Century Company, 1922), 172–74.

5. Ricardo Trota Jose, "The Philippine National Guard in World War I," *Philippine Studies* 36, no. 3 (1988): 275–99.

6. Frank Hindman Golay, *Face of Empire: United States-Philippine Relations, 1898–1946* (Ateneo de Manila University Press, 1997).

7. Tarak Barkawi, "States, Armies and Wars in Global Context," in *Global Historical Sociology*, ed. Julian Go and George Lawson (Cambridge University Press, 2017), 58–76; Jane Burbank and Frederick Cooper, *Empires in World History: Power and the Politics of Difference* (Princeton University Press, 2011), 369–76; Anthony Clayton, *France, Soldiers, and Africa* (Brassey's Defence Publishers, 1988); Frederick William Perry, *The Commonwealth Armies: Manpower and Organisation in Two World Wars* (Manchester University Press, 1988).

8. Golay, *Face of Empire: United States-Philippine Relations*, 233–34.

9. Woodrow Wilson, "Address to a Joint Session of Congress, February 11, 1918." The League rejected Wilson's language of self-determination. See Adom Getachew, *Worldmaking after Empire: The Rise and Fall of Self-Determination* (Princeton University Press, 2019), 39–45. Although Wilson was not an anti-imperial politician, his calls for self-determination did inspire contestation from colonial peoples. See Getachew, *Worldmaking after Empire*; Erez Manela, *The Wilsonian Moment: Self-Determination and the International Origins of Anticolonial Nationalism* (Oxford University Press, 2007).

10. *Declaration on the Granting of Independence to Colonial Countries and Peoples,* United Nations General Assembly Resolution 1514 (XV) (1960). See Adom Getachew, *Worldmaking after Empire*.

11. John Lewis Gaddis, *We Now Know: Rethinking Cold War History* (Clarendon Press, 1997).

12. Gerald E. Wheeler, "The United States Navy and the Japanese 'Enemy': 1919–1931," *Military Affairs* 21, no. 2 (1957): 61–74.

13. Paul A. Kramer, *The Blood of Government: Race, Empire, the United States, and the Philippines* (University of North Carolina Press, 2006); Gerald E. Wheeler, "Republican Philippine Policy, 1921–1933," *Pacific Historical Review* 28, no. 4 (1959): 377–90.

14. Wheeler, "Republican Philippine Policy, 1921–1933."

15. Henry William Brands, *Bound to Empire: The United States and the Philippines* (Oxford University Press, 1992), 132–36; Golay, *Face of Empire: United States-Philippine Relations*, 250.

16. See Memorandum on Nationality and Citizenship; Status of Inhabitants of the Outlying Possessions of the United States, 1928, *Proposed Amendment of Nationality Laws of the United States*, Report of the Committee Appointed by the Secretary of State, RG 350 Entry I3 5B Box 310 GCF Boundaries 1444, National Archives II, College Park, MD.

17. Senators Tydings and Copeland, speaking on H.R. 7233, "Philippine Independence," on December 8, 1932, 72nd Congress, 2nd Session, *Congressional Record* 76, pt. 1: 186.

18. Fred A. Feliciano, "Filipinos and the Census," letter to the editor, *New York Times*, April 14, 1930.

Chapter 4

1. In the Matter of Aclang, Ambrocio B., Filipino, At a Meeting of a Board of Special Inquiry, Hearing for Testimony, U.S. Department of Labor, Immigration Service, May 17, 1934: 3208; Aclang, Box 34028, SS *President Hoover*, RG 85, NARA–San Bruno, San Bruno, CA.

2. *Philippines Independence Act*, Public Law 73-127 (1934).

3. Extract from BIA Radio to the Governor General of the Philippines, April 24, 1934, RG 350 Entry I3 5B GCF 25051 Immigration Box 1027, National Archives II, College Park, MD.

4. Cybelle Fox, *Three Worlds of Relief: Race, Immigration, and the American Welfare State from the Progressive Era to the New Deal* (Princeton University Press, 2012); Natalia Molina, *How Race Is Made in America: Immigration, Citizenship, and the Historical Power of Racial Scripts* (University of California Press, 2014); Mae M. Ngai, *Impossible Subjects: Illegal Aliens and the Making of Modern America* (Princeton University Press, 2004); George J. Sanchez, *Becoming Mexican American: Ethnicity, Culture, and Identity in Chicano Los Angeles, 1900–1945* (Oxford University Press, USA, 1995).

5. Bruno Lasker, *Filipino Immigration to Continental United States and to Hawaii* (University of Chicago Press, 1931), 31. Lasker notes it was hard to estimate the Filipino population in the United States because many were migrant laborers. Estimates by the Industrial Relations Department of California were in the 31,000 to 34,000 range for California alone (Francis Parker, to Dwight Davis, BIA Radiogram, April 15, 1930, RG 350 Entry I3 5B GCF Box 1027 25051 Immigration, National Archives II, College Park, MD).

6. April Merleaux, *Sugar and Civilization: American Empire and the Cultural Politics of Sweetness* (UNC Press, 2015); JoAnna Poblete, *Islanders in the Empire: Filipino and Puerto Rican Laborers in Hawai'i* (University of Illinois Press, 2014).

7. Ngai, *Impossible Subjects*, 103.

8. Emory S. Bogardus, *Anti-Filipino Race Riots: A Report Made to the Ingram Institute of Social Science of San Diego* (Ingram Institute, 1930), 20–22; Emory S. Bogardus, "Filipino Repatriation," *Sociology and Social Research* 21, no. 1 (1936): 67–71; Ruby C. Tapia, "'Just Ten Years Removed from a Bolo and a Breech-Cloth': The Sexualization of the Filipino 'Menace,'" in *Positively No Filipinos Allowed: Building Communities and Discourse*, ed. Antonio T. Tiongson et al. (Temple University Press, 2006), 63.

9. Ronald Takaki notes that 25 percent of Filipinos in the mainland United States in 1930 were service workers. Ronald Takaki, "Dollar a Day, Dime a Dance: The Forgotten Filipinos," in *Strangers from a Different Shore: A History of Asian Americans* (Penguin, 1989), 317–18.

10. Ngai, *Impossible Subjects*, 109.

11. Rick Baldoz, *The Third Asiatic Invasion: Migration and Empire in Filipino America, 1898–1946* (NYU Press, 2011), 136.

12. Bogardus, "Filipino Repatriation," 4.

13. Baldoz, *The Third Asiatic Invasion*; Louis Bloch, *Facts about Filipino Immigration into California*, Special Bulletin, no. 3 (San Francisco: State Department of Industrial Relations, 1930); Paul Scharrenberg, "The Philippine Problem: Attitude of

American Labor Toward Filipino Immigration and Philippine Independence," *Pacific Affairs* 2, no. 2 (1929): 49.

14. As quoted in Baldoz, *The Third Asiatic Invasion*, 70.

15. See Johann Friedrich Blumenbach, "On the Natural Variety of Mankind," in *The Idea of Race*, ed. Robert Bernasconi and Tommy L. Lott (Hackett Publishing Company, 2000), 27–37.

16. See Ian Haney-López, *White by Law: The Legal Construction of Race* (NYU Press, 1996); Ngai, *Impossible Subjects*.

17. Baldoz, *The Third Asiatic Invasion*, 93–101; Ngai, *Impossible Subjects*, 115.

18. *Roldan v. Los Angeles County*, 129 Cal. App. 267, 18 P.2d 706 (Cal. Ct. App. 1933).

19. Baldoz, *The Third Asiatic Invasion*, 101.

20. Chas C. Walcutt, to A. S. Espinosa, November 9, 1922, RG 350 GCF 1914–1945 Box 309 Citizenship PI Boundaries 1444, National Archives II, College Park, MD.

21. RG 350 GCF 1914–1945 Boxes 309–310, Citizenship PI Boundaries 1444, Entry I3 5B Box 310 GCF Boundaries 1444, National Archives II, College Park, MD.

22. Baldoz, *The Third Asiatic Invasion*, 113.

23. Filipinos mostly worked in lettuce and asparagus harvest, whereas the whites who were migrant farmworkers harvested figs and apples. See Ngai, *Impossible Subjects*, 108. Lasker too notes that there was no direct competition between whites and Filipinos. See Lasker, *Filipino Immigration to Continental United States and to Hawaii*, 15, 35.

24. Commonwealth Club of California Transactions 5: 352–53, November 5, 1929, as cited in Casiano Coloma, "A Study of the Filipino Repatriation Movement" (master's thesis, University of Southern California, 1939).

25. Ngai, *Impossible Subjects*; Antonio T. Tiongson et al., eds., *Positively No Filipinos Allowed: Building Communities and Discourse* (Temple University Press, 2006).

26. Matthew Frye Jacobson, *Barbarian Virtues: The United States Encounters Foreign Peoples at Home and Abroad, 1876–1917* (Macmillan, 2001).

27. Lasker, *Filipino Immigration to Continental United States and to Hawaii*, 34.

28. Frank McIntyre, to F. C. Fisher, February 27, 1928, In Memorandum for General Parker on H.R. 8708, RG 350 Entry I3 5B GCF Box 1027 25051 Immigration, National Archives II, College Park, MD.

29. Francis Parker, November 29, 1930, "Filipino Immigration," Memorandum for the Secretary of War, RG 350 Entry I3 5B GCF Box 1027 25051 Immigration, National Archives II, College Park, MD.

30. In both the acts of 1917 and 1924, the term "alien" did not apply to Native Americans or citizens of the islands of the United States. *Immigration Act of 1917*, Public Law 64-301 (1917); *Immigration Act of 1924*, Public Law 68-139 (1924).

31. See *United States v. Tod*, 285 Fed. 523.

32. E. A. Kreger, to Francis Parker, April 9, 1930, RG 350 Entry I3 5B GCF Box 1027 25051 Immigration, National Archives II, College Park, MD.

33. *Philippine Independence Act of 1934*, Public Law 73-127 (1934).

34. U.S. Congress, House, *A Bill to provide for full and complete independence for the Philippine Islands*, H.R. 5462, 72nd Congress, 1st Session, December 11, 1931.

35. U.S. Congress, House, Committee on Insular Affairs, *Independence for the Philippine Islands: Hearings before the Committee on Insular Affairs,* 72nd Congress, 1st Session, January 28, 1932, 123–24.

36. Bureau of Insular Affairs, "Power of Congress to limit immigration from the Philippines to continental United States," by Blanton Winship for Chief, February 18, 1932, RG 350 Entry I3 5B GCF 25051 Immigration Box 1027, National Archives II, College Park, MD.

37. U.S. Congress, House, Committee on Insular Affairs, *Independence for the Philippine Islands: Hearings before the Committee on Insular Affairs,* 72nd Congress, 1st Session, January 22, 1932, 4–5.

38. Stimson to Hoover, January 3, 1933. As quoted in Theodore W. Friend, "Veto and Repassage of the Hare–Hawes–Cutting Act: A Catalogue of Motives," *Philippine Studies* 12, no. 4 (1964): 668.

39. Friend, "Veto and Repassage of the Hare–Hawes–Cutting Act," 672.

40. Friend, "Veto and Repassage of the Hare–Hawes–Cutting Act," 669. Hoover's views were more complicated than his publicly stated opinion, however; Friend documents that Hoover was opposed to colonies and large navies and that he was not interested in the Philippine sugar industry. Nevertheless, he vetoed the bill.

41. The existence of the two versions of the act reflects political maneuvering on the part of Quezon more than any difference in definitions of sovereignty or territorial status.

42. Bogardus, "Filipino Repatriation"; Benicio T. Catapusan, *The Social Adjustment of Filipinos in the United States* (master's thesis, University of Southern California, 1940); Ngai, *Impossible Subjects.*

43. *Filipino Emigration to Philippine Islands Extension,* Public Law 74-645 (1936).

44. These positions still exist for Puerto Rico, Washington, D.C., Guåhan the Northern Marianas, and other U.S. territories.

45. U.S. Congress, House, Committee on Immigration and Naturalization, *Extending the Time for Voluntary Return of Unemployed Filipinos to the Philippines: Hearings before the Committee on Immigration and Naturalization,* 74th Congress, 1st Session, February 6, 1935, 2.

46. *Alien Registration Act,* Section 37b1, Public Law 76-670 (1940).

47. *Alien Registration Act,* Public Law 76-670 (1940).

48. *Immigration Act,* Public Law 68-139 (1924).

49. Thomas Tabanda, to Ruth Hampton, January 2, 1941, RG 350 I3 5B GCF Aliens Box 842, National Archives II, College Park, MD.

50. Ruth Hampton, to Thomas Tabanda, January 6, 1941, RG 350 I3 5B GCF Aliens Box 842, National Archives II, College Park, MD.

51. Ruth Hampton, to A. M. Dandoy, December 26, 1940, RG 350 I3 5B GCF Aliens Box 842, National Archives II, College Park, MD.

52. U.S. Congress, Senate, *A Bill to Enable the people of the Philippine Islands to adopt a constitution and form a government for the Philippine Islands, to provide independence of the same, and or other purposes,* Sec. 8 of S. 3377, 72nd Congress, 1st Session, January 26, 1932. Exceptions to this included migration to Hawai'i, and

government officials, ministers, religious teachers, missionaries, lawyers, physicians, chemists, engineers, teachers, students, authors, artists, merchants, "travelers for curiosity or pleasure," as well as their legal wives and children under sixteen.

53. Mr. Dill, speaking on 71. S. 51, on April 22, 1930, 71st Congress, 2nd Session, *Congressional Record* 72, pt. 7: 7425

54. Francis Parker, radiogram to Dwight Davis, April 24, 1930, RG 350 Entry I3 5B GCF Box 1027 25051 Immigration, National Archives II, College Park, MD.

55. U.S. Congress, Senate and House, Committee on Territories and Insular Affairs and Committee on Insular Affairs, *Independence for the Philippine Islands: Hearings before the Committee on Territories and Insular Affairs* and *Hearings before the Committee on Insular Affairs*, 72nd Congress, 1st Session, February 11 and 13, 1932, 132.

56. In the 1910s, nativist legislators proposed literacy tests as means to keep out unwanted immigrants. Presidents Taft and Wilson, however, vetoed these bills. In 1917, a quota bill succeeded, but many southern and eastern Europeans still passed the test. Then, nativists in Congress turned to quotas. The Emergency Quota Act of 1921 established quotas based on the number of residents living in the United States from the 1910 Census. Three percent of that number would be allowed entry each year. For more discussion, see David Scott FitzGerald and David Cook-Martín, *Culling the Masses* (Harvard University Press, 2014), 98–102.

57. "Provisions for restriction of Philippine Immigration contained in Sec. 8-S-3377, Hawes–Cutting Bill," January 29, 1932, Memorandum for General Parker, RG 350 Entry I3 5B GCF 25051 Immigration Box 1027, National Archives II, College Park, MD.

58. U.S. Congress, House, *A Bill to enable the people of the Philippine Islands to adopt a constitution and form a government for the Philippine Islands and to provide for the future political status of the same*, H.R. 3080, 72nd Congress, 1st Session, January 18, 1932.

59. U.S. Congress, House, Committee on Insular Affairs, *Independence for the Philippine Islands: Hearings before the Committee on Insular Affairs*, 72nd Congress, 1st Session, January 25, 1932, 80.

60. U.S. Congress, House, Committee, *Independence for the Philippine Islands*, 122.

61. U.S. Congress, House, *A Bill to provide for the withdrawal of the sovereignty of the United States over the Philippine Islands and for the recognition of their independence*, Sec. 8.a. of H.R. 7233, 72nd Congress, 1st Session, March 15, 1932.

62. "Philippine Independence," H.R. 7233, on June 29, 1932, 72nd Congress, 1st Session, *Congressional Record* 75, pt. 13: 14274.

63. U.S. Congress, House, Committee on Immigration and Naturalization, *Extending the Time for Voluntary Return of Unemployed Filipinos to the Philippines: Hearings before the Committee on Immigration and Naturalization*, 74th Congress, 1st Session, February 6, 1935.

64. U.S. Congress, Senate, Committee on Territories and Insular Affairs, *Complete Independence of the Philippine Islands: Hearings before the Senate Committee on Territories and Insular Affairs*, 76th Congress, 1st Session, February 16, 1939; J. Weldon Jones Papers, Box 7, 1939 Independence Bill, Truman Library, Independence, MO.

65. Coloma, "A Study of the Filipino Repatriation Movement."

66. U.S. Congress, House, Committee on Immigration and Naturalization, *To Return to the Philippine Islands Unemployed Filipinos: Hearings before the Committee on Immigration and Naturalization*, 73rd Congress, 1st Session, January 25, 1933, 46. See Fox, *Three Worlds of Relief*, for a discussion of Mexican Repatriation and the role of local bureaucrats and charities in repatriating Mexicans and Mexican Americans.

67. According to ProQuest Congressional, there is no available history for this law. From my research at NARA–San Bruno, I discovered files related to the repatriation were destroyed under the authority of National Archives disposal job 347-258, item 55, and job 347-258, item 49.

68. Case Inspector R. I. Davis, May 21, 1934, In the Matter of Aglipay, Lorenzo, At a meeting of the Board of Special Inquiry, Held at Angel Island Station, CA. RG 85, NARA–San Bruno, San Bruno, CA.

69. Case Inspector F. Arnold, May 15, 1934, In the Matter of Crispolo, Antonio, At a meeting of the Board of Special Inquiry, Held at Angel Island Station, CA. RG 85, NARA–San Bruno, San Bruno, CA.

70. Ugo Carusi, to W. F. Kelly, March 7, 1946, Filipinos under Deportation Proceedings, RG 85, NARA–San Bruno, San Bruno, CA.

71. U.S. Congress, House, Committee on Immigration and Naturalization, *To Return to the Philippine Islands Unemployed Filipinos: Hearings before the Committee on Immigration and Naturalization*, 72nd Congress, 1st Session, January 18, 1933, 4.

72. U.S. Congress, House, Committee on Immigration and Naturalization, *Extending the Time for Voluntary Return of Unemployed Filipinos to the Philippines: Hearings before the Committee on Immigration and Naturalization*, 74th Congress, 1st Session, February 5, 1935.

73. U.S. Congress, House, Committee on Immigration and Naturalization, *Extending the Time for Voluntary Return of Unemployed Filipinos to the Philippines: Hearings before the Committee on Immigration and Naturalization*, 74th Congress, 1st Session, February 6, 1935, 2.

74. For discussion of earlier debates and crises over public health, race, citizenship, and exclusion see: Nayan Shah, *Contagious Divides: Epidemics and Race in San Francisco's Chinatown*, American Crossroads (University of California Press, 2001).

75. Statement of W. C. Hushing, January 29, 1930, "Independence for the Philippine Islands," Committee on Territories and Insular Affairs, Senate: 114–17.

76. Mr. Dill, speaking on 71. S. 51, on April 22, 1930, 71st Congress, 2nd Session, *Congressional Record*: 7425.

77. Francis Parker, to Hiram Bingham, April 23, 1930, RG 350 Entry I3 5B GCF Box 1027 25051 Immigration, National Archives, College Park, MD.

78. Francis Parker, to Hiram Bingham, April 23, 1930, RG 350 Entry I3 5B GCF Box 1027 25051 Immigration, National Archives, College Park, MD.

79. H. S. Cumming, to Francis Parker, April 23, 1930, RG 350 Entry I3 5B GCF Box 1027 25051 Immigration, National Archives, College Park, MD.

80. Bogardus, *Anti-Filipino Race Riots*, 24.

81. Ngai, *Impossible Subjects*, 110.

82. P. G. Cressey, *The Taxi-Dance Hall: A Sociological Study in Commercialized Recreation and City Life* (University of Chicago Press, 1932).

83. Bogardus, *Anti-Filipino Race Riots*; Catapusan, *The Social Adjustment of Filipinos in the United States*.

84. Bogardus, *Anti-Filipino Race Riots*, 24–25. Bogardus was famous for his studies of migration and social distance among ethno-racial groups.

85. Bogardus, *Anti-Filipino Race Riots*, 25.

86. Commonwealth Club of California Transactions 5: 352–53, November 5, 1929, as cited in Coloma, "A Study of the Filipino Repatriation Movement."

87. U.S. Congress, House, Committee on Insular Affairs, *Independence for the Philippine Islands: Hearings before the Committee on Insular Affairs*, 72nd Congress, 1st Session, February 5, 1932, 271.

88. U.S. Congress, House, Committee on Immigration and Naturalization, *To Extend the Time for Applying for and Receiving Benefits Under the Act Entitled "An Act To Provide Means by Which Certain Filipinos Can Emigrate from the U.S.": Hearings before the Committee on Immigration and Naturalization*, 74th Congress, 2nd Session, February 12, 1936.

89. U.S. Congress, House, Committee on Insular Affairs, *Independence for the Philippine Islands: Hearings before the Committee on Insular Affairs*, 72nd Congress, 1st Session, February 2, 1932, 233.

90. U.S. Congress, House, Committee on Immigration and Naturalization, *To Extend the Time for Applying for and Receiving Benefits Under the Act Entitled "An Act To Provide Means by Which Certain Filipinos Can Emigrate from the U.S.": Hearings before the Committee on Immigration and Naturalization*, 74th Congress, 2nd Session, February 12, 1936.

91. U.S. Congress, House, Committee on Insular Affairs, *Independence for the Philippine Islands: Hearings before the Committee on Insular Affairs*, 72nd Congress, 1st Session, January 25, 1932, 80–82.

92. Senator Shortridge, speaking on H.R. 7233, "Philippine Independence," on December 19, 1932, 72nd Congress, 2nd Session: *Congressional Record* 76, pt. 1: 14273.

93. U.S. Congress, House, Committee on Immigration and Naturalization, *To Authorize the Naturalization of Filipinos Who Are Permanent Residents of the U.S.: Hearings before the Committee on Immigration and Naturalization*, 76th Congress, 3rd Session, March 29, 1940, 8.

94. U.S. Congress, House, Committee on Immigration and Naturalization, *To Authorize the Naturalization of Filipinos Who Are Permanent Residents of the U.S.: Hearings before the Committee on Immigration and Naturalization*, 76th Congress, 3rd Session, April 10, 1940, 6.

95. U.S. Congress, House, Committee, *To Authorize the Naturalization of Filipinos Who Are Permanent Residents of the U.S.*, 41.

96. Marcantonio represents the rise of progressive labor and U.S. socialist politics in the United States.

97. U.S. Congress, House, Committee on Immigration and Naturalization, *To Authorize the Naturalization of Filipinos Who Are Permanent Residents of the U.S.:*

Hearings before the Committee on Immigration and Naturalization, 76th Congress, 3rd Session, March 28, 1940, 44.

98. U.S. Congress, House, Committee, *To Authorize the Naturalization of Filipinos Who Are Permanent Residents of the U.S.,* 45–47.

99. U.S. Congress, House, Committee, *To Authorize the Naturalization of Filipinos Who Are Permanent Residents of the U.S.,* 50.

100. U.S. Congress, House, Committee on Immigration and Naturalization, *To Authorize the Naturalization of Filipinos Who Are Permanent Residents of the United States: Hearings before the Committee on Immigration and Naturalization,* 77th Congress, 2nd Session, January 21, 1942, 22.

101. U.S. Congress, House, Committee, *To Authorize the Naturalization of Filipinos Who Are Permanent Residents of the United States,* 2.

102. U.S. Congress, House, Committee, *To Authorize the Naturalization of Filipinos Who are Permanent Residents of the United States,* 5.

103. U.S. Congress, House, Committee, *To Authorize the Naturalization of Filipinos Who Are Permanent Residents of the United States,* 14–15. Young was, of course, incorrect in arguing that the Bill of Rights and the original Constitution guaranteed equality for all.

Chapter 5

1. Samuel R. Molina, to Senator Daniel K. Inouye, July 10, 1977, Box LF 45, Folder 1, Senator Daniel K. Inouye Papers, University of Hawai'i–Manoa, Manoa, Hawai'i.

2. The most conservative estimate of the number of Filipino veterans who served in World War II and did not receive benefits is 200,000. According to Franco Arcebal and Arturo Garcia, of Justice for Filipino American Veterans, the numbers from the Philippine government are closer to 425,000. Some numbers even suggest that there were over 700,000 people who served, including the unrecognized guerrillas.

3. *Neutrality Act of 1935,* 74 S.J. Res 173 (1935); *Neutrality Act of 1936,* 74 H.J. Res. 491 (1936); *Neutrality Act of 1937,* 75 S.J. Res. 51 (1937); *Neutrality Act of 1939,* 76 H.J. Res 306 (1939).

4. Theodore Friend, *Between Two Empires: The Ordeal of the Philippines, 1929–1960* (Yale University Press, 1965).

5. Claro Recto, *Philippine Magazine,* October 31, 1934: 412, as cited in Friend, *Between Two Empires.*

6. Friend, *Between Two Empires;* Frank Hindman Golay, *Face of Empire: United States–Philippine Relations, 1898–1946* (Ateneo de Manila University Press, 1997).

7. J. Weldon Jones, Address for Fourth of July Exercises, J. Weldon Jones Papers, Box 54, 1934–1936 Philippine Speeches, Truman Library, Independence, MO.

8. Friend, *Between Two Empires;* Golay, *Face of Empire.*

9. Douglas MacArthur, "Can the Philippines Be Defended?," *Christian Science Monitor,* November 2, 1938.

10. J. Weldon Jones, Address for Fourth of July Exercises, 1936, J. Weldon Jones Papers, Box 54, 1934–1936 Philippine Speeches, Truman Library, Independence, MO.

11. Most cite the start of World War II as September 1, 1939, when Germany invaded Poland, but in Asia the July 7, 1937, Marco Polo Bridge incident marks the start of the Second Sino-Japanese War. Hiro Saito, "Cross-National Fragmentation, 1945–1964," in *The History Problem, The Politics of War Commemoration in East Asia* (University of Hawai'i Press, 2017), 22.

12. President Roosevelt, Message to Congress, September 21, 1939, Master Speech File, Roosevelt Library, Hyde Park, NY.

13. President Roosevelt, Fireside Chat, December 29, 1940, Roosevelt Library, Hyde Park, NY.

14. Roosevelt, Fireside Chat, December 29, 1940.

15. R House Roll Call Vote H.R. 1776, on February 8, 1941, 77th Congress, 1st Session, *Congressional Record* 87, pt. 1: 815. Senate Roll Call Vote H.R. 1776, on March 8, 1941, 77th Congress, 1st Session, *Congressional Record* 87, pt. 2: 2097.

16. The 1939 Neutrality Act passed with 243 yeas, 172 nays, and 14 not voting in the House and 55 yeas, 24 nays, and 17 not voting in the Senate. House Roll Call H.J. Res. 306, on November 3, 1939, 76th Congress, 2nd Session, *Congressional Record* 85, pt. 2: 1389. Senate Roll Call. H.J. Res 306, on November 3, 1939, 76th Congress, 2nd Session, *Congressional Record* 85, pt. 2: 1356.

17. *An Act Further to Promote the Defense of the United States, and for other purposes*, Public Law 77-11 (1941).

18. Friend, *Between Two Empires*; Golay, *Face of Empire*.

19. Japan attacked the Philippines on December 8 in the Philippines, which was December 7 in Hawai'i.

20. House Roll Call H.J. Res. 254, on December 8, 1941, 77th Congress, 1st Session, *Congressional Record* 87, pt. 9: 9536. Senate Roll Call. S.J. Res 116. 1941, on December 8, 1941, 77th Congress, 1st Session, *Congressional Record* 87, pt. 9: 9505.

21. Hanson W. Baldwin, "Wanted: A Plan for Defense," July 24, 1940, in *Harper's Magazine*, August, as cited in U.S. Congress, House, Committee on Military Affairs, *Selective Compulsory Military Training and Service: Hearings before the Committee on Military Affairs*, 76th Congress, 3rd Session, July 25, 1940, 142.

22. Baldwin, "Wanted: A Plan for Defense."

23. President Roosevelt, Message on Philippine Independence, March 2, 1934, Master Speech File, Roosevelt Library, Hyde Park, NY.

24. *Philippines Independence Act of 1934*, Public Law 73-127 (1934).

25. Manuel Elizalde, to Quezon, Radio 407, August 2, 1940, Reel 20, Quezon papers. Ricardo Jose (1992) suggests the former bill won out, but actually these acts and competing definitions of the Philippines coexisted. See Jose, "The Philippine National Guard in World War I," 166–71.

26. 76 S.J. Res 286 (1940).

27. *Selective Training and Service Act of 1940*, Public Law 76-783 (1940).

28. Manuel Elizalde, to Quezon, November 19, 1940, Reel 20, Quezon papers.

29. For discussion of how, between 1903 and 1924, the reach of the U.S. National Guard extended globally, whereas U.S. citizenship did not, see Christopher Capozzola,

"Minutemen for the World: Empire, Citizenship, and the National Guard, 1903–1924," in *Colonial Crucible: Empire in the Making of the Modern American State*, ed. Alfred W. McCoy and Francisco A. Scarano (University of Wisconsin Press, 2009), 421–30.

30. U.S. Congress, Senate, Committee on Military Affairs, *Ordering Reserve Components and Retired Personnel into Active Military Service: Hearings before the Committee on Military Affairs*, 76th Congress, 3rd Session, July 30, 1940, 11–12.

31. Senators Ashurst and Gillette, speaking on S.J. Res 28, on August 6, 1940, 76th Congress, 3rd Session, *Congressional Record* 86, pt. 9: 9915–17.

32. Representative Stefan, speaking on War Department Appropriation Bill, 1937, on February 11, 1936, 74th Congress, 2nd Session, *Congressional Record* 80, pt. 2: 1825.

33. Mr. Pierce, speaking on "Report on Advisory Commission to Council of National Defense," on July 25, 1940, 76th Congress, 3rd Session, *Congressional Record* 86, pt. 9: 9620–24.

34. Senator George, speaking on S.J. Res. 286, on August 7, 1940, 76th Congress, 3rd Session, *Congressional Record* 86, pt. 9: 9982–83.

35. J. Weldon Jones, Memorandum for His Excellency, the Governor-General on Defense forces for P.I. Commonwealth, 1933, J. Weldon Jones Papers, Box 53, 1933–1934 May, Truman Library, Independence, MO.

36. Stimson to Hoover, January 3, 1933. As quoted in Theodore W. Friend, "Veto and Repassage of the Hare–Hawes–Cutting Act: A Catalogue of Motives," *Philippine Studies* 12, no. 4 (1964): 668.

37. Douglas MacArthur, as quoted in Sixth Weekly Report by J. Weldon Jones for Week ending June 21, 1936, J. Weldon Jones Papers, Box 53, 1937–1948, Truman Library, Independence, MO.

38. U.S. Congress, House, Committee on Military Affairs, *Selective Compulsory Military Training and Service: Hearings before the Committee on Military Affairs*, 76th Congress, 3rd Session, July 31, 1940, 380.

39. Representative Harlan, speaking on "Reciprocal Trade Agreements," on January 28, 1936, 74th Congress, 2nd Session, *Congressional Record* 80, pt. 1: 1111.

40. U.S. Congress, Senate, Committee on Territories and Insular Affairs, *Complete Independence of the Philippine Islands: Hearings before the Committee on Territories and Insular Affairs*, 76 Congress, 1st Session, February 21, 1939, 46.

41. Representative Alexander, speaking on H.J. Res 306, "Our Real Problem Not Considered," on June 28, 1939, 76th Congress, 1st Session, *Congressional Record* 84, pt. 8: 8150.

42. Representative Faddis, speaking on H.R. 10132, on September 6, 1940, 76th Congress, 3rd Session, *Congressional Record* 86, pt. 10: 11662.

43. Senator Mead, speaking on "War with Japan," on December 8, 1941, 77th Congress, 1st Session, *Congressional Record* 87, pt. 9: 9514.

44. Representative Thill, speaking on "War Resolution," on December 8, 1941, 77th Congress, 1st Session, *Congressional Record* 87, pt. 9: 9524.

45. Representative Sweeney, speaking on "War Resolution," on December 8, 1941, 77th Congress, 1st Session, *Congressional Record* 87, pt. 9: 9523.

46. Sweeney, speaking on "War Resolution," 9524.

47. Representative Rankin, speaking on "War Resolution," on December 8, 1941, 77th Congress, 1st Session, *Congressional Record* 87, pt. 9: 9524.

48. Representative Angell, speaking on "War Resolution," on December 8, 1941, 77th Congress, 1st Session, *Congressional Record* 87, pt. 9: 9530.

49. Representative Sabath, speaking on "War Resolution," on December 8, 1941, 77th Congress, 1st Session, *Congressional Record* 87, pt. 9: 9534.

50. Representative Van Zandt, speaking on "War Resolution," on December 8, 1941, 77th Congress, 1st Session, *Congressional Record* 87, pt. 9: 9532.

51. Representative Plumley, speaking on "War Resolution," on December 8, 1941, 77th Congress, 1st Session, *Congressional Record* 87, pt. 9: 9524.

52. *United States v. Bhagat Singh Thind (1923)*; *Toyota v. United States* (1925). See Ian Haney-López, *White by Law: The Legal Construction of Race* (NYU Press, 1996), for a discussion of how these opinions relied on pseudo-scientific notions of racial difference.

53. Lucy E. Salyer, "Baptism by Fire: Race, Military Service, and US Citizenship Policy, 1918–1935," *The Journal of American History* 91, no. 3 (2004): 847–76; Deenesh Sohoni and Amin Vafa, "The Fight to Be American: Military Naturalization and Asian Citizenship," *Asian American Law Journal* 17 (2010): 119.

54. For more information see U.S. Department of Veterans Affairs, *VA Benefits for Filipino Veterans* (Washington, D.C., 2008).

55. The 1917 Jones Act gave Puerto Ricans U.S. citizenship.

56. Rick Baldoz, *The Third Asiatic Invasion: Migration and Empire in Filipino America, 1898–1946* (NYU Press, 2011), 82.

57. Olivier Burtin, "Veterans as a Social Movement: The American Legion, the First Hoover Commission, and the Making of the American Welfare State," *Social Science History* 44, no. 2 (2020): 329–54; Margot Canaday, *The Straight State: Sexuality and Citizenship in Twentieth-Century America* (Princeton University Press, 2009); Suzanne Mettler, *Soldiers to Citizens: The GI Bill and the Making of the Greatest Generation* (Oxford University Press, 2005); David R. Segal, *Recruiting for Uncle Sam: Citizenship and Military Manpower Policy* (University Press of Kansas, 1989); Theda Skocpol, *Protecting Soldiers and Mothers* (Harvard University Press, 1992); Theda Skocpol, "The GI Bill and US Social Policy, Past and Future," *Social Philosophy and Policy* 14, no. 2 (1997): 95–115; Sohoni and Vafa, "The Fight to Be American."

58. See, for example, Morris Janowitz and Charles C. Moskos, Jr., "Racial Composition in the All-Volunteer Force," *Armed Forces & Society* 1, no. 1 (1974): 109–23; Charles C. Moskos, Jr., "Racial Integration in the Armed Forces," *American Journal of Sociology* 72, no. 2 (1966): 132–48. For critiques of the military as a race-blind institution, see: Thomas A. Guglielmo, *Divisions: The Untold Story of Racism and Resistance in America's World War II Military* (Oxford University Press, 2021); Victor Ray, "Militarism as a Racial Project," in *Handbook of the Sociology of Racial and Ethnic Relations*, ed. Pinar Batur and Joe R. Feagin (Springer International Publishing, 2018), 161–68.

59. 6 Fed. Reg. 3825 (1941).

60. U.S. Department of Veterans Affairs in cooperation with the Office of Management and Budget, Department of State, Department of Defense, "A Study of Services and Benefits for Filipino Veterans," Box LF 135, Folder S.120, Daniel K. Inouye Papers, University of Hawai'i–Manoa, Manoa, Hawai'i: 5.

61. The topic of recognition is thorny. Amidst the chaos of post-war administration and bureaucracy in the Philippines, charges of political corruption and deceit, and favoritism for units led by Americans, some veterans claim that they were unjustly ignored and that people who did not serve benefited. While this is an important part of Filipino veteran history, the issue of recognition and what is owed to unrecognized guerrillas is beyond the scope of what I address here. See Christopher Capozzola, *Bound by War: How the United States and the Philippines Built America's First Pacific Century* (Basic Books, 2020); Vina A. Lanzona, *Amazons of the Huk Rebellion: Gender, Sex, and Revolution in the Philippines* (University of Wisconsin Press, 2009); Alfred W. McCoy, *Closer Than Brothers: Manhood at the Philippine Military Academy* (Yale University Press, 2002).

62. By the Armed Forces Voluntary Recruitment Act of 1945 (PL79-190), U.S. Congress authorized 50,000 new Philippine Scouts.

63. Satoshi Nakano, "Nation and Citizenship in the Filipino World War II Veterans Equity Movement,1945–2011," in *"We the People" in the Global Age: Re-Examination of Nationalism and Citizenship* (The Japan Center for Area Studies, 2002), 208.

64. After the amendment to the 1940 Selective Service Act that allowed for the enlistment of Filipinos, these Filipinos were recruited and served in the United States. The First Filipino Infantry Battalion was formed in San Luis Obispo, California, in January 1942, and expanded to include a second regiment. Together, they were made of about seven thousand men. Rick Baldoz, *The Third Asiatic Invasion: Migration and Empire in Filipino America, 1898–1946* (NYU Press, 2011), 211–13. Capozzola, *Bound by War*, 166.

65. Capozzola, *Bound by War*, 164.

66. Statement of service, First Filipino Regiment, History of the U.S. Army's 1st Filipino REG and 2nd Filipino BN, U.S. Army Center of Military History, Washington, D.C.; Statement of service, Second Filipino Regiment, History of the U.S. Army's 1st Filipino REG and 2nd Filipino BN, U.S. Army Center of Military History; Statement of service, Second Filipino Regiment (Separate), History of the U.S. Army's 1st Filipino REG and 2nd Filipino BN, U.S. Army Center of Military History; Statement of service, Second Filipino Battalion (Separate), History of the U.S. Army's 1st Filipino REG and 2nd Filipino BN, U.S. Army Center of Military History.

67. *Second War Powers Act of 1942*, Public Law 77-507 (1942). Sections 701 and 702 provided for expedited naturalization of noncitizen veterans.

68. Satoshi Nakano, "The Filipino World War II Veterans Equity Movement and the Filipino American Community," in *International Philippine Studies Conference*, 2004, 1–34; Lucy E. Salyer, "Baptism by Fire: Race, Military Service, and US Citizenship Policy, 1918–1935," *The Journal of American History* 91, no. 3 (2004): 847–76.

69. *National Service Life Insurance Act of 1940*, Public Law 76-801 (1940).

70. Francis Biddle, to Omar Bradley, April 27, 1942. RG 126, Entry PI-151-1, Box 1 Army and Scouts, Philippine 1942–1946, National Archives II, College Park, MD.

71. Robert P. Patterson, to Harry S. Truman, December 29, 1945, WHCF: OF 1055. Truman Papers, Truman Library, Independence, MO.

72. Paul V. McNutt, to Harry S. Truman, February 11, 1947, WHCF: OF 1055, Truman Papers, Truman Library, Independence, MO.

73. Ugo Carusi, to Paul McNutt, December 4, 1945, RG 12, Entry PI-151-1, Box 1 Army and Scouts, Philippine 1942–1946, National Archives II, College Park, MD.

74. *An Act to provide for the complete independence of the Philippine Islands, to provide for the adoption of a constitution and a form of government for the Philippine Islands, and for other purposes,* Section 2(a)2, Public Law 73-127 (1934).

75. Richard Ely, to Felix Cohen, October 11, 1945, RG 126, Entry PI-151-1; Box 1 Army and Scouts, Philippine 1942–1946, National Archives II, College Park, MD.

76. Dwight Davis, to Francis Parker, January 27, 1930, RG 350 Entry I3 5B GCF Box 1027 25051 Immigration, National Archives II, College Park, MD.

77. U.S. Congress, House, Committee on Immigration and Naturalization, *To Authorize the Naturalization of Filipinos Who Are Permanent Residents of the U.S.: Hearings before the Committee on Immigration and Naturalization,* 77th Congress, 2nd Session, January 21, 1942, 5.

78. Senator King, speaking on H.R. 9980, "Revision and Codification of Nationality Laws—Conference Report," October 4, 1940, 76th Congress, 3rd Session, *Congressional Record* 86, pt. 12: 13184.

79. U.S. Congress, House, Committee on Military Affairs, *Selective Compulsory Military Training and Service: Hearings before the Committee on Military Affairs,* 76th Congress, 3rd Session, July 30, 1940, 389–90.

80. According to Paul V. McNutt. McNutt, to Harry S. Truman, February 11, 1947, WHCF: OF 1055. Truman Papers, Truman Library, Independence, MO.

81. Lieutenant-Colonel Carpenter, speaking on S. 2340, "To Expedite Naturalization of Persons Serving Honorably in Military Naval Forces," on March 13, 1942, Senate Subcommittee of the Committee on Immigration: 10.

82. *An Act to Amend the Selective Training and Service Act of 1940,* Public Law 77-360 (1941).

83. See Baldoz, *The Third Asiatic Invasion,* 206.

Part 3

1. Jane Burbank and Frederick Cooper, *Empires in World History: Power and the Politics of Difference* (Princeton University Press, 2011), 404–11.

2. See John Dower, *War without Mercy: Race and Power in the Pacific War* (Knopf Doubleday Publishing Group, 2012).

3. Dower, *War without Mercy,* 3.

4. Christopher Capozzola, *Bound by War: How the United States and the Philippines Built America's First Pacific Century* (Basic Books, 2020); Frank Hindman Golay, *Face of Empire: United States-Philippine Relations, 1898–1946* (Ateneo de Manila University Press, 1997); Louis Morton, *The Fall of the Philippines* (Office of the Chief of Military History, Department of the Army, 1953).

5. As quoted in Capozzola, *Bound by War,* 185–86.

6. Joseph Clark Grew, *Report from Tokyo: A Message to the American People* (Simon and Schuster, 1942). As quoted in Dower, *War without Mercy*, 113.

7. Office of War Information, Overseas Branch, "Publications Plan for Philippines," September 15, 1944 (Revised), Records of the Office of the Director and Predecessor Agencies, Records of the Historian Area File, 1943–1945, entry 6c, Box 1, Records of the Office of War Information, RG 208: 1. As quoted in Takashi Fujitani, *Race for Empire: Koreans as Japanese and Japanese as Americans during World War II* (University of California Press, 2011), 220–21.

8. Gunnar Myrdal, *An American Dilemma: The Negro Problem and Modern Democracy* (Routledge, 1944).

9. Peter Duus, "The Greater East Asian Co-Prosperity Sphere: Dream and Reality," *Journal of Northeast Asian History* 5, no. 1 (2008): 143–54; Xiaohua Ma, "The Sino-American Alliance During World War II and the Lifting of the Chinese Exclusion Acts," *American Studies International* 38, no. 2 (2000): 39–61.

10. Dower, *War without Mercy*, 173–74.

11. Karen J. Leong, "Foreign Policy, National Identity, and Citizenship: The Roosevelt White House and the Expediency of Repeal," *Journal of American Ethnic History* (2003): 16.

12. See: Lon Kurashige, *Two Faces of Exclusion: The Untold History of Anti-Asian Racism in the United States* (UNC Press, 2016), especially Chapter 7.

13. Neil Gotanda, "Towards Repeal of Asian Exclusion, 1943–1950," in *Asian Americans and Congress*, ed. Hyung-Chan Kim (Greenwood Press, 1996), 309–11; Jane Hong, "Manila Prepares for Independence: Filipina/o Campaigns for US Citizenship and the Reorienting of American Ethnic Histories," *Journal of American Ethnic History* 38, no. 1 (2018): 5–33; Ma, "The Sino-American Alliance During World War II and the Lifting of the Chinese Exclusion Acts"; Fred Warren Riggs, *Pressures on Congress: A Study of the Repeal of Chinese Exclusion* (Greenwood Press, 1972).

14. Hong, "Manila Prepares for Independence"; David M. Reimers, *Still the Golden Door: The Third World Comes to America* (Columbia University Press, 1985), 11–12.

15. Hong, "Manila Prepares for Independence."

16. Pearl S. Buck, "Tinder for Tomorrow," delivered at the Book & Author Luncheon, Astor Hotel, New York, February 10, 1942, reprinted in *Asia*, March 1942: 153–55. For more examples, see Ma, "The Sino-American Alliance During World War II and the Lifting of the Chinese Exclusion Acts."

17. Ellen D. Wu, *The Color of Success: Asian Americans and the Origins of the Model Minority* (Princeton University Press, 2013), 11. See also Elena Tajima Creef, *Imaging Japanese America: The Visual Construction of Citizenship, Nation, and the Body* (NYU Press, 2004).

18. Franklin D. Roosevelt, Message to Congress, October 11, 1943, OF 133 Immigration 1943–1945, Roosevelt Papers, Roosevelt Library, Hyde Park, NY. See Leong, "Foreign Policy, National Identity, and Citizenship," for discussion of Roosevelt's shifting orientation to China and the Chinese.

19. Representative Dickstein to the House, on April 15, 1943, 78th Congress, 1st Session, *Congressional Record* 89, pt. 3: 3410. Notably, the language used here by Dickstein

is like that used by Paul McNutt nearly three years later in reference to the 1946 Rescission Act, discussed in the next chapter. Whereas there would be an end to Chinese exclusion, McNutt was not successful in arguing for rights for Filipino veterans.

20. For discussion of the possible factors related to the repeal of Asian exclusion laws, see: Cindy I-Fen Cheng, *Citizens of Asian America: Democracy and Race During the Cold War* (NYU Press, 2014); Mary L. Dudziak, "Desegregation as a Cold War Imperative," *Stanford Law Review* (1988), 61–120; Jane H. Hong, *Opening the Gates to Asia: A Transpacific History of How America Repealed Asian Exclusion* (UNC Press, 2019); Brenda Gayle Plummer, *Rising Wind: Black Americans and US Foreign Affairs, 1935–1960* (UNC Press, 1996); John Hayakawa Torok, "Asians and the Reconstruction Era Constitutional Amendments and Civil Rights Laws" in Asian *Americans and Congress: A Documentary History*, ed. Hyung-Chan Kim (Greenwood Publishing Group, 1996), 13.

21. Mae M. Ngai, *Impossible Subjects: Illegal Aliens and the Making of Modern America* (Princeton University Press, 2004); Ronald Takaki, *Double Victory: A Multicultural History of America in World War II* (Back Bay Books, 2000).

22. Colleen Woods, *Freedom Incorporated: Anticommunism and Philippine Independence in the Age of Decolonization* (Cornell University Press, 2020), 21, 25. Yet, as Woods documents, the Partido Komunista ng Pilipinas (PKP) challenged U.S. imperialists by 1930. See also: Moon-Ho Jung, *Menace to Empire: Anticolonial Solidarities and the Transpacific Origins of the US Security State* (University of California Press, 2022).

23. Vina A. Lanzona, *Amazons of the Huk Rebellion: Gender, Sex, and Revolution in the Philippines* (University of Wisconsin Press, 2009); Woods, *Freedom Incorporated*, 67–68.

24. Woods, *Freedom Incorporated*, 70.

25. Benedict J. Kerkvliet, *The Huk Rebellion: A Study of Peasant Revolt in the Philippines* (Rowman & Littlefield, 2002), 115; Woods, *Freedom Incorporated*, 72.

26. Golay, *Face of Empire*, 480.

27. Burbank and Cooper, *Empires in World History*, 402–4; Adom Getachew, *Worldmaking after Empire: The Rise and Fall of Self-Determination* (Princeton University Press, 2019); Erez Manela, *The Wilsonian Moment: Self-Determination and the International Origins of Anticolonial Nationalism* (Oxford University Press, 2007).

28. David Scott FitzGerald and David Cook-Martín, *Culling the Masses* (Harvard University Press, 2014), 28.

29. Woods, *Freedom Incorporated*, 53.

30. Justin Hart, *Empire of Ideas: The Origins of Public Diplomacy and the Transformation of U.S. Foreign Policy* (Oxford University Press, 2013), 8–9.

31. Odd Westad, *The Global Cold War: Third World Interventions and the Making of Our Times* (Cambridge University Press, 2005).

32. Erika Lee, *The Making of Asian America: A History* (Simon and Schuster, 2015), 252.

Chapter 6

1. *An Act Reducing certain appropriations and contract authorizations available for the fiscal year 1946, and for other purposes,* Public Law 79-301 (1946).

2. Harry Truman, Proclamation 2696: Immigration Quota for the Philippines, July 4, 1946.

3. Dawn Bohulano Mabalon, *Little Manila Is in the Heart: The Making of the Fili-pina/o American Community in Stockton, California* (Duke University Press, 2013), 5.

4. Neil Gotanda, "Towards Repeal of Asian Exclusion, 1943–1950," in *Asian Americans and Congress*, ed. Hyung-Chan Kim (Greenwood Press, 1996), 309–11. As Gotanda notes, the repeal of Asian exclusion as a whole actually had little effect on the number of immigrants to the United States, as Congress, in repealing exclusion, also implemented immigration quotas.

5. Carl Hayden, to Omar Bradley, August 27, 1945, RG 126, Entry PI-151-2, Box 9 Pensions, National Archives II, College Park, MD.

6. Harry S. Truman, October 25, 1945, OF 1055, Truman Papers, Truman Library, Independence, MO.

7. Harry S. Truman, to General Omar N. Bradley, October 25, 1945, OF 1055, Truman Papers, Truman Library, Independence, MO. While both Patterson and Bradley reference Truman's October 1945 request to study veterans' issues, the histor-ical record does not reflect whether Truman asked anything similar of the Philippine government or high commissioner of the Philippines, Paul V. McNutt.

8. The veto was primarily in response to lobbyists and the recommendation of the director of the Bureau of the Budget, Harold D. Smith, about returning the Employ-ment Service to the states.

9. Carlos P. Romulo, telegraph to Hon. Sergio Osmeña, President of the Philip-pines, November 25, 1945, S1B8, Osmeña Papers, National Library of the Philippines, Manila, Philippines.

10. See Michael A. Cabotaje, "Equity Denied: Historical and Legal Analyses in Support of the Extension of US Veterans' Benefits to Filipino World War II Veterans," *Asian Law Journal* 6, no. 1 (1999): 67–97. Note also that in 1948 Congress did approve construction of a veteran hospital in Manila. The Philippine government and Con-gress do provide their own benefits at reduced rates under the Philippines G.I. Act. In 1951, veterans received funeral benefits and burial flags. See Satoshi Nakano, "Nation and Citizenship in the Filipino World War II Veterans Equity Movement, 1945–2011," in *"We the People" in the Global Age: Re-Examination of Nationalism and Citizen-ship* (The Japan Center for Area Studies, 2002), 205–28. Despite the slow rolling out of benefits, inflation in the Philippines devalued the peso to the dollar, resulting in a decrease in pensions (Nakano, "Nation and Citizenship in the Filipino World War II Veterans Equity Movement," 205–28).

11. Harry S. Truman, to Robert P. Patterson, February 12, 1946, WHCF: OF 1055, Truman Papers, Truman Library, Independence, MO; Harry S. Truman, to Omar N. Bradley, February 12, 1946, WHCF: OF 1055, Truman Papers, Truman Library, Inde-pendence, MO.

12. Omar N. Bradley, to Harry S. Truman, October 31, 1945, WHCF: OF 1055, Truman Papers, Truman Library, Independence, MO.

13. *An Act to provide for the complete independence of the Philippine Islands, to provide for the adoption of a constitution and a form of government for the Philippine Islands, and for other purposes,* Public Law 73-127 (1934).

14. 78 H.R. 2012, H.R. 2776, H.R. 3633, H.R. 4003, H.R. 4229, H.R. 4826.

15. U.S. Congress, House, Committee of Insular Affairs, *Independence of the Philippine Islands, Hearings before the Committee of Insular Affairs,* 78th Congress, 2nd Session, March 22, 1944.

16. U.S. Congress, House, Committee, *Independence of the Philippine Islands.*

17. Jane H. Hong, *Opening the Gates to Asia: A Transpacific History of How America Repealed Asian Exclusion* (UNC Press, 2019), 97–98.

18. *Luce–Celler Act,* Public Law 79-483 (1946). The Nationality Act only allowed for the naturalization of Filipinos who served in the U.S. Army, Navy, Marine Corps, or Coast Guard.

19. *Nationality Act,* Public Law 76-853 (1940).

20. Because the United States Immigration and Naturalization Service did not keep records on Filipinos' declaration of intent (owing to the fact that Filipino illegal migration was not possible prior to 1934), the Department of the Interior and the State Department suggested waiving the declaration of intent was important. WHRO 79 H.R. 3517, Truman Library, Independence, MO; "Amendment to Section 401 (a) of The Nationality Act Of 1940," on April 17, 1945, 79th Congress, 1st Session, *Congressional Record* 91, pt. 3: 3454.

21. Hong, *Opening the Gates to Asia,* 48–49.

22. Hong, *Opening the Gates to Asia.* Hong notes that the Celler bill "harped on the promise of the Indian market for American goods, while Luce focused on the legislation's 'political expediency' during a time when 'Asiatic colonial peoples' were 'shopping for political ideologies' and 'inclined' to look to 'Moscow'" (75; citing *Congressional Record,* October 10, 1945: 9526–27).

23. Rick Baldoz, *The Third Asiatic Invasion: Migration and Empire in Filipino America, 1898–1946* (NYU Press, 2011), 227.

24. Representatives McCowen, Allen, and Murdock speaking on Immigration and Naturalization of Persons Indigenous to India, October 10, 1945, 79th Congress, 1st Session, *Congressional Record* 91, pt. 7: 9523–44.

25. "Naturalization of Natives of India," in *CQ Almanac 1945,* 1st ed., 07-710-07-711, Washington, D.C.: Congressional Quarterly, 1946. For more discussion on Asian Indian naturalization, see Hong, *Opening the Gates to Asia.*

26. Hong, *Opening the Gates to Asia,* 100–104.

27. June 14, 1946, 79th Congress, 2nd Session, *Congressional Record* 92, pt. 6: 6918–19.

28. U.S. Congress, House, Committee on Immigration and Naturalization, *Naturalization of Filipinos: Hearings before the Committee on Immigration and Naturalization,* 78th Congress, 2nd Session, November 22, 1944, 6.

29. The 1934 Tydings–McDuffie Act allowed for fifty Filipinos per year to migrate to the United States. Even without accounting for the Filipinos already in the United States prior to the act, between 1934 and 1946, six hundred Filipinos could have migrated to the United States, but not all of them would have been eligible for naturalization.

30. President Truman, Statement Concerning Provisions in Bill Affecting Philippine Army Veterans, February 20, 1946, Statement 38, Public Papers of the President, Truman Library, Independence, MO.

31. U.S. Congress, Senate, Subcommittee of the Committee on Appropriations, *Second Supplemental Surplus Appropriation Rescission Bill, 1946: Hearings before the Subcommittee of the Committee on Appropriations,* 79th Congress, 2nd Session, March 25, 1946, 45.

32. Paul V. McNutt to Harry S. Truman, February 11, 1946, WHCF: OF 1055, Truman Papers, Truman Library, Independence, MO.

33. The United States High Commissioner in the Philippines (McNutt), to President Harry S. Truman, January 18, 1946, U.S. Department of State, *Foreign Relations of the United States,* 1946, Volume VIII, The Far East (Washington, D.C.: Government Printing Office, 1971).

34. Mr. Gearhart, speaking on Immigration and Naturalization of Persons Indigenous to India, on October 10, 1945, 79th Congress, 1st Session, *Congressional Record* 91, pt. 7: 9530.

35. Representative McGehee, Senate Joint Resolutions 93 and 94, Executive Session, Committee of Insular Affairs, House of Representatives, Washington, D.C. May 18, 1944.

36. Representative Judd, speaking on H.R. 3517, "Minorities Views on H.R. 3517," on October 10, 1945, 29th Congress, 1st Session, *Congressional Record* 91, pt. 7: 9541.

37. U.S. Congress, House, Committee on Immigration and Naturalization. *Authorizing the Naturalization of Filipinos: Report (to Accompany H.R. 4826).* 78th Congress, 2nd Session: 2. H. Rep. 1940.

38. U.S. Congress, House, Committee on Immigration and Naturalization. *Authorizing the Naturalization of Filipinos: Report (to Accompany H.R. 4826).* 79th Congress, 1st Session: 1–2. H. Rep. 252.

39. U.S. Congress, House, Committee on Immigration and Naturalization, *Naturalization of Filipinos: Hearings before the Committee on Immigration and Naturalization,* 78th Congress, 2nd Session, November 22, 1944, 28; "Immigration and Naturalization of Persons Indigenous to India," on October 10, 1945, 79th Congress, 1st Session, *Congressional Record* 91, pt. 7.

40. U.S. Congress, House, Committee on Immigration and Naturalization, *Naturalization of Filipinos: Hearings before the Committee on Immigration and Naturalization,* 78th Congress, 2nd Session, November 22, 1944, 28.

41. U.S. Congress, House, Committee, *Naturalization of Filipinos,* 6.

42. U.S. Congress, House, Committee, *Naturalization of Filipinos,* 10.

43. U.S. Congress, House, Committee, *Naturalization of Filipinos,* 14.

44. Richard Ely, to Carl Hayden, October 3, 1945, RG 126 PI 151 2 Box 14 Rehab Veterans Admin, National Archives II, College Park, MD.

45. Omar N. Bradley, to Harry S. Truman, October 31, 1945, WHCF: OF 1055; Truman Papers, Truman Library, Independence, MO.

46. Between July 1, 1940, and August 31, 1945, 62,000 Puerto Ricans were inducted into the U.S. Army. See Edward Witsell, to Dorothy Gordon, Dec 2, 1948, RG 407 201 Puerto Rico, National Archives II, College Park, MD. For a discussion of Puerto Rican military service for the U.S., see: Harry Franqui-Rivera, *Soldiers of the Nation: Military Service and Modern Puerto Rico, 1868–1952* (University of Nebraska Press, 2018);

Che Paralitici, *No Quiero Mi Cuerpo Pa'tambor: El Servicio Militar Obligatorio En Puerto Rico* (Ediciones Puerto, 1998).

47. For Nakano's interpretation see Nakano, "Nation and Citizenship in the Filipino World War II Veterans Equity Movement," 209.

48. In my archival research, I likewise found no such document or evidence that Filipino elites supported the revocation of benefits.

49. In 1975, the Court did not decide in favor of the Filipino Veterans, instead arguing that the terms of the Nationality Act made them ineligible for naturalization.

50. Jane Hong, "Manila Prepares for Independence: Filipina/o Campaigns for US Citizenship and the Reorienting of American Ethnic Histories," *Journal of American Ethnic History* 38, no. 1 (2018): 7.

51. Two million in 1920s and five million in the 1930s. Miriam Sharma, "Labor Migration and Class Formation among the Filipinos in Hawaii, 1906–1946," in *Labor Immigration under Capitalism: Asian Workers in the United States before World War II*, ed. Lucie Cheng and Edna Bonacich (University of California Press, 1984), 579–615.

52. Hong, "Manila Prepares for Independence."

53. Carl Hayden, to Robert Patterson, October 9, 1945, RG 126, Entry PI 151 1, Box 1 Army and Scouts, Philippine 1942–1946, National Archives II, College Park, MD.

54. Richard Ely, "Memorandum for the High Commissioner," December 7, 1945, RG 126, Entry PI 151 1, Box 1 Army and Scouts, Philippine 1942–1946, National Archives II, College Park, MD.

55. Omar N. Bradley, to Harry S. Truman, October 31, 1945, WHCF: OF 1055, Truman Papers, Truman Library, Independence, MO.

56. Paul V. McNutt to Harry S. Truman, February 11, 1946, WHCF: OF 1055, Truman Papers, Truman Library, Independence, MO.

57. U.S. Congress, Senate, *Hearing before the Subcommittee of the Committee on Appropriations*, 79th Congress, 1st Session, October 30, 1945.

58. RG 59 CDF 103.9992, National Archives, College Park, MD.

59. U.S. Congress, Senate, Subcommittee of the Committee on Appropriations, *Second Supplemental Surplus Appropriation Rescission Bill, 1946: Hearings before the Subcommittee of the Committee on Appropriations,* 79th Congress, 2nd Session, March 25, 1946, 61.

60. Cybelle Fox, *Three Worlds of Relief: Race, Immigration, and the American Welfare State from the Progressive Era to the New Deal* (Princeton University Press, 2012); Ira Katznelson, *When Affirmative Action Was White: An Untold History of Racial Inequality in Twentieth-Century America* (W. W. Norton, 2005).

61. Representative Luce, speaking on H.R. 3517, "Immigration and Naturalization of Persons Indigenous to India," on October 10, 1945, 79th Congress, 1st Session, *Congressional Record* 91, pt. 7: 9529–30.

62. Representatives Luce and Celler, "Immigration and Naturalization of Persons Indigenous to India," on October 10, 1945, 79th Congress, 1st Session, Congressional Record 91, pt. 7: 9530–31.

63. Representative Johnson of California, speaking on H.R. 3517, "Immigration and Naturalization of Persons Indigenous to India," on October 10, 1945, 79th Congress, 1st Session, *Congressional Record* 91, pt. 7: 9536.

64. Representative Welch, speaking on "Filipino Rehabilitation Commission," on June 19, 1944, 78th Congress, 2nd Session, *Congressional Record* 90, pt. 5: 6211.

65. Representative Mason, speaking on H.R. 3517, "Immigration and Naturalization of Persons Indigenous to India," on October 10, 1945, 79th Congress, 1st Session, Congressional Record 91, pt. 7: 9521.

66. U.S. Congress, House, Committee on Immigration and Naturalization, *Naturalization of Filipinos: Hearings before the Committee on Immigration and Naturalization*, 78th Congress, 2nd Session, November 22, 1944.

67. U.S. Congress, House, Committee, *Naturalization of Filipinos*, 1944.

68. As of 1940, there were 45,321 noncitizen Filipinos in the continental United States and 38,735 in the U.S. possessions, mostly in Hawai'i. U.S. Congress, House, Committee on Immigration and Naturalization. *Authorizing the Naturalization of Filipinos: Report (to Accompany H.R. 4826)*. 79th Congress, 1st Session: 1–2. H. Rep. 252.

69. Press Release of Sergio Osmeña relayed by Representative McCormack, speaking on "Filipino Rehabilitation Commission," on June 19, 1944, 78th Congress, 2nd Session, *Congressional Record* 90, pt. 5: 6210.

Chapter 7

1. Harry S. Truman, Message of the President to the People of the Philippines, July 3, 1946, *Department of State Bulletin*: 68.

2. William E. Berry, *U.S. Bases in the Philippines: The Evolution of the Special Relationship* (Westview Press, 1989); Theodore Friend, *Between Two Empires: The Ordeal of the Philippines, 1929–1946* (Yale University Press, 1965); Frank Hindman Golay, *Face of Empire: United States-Philippine Relations, 1898–1946* (Ateneo de Manila University Press, 1997); Stephen Rosskamm Shalom, *The United States and the Philippines: A Study of Neocolonialism* (New Day Publishers, 1986).

3. Louis A. Pérez, *The War of 1898: The United States and Cuba in History and Historiography* (UNC Press, 1998), 34–35.

4. Julian Go, *Patterns of Empire: The British and American Empires, 1688 to the Present* (Cambridge University Press, 2011), 123.

5. In 1939, the BIA moved from the War Department to the Interior, with a complete transfer of the powers, duties, and functions of the high commissioner of the Philippines transferred in 1942 (when the Philippines was under Japanese occupation).

6. Ickes was particularly concerned about collaborators and did not support the political career of Roxas, who signed the constitution of the Japanese-occupied Philippines. E. D. Hester noted that Roxas was a brigadier general in the Philippine Army "called to colors and command of U.S. Army at the time he signed the constitution of the puppet government" (E. D. Hester, July 3, 1945, RG 126 OHC PE matters Box 2 ED Hester, National Archives II, College Park, MD). Later, General MacArthur cleared his name. Ickes and MacArthur were often at odds over the future of Philippine politics and rehabilitation.

7. Harold Ickes, to Truman, May 1945, RG 126 Box 2 Folder Economic Survey and Elections.

8. Harold Ickes, First Draft of "The Philippines Comes of Age," April 23, 1945, Box 117, Secretary of the Interior File: Can the Philippines Stand Alone? Harold Ickes Papers, Library of Congress, Washington, D.C.

9. See for example: Henry William Brands, *Bound to Empire: The United States and the Philippines* (Oxford University Press, 1992); Keith Thor Carlson, "The Twisted Road to Freedom: America's Granting of Independence to the Philippines in 1946" (master's thesis, University of Victoria (Canada), 1992); Daniel Immerwahr, "Philippine Independence in U.S. History: A Car, Not a Train," *Pacific Historical Review* 91, no. 2 (May 1, 2022): 220–48.

10. The United States High Commissioner in the Philippines (McNutt), to Mr. Richard R. Ely, of the Office of United States High Commissioner, January 18, 1946, Washington, *Foreign Relations of the United States*, 1946, Volume VIII, The Far East (Washington, D.C.: Government Printing Office, 1971), Document 651. 611.11B31/1–1046.

11. Secretary of Interior File Philippines, 1945–1946, Box 226, Harold Ickes Papers, Library of Congress, Washington, D.C.

12. Harold Ickes, First Draft of "The Philippines Comes of Age," April 23, 1945, Box 117, Secretary of the Interior File: Can the Philippines Stand Alone? Harold Ickes Papers, Library of Congress, Washington, D.C.

13. Simeon Man, *Soldiering Through Empire: Race and the Making of the Decolonizing Pacific* (University of California Press, 2018); Colleen Woods, *Freedom Incorporated: Anticommunism and Philippine Independence in the Age of Decolonization* (Cornell University Press, 2020).

14. Acting Secretary of State, Memorandum to President Truman, June 26, 1946, *Foreign Relations of the United States*, 1946, Volume VIII, The Far East (Washington, D.C.: Government Printing Office, 1971), Document 676. 611.11B31/6–2646.

15. Director of the Office of Far Eastern Affairs, Memorandum to Secretary of State, June 6, 1946, U.S. Department of State *Foreign Relations of the United States*, 1946, Volume VIII, The Far East (Washington, D.C.: Government Printing Office, 1971), Document 666. 811.24596/6–646.

16. Director of the Office of Far Eastern Affairs, Memorandum to Secretary of State, June 6, 1946, U.S. Department of State *Foreign Relations of the United States*, 1946, Volume VIII, The Far East (Washington, D.C.: Government Printing Office, 1971), Document 666. 811.24596/6–646.

17. Other key provisions of the act included: absolute quotas on cordage and coconut oil imported into the United States; option for the United States to establish new quotas if Philippine products compete with U.S. ones; no export taxes for either country; and a fixed currency exchange rate.

18. "Philippine Trade Bill," in *CQ Almanac 1946*, 2nd ed., 08-117-08-118, Washington, D.C.: Congressional Quarterly, 1947.

19. Nick Cullather, *Illusions of Influence: The Political Economy of United States-Philippines Relations, 1942–1960* (Stanford University Press, 1994), 24–27.

20. Cullather, *Illusions of Influence*, 29–31.

21. Cullather, *Illusions of Influence*, 29–33.

22. Cullather, *Illusions of Influence*, 34–36.

23. See Philippine Constitution, article 12, section 1, article 13, section 8.

24. Chief of the Division of Commercial Policy (Brown), Memorandum of Telephone Conversation, June 25, 1946, U.S. Department of State, *Foreign Relations of the United States*, 1946, Volume VIII, The Far East (Washington, D.C.: Government Printing Office, 1971), Document 675. 711.11B/6–2546.

25. Shalom, *The United States and the Philippines*, 53.

26. Secretary of State, Memorandum to President Truman, April 18, 1946, *Foreign Relations of the United States*, 1946, Volume VIII, The Far East (Washington, D.C.: Government Printing Office, 1971), Document 659. 611.11B31/4–1846.

27. Acting Secretary of State, Memorandum to President Truman, June 26, 1946, *Foreign Relations of the United States*, 1946, Volume VIII, The Far East (Washington, D.C.: Government Printing Office, 1971), Document 676. 611.11B31/6–2646.

28. President Truman, Statement on Independence for the Philippines, May 6, 1945, *Foreign Relations of the United States: Diplomatic Papers*, 1945, Volume VI , The British Commonwealth, The Far East (Washington, D.C.: Government Printing Office, 1969), Document 883.

29. "Philippine Islands Trade and Rehabilitation Acts," in *CQ Almanac 1946*, 2nd ed., 08-359, Washington, D.C.: Congressional Quarterly, 1947.

30. *The Philippine Rehabilitation Act of 1946*, Public Law 79-370 (1946).

31. *The Philippine Rehabilitation Act of 1946*, Public Law 79-370 (1946).

32. The Ambassador in the Philippines (McNutt), to the Secretary of State, Manila, September 13, 1946—11 a.m. [Received September 14—9:55 a.m.], *Foreign Relations of the United States*, 1946, Volume VIII, The Far East (Washington, D.C.: Government Printing Office, 1971), Document 703. 896.51/9–1346: Telegram.

33. The United States also allocated $800 million for various war damages to the Philippines and $70 million for budgetary assistance. See: *The Philippine Rehabilitation Act of 1946*, Public Law 79-370 (1946); Golay, *Face of Empire*, 472, 483.

34. Richard Ely, "Memorandum for the High Commissioner," December 7, 1945, RG 126, Entry PI 151 1, Box 1 Army and Scouts, Philippine 1942–1946, National Archives II, College Park, MD.

35. Cullather, *Illusions of Influence*, 18–19. Cullather quotes Capt. John L. McCrea to Adm William D. Leahy, Dec. 28, 1942, CCS decimal file, 686.9 Philippine Islands (11-7-43), USNA, RG 218, Box 264; "Post War Military Problems with Particular Relation to Air Bases," March 15, 1943, CCS decimal file, 686.9 Philippine Islands (11-7-43), USNA, RG 218, Box 264; "Air Routes across the Pacific and Air Facilities for International Police Force," JCS 183/5, March 25, 1943, CCS decimal file, 686.9 Philippine Islands (11-7-43), USNA, RG 218, Box 264.

36. "Liberation of the Philippines," JCS 1027/1, September 8, 1944, RG 218 Box 179 Philippine Islands 11-7-43 Bases Sec 1, National Archives II, College Park, MD.

37. The JCS also considered bases around the world as part of securing U.S. domination. See Chapter 2 in Melvyn P. Leffler, *A Preponderance of Power: National Security, the Truman Administration, and the Cold War* (Stanford University Press, 1992).

38. JCS 138th Meeting December 21, 1943, RG 218 Box 179 Philippine Islands 11-7-43 Bases Sec, National Archives II, College Park, MD.

39. *Declaring the policy of the Congress with respect to the independence of the Philippine Islands, and for other purposes,* Public Law 78-380 (1944).

40. J.C.S. 1027/3. See Appendix B "Facts Bearing on the Problem" in "Negotiations for the Retention of American Bases in the Philippines after Independence," Report by the Joint Staff Planners in collaboration with the Joint Post-War Committee, September 20, 1945, RG 218 Box 179 Philippine Islands 11-7-43 Bases, National Archives II, College Park, MD.

41. "Preliminary Statement of General Principles Pertaining to the U.S. Military and Naval Base System in the Philippines to be used as a basis for detailed discussions and staff studies," May 14, 1945, RG 218 Box 179 Philippine Islands 11-7-43 Bases, National Archives II, College Park, MD.

42. Director of the Office of Far Eastern Affairs, Memorandum to Secretary of State, June 6, 1946, U.S. Department of State, *Foreign Relations of the United States, 1946,* Volume VIII, The Far East (Washington, D.C.: Government Printing Office, 1971), Document 666. 811.24596/6–646.

43. U.S. Congress, House, Committee on Foreign Affairs, *United States Policy in the Far East: Hearings before the Committee on Foreign Affairs,* 79th Congress, 2nd Session, June 7, 1946, 12.

44. JCS 1027/5, September 20, 1945, "Negotiations for the Retention of American Bases in the Philippines After Independence," annex A to appendix A: "Special instructions Regarding Selection of U.S. Military Bases in the Philippines," RG 218, File: CCS 686.9 Philippine Islands (11-7-43), Sec 1, National Archives II, College Park, MD.

45. JCS 1027/5, September 20, 1945, "Negotiations for the Retention of American Bases in the Philippines after Independence," Report by the Joint Staff Planners in collaboration with the Joint Post-War Committee, RG 218 Box 179 Philippine Islands 11-7-43 Bases Sec 1, National Archives II, College Park, MD.

46. Appendix to *Congressional Record,* July 3, 1946: 3922.

47. *An Act to provide military assistance to the Republic of the Philippines in establishing and maintaining national security and to form a basis for participation by that government in such defensive military operations as the future may require,* Public Law 79-454 (1946).

48. James F. Byrnes, to Sam Rayburn, May 24, 1946, in U.S. Congress, House, Committee on Foreign Affairs. *Republic of the Philippines Military Assistance Act: Report (to Accompany H.R. 6572),* 79th Congress, 2nd Session, 2. H. Rep. 2243.

49. "Appendix E" RG 218 Box 46 Philippines 11-7-43 Bases Sec 5, National Archives II, College Park, MD.

50. See, for example: Acting Chief of the Division of Philippine Affairs (Ely), Memorandum of Conversation, November 19, 1946, *Foreign Relations of the United States, 1946,* Volume VIII, The Far East (Washington, D.C.: Government Printing Office, 1971), Document 723, 811.24596/11–1946 and The Ambassador in the Philippines (McNutt), to the Secretary of State, November 7, 1946, *Foreign Relations of the United*

States, 1946, Volume VIII, The Far East (Washington, D.C.: Government Printing Office, 1971), Document 716. 811.24596/11–746.

51. The Ambassador in the Philippines (McNutt), to the Secretary of State, November 7, 1946, *Foreign Relations of the United States*, 1946, Volume VIII, The Far East (Washington, D.C.: Government Printing Office, 1971), Document 716. 811.24596/11–746.

52. The Ambassador in the Philippines (McNutt), to the Secretary of State, November 7, 1946, *Foreign Relations of the United States*, 1946, Volume VIII, The Far East (Washington, D.C.: Government Printing Office, 1971), Document 716. 811.24596/11–746: Telegram; 811.0011 Three Secretaries/1–2446.

53. The Secretary of War (Patterson), to the Secretary of State, November 29, 1946, *Foreign Relations of the United States*, 1946, Volume VIII, The Far East (Washington, D.C.: Government Printing Office, 1971), Document 726. 811.24596/11–2946.

54. The Ambassador in the Philippines (McNutt), to the Secretary of State, December 23, 1946, *Foreign Relations of the United States*, 1946, Volume VIII, The Far East (Washington, D.C.: Government Printing Office, 1971), Document 732. 811.24596/12–2346.

55. In 1966, this was amended to a shortened lease that ended until 1991. See Daniel B. Schirmer and Stephen Rosskamm Shalom, "Independence with Strings," in *The Philippines Reader: A History of Colonialism, Neocolonialism, Dictatorship, and Resistance* (South End Press, 1987), 97.

56. "Military Bases: Agreement Between the United States and the Republic of the Philippines, March 14, 1947," in U.S. Senate, *A Decade of American Foreign Policy: Basic Documents, 1941–49*. For a discussion of the postcolonial effects of U.S. jurisdiction on military bases, see Victoria Reyes, "Global Borderlands: A Case Study of the Subic Bay Freeport Zone, Philippines," *Theory and Society* 44, no. 4 (2015): 355–84.

57. "Military Bases: Agreement Between the United States and the Republic of the Philippines, March 14, 1947," in U.S. Senate, *A Decade of American Foreign Policy: Basic Documents, 1941–49*: Article XXV.

58. William E. Berry, *US Bases in the Philippines: The Evolution of the Special Relationship* (Boulder, CO: Westview Press, 1989); Catherine Lutz and Cynthia Enloe, *The Bases of Empire: The Global Struggle against US Military Posts* (NYU Press, 2009); Simeon Man, *Soldiering Through Empire: Race and the Making of the Decolonizing Pacific* (University of California Press, 2018); Colleen Woods, *Freedom Incorporated: Anticommunism and Philippine Independence in the Age of Decolonization* (Cornell University Press, 2020).

59. The United States High Commissioner in the Philippines (McNutt), to Mr. Richard R. Ely, of the Office of United States High Commissioner, Washington, January 18, 1946, *Foreign Relations of the United States*, 1946, Volume VIII, The Far East (Washington, D.C.: Government Printing Office, 1971), Document 651. 611.11B31/1–1046.

60. Francis B. Sayre, "Freedom Comes to the Philippines," *The Atlantic*, March 1, 1945.

61. Representative Robertson, speaking on H.R. 5856, "Philippine Trade Act of 1946," on March 28, 1946, 79th Congress, 2nd Session, *Congressional Record* 92, pt. 3: 2763.

62. U.S. Congress, Senate, Committee on Finance, *Philippine Trade Act of 1946: Report (to Accompany H.R. 5856), 79th Congress, 2nd Session, 6. S. Rep. 1145.

63. Representative Stefan, speaking on H.R. 5856, "The Philippines—Mercy and Justice for our Friends," on March 29, 1946, 79th Congress, 2nd Session, *Congressional Record* 92, pt. 3: 2830.

64. Representative Douglas, speaking on H.R. 5856, "Philippine Trade Act of 1946," on March 28, 1946, 79th Congress, 2nd Session, *Congressional Record* 92, pt. 3: 2767.

65. Dingell also proposed his own bill 79 H.R. 3142 to postpone for twenty years the imposition of import duties and other import restrictions on articles imported into the United States from the Philippine Islands. In effect, this act would extend the terms of trade under the Tydings–McDuffie Act.

66. Representative Dingell, speaking on H.R. 5856, "Philippine Trade Act of 1946," on March 28, 1946, 79th Congress, 2nd Session, *Congressional Record* 92, pt. 3: 2773.

67. Representative Bell, speaking on S. 1610, "Philippine Rehabilitation Act, 1946," in *Congressional Record* 79th Congress, 2nd Session, April 10, 1946: 3438.

68. Representative Bell, speaking on S. 1610. "Philippine Rehabilitation Act, 1946," in *Congressional Record* 79th Congress, 2nd Session, April 10, 1946: 3438.

69. Representative Dingell, speaking on H.R. 5856. "Philippine Trade Act of 1946," on March 28, 1946, 79th Congress, 2nd Session, *Congressional Record* 92, pt. 3: 2771-2773.

70. Harold Ickes, First Draft of "The Philippines Comes of Age," April 23, 1945, Box 117, Secretary of the Interior File: Can the Philippines Stand Alone? Harold Ickes Papers, Library of Congress, Washington, D.C.

71. Harold Ickes, First Draft of "The Philippines Comes of Age," April 23, 1945, Box 117, Secretary of the Interior File: Can the Philippines Stand Alone? Harold Ickes Papers, Library of Congress. Washington, D.C.

72. Representative Robertson, speaking on H.R. 5856, "Philippine Trade Act of 1946," on March 28, 1946, 79th Congress, 2nd Session, *Congressional Record* 92, pt. 3: 2764.

73. Manuel Roxas, *Message of His Excellency Manual Roxas, President of the Philippines to the Filipino People Urging Approval of the Constitutional Amendment on Parity at the Plebiscite,* March 11, 1947.

74. Manuel Roxas, "The Case for Parity," *The Parity Question: A Presentation of Arguments for and Against This Momentous Issue in Our National Life,* 1947: 7-26.

75. Statement by the President, October 3, 1945, RG 126 Box 5 Folder Independence, Political, National Archives II, College Park, MD.

76. Representative Stefan, speaking on H.R. 5856, "The Philippines—Mercy and Justice for our Friends," on March 29, 1946, 79th Congress, 2nd Session, *Congressional Record* 92, pt. 3: 2830.

77. Harold Ickes, First Draft of "The Philippines Comes of Age," April 23, 1945, Box 117, Secretary of the Interior File: Can the Philippines Stand Alone? Harold Ickes Papers, Library of Congress. Washington, D.C.

78. The United States High Commissioner in the Philippines (McNutt), to Mr. Richard R. Ely, of the Office of United States High Commissioner, January 18, 1946,

Washington, *Foreign Relations of the United States*, 1946, Volume VIII, The Far East (Washington, D.C.: Government Printing Office, 1971), Document 651.

79. McNutt was in favor of U.S. empire throughout his career. Senator Tydings even remarked that McNutt was "opposed to Philippine independence, and if you would ask him he would tell you so" (U.S. Congress, House, Committee on Ways and Means, *Philippine Trade Act of 1945: Hearings before the Committee on Ways and Means,* 79th Congress, 1st Session, October 17, 1945, 90). McNutt's position on U.S. sovereignty in the Philippines not only led him to support the parity act but also, as I mention in the above section, was the source of his defense of benefits for Filipino veterans.

80. McNutt, Radio Address, March 30, 1946, Box 11, Paul V. McNutt Papers, Lilly Library, Indiana University, Bloomington, IN.

81. Draft Statement of the Secretary of the Interior to the Senate Committee on Appropriations: c. April 1945, Box 226, Secretary of the Interior File, Philippines, 1945–1946, Harold Ickes Papers, Library of Congress, Washington D.C.

82. Senator Tydings, speaking on S. 1610, "Rehabilitation of the Philippine Islands," on December 5, 1945, 79th Congress, 1st Session, *Congressional Record* 91, pt. 9: 11469.

83. Representative Bell, speaking on H.R. 5856, "Philippine Trade Act of 1946," on March 28, 1946, 79th Congress, 2nd Session, *Congressional Record* 92, pt. 2: 2763.

84. Representative Johnson, speaking on H.R. 5856, "Philippine Trade Act of 1946," on March 29, 1946, 79th Congress, 2nd Session, *Congressional Record* 92, pt. 2: 2829.

85. On pages 66–7 of *The United States and the Philippines: A Study of Neocolonialism*, Shalom also argues that neocolonialism did not simply replace colonialism. Neocolonialism gave the Philippines more freedom to maneuver and placed greater constraint on the United States. So, even if the difference is a legal one (i.e., the specific locus of sovereignty), the difference can have important implications for the behavior of nation states (183).

86. *Downes v. Bidwell*, 182 U.S. 244 (1901).

Conclusion

1. Frederick Cooper, *Citizenship Between Empire and Nation: Remaking France and French Africa, 1945–1960* (Princeton University Press, 2014); Martin Shipway, *The Road to War: France and Vietnam 1944–1947* (Berghahn Books, 2003).

2. Frederick Cooper, "Decolonization and Citizenship: Africa between Empires and a World of Nations," in *Beyond Empire and Nation: The Decolonization of African and Asian Societies, 1930s–1970s*, ed. Els Bogaerts and Remco Raben (Brill, 2012), 39–68; Kathleen Paul, *Whitewashing Britain: Race and Citizenship in the Postwar Era* (Cornell University Press, 1997).

3. Christopher Alan Bayly and Timothy Norman Harper, *Forgotten Wars: Freedom and Revolution in Southeast Asia* (Harvard University Press, 2007); Muriam Haleh Davis, *Markets of Civilization: Islam and Racial Capitalism in Algeria* (Duke University Press, 2022).

4. Ulbe Bosma, "Decolonization, Nation Building, and Migration Crises in Southeast Asia," in *The Oxford Handbook of Migration Crises* (Oxford University Press,

2019), 73–92; Wen-Qing Ngoei, *Arc of Containment: Britain, the United States, and Anticommunism in Southeast Asia* (Cornell University Press, 2019).

5. Paul Bijl, "Colonial Memory and Forgetting in the Netherlands and Indonesia," *Journal of Genocide Research* 14, nos. 3–4 (2012): 441–61.

6. William H. Taft to the Senate, on April 12, 1946, 79th Congress, 2nd Session, *Congressional Record* 92, pt. 3: 3537.

7. Keith L. Camacho, *Sacred Men: Law, Torture, and Retribution in Guam* (Duke University Press, 2019); Takashi Fujitani, *Race for Empire: Koreans as Japanese and Japanese as Americans during World War II* (University of California Press, 2011); Jim Glassman, *Drums of War, Drums of Development: The Formation of a Pacific Ruling Class and Industrial Transformation in East and Southeast Asia, 1945–1980* (Brill, 2018); Juliet Nebolon, "'Life Given Straight from the Heart': Settler Militarism, Biopolitics, and Public Health in Hawai'i during World War II," *American Quarterly* 69, no. 1 (2017): 23–45.

8. I am not suggesting that these strategies are unique to the United States. Other empires, like Great Britain, have also relied on these strategies during what Julian Go (2011) refers to as periods of hegemonic maturity. The United States laid down these systems in the Philippines during the period of formal empire and then expanded during informal empire. See Julian Go, *Patterns of Empire: The British and American Empires, 1688 to the Present* (Cambridge University Press, 2011).

9. Leonard Frederick Giesecke, Jr., *History of American Economic Policy in the Philippines During the American Colonial Period: 1900–1935* (PhD diss., The University of Texas at Austin, 1975).

10. Nick Cullather, *Illusions of Influence: The Political Economy of United States-Philippines Relations, 1942–1960* (Stanford University Press, 1994), 4.

11. Walter Hatch, "European Integration, Asian Subordination: U.S. Identity and Power in Two Regions," in *Power Relations and Comparative Regionalism* (Routledge, 2021); Christopher Hemmer and Peter J. Katzenstein, "Why Is There No NATO in Asia? Collective Identity, Regionalism, and the Origins of Multilateralism," *International Organization* 56, no. 3 (July 2002): 575–607.

12. Megan Black, "Interior's Exterior: The State, Mining Companies, and Resource Ideologies in the Point Four Program," *Diplomatic History* 40, no. 1 (January 1, 2016): 81–110; Stephen Macekura, "The Point Four Program and U.S. International Development Policy," *Political Science Quarterly* 128, no. 1 (2013): 127–60.

13. Laleh Khalili, *Time in the Shadows: Confinement in Counterinsurgencies* (Stanford University Press, 2012).

14. For discussion of colonies as laboratories, see Alfred W. McCoy and Francisco A. Scarano, eds., *Colonial Crucible: Empire in the Making of the Modern American State* (University of Wisconsin Press, 2009).

15. Colleen Woods, *Freedom Incorporated: Anticommunism and Philippine Independence in the Age of Decolonization* (Cornell University Press, 2020), 13. Quoting "We Smashed the Communists," *U.S. News and World Report*, February 13, 1953.

16. Simeon Man, *Soldiering Through Empire: Race and the Making of the Decolonizing Pacific* (University of California Press, 2018); Woods, *Freedom Incorporated*.

17. Wesley Attewell, *The Quiet Violence of Empire: How USAID Waged Counterinsurgency in Afghanistan* (University of Minnesota Press, 2023).

18. Lisa Bhungalia, *Elastic Empire: Refashioning War through Aid in Palestine* (Stanford University Press, 2023).

19. Stephen Rosskamm Shalom, *The United States and the Philippines: A Study of Neocolonialism* (Institute for the Study of Human Issues, 1981), 63; Victoria Reyes, *Global Borderlands Fantasy, Violence, and Empire in Subic Bay, Philippines* (Stanford University Press, 2019).

20. Victoria Reyes, "Legacies of Place and Power: From Military Base to Freeport Zone," *City & Community* 14, no. 1 (2015): 1–26; Roland G. Simbulan, "People's Movement Responses to Evolving US Military Activities in the Philippines," in *The Bases of Empire: The Global Struggle Against US Military Posts* (NYU Press, 2009), 145–80.

21. Woods, *Freedom Incorporated*, 4.

22. Catherine Lutz and Cynthia Enloe, *The Bases of Empire: The Global Struggle Against US Military Posts* (NYU Press, 2009); Chalmers Johnson, *The Sorrows of Empire: Militarism, Secrecy, and the End of the Republic* (Verso, 2004).

23. Jodi Kim, *Settler Garrison: Debt Imperialism, Militarism, and Transpacific Imaginaries* (Duke University Press, 2022).

24. Daniel Immerwahr, "The Greater United States: Territory and Empire in U.S. History," *Diplomatic History* 40, no. 3 (June 1, 2016): 373–91; Daniel Immerwahr, *How to Hide an Empire: A History of the Greater United States* (Farrar, Straus and Giroux, 2019).

25. Cynthia Enloe, *Bananas, Beaches and Bases: Making Feminist Sense of International Politics* (University of California Press, 2014); Stewart Firth, "Sovereignty and Independence in the Contemporary Pacific," *The Contemporary Pacific* 1, no. 1/2 (1989): 75–96; Amy Kaplan, "Where Is Guantanamo?," *American Quarterly* 57, no. 3 (2005): 831–58; Lutz and Enloe, *The Bases of Empire*; Simon Reid-Henry, "Exceptional Sovereignty? Guantánamo Bay and the Re-Colonial Present," *Antipode* 39, no. 4 (2007): 627–48; Setsu Shigematsu and Keith L. Camacho, *Militarized Currents: Toward a Decolonized Future in Asia and the Pacific* (University of Minnesota Press, 2010); Rachel Woodward, *Military Geographies*, vol. 45 (John Wiley & Sons, 2004).

26. Sasha Davis, "The US Military Base Network and Contemporary Colonialism: Power Projection, Resistance and the Quest for Operational Unilateralism," *Political Geography* 30, no. 4 (2011): 215–24; Masamichi S. Inoue, *Okinawa and the US Military: Identity Making in the Age of Globalization* (Columbia University Press, 2007); Lutz and Enloe, *The Bases of Empire*.

27. Bianca Freeman, "Racial Hierarchy and Jurisdiction in U.S. Status of Forces Agreements," *Security Studies* 32, no. 4–5 (October 20, 2023): 748–74.

28. Ken Fuller, *Forcing the Pace: The Partido Komunista Ng Pilipinas: From Foundation to Armed Struggle* (University of the Philippines Press, 2007); Karen Buenavista Hanna, "Makibaka!: Feminist Social Histories of the Transnational Filipina/o American Anti-Imperialist Left, 1968–1992," *ProQuest Dissertations and Theses* (PhD diss., University of California, Santa Barbara, 2018); Moon-Ho Jung, *Menace to Empire: Anticolonial Solidarities and the Transpacific Origins of the US Security State* (University

of California Press, 2022); Vina A. Lanzona, *Amazons of the Huk Rebellion: Gender, Sex, and Revolution in the Philippines* (University of Wisconsin Press, 2009); Resil B. Mojares, "Apolinario Mabini, Isabelo de Los Reyes, and the Emergence of a 'Public,'" *PLARIDEL* 13, no. 1 (2016): 1–15; Joy Nicolas Sales, "Diasporic Struggle: Transnational Activism, Migration, and Anti-Imperialism in Filipino America, 1964–1991," *ProQuest Dissertations and Theses* (PhD diss., Northwestern University, 2019); Mark John Sanchez, "Let the People Speak: Solidarity Culture and the Making of a Transnational Opposition to the Marcos Dictatorship, 1972–1986," *ProQuest Dissertations and Theses* (PhD diss., University of Illinois at Urbana-Champaign, 2018); Motoe Terami, *Sakdalistas' Struggle for Philippine Independence, 1930–1945* (Ateneo de Manila University Press, 2014).

INDEX

Page numbers in *italics* refer to figures and tables.

and, 191, 196, 198; dispossession and
exclusion linked to, 11, 189, 202, 228;
institutional bifurcation linked to,
49–50, 191, 264; persistence of, 24, 27,
31–32, 39–40, 59, 90, 231, 232, 257, 266,
269, 271; racial classification linked
to, 100; slavery and Reconstruction
linked to, 12–16; war-making linked
to, 7, 9, 10, 16, 17, 119, 164, 186, 265;
whitewashing of, 23, 28, 33–34, 63,
66, *78*, 118, 125, 191, 199, 218, 254, 258,
261, 265, 268
racial knowledge, 89–90, 98–99,
103, 116
racial threat, 9, 52, 71, 140, 144, 175–76,
186, 224, 264
Randolph, Carman F., 66
Randolph, Jennings, 210
Rankin, John Elliot, 175
Rawlins, Joseph L., 97, 98
Reconstruction, 9, 14, 15, 16, 88
repatriation, *124*, *134*, 140–41, 150,
151, 216
Repatriation Act (Philippines, 1935), *126*,
140, 144, 146, 151
Rescission Act (1946), *199*, 200–209, 213,
214, 217, 218, 219, 238
Richards (general), 221
Richardson, James Daniel, 95
riots, 131
Robertson, A. Willis, 249–50, 253
*Roldan v. Los Angeles County and the
State of California* (1933), 132
Romulo, Carlos, 207, 221
Roosevelt, Franklin D., 31, 162–63,
165–66, 186, 195–96
Roosevelt, Theodore, 25–26, 42, 55, 57,
61–62, 66, 100–101, 121
Root, Elihu, 58, 66, 67, 89–94, 96, 98, 100,
106, 232–33
Rough Riders, 42
Roxas, Manuel, 122, 138, 143, 229, 233,
234, 248; alien status denounced by,
144, 151; communists denounced

by, 247; constitutional amendments
passed under, 241; Philippine rehabilitation backed by, 240,
243, 253
Russell, Richard, 212
Russia, 120, 173

Sabath, Adolph J., 146, 175–76
Sand Creek massacre (1864), 11
Santo Domingo, 40
Sayre, Francis B., 173, 249
Scharrenberg, Paul, 152
Second War Powers Act (1942), *124*, *179*,
181, 182, 184
segregation, 15, 95
Selective Service Act (1940), *124*, *126*, *166*,
182, 184–85
self-determination, 105, 120, 231
self-government, 3, 64, 79, 86, 100, 102;
British promises of, 260; self-
determination distinguished from,
231; tutelage in, 82, 101, 106, 115, 120,
262–65
self-rule, 19, 29, 105, 113, 120
settler colonialism, 15, 16, 65
Shalom, Stephen R., 257
Sheppard, Harry, 210, 211
Sheppard, Morris, 166
Sherman, Forrest P., 246
Shiras, George, Jr., 73, 75, *78*, 86
Shortridge, Samuel M., 143,
151–52
Simmons, Furnifold McLendel, 2–3, 4,
59, 64–65
Singh, Anup, *202*
Singh, J. J., *202*
Singh, Nikhil, 9
Sioux, 16
Sitting Bull, 67
slavery, 3, 12–14
Smith, Howard, 141
Smith Act (Alien Registration Act, 1940),
124, *126*, 141–42
Soriano, Andrés, 234

ARTICULATIONS STUDIES IN RACE,
IMMIGRATION,
AND CAPITALISM

EDITORS
Cedric de Leon
Pawan Dhingra

Change is afoot in sociology and related fields. Motivated by mounting social inequality and the latest groundbreaking research, a new generation of scholars is pushing for a more synthetic and empirically rigorous approach to race, immigration, and capitalism. This book series seeks work at the intersection of these three fields. The series is a space to push forward a positive research agenda that articulates immigration, race, and capitalism together as overlapping systems that are experienced in people's everyday lives. Such studies will allow us to offer more nuanced analyses on topics such as immigrant assimilation, the pervasiveness of white supremacy, and the governing economic structures that surround all forms of discrimination. With an emphasis on sociological and qualitative work, the series will also be interested in interdisciplinary work across the social sciences and humanities, with a range of methodological approaches.

Language Brokers: Children of Immigrants Translating Inequality and Belonging for Their Families
HYEYOUNG KWON 2024

The Borders of Privilege: 1.5-Generation Brazilian Migrants Navigating Power Without Papers
KARA B. CEBULKO 2024

The authorized representative in the EU for product safety and compliance is:
Mare Nostrum Group
B.V Doelen 72
4831 GR Breda
The Netherlands

www.ingramcontent.com/pod-product-compliance
Lightning Source LLC
Chambersburg PA
CBHW020454270326
41926CB00008B/594